# Machine Learning with R

Learn how to use R to apply powerful machine learning
methods and gain an insight into real-world applications

**Brett Lantz**

**[PACKT]** open source*
**PUBLISHING**  community experience distilled

BIRMINGHAM - MUMBAI

# Machine Learning with R

First published: October 2013

Production Reference: 1211013

Published by Packt Publishing Ltd.
Livery Place
35 Livery Street
Birmingham B3 2PB, UK.

ISBN 978-1-78216-214-8

www.packtpub.com

Cover Image by Abhishek Pandey (abhishek.pandey1210@gmail.com)

# Credits

**Author**
Brett Lantz

**Reviewers**
Jia Liu
Mzabalazo Z. Ngwenya
Abhinav Upadhyay

**Acquisition Editor**
James Jones

**Lead Technical Editor**
Azharuddin Sheikh

**Technical Editors**
Pooja Arondekar
Pratik More
Anusri Ramchandran
Harshad Vairat

**Project Coordinator**
Anugya Khurana

**Proofreaders**
Simran Bhogal
Ameesha Green
Paul Hindle

**Indexer**
Tejal Soni

**Graphics**
Ronak Dhruv

**Production Coordinator**
Nilesh R. Mohite

**Cover Work**
Nilesh R. Mohite

# About the Author

**Brett Lantz** has spent the past 10 years using innovative data methods to understand human behavior. A sociologist by training, he was first enchanted by machine learning while studying a large database of teenagers' social networking website profiles. Since then, he has worked on interdisciplinary studies of cellular telephone calls, medical billing data, and philanthropic activity, among others. When he's not spending time with family, following college sports, or being entertained by his dachshunds, he maintains `dataspelunking.com`, a website dedicated to sharing knowledge about the search for insight in data.

This book could not have been written without the support of my family and friends. In particular, my wife Jessica deserves many thanks for her patience and encouragement throughout the past year. My son Will (who was born while *Chapter 10* was underway), also deserves special mention for his role in the writing process; without his gracious ability to sleep through the night, I could not have strung together a coherent sentence the next morning. I dedicate this book to him in the hope that one day he is inspired to follow his curiosity wherever it may lead.

I am also indebted to many others who supported this book indirectly. My interactions with educators, peers, and collaborators at the University of Michigan, the University of Notre Dame, and the University of Central Florida seeded many of the ideas I attempted to express in the text. Additionally, without the work of researchers who shared their expertise in publications, lectures, and source code, this book might not exist at all. Finally, I appreciate the efforts of the R team and all those who have contributed to R packages, whose work ultimately brought machine learning to the masses.

# About the Reviewers

**Jia Liu** holds a Master's degree in Statistics from the University of Maryland, Baltimore County, and is presently a PhD candidate in statistics from Iowa State University. Her research interests include mixed-effects model, Bayesian method, Boostrap method, reliability, design of experiments, machine learning and data mining. She has two year's experience as a student consultant in statistics and two year's internship experience in agriculture and pharmaceutical industry.

**Mzabalazo Z. Ngwenya** has worked extensively in the field of statistical consulting and currently works as a biometrician. He holds an MSc in Mathematical Statistics from the University of Cape Town and is at present studying for a PhD (at the School of Information Technology, University of Pretoria), in the field of Computational Intelligence. His research interests include statistical computing, machine learning, and spatial statistics. Previously, he was involved in reviewing *Learning RStudio for R Statistical Computing* (*Van de Loo and de Jong*, 2012), and *R Statistical Application Development by Example beginner's guide* (*Prabhanjan Narayanachar Tattar* , 2013).

**Abhinav Upadhyay** finished his Bachelor's degree in 2011 with a major in Information Technology. His main areas of interest include machine learning and information retrieval.

In 2011, he worked for the NetBSD Foundation as part of the Google Summer of Code program. During that period, he wrote a search engine for Unix manual pages. This project resulted in a new implementation of the apropos utility for NetBSD.

Currently, he is working as a Development Engineer for SocialTwist. His day-to-day work involves writing system level tools and frameworks to manage the product infrastructure.

He is also an open source enthusiast and quite active in the community. In his free time, he maintains and contributes to several open source projects.

# www.PacktPub.com

## Support files, eBooks, discount offers and more

You might want to visit www.PacktPub.com for support files and downloads related to your book.

Did you know that Packt offers eBook versions of every book published, with PDF and ePub files available? You can upgrade to the eBook version at www.PacktPub.com and as a print book customer, you are entitled to a discount on the eBook copy. Get in touch with us at service@packtpub.com for more details.

At www.PacktPub.com, you can also read a collection of free technical articles, sign up for a range of free newsletters and receive exclusive discounts and offers on Packt books and eBooks.

 PACKTLIB

http://PacktLib.PacktPub.com

Do you need instant solutions to your IT questions? PacktLib is Packt's online digital book library. Here, you can access, read and search across Packt's entire library of books.

## Why Subscribe?
- Fully searchable across every book published by Packt
- Copy and paste, print and bookmark content
- On demand and accessible via web browser

## Free Access for Packt account holders

If you have an account with Packt at www.PacktPub.com, you can use this to access PacktLib today and view nine entirely free books. Simply use your login credentials for immediate access.

# Table of Contents

# Preface

Machine learning, at its core, is concerned with algorithms that transform information into actionable intelligence. This fact makes machine learning well-suited to the present day era of Big Data. Without machine learning, it would be nearly impossible to keep up with the massive stream of information.

Given the growing prominence of R—a cross-platform, zero-cost statistical programming environment—there has never been a better time to start using machine learning. R offers a powerful but easy-to-learn set of tools that can assist you with finding data insights.

By combining hands-on case studies with the essential theory that you need to understand how things work under the hood, this book provides all the knowledge that you will need to start applying machine learning to your own projects.

## What this book covers

*Chapter 1, Introducing Machine Learning,* presents the terminology and concepts that define and distinguish machine learners, as well as a method for matching a learning task with the appropriate algorithm.

*Chapter 2, Managing and Understanding Data,* provides an opportunity to get your hands dirty working with data in R. Essential data structures and procedures used for loading, exploring, and understanding data are discussed.

*Chapter 3, Lazy Learning – Classification Using Nearest Neighbors,* teaches you how to understand and apply a simple yet powerful learning algorithm to your first machine learning task: identifying malignant samples of cancer.

*Chapter 4, Probabilistic Learning – Classification Using Naive Bayes,* reveals the essential concepts of probability that are used in cutting-edge spam filtering systems. You'll learn the basics of text mining in the process of building your own spam filter.

*Chapter 5, Divide and Conquer – Classification Using Decision Trees and Rules*, explores a couple of learning algorithms whose predictions are not only accurate but easily explained. We'll apply these methods to tasks where transparency is important.

*Chapter 6, Forecasting Numeric Data – Regression Methods*, introduces machine learning algorithms used for making numeric predictions. As these techniques are heavily embedded in the field of statistics, you will also learn the essential metrics needed to make sense of numeric relationships.

*Chapter 7, Black Box Methods – Neural Networks and Support Vector Machines*, covers two extremely complex yet powerful machine learning algorithms. Though the mathematics may appear intimidating, we will work through examples that illustrate their inner workings in simple terms.

*Chapter 8, Finding Patterns – Market Basket Analysis Using Association Rules*, exposes the algorithm for the recommendation systems used at many retailers. If you've ever wondered how retailers seem to know your purchasing habits better than you know them yourself, this chapter will reveal their secrets.

*Chapter 9, Finding Groups of Data – Clustering with k-means*, is devoted to a procedure that locates clusters of related items. We'll utilize this algorithm to identify segments of profiles within a web-based community.

*Chapter 10, Evaluating Model Performance*, provides information on measuring the success of a machine learning project, and obtaining a reliable estimate of the learner's performance on future data.

*Chapter 11, Improving Model Performance*, reveals the methods employed by the teams found at the top of machine learning competition leader boards. If you have a competitive streak, or simply want to get the most out of your data, you'll need to add these techniques to your repertoire.

*Chapter 12, Specialized Machine Learning Topics*, explores the frontiers of machine learning. From working with Big Data to making R work faster, the topics covered will help you push the boundaries of what is possible with R.

# What you need for this book

The examples in this book were written for and tested with R Version 2.15.3 on both Microsoft Windows and Mac OS X, though they are likely to work with any recent version of R.

# Who this book is for

This book is intended for anybody hoping to use data for action. Perhaps you already know a bit about machine learning, but have never used R; or perhaps you know a little R but are new to machine learning. In any case, this book will get you up and running quickly. It would be helpful to have a bit of familiarity with basic math and programming concepts, but no prior experience is required. You need only curiosity.

# Conventions

In this book, you will find a number of styles of text that distinguish between different kinds of information. Here are some examples of these styles, and an explanation of their meaning.

Code words in text, database table names, folder names, filenames, file extensions, pathnames, dummy URLs, user input, and Twitter handles are shown as follows: "To fit a linear regression model to data with R, the lm() function can be used."

Any command-line input or output is written as follows:

```
> pairs.panels(insurance[c("age", "bmi", "children", "charges")])
```

**New terms** and **important words** are shown in bold. Words that you see on the screen, in menus or dialog boxes for example, appear in the text like this: "Instead, ham messages use words such as **can, sorry, need**, and **time**."

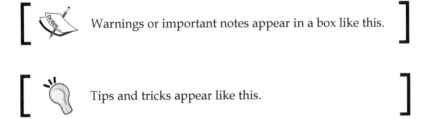

Warnings or important notes appear in a box like this.

Tips and tricks appear like this.

# Reader feedback

Feedback from our readers is always welcome. Let us know what you think about this book—what you liked or may have disliked. Reader feedback is important for us to develop titles that you really get the most out of.

To send us general feedback, simply send an e-mail to feedback@packtpub.com, and mention the book title via the subject of your message.

If there is a topic that you have expertise in and you are interested in either writing or contributing to a book, see our author guide on www.packtpub.com/authors.

# Customer support

Now that you are the proud owner of a Packt book, we have a number of things to help you to get the most from your purchase.

# Downloading the example code

You can download the example code files for all Packt books you have purchased from your account at http://www.packtpub.com. If you purchased this book elsewhere, you can visit http://www.packtpub.com/support and register to have the files e-mailed directly to you.

# Errata

Although we have taken every care to ensure the accuracy of our content, mistakes do happen. If you find a mistake in one of our books—maybe a mistake in the text or the code—we would be grateful if you would report this to us. By doing so, you can save other readers from frustration and help us improve subsequent versions of this book. If you find any errata, please report them by visiting http://www.packtpub.com/submit-errata, selecting your book, clicking on the **errata submission form** link, and entering the details of your errata. Once your errata are verified, your submission will be accepted and the errata will be uploaded on our website, or added to any list of existing errata, under the Errata section of that title. Any existing errata can be viewed by selecting your title from http://www.packtpub.com/support.

# Piracy

Piracy of copyright material on the Internet is an ongoing problem across all media. At Packt, we take the protection of our copyright and licenses very seriously. If you come across any illegal copies of our works, in any form, on the Internet, please provide us with the location address or website name immediately so that we can pursue a remedy.

Please contact us at copyright@packtpub.com with a link to the suspected pirated material.

We appreciate your help in protecting our authors, and our ability to bring you valuable content.

# Questions

You can contact us at questions@packtpub.com if you are having a problem with any aspect of the book, and we will do our best to address it.

# Introducing Machine Learning 1

If science fiction stories are to be believed, teaching machines to learn will inevitably lead to apocalyptic wars between machines and their makers. In the early stages, computers are taught to play simple games of tic-tac-toe and chess. Later, machines are given control of traffic lights and communications, followed by military drones and missiles. The machines' evolution takes an ominous turn once the computers become sentient and learn how to teach themselves. Having no more need for human programmers, humankind is then "deleted."

Thankfully, at the time of this writing, machines still require user input.

Your impressions of machine learning may be very heavily influenced by these types of mass media depictions of artificial intelligence. And even though there may be a hint of truth to such tales; in reality, machine learning is focused on more practical applications. The task of teaching a computer to learn is tied more closely to a specific problem that would be a computer that can play games, ponder philosophy, or answer trivial questions. Machine learning is more like training an employee than raising a child.

Putting these stereotypes aside, by the end of this chapter, you will have gained a far more nuanced understanding of machine learning. You will be introduced to the fundamental concepts that define and differentiate the most commonly used machine learning approaches.

You will learn:

- The origins and practical applications of machine learning
- How knowledge is defined and represented by computers
- The basic concepts that differentiate machine learning approaches

In a single sentence, you could say that machine learning provides a set of tools that use computers to transform data into actionable knowledge. To learn more about how the process works, read on.

# The origins of machine learning

Since birth, we are inundated with data. Our body's sensors—the eyes, ears, nose, tongue, and nerves—are continually assailed with raw data that our brain translates into sights, sounds, smells, tastes, and textures. Using language, we are able to share these experiences with others.

The earliest databases recorded information from the observable environment. Astronomers recorded patterns of planets and stars; biologists noted results from experiments crossbreeding plants and animals; and cities recorded tax payments, disease outbreaks, and populations. Each of these required a human being to first observe and second, record the observation. Today, such observations are increasingly automated and recorded systematically in ever-growing computerized databases.

The invention of electronic sensors has additionally contributed to an increase in the richness of recorded data. Specialized sensors see, hear, smell, or taste. These sensors process the data far differently than a human being would, and in many ways, this is a benefit. Without the need for translation into human language, the raw sensory data remains objective.

It is important to note that although a sensor does not have a subjective component to its observations, it does not necessarily report truth (if such a concept can be defined). A camera taking photographs in black and white might provide a far different depiction of its environment than one shooting pictures in color. Similarly, a microscope provides a far different depiction of reality than a telescope.

Between databases and sensors, many aspects of our lives are recorded. Governments, businesses, and individuals are recording and reporting all manners of information from the monumental to the mundane. Weather sensors record temperature and pressure data, surveillance cameras watch sidewalks and subway tunnels, and all manner of electronic behaviors are monitored: transactions, communications, friendships, and many others.

This deluge of data has led some to state that we have entered an era of Big Data, but this may be a bit of a misnomer. Human beings have always been surrounded by data. What makes the current era unique is that we have easy data. Larger and more interesting data sets are increasingly accessible through the tips of our fingers, only a web search away. We now live in a period with vast quantities of data that can be directly processed by machines. Much of this information has the potential to inform decision making, if only there was a systematic way of making sense from it all.

The field of study interested in the development of computer algorithms for transforming data into intelligent action is known as **machine learning**. This field originated in an environment where the available data, statistical methods, and computing power rapidly and simultaneously evolved. Growth in data necessitated additional computing power, which in turn spurred the development of statistical methods for analyzing large datasets. This created a cycle of advancement allowing even larger and more interesting data to be collected.

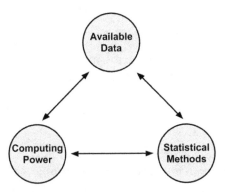

A closely related sibling of machine learning, **data mining**, is concerned with the generation of novel insight from large databases (not to be confused with the pejorative term "data mining," describing the practice of cherry-picking data to support a theory). Although there is some disagreement over how widely the two fields overlap, a potential point of distinction is that machine learning tends to be focused on performing a known task, whereas data mining is about the search for hidden nuggets of information. For instance, you might use machine learning to teach a robot to drive a car, whereas you would utilize data mining to learn what type of cars are the safest.

Machine learning algorithms are virtually a prerequisite for data mining but the opposite is not true. In other words, you can apply machine learning to tasks that do not involve data mining, but if you are using data mining methods, you are almost certainly using machine learning.

# Uses and abuses of machine learning

At its core, machine learning is primarily interested in making sense of complex data. This is a broadly applicable mission, and largely application agnostic. As you might expect, machine learning is used widely. For instance, it has been used to:

- Predict the outcomes of elections
- Identify and filter spam messages from e-mail
- Foresee criminal activity
- Automate traffic signals according to road conditions
- Produce financial estimates of storms and natural disasters
- Examine customer churn
- Create auto-piloting planes and auto-driving cars
- Identify individuals with the capacity to donate
- Target advertising to specific types of consumers

For now, don't worry about exactly how the machines learn to perform these tasks; we will get into the specifics later. But across each of these contexts, the process is the same. A machine learning algorithm takes data and identifies patterns that can be used for action. In some cases, the results are so successful that they seem to reach near-legendary status.

One possibly apocryphal tale is of a large retailer in the United States, which employed machine learning to identify expectant mothers for targeted coupon mailings. If mothers-to-be were targeted with substantial discounts, the retailer hoped they would become loyal customers who would then continue to purchase profitable items like diapers, formula, and toys.

By applying machine learning methods to purchase data, the retailer believed it had learned some useful patterns. Certain items, such as prenatal vitamins, lotions, and washcloths could be used to identify with a high degree of certainty not only whether a woman was pregnant, but also when the baby was due.

After using this data for a promotional mailing, an angry man contacted the retailer and demanded to know why his teenage daughter was receiving coupons for maternity items. He was furious that the merchant seemed to be encouraging teenage pregnancy. Later on, as a manager called to offer an apology, it was the father that ultimately apologized; after confronting his daughter, he had discovered that she was indeed pregnant.

Whether completely true or not, there is certainly an element of truth to the preceding tale. Retailers, do in fact, routinely analyze their customers' transaction data. If you've ever used a shopper's loyalty card at your grocer, coffee shop, or another retailer, it is likely that your purchase data is being used for machine learning.

Retailers use machine learning methods for advertising, targeted promotions, inventory management, or the layout of the items in the store. Some retailers have even equipped checkout lanes with devices that print coupons for promotions based on the items in the current transaction. Websites also routinely do this to serve advertisements based on your web browsing history. Given the data from many individuals, a machine learning algorithm learns typical patterns of behavior that can then be used to make recommendations.

Despite being familiar with the machine learning methods working behind the scenes, it still feels a bit like magic when a retailer or website seems to know me better than I know myself. Others may be less thrilled to discover that their data is being used in this manner. Therefore, any person wishing to utilize machine learning or data mining would be remiss not to at least briefly consider the ethical implications of the art.

# Ethical considerations

Due to the relative youth of machine learning as a discipline and the speed at which it is progressing, the associated legal issues and social norms are often quite uncertain and constantly in flux. Caution should be exercised when obtaining or analyzing data in order to avoid breaking laws, violating terms of service or data use agreements, abusing the trust, or violating privacy of the customers or the public.

> The informal corporate motto of Google, an organization, which collects perhaps more data on individuals than any other, is "don't be evil." This may serve as a reasonable starting point for forming your own ethical guidelines, but it may not be sufficient.

Certain jurisdictions may prevent you from using racial, ethnic, religious, or other protected class data for business reasons, but keep in mind that excluding this data from your analysis may not be enough—machine learning algorithms might inadvertently learn this information independently. For instance, if a certain segment of people generally live in a certain region, buy a certain product, or otherwise behave in a way that uniquely identifies them as a group, some machine learning algorithms can infer the protected information from seemingly innocuous data. In such cases, you may need to fully "de-identify" these people by excluding any potentially identifying data in addition to the protected information.

Apart from the legal consequences, using data inappropriately may hurt your bottom line. Customers may feel uncomfortable or become spooked if aspects of their lives they consider private are made public. Recently, several high-profile web applications have experienced a mass exodus of users who felt exploited when the applications' terms of service agreements changed and their data was used for purposes beyond what the users had originally agreed upon. The fact that privacy expectations differ by context, by age cohort, and by locale, adds complexity to deciding the appropriate use of personal data. It would be wise to consider the cultural implications of your work before you begin on your project.

> The fact that you *can* use data for a particular end does not always mean that you *should*.

# How do machines learn?

A commonly cited formal definition of machine learning, proposed by computer scientist *Tom M. Mitchell*, says that a machine is said to learn if it is able to take experience and utilize it such that its performance improves up on similar experiences in the future. This definition is fairly exact, yet says little about how machine learning techniques actually learn to transform data into actionable knowledge.

> Although it is not strictly necessary to understand the theoretical basis of machine learning prior to using it, this foundation provides an insight into the distinctions among machine learning algorithms. Because machine learning algorithms are modeled in many ways on human minds, you may even discover yourself examining your own mind in a different light.

Regardless of whether the learner is a human or a machine, the basic learning process is similar. It can be divided into three components as follows:

- **Data input**: It utilizes observation, memory storage, and recall to provide a factual basis for further reasoning.
- **Abstraction**: It involves the translation of data into broader representations.
- **Generalization**: It uses abstracted data to form a basis for action.

To better understand the learning process, think about the last time you studied for a difficult test, perhaps for a university final exam or a career certification. Did you wish for an eidetic (that is, photographic) memory? If so, you may be disappointed to learn that perfect recall is unlikely to save you much effort. Without a higher understanding, your knowledge is limited exactly to the data input, meaning only what you had seen before and nothing more. Therefore, without knowledge of all the questions that could appear on the exam, you would be stuck attempting to memorize answers to every question that could conceivably be asked. Obviously, this is an unsustainable strategy.

Instead, a better strategy is to spend time selectively managing only a smaller set of key ideas. The commonly used learning strategies of creating an outline or a concept map are similar to how a machine performs knowledge abstraction. The tools define relationships among information and in doing so, depict difficult ideas without needing to memorize them word-for-word. It is a more advanced form of learning because it requires that the learner puts the topic into his or her own words.

It is always a tense moment when the exam is graded and the learning strategies are either vindicated or implicated with a high or low mark. Here, one discovers whether the learning strategies generalized to the questions that the teacher or professor had selected. Generalization requires a breadth of abstracted data, as well as a higher-level understanding of how to apply such knowledge to unforeseen topics. A good teacher can be quite helpful in this regard.

Keep in mind that although we have illustrated the learning process as three distinct steps, they are merely organized this way for illustrative purposes. In reality, the three components of learning are inextricably linked. In particular, the stages of abstraction and generalization are so closely related that it would be impossible to perform one without the other. In human beings, the entire process happens subconsciously. We recollect, deduce, induct, and intuit. Yet for a computer, these processes must be made explicit. On the other hand, this is a benefit of machine learning. Because the process is transparent, the learned knowledge can be examined and utilized for future action.

# Abstraction and knowledge representation

Representing raw input data in a structured format is the quintessential task for a learning algorithm. Prior to this point, the data is merely ones and zeros on a disk or in memory; they have no meaning. The work of assigning a meaning to data occurs during the **abstraction** process.

The connection between ideas and reality is exemplified by the famous *René Magritte* painting *The Treachery of Images* shown as follows:

Source: http://collections.lacma.org/node/239578

The painting depicts a tobacco pipe with the caption *Ceci n'est pas une pipe* ("this is not a pipe"). The point *Magritte* was illustrating is that a representation of a pipe is not truly a pipe. In spite of the fact that the pipe is not real, anybody viewing the painting easily recognizes that the picture is a pipe, suggesting that observers' minds are able to connect the picture of a pipe to the idea of a pipe, which can then be connected to an actual pipe that could be held in the hand. Abstracted connections like this are the basis of **knowledge representation**, the formation of logical structures that assist with turning raw sensory information into a meaningful insight.

During the process of knowledge representation, the computer summarizes raw inputs in a **model**, an explicit description of the structured patterns among data. There are many different types of models. You may already be familiar with some. Examples include:

- Equations
- Diagrams such as trees and graphs
- Logical if/else rules
- Groupings of data known as clusters

The choice of model is typically not left up to the machine. Instead, the model is dictated by the learning task and the type of data being analyzed. Later in this chapter, we will discuss methods for choosing the type of model in more detail.

The process of fitting a particular model to a dataset is known as **training**. Why is this not called learning? First, note that the learning process does not end with the step of data abstraction. Learning requires an additional step to generalize the knowledge to future data. Second, the term training more accurately describes the actual process undertaken when the model is fitted to the data. Learning implies a sort of inductive, bottom-up reasoning. Training better connotes the fact that the machine learning model is imposed by the human teacher onto the machine student, providing the computer with a structure it attempts to model after.

When the model has been trained, the data has been transformed into an abstract form that summarizes the original information. It is important to note that the model does not itself provide additional data, yet it is sometimes interesting on its own. How can this be? The reason is that by imposing an assumed structure on the underlying data, it gives insight into the unseen and provides a theory about how the data is related. Take for instance the discovery of gravity. By fitting equations to observational data, *Sir Isaac Newton* deduced the concept of gravity. But gravity was always present. It simply wasn't recognized as a concept until the model noted it in abstract terms — specifically, by becoming the $g$ term in a model that explains observations of falling objects.

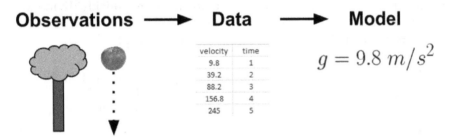

Most models will not result in the development of theories that shake up scientific thought for centuries. Still, your model might result in the discovery of previously unseen relationships among data. A model trained on genomic data might find several genes that when combined are responsible for the onset of diabetes; banks might discover a seemingly innocuous type of transaction that systematically appears prior to fraudulent activity; psychologists might identify a combination of characteristics indicating a new disorder. The underlying relationships were always present; but in conceptualizing the information in a different format, a model presents the connections in a new light.

# Generalization

Recall that the learning process is not complete until the learner is able to use its abstracted knowledge for future action. Yet an issue remains before the learner can proceed — there are countless underlying relationships that might be identified during the abstraction process and myriad ways to model these relationships. Unless the number of potential theories is limited, the learner will be unable to utilize the information. It would be stuck where it started, with a large pool of information but no actionable insight.

The term **generalization** describes the process of turning abstracted knowledge into a form that can be utilized for action. Generalization is a somewhat vague process that is a bit difficult to describe. Traditionally, it has been imagined as a search through the entire set of models (that is, theories) that could have been abstracted during training. Specifically, if you imagine a hypothetical set containing every possible theory that could be established from the data, generalization involves the reduction of this set into a manageable number of important findings.

Generally, it is not feasible to reduce the number of potential concepts by examining them one-by-one and determining which are the most useful. Instead, machine learning algorithms generally employ shortcuts that more quickly divide the set of concepts. Toward this end, the algorithm will employ **heuristics**, or educated guesses about the where to find the most important concepts.

 Because the heuristics utilize approximations and other rules of thumb, they are not guaranteed to find the optimal set of concepts that model the data. However, without utilizing these shortcuts, finding useful information in a large dataset would be infeasible.

Heuristics are routinely used by human beings to quickly generalize experience to new scenarios. If you have ever utilized gut instinct to make a snap decision prior to fully evaluating your circumstances, you were intuitively using mental heuristics.

For example, the availability heuristic is the tendency for people to estimate the likelihood of an event by how easily examples can be recalled. The availability heuristic might help explain the prevalence of the fear of airline travel relative to automobile travel, despite automobiles being statistically more dangerous. Accidents involving air travel are highly publicized and traumatic events, and are likely to be very easily recalled, whereas car accidents barely warrant a mention in the newspaper.

The preceding example illustrates the potential for heuristics to result in illogical conclusions. Browsing a list of common logical fallacies, one is likely to note many that seem rooted in heuristic-based thinking. For instance, the gambler's fallacy, or the belief that a run of bad luck implies that a stretch of better luck is due, may be resultant from the application of the representativeness heuristic, which erroneously led the gambler to believe that all random sequences are balanced since most random sequences are balanced.

The folly of misapplied heuristics is not limited to human beings. The heuristics employed by machine learning algorithms also sometimes result in erroneous conclusions. If the conclusions are systematically imprecise, the algorithm is said to have a **bias**. For example, suppose that a machine learning algorithm learned to identify faces by finding two circles, or eyes, positioned side-by-side above a line for a mouth. The algorithm might then have trouble with, or be biased against faces that do not conform to its model. This may include faces with glasses, turned at an angle, looking sideways, or with darker skin tones. Similarly, it could be biased toward faces with lighter eye colors or other characteristics that do not conform to its understanding of the world.

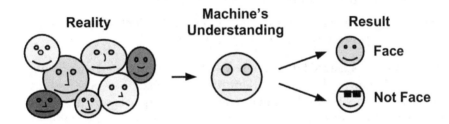

In modern usage, the word bias has come to carry quite negative connotations. Various forms of media frequently claim to be free from bias, and claim to report the facts objectively, untainted by emotion. Still, consider for a moment the possibility that a little bias might be useful. Without a bit of arbitrariness, might it be a bit difficult to decide among several competing choices, each with distinct strengths and weaknesses? Indeed, some recent studies in the field of psychology have suggested that individuals born with damage to portions of the brain responsible for emotion are ineffectual at decision making, and might spend hours debating simple decisions such as what color shirt to wear or where to eat lunch. Paradoxically, bias is what blinds us from some information while also allowing us to utilize other information for action.

# Assessing the success of learning

Bias is a necessary evil associated with the abstraction and generalization process inherent in any machine learning task. Every learner has its weaknesses and is biased in a particular way; there is no single model to rule them all. Therefore, the final step in the generalization process is to determine the model's success in spite of its biases.

After a model has been trained on an initial dataset, the model is tested on a new dataset, and judged on how well its characterization of the training data generalizes to the new data. It's worth noting that it is exceedingly rare for a model to perfectly generalize to every unforeseen case.

In part, the failure for models to perfectly generalize is due to the problem of **noise**, or unexplained variations in data. Noisy data is caused by seemingly random events, such as:

- Measurement error due to imprecise sensors that sometimes add or subtract a bit from the reading

- Issues with reporting data, such as respondents reporting random answers to survey questions in order to finish more quickly

- Errors caused when data is recorded incorrectly, including missing, null, truncated, incorrectly coded, or corrupted values

Trying to model the noise in data is the basis of a problem called **overfitting**. Because noise is unexplainable by definition, attempting to explain the noise will result in erroneous conclusions that do not generalize well to new cases. Attempting to generate theories to explain the noise also results in more complex models that are more likely to ignore the true pattern the learner is trying to identify. A model that seems to perform well during training but does poorly during testing is said to be overfitted to the training dataset as it does not generalize well.

Solutions to the problem of overfitting are specific to particular machine learning approaches. For now, the important point is to be aware of the issue. How well models are able to handle noisy data is an important source of distinction among them.

# Steps to apply machine learning to your data

Any machine learning task can be broken down into a series of more manageable steps. This book has been organized according to the following process:

1. **Collecting data**: Whether the data is written on paper, recorded in text files and spreadsheets, or stored in an SQL database, you will need to gather it in an electronic format suitable for analysis. This data will serve as the learning material an algorithm uses to generate actionable knowledge.

2. **Exploring and preparing the data**: The quality of any machine learning project is based largely on the quality of data it uses. This step in the machine learning process tends to require a great deal of human intervention. An often cited statistic suggests that 80 percent of the effort in machine learning is devoted to data. Much of this time is spent learning more about the data and its nuances during a practice called data exploration.

3. **Training a model on the data**: By the time the data has been prepared for analysis, you are likely to have a sense of what you are hoping to learn from the data. The specific machine learning task will inform the selection of an appropriate algorithm, and the algorithm will represent the data in the form of a model.

4. **Evaluating model performance**: Because each machine learning model results in a biased solution to the learning problem, it is important to evaluate how well the algorithm learned from its experience. Depending on the type of model used, you might be able to evaluate the accuracy of the model using a test dataset, or you may need to develop measures of performance specific to the intended application.

5. **Improving model performance**: If better performance is needed, it becomes necessary to utilize more advanced strategies to augment the performance of the model. Sometimes, it may be necessary to switch to a different type of model altogether. You may need to supplement your data with additional data, or perform additional preparatory work as in step two of this process.

After these steps have been completed, if the model appears to be performing satisfactorily, it can be deployed for its intended task. As the case may be, you might utilize your model to provide score data for predictions (possibly in real time), for projections of financial data, to generate useful insight for marketing or research, or to automate tasks such as mail delivery or flying aircraft. The successes and failures of the deployed model might even provide additional data to train the next generation of your model.

# Choosing a machine learning algorithm

The process of choosing a machine learning algorithm involves matching the characteristics of the data to be learned to the biases of the available approaches. Since the choice of a machine learning algorithm is largely dependent upon the type of data you are analyzing and the proposed task at hand, it is often helpful to be thinking about this process while you are gathering, exploring, and cleaning your data.

 It may be tempting to learn a couple of machine learning techniques and apply them to everything, but resist this temptation. No machine learning approach is best for every circumstance. This fact is described by the **No Free Lunch** theorem, introduced by *David Wolpert* in 1996. For more information, visit: http://www.no-free-lunch.org.

# Thinking about the input data

All machine learning algorithms require input training data. The exact format may differ, but in its most basic form, input data takes the form of examples and features.

An **example** is literally a single exemplary instance of the underlying concept to be learned; it is one set of data describing the atomic unit of interest for the analysis. If you were building a learning algorithm to identify spam e-mail, the examples would be data from many individual electronic messages. To detect cancerous tumors, the examples might comprise biopsies from a number of patients.

The phrase **unit of observation** is used to describe the units that the examples are measured in. Commonly, the unit of observation is in the form of transactions, persons, time points, geographic regions, or measurements. Other possibilities include combinations of these such as person years, which would denote cases where the same person is tracked over multiple time points.

A **feature** is a characteristic or attribute of an example, which might be useful for learning the desired concept. In the previous examples, attributes in the spam detection dataset might consist of the words used in the e-mail messages. For the cancer dataset, the attributes might be genomic data from the biopsied cells, or measured characteristics of the patient such as weight, height, or blood pressure.

The following spreadsheet shows a dataset in **matrix format**, which means that each example has the same number of features. In matrix data, each row in the spreadsheet is an example and each column is a feature. Here, the rows indicate examples of automobiles while the columns record various features of the cars such as the price, mileage, color, and transmission. Matrix format data is by far the most common form used in machine learning, though as you will see in later chapters, other forms are used occasionally in specialized cases.

**features**

| | A | B | C | D | E | F |
|---|---|---|---|---|---|---|
| 1 | year | model | price | mileage | color | transmission |
| 2 | 2011 | SEL | 21992 | 7413 | Yellow | AUTO |
| 3 | 2011 | SEL | 20995 | 10926 | Gray | AUTO |
| 4 | 2011 | SEL | 19995 | 7351 | Silver | AUTO |
| 5 | 2011 | SEL | 17809 | 11613 | Gray | AUTO |
| 6 | 2012 | SE | 17500 | 8367 | White | AUTO |
| 7 | 2010 | SEL | 17495 | 25125 | Silver | AUTO |
| 8 | 2011 | SEL | 17000 | 27393 | Blue | AUTO |
| 9 | 2010 | SEL | 16995 | 21026 | Silver | AUTO |
| 10 | 2011 | SES | 16995 | 32655 | Silver | AUTO |

**examples**

Features come in various forms as well. If a feature represents a characteristic measured in numbers, it is unsurprisingly called **numeric**. Alternatively, if it measures an attribute that is represented by a set of categories, the feature is called **categorical** or **nominal**. A special case of categorical variables is called **ordinal**, which designates a nominal variable with categories falling in an ordered list. Some examples of ordinal variables include clothing sizes such as small, medium, and large, or a measurement of customer satisfaction on a scale from 1 to 5. It is important to consider what the features represent because the type and number of features in your dataset will assist with determining an appropriate machine learning algorithm for your task.

# Thinking about types of machine learning algorithms

Machine learning algorithms can be divided into two main groups: supervised learners that are used to construct predictive models, and unsupervised learners that are used to build descriptive models. Which type you will need to use depends on the learning task you hope to accomplish.

A **predictive model** is used for tasks that involve, as the name implies, the prediction of one value using other values in the dataset. The learning algorithm attempts to discover and model the relationship among the **target** feature (the feature being predicted) and the other features. Despite the common use of the word "prediction" to imply forecasting predictive models need not necessarily foresee future events. For instance, a predictive model could be used to predict past events such as the date of a baby's conception using the mother's hormone levels; or, predictive models could be used in real time to control traffic lights during rush hours.

Because predictive models are given clear instruction on what they need to learn and how they are intended to learn it, the process of training a predictive model is known as **supervised learning**. The supervision does not refer to human involvement, but rather the fact that the target values provide a supervisory role, which indicates to the learner the task it needs to learn. Specifically, given a set of data, the learning algorithm attempts to optimize a function (the model) to find the combination of feature values that result in the target output.

The often used supervised machine learning task of predicting which category an example belongs to is known as **classification**. It is easy to think of potential uses for a classifier. For instance, you could predict whether:

- A football team will win or lose
- A person will live past the age of 100
- An applicant will default on a loan
- An earthquake will strike next year

The target feature to be predicted is a categorical feature known as the **class** and is divided into categories called **levels**. A class can have two or more levels, and the levels need not necessarily be ordinal. Because classification is so widely used in machine learning, there are many types of classification algorithms.

Supervised learners can also be used to predict numeric data such as income, laboratory values, test scores, or counts of items. To predict such numeric values, a common form of **numeric prediction** fits linear regression models to the input data. Although regression models are not the only type of numeric models, they are by far the most widely used. Regression methods are widely used for forecasting, as they quantify in exact terms the association between the inputs and the target, including both the magnitude and uncertainty of the relationship.

Since it is easy to convert numbers to categories (for example, ages 13 to 19 are teenagers) and categories to numbers (for example, assign 1 to all males, 0 to all females), the boundary between classification models and numeric prediction models is not necessarily firm.

A **descriptive model** is used for tasks that would benefit from the insight gained from summarizing data in new and interesting ways. As opposed to predictive models that predict a target of interest; in a descriptive model, no single feature is more important than any other. In fact, because there is no target to learn, the process of training a descriptive model is called **unsupervised learning**. Although it can be more difficult to think of applications for descriptive models — after all, what good is a learner that isn't learning anything in particular — they are used quite regularly for data mining.

For example, the descriptive modeling task called **pattern discovery** is used to identify frequent associations within data. Pattern discovery is often used for **market basket analysis** on transactional purchase data. Here, the goal is to identify items that are frequently purchased together, such that the learned information can be used to refine the marketing tactics. For instance, if a retailer learns that swimming trunks are commonly purchased at the same time as sunscreen, the retailer might reposition the items more closely in the store, or run a promotion to "up-sell" customers on associated items.

Originally used only in retail contexts, pattern discovery is now starting to be used in quite innovative ways. For instance, it can be used to detect patterns of fraudulent behavior, screen for genetic defects, or prevent criminal activity.

The descriptive modeling task of dividing a dataset into homogeneous groups is called **clustering**. This is sometimes used for segmentation analysis that identifies groups of individuals with similar purchasing, donating, or demographic information so that advertising campaigns can be tailored to particular audiences. Although the machine is capable of identifying the groups, human intervention is required to interpret them. For example, given five different clusters of shoppers at a grocery store, the marketing team will need to understand the differences among the groups in order to create a promotion that best suits each group. However, this is almost certainly easier than trying to create a unique appeal for each customer.

# Matching your data to an appropriate algorithm

The following table lists the general types of machine learning algorithms covered in this book, each of which may be implemented in several ways. Although this covers only some of the entire set of all machine learning algorithms, learning these methods will provide a sufficient foundation for making sense of other methods as you encounter them.

| Model | Task | Chapter |
|---|---|---|
| **Supervised Learning Algorithms** | | |
| Nearest Neighbor | Classification | *Chapter 3* |
| naive Bayes | Classification | *Chapter 4* |
| Decision Trees | Classification | *Chapter 5* |
| Classification Rule Learners | Classification | *Chapter 5* |
| Linear Regression | Numeric prediction | *Chapter 6* |
| Regression Trees | Numeric prediction | *Chapter 6* |
| Model Trees | Numeric prediction | *Chapter 6* |
| Neural Networks | Dual use | *Chapter 7* |
| Support Vector Machines | Dual use | *Chapter 7* |
| **Unsupervised Learning Algorithms** | | |
| Association Rules | Pattern detection | *Chapter 8* |
| k-means Clustering | Clustering | *Chapter 9* |

To match a learning task to a machine learning approach, you will need to begin with one of the four types of tasks: classification, numeric prediction, pattern detection, or clustering. Certain tasks make the choice of algorithm simpler. For instance, if you are undertaking pattern detection, you will likely employ association rules. Similarly, a clustering problem will likely utilize the k-means algorithm while numeric prediction will utilize regression analysis or regression trees.

For classification, more thought is needed to match a learning problem to an appropriate classifier. In these cases, it is helpful to consider the various distinctions among the algorithms. For instance, within classification problems, decision trees result in models that are readily understood, while the models of neural networks are notoriously difficult to interpret. If you were designing a credit-scoring model, this could be an important distinction because law often requires that the applicant must be notified about the reasons he or she was rejected for the loan. Even if the neural network was better at predicting loan defaults if the predictions cannot be explained, then it is useless.

In each chapter, the key strengths and weaknesses of each approach will be listed. Although you will sometimes find that these characteristics exclude certain models from consideration in most cases, the choice of model is arbitrary. In this case, feel free to use whichever algorithm you are most comfortable with. Other times, when predictive accuracy is primary, you may need to test several and choose the one that fits best. In later chapters, we will even look at methods of combining models that utilize the best properties of each.

# Using R for machine learning

Many of the algorithms needed for machine learning in R are not included as part of the base installation. Thanks to R being free open source software, there is no additional charge for this functionality. The algorithms needed for machine learning were added to base R by a large community of experts who contributed to the software. A collection of R functions that can be shared among users is called a **package**. Free packages exist for each of the machine learning algorithms covered in this book. In fact, this book only covers a small portion of the more popular machine learning packages.

If you are interested in the breadth of R packages (4,209 packages were available at the time of writing this), you can view a list at the **Comprehensive R Archive Network (CRAN)** collection of web and FTP sites located around the world to provide the most up-to-date versions of R software and R packages for download. If you obtained the R software via download, it was most likely from CRAN. The CRAN website is available at:

```
http://cran.r-project.org/index.html.
```

> If you do not already have R, the CRAN website also provides installation instructions and information on where to find help if you have trouble.

The **Packages** link on the left side of the page will take you to a page where you can browse the packages in alphabetical order or sorted by publication date. Perhaps even better, the **CRAN Task Views** provide organized lists of packages by subject area. The task view for machine learning, which lists the packages covered in this book (and many more), is available at:

```
http://cran.r-project.org/web/views/MachineLearning.html
```

# Installing and loading R packages

Despite the vast set of available R add-ons, the package format makes installation and use a virtually effortless process. To demonstrate the use of packages, we will install and load the RWeka package, which was developed by *Kurt Hornik, Christian Buchta*, and *Achim Zeileis* (see *Open-Source Machine Learning: R Meets Weka* in Computational Statistics 24: 225-232 for more information). The RWeka package provides a collection of functions that give R access to the machine learning algorithms in the Java-based Weka software package by *Ian H. Witten* and *Eibe Frank*. For more information on Weka, see:

```
http://www.cs.waikato.ac.nz/~ml/weka/.
```

> To use the RWeka package, you will need to have Java installed if it isn't already (many computers come with Java preinstalled). Java is a set of programming tools, available for free, which allow for the use of cross-platform applications such as Weka. For more information and to download Java for your system, visit: http://java.com.

# Installing an R package

The most direct way to install a package is via the install.packages() function. To install the RWeka package, at the R command prompt simply type:

```
> install.packages("RWeka")
```

R will then connect to CRAN and download the package in the correct format for your operating system. Some packages such as RWeka require additional packages to be installed before they can be used (these are called dependencies). By default, the installer will automatically download and install any dependencies.

> The first time you install a package, R may ask you to choose a CRAN mirror. If this happens, choose the mirror residing at a location close to you. This will generally provide the fastest download speed.

The default installation options are appropriate for most systems. However, in some cases, you may want to install a package to another location. For example, if you do not have root or administrator privileges on your system, you may need to specify an alternative installation path. This can be accomplished using the `lib` option, as follows:

```
> install.packages("RWeka", lib="/path/to/library")
```

The installation function also provides additional options for installing from a local file, installing from source, or using experimental versions. You can read about these options in the help file by using the following command:

```
> ?install.packages
```

## Installing a package using the point-and-click interface

As an alternative to typing the `install.packages()` command, R provides a graphical user interface (GUI) for package installation. On a Microsoft Windows system, this can be accessed from the **Install package(s)** command item under the **Packages** menu, as shown in the following screenshot. On Mac OS X, the command is labeled **Package Installer** and is located under the **Packages & Data** menu.

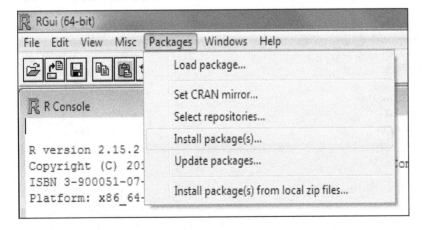

On Windows, after launching the package installer (and choosing a CRAN mirror location if you haven't already), a large list of packages will appear. Simply scroll to the RWeka package and click on the **OK** button to install the package and all dependencies to the default location.

On Mac OS X, the package installer menu provides additional options. To load the list of packages, click on the **Get List** button. Scroll to the RWeka package (or use the **Package Search** feature) and click on **Install Selected**. Note that by default, the Mac OS X Package Installer does not install dependencies unless the **Install Dependencies** checkbox is selected, as shown in the following screenshot:

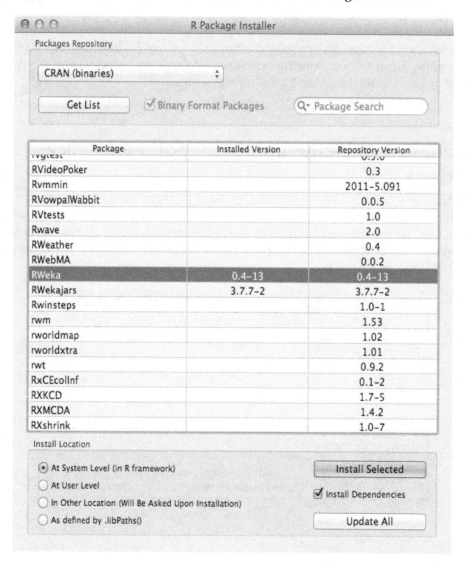

## Loading an R package

In order to conserve memory, R does not load every installed package by default. Instead, packages are loaded by users as they are needed using the `library()` function.

 The name of this function leads some people to incorrectly use the terms library and package interchangeably. However, to be precise, a library refers to the location where packages are installed and never to a package itself.

To load the RWeka package we installed previously, you would type the following:

```
> library(RWeka)
```

Aside from RWeka, there are several other R packages that will be used in later chapters. Installation instructions will be provided as additional packages are used.

# Summary

Machine learning originated at the intersection of statistics, database science, and computer science. It is a powerful tool, capable of finding actionable insight in large quantities of data. Still, caution must be used in order to avoid common abuses of machine learning in the real world.

In conceptual terms, learning involves the abstraction of data into a structured representation, and the generalization of this structure into action. In more practical terms, a machine learner uses data containing examples and features of the concept to be learned, and summarizes this data in the form of a model, which is then used for predictive or descriptive purposes. These can be further divided into specific tasks including classification, numeric prediction, pattern detection, and clustering. Among the many options, machine learning algorithms are chosen on the basis of the input data and the learning task.

R provides support for machine learning in the form of community-authored packages. These powerful tools are free to download, but need to be installed before they can be used. In the next chapter, we will further introduce the basic R commands that are used to manage and prepare data for machine learning.

# 2
# Managing and Understanding Data

A key early component of any machine learning project involves managing and understanding the data you have collected. Although you may not find it as gratifying as building and deploying models — the stages in which you begin to see the fruits of your labor — you cannot ignore the preparatory work.

Any learning algorithm is only as good as its input data, and in many cases, input data is complex, messy, and spread across multiple sources and formats. Because of this complexity, the largest portion of effort invested in machine learning projects is spent on the data preparation and exploration process.

This chapter is divided into three main sections. The first section discusses the basic data structures R uses to store data. You will become very familiar with these structures as you create and manipulate datasets. The second section is practical, as it covers several functions that are useful for getting data in and out of R. In the third section, methods for understanding data are illustrated throughout the process of exploring a real-world dataset.

By the end of this chapter, you will understand:

- The basic R data structures and how to use them to store and extract data
- How to get data into R from a variety of source formats
- Common methods for understanding and visualizing complex data

Since the way R thinks about data will define the way you think about data, it is helpful to understand the basic R data structures before jumping into data preparation. However, if you are already familiar with R data structures, feel free to skip ahead to the section on data preprocessing.

# R data structures

There are numerous types of data structures across programming languages, each
with strengths and weaknesses specific to particular tasks. Since R is a programming
language used widely for statistical data analysis, the data structures it utilizes
are designed to make it easy to manipulate data for this type of work. The R data
structures used most frequently in machine learning are vectors, factors, lists, arrays,
and data frames. Each of these data types is specialized for a specific data management
task, which makes it important to understand how they will interact in your R project.

# Vectors

The fundamental R data structure is the **vector**, which stores an ordered set of
values called **elements**. A vector can contain any number of elements. However, all
the elements must be of the same type; for instance, a vector cannot contain both
numbers and text.

There are several vector types commonly used in machine learning: `integer`
(numbers without decimals), `numeric` (numbers with decimals), `character` (text data),
or `logical` (TRUE or FALSE values). There are also two special values: NULL, which is
used to indicate the absence of any value, and NA, which indicates a missing value.

It is tedious to enter large amounts of data manually, but simple vectors can be
created by using the combine function `c()`. The vector can also be given a name
using the arrow `<-` operator, which is R's assignment operator, used in a similar
way to the `=` assignment operator in many other programming languages.

For example, let's construct a set of vectors containing data on three medical patients.
We'll create a character vector named `subject_name`, which contains the three
patient names, a numeric vector named `temperature` containing each patient's body
temperature, and a logical vector `flu_status` containing each patient's diagnosis;
TRUE if he or she has influenza, FALSE otherwise. As shown in the following listing,
the three vectors are:

```
> subject_name <- c("John Doe", "Jane Doe", "Steve Graves")
> temperature <- c(98.1, 98.6, 101.4)
> flu_status <- c(FALSE, FALSE, TRUE)
```

Because R vectors are inherently ordered, the records can be accessed by counting
the item's number in the set, beginning at 1, and surrounding this number with
square brackets (for example, [ and ]) after the name of the vector. For instance, to
obtain the body temperature for patient Jane Doe, or element 2 in the temperature
vector simply type:

```
> temperature[2]
[1] 98.6
```

R offers a variety of convenient methods for extracting data from vectors. A range of values can be obtained using the colon operator. For instance, to obtain the body temperature of Jane Doe and Steve Graves, type:

```
> temperature[2:3]
[1] 98.6 101.4
```

Items can be excluded by specifying a negative item number. To exclude Jane Doe's temperature data, type:

```
> temperature[-2]
[1]   98.1 101.4
```

Finally, it is also sometimes useful to specify a logical vector indicating whether each item should be included. For example, to include the first two temperature readings but exclude the third, type:

```
> temperature[c(TRUE, TRUE, FALSE)]
[1] 98.1 98.6
```

As you will see shortly, the vector provides the foundation for many other R data structures. Therefore, knowing the various vector operations is crucial for working with data in R.

**Downloading the example code**

You can download the example code files for all Packt books you have purchased from your account at http://www.packtpub.com. If you purchased this book elsewhere, you can visit http://www.packtpub.com/support and register to have the files e-mailed directly to you.

# Factors

If you recall from *Chapter 1, Introducing Machine Learning*, features that represent a characteristic with categories of values are known as **nominal**. Although it is possible to use a character vector to store nominal data, R provides a data structure known as a **factor** specifically for this purpose. A factor is a special case of vector that is solely used for representing nominal variables. In the medical dataset we are building, we might use a factor to represent gender, because it uses two categories: MALE and FEMALE.

Why not use `character` vectors? An advantage of using factors is that they are generally more efficient than `character` vectors because the category labels are stored only once. Rather than storing MALE, MALE, FEMALE, the computer may store 1, 1, 2. This can save memory. Additionally, certain machine learning algorithms use special routines to handle categorical variables. Coding categorical variables as factors ensures that the model will treat this data appropriately.

To create a factor from a `character` vector, simply apply the `factor()` function. For example:

```
> gender <- factor(c("MALE", "FEMALE", "MALE"))
> gender
[1] MALE    FEMALE MALE
Levels: FEMALE MALE
```

Notice that when the gender data was displayed, R printed additional information indicating the levels of the gender factor. The levels comprise the set of possible categories the data could take, in this case MALE or FEMALE.

When factors are created, we can add additional levels that may not appear in the data. Suppose we added another factor for blood type as shown in the following example :

```
> blood <- factor(c("O", "AB", "A"),
                   levels = c("A", "B", "AB", "O"))
> blood
[1] O  AB A
Levels: A B AB O
```

Notice that when we defined the `blood` factor for the three patients, we specified an additional vector of four possible blood types using the `levels` = statement. As a result, even though our data include only types O, AB, and A, all four types are stored with the `blood` factor as indicated by the output Levels: A B AB O. Storing the additional level allows for the possibility of adding data with the other blood type in the future. It also ensures that if we were to create a table of blood types, we would know that type B exists, despite it not being recorded in our data.

# Lists

Another special type of vector, a list, is used for storing an ordered set of values. However, unlike a vector that requires all elements to be the same type, a list allows different types of values to be collected. Due to this flexibility, lists are often used to store various types of input and output data and sets of configuration parameters for machine learning models.

To illustrate lists, consider the medical patient dataset we have been constructing, with data for three patients stored in five vectors. If we wanted to display all the data on John Doe (subject 1), we would need to enter five R commands:

```
> subject_name[1]
[1] "John Doe"
> temperature[1]
[1] 98.1
> flu_status[1]
[1] FALSE
> gender[1]
[1] MALE
Levels: FEMALE MALE
> blood[1]
[1] O
Levels: A B AB O
```

This seems like a lot of work to display one patient's medical data. The list structure allows us to group all of a patient's data into one object we can use repeatedly.

Similar to creating a vector with `c()`, a list is created using the `list()` function as shown in the following example. One notable difference is that when a list is constructed, you have the option of providing names (`fullname` in the following example), for each value in the sequence of items. The names are not required, but allow the list's values to be accessed later on by name, rather than by the numbered position as with vectors:

```
> subject1 <- list(fullname = subject_name[1],
                   temperature = temperature[1],
                   flu_status = flu_status[1],
                   gender = gender[1],
                   blood = blood[1])
```

Printing a patient's data is now a matter of typing a single command:

```
> subject1
$fullname
[1] "John Doe"

$temperature
[1] 98.1
```

```
$flu_status
[1] FALSE

$gender
[1] MALE
Levels: FEMALE MALE

$blood
[1] O
Levels: A B AB O
```

Note that the values are labeled with the names we specified in the preceding command. Although a list can be accessed using the same methods as a vector, the names give additional clarity for accessing the values, rather than needing to remember the position of the temperature value, like this:

```
> subject1[2]
$temperature
[1] 98.1
```

It is often easier to access temperature directly, by appending a $ and the value's name to the name of the list:

```
> subject1$temperature
[1] 98.1
```

Accessing the value by name also ensures that if you add or remove values from the list, you will not accidentally retrieve the wrong list item when the ordering changes.

It is possible to obtain several items in a list by specifying a vector of names:

```
> subject1[c("temperature", "flu_status")]
$temperature
[1] 98.1

$flu_status
[1] FALSE
```

Although entire datasets could be constructed using lists (or lists of lists), constructing a dataset is common enough that R provides a specialized data structure specifically for this task.

# Data frames

By far the most important R data structure utilized in machine learning is the **data frame**, a structure analogous to a spreadsheet or database since it has both rows and columns of data. In R terms, a data frame can be understood as a list of vectors or factors, each having exactly the same number of values. Because the data frame is literally a list of vectors, it combines aspects of both vectors and lists.

Let's create a data frame for our patient dataset. Using the patient data vectors we created previously, the `data.frame()` function combines them into a data frame:

```
> pt_data <- data.frame(subject_name, temperature, flu_status,
    gender, blood, stringsAsFactors = FALSE)
```

You might notice something new in the preceding code; we included an additional parameter: `stringsAsFactors = FALSE`. If we do not specify this option, R will automatically convert every character vector to a factor; this a feature which is occasionally useful, but is also sometimes excessive. Here, for example, the `subject_name` field is definitely not categorical data; names are not categories of values. Therefore, setting the `stringsAsFactors` option to `FALSE` allows us to convert to factors only where it makes sense for the project.

When we display the `pt_data` data frame, we see that the structure is quite different from the data structures we worked with previously:

```
> pt_data
  subject_name temperature flu_status gender blood
1     John Doe        98.1 FALSE       MALE      O
2     Jane Doe        98.6 FALSE       FEMALE    AB
3 Steve Graves       101.4  TRUE       MALE      A
```

Compared to the one-dimensional vectors, factors, and lists, a data frame has two dimensions and it is therefore displayed in matrix format. The data frame has one column for each vector of patient data and one row for each patient. In machine learning terms, the columns are the features or attributes and the rows are the examples.

To extract entire columns (vectors) of data, we can take advantage of the fact that a data frame is simply a list of vectors. Similar to lists, the most direct way to extract a single element, in this case a vector or column of data, is by referring to it by name. For example, to obtain the `subject_name` vector, type:

```
> pt_data$subject_name
[1] "John Doe"     "Jane Doe"      "Steve Graves"
```

Also similar to lists, a vector of names can be used to extract several columns from a data frame:

```
> pt_data[c("temperature", "flu_status")]
  temperature flu_status
1        98.1 FALSE
2        98.6 FALSE
3       101.4  TRUE
```

When we access the data frame in this way, the result is a data frame containing all rows of data for the requested columns. You could also enter `pt_data[2:3]` to extract the `temperature` and `flu_status` columns, but listing the columns by name results in clear and easy-to-maintain R code.

To extract values in the data frame, we can use methods like those we learned for accessing values in vectors, with an important exception; because the data frame is two-dimensional, you will need to specify the position of both the rows and columns you would like to extract. Rows are specified first, followed by a comma, followed by the columns in a format like this: `[rows, columns]`, starting from the number 1.

For instance, to extract the value in the first row and second column of the patient data frame (the temperature value for John Doe), you would enter:

```
> pt_data[1, 2]
[1] 98.1
```

If you would like more than one row or column of data, this can be done by specifying vectors for the row and column numbers you would like. The following statement will pull data from rows 1 and 3, and columns 2 and 4:

```
> pt_data[c(1, 3), c(2, 4)]
  temperature gender
1        98.1   MALE
3       101.4   MALE
```

To extract all of the rows or columns, rather than listing every one, simply leave the row or column portion blank. For example, to extract all rows of the first column:

```
> pt_data[, 1]
[1] "John Doe"     "Jane Doe"     "Steve Graves"
```

To extract all columns for the first row:

```
> pt_data[1, ]
  subject_name temperature flu_status gender blood
1    John Doe        98.1      FALSE   MALE     O
```

And to extract everything:

```
> pt_data[ , ]
  subject_name temperature flu_status gender blood
1    John Doe        98.1      FALSE   MALE     O
2    Jane Doe        98.6      FALSE FEMALE    AB
3 Steve Graves      101.4       TRUE   MALE     A
```

The methods we have learned for accessing values in lists and vectors can also be used for retrieving data frame rows and columns. For example, columns can be accessed by name rather than position, and negative signs can be used to exclude rows or columns of data. Therefore, the statement:

```
> pt_data[c(1, 3), c("temperature", "gender")]
```

Is equivalent to:

```
> pt_data[-2, c(-1, -3, -5)]
```

To become familiar working with data frames, try practicing these operations with the patient data, or better yet, use your own dataset. These types of operations are crucial to much of the work we will do in later chapters.

# Matrixes and arrays

In addition to data frames, R provides other structures that store values in tabular form. A **matrix** is a data structure that represents a two-dimensional table, with rows and columns of data. R matrixes can contain any single type of data, although they are most often used for mathematical operations and therefore typically store only numeric data.

To create a matrix, simply supply a vector of data to the matrix() function, along with a parameter specifying the number of rows (nrow) or number of columns (ncol). For example, to create a 2x2 matrix storing the first four letters of the alphabet, we can use the nrow parameter to request the data to be divided into two rows:

```
> m <- matrix(c('a', 'b', 'c', 'd'), nrow = 2)
> m
     [,1] [,2]
[1,] "a"  "c"
[2,] "b"  "d"
```

This is equivalent to the matrix produced using `ncol = 2`:

```
> m <- matrix(c('a', 'b', 'c', 'd'), ncol = 2)
> m
     [,1] [,2]
[1,] "a"  "c"
[2,] "b"  "d"
```

You will notice that R loaded the first column of the matrix first, then loaded the second column. This is called **column-major order**. To illustrate this further, let's see what happens if we add a few more values to the matrix.

With six values, requesting two rows creates a matrix with three columns:

```
> m <- matrix(c('a', 'b', 'c', 'd', 'e', 'f'), nrow = 2)
> m
     [,1] [,2] [,3]
[1,] "a"  "c"  "e"
[2,] "b"  "d"  "f"
```

Similarly, requesting two columns creates a matrix with three rows:

```
> m <- matrix(c('a', 'b', 'c', 'd', 'e', 'f'), ncol = 2)
> m
     [,1] [,2]
[1,] "a"  "d"
[2,] "b"  "e"
[3,] "c"  "f"
```

As with data frames, values in matrixes can be extracted using `[row, column]` notation. For instance, `m[1, 1]` will return the value a and `m[3, 2]` will extract f from the m matrix. Similarly, entire rows or columns can be requested:

```
> m[1, ]
[1] "a" "d"
> m[, 1]
[1] "a" "b" "c"
```

Closely related to the matrix structure is the **array**, which is a multi-dimensional table of data. Where a matrix has rows and columns of values, an array has rows, columns, and any number of additional layers of values. Although we will occasionally use matrixes in later chapters, the use of arrays is outside the scope of this book.

# Managing data with R

One of the challenges faced when working with massive datasets involves gathering, preparing, and otherwise managing data from a variety of sources. This task is facilitated by R's tools for loading data from many common formats.

# Saving and loading R data structures

When you have spent a lot of time getting a particular data frame into the format that you want, you shouldn't need to recreate your work each time you restart your R session. To save a particular data structure to a file that can be reloaded later or transferred to another system, you can use the save() function. The save() function writes R data structures to the location specified by the file parameter. R data files have the file extension .RData.

If we had three objects named x, y, and z, we could save them to a file mydata.RData using the following command:

```
> save(x, y, z, file = "mydata.RData")
```

Regardless of whether x, y, and z are vectors, factors, lists, or data frames, they will be saved to the file.

The load() command will recreate any data structures already saved that were to an .RData file. To load the mydata.RData file we saved in the preceding code, simply type:

```
> load("mydata.RData")
```

This will recreate the x, y, and z data structures.

 Be careful what you are loading! All data structures stored in the file you are importing with the load() command will be added to your workspace, even if they overwrite something else you are working on.

If you need to wrap up your R session in a hurry, the save.image() command will write your entire session to a file simply called .RData. By default, R will look for this file the next time when you start R, and your session will be recreated just as you had left it.

# Importing and saving data from CSV files

It is very common for publically-available data to be stored in text files. Text files can be read on virtually any computer or operating system, making the format nearly universal. They can also be exported and imported from/to programs such as Microsoft Excel, providing a quick and easy way to work with spreadsheet data.

A **tabular** (as in "table") data file is structured in matrix form, in such a way that each line of text reflects one example, and each example has the same number of features. The feature values on each line are separated by a predefined symbol known as a **delimiter**. Often, the first line of a tabular data file lists the names of the columns of data. This is called a **header** line.

Perhaps the most common tabular text file format is the **Comma-Separated Values** (**CSV**) file, which as the name suggests, uses the comma as a delimiter. The CSV files can be imported to and exported from many common applications. A CSV file representing the medical dataset constructed previously would look as follows:

```
subject_name,temperature,flu_status,gender,blood_type
John Doe,98.1,FALSE,MALE,O
Jane Doe,98.6,FALSE,FEMALE,AB
Steve Graves,101.4,TRUE,MALE,A
```

To load this CSV file into R, the `read.csv()` is used as follows:

```
> pt_data <- read.csv("pt_data.csv", stringsAsFactors = FALSE)
```

Given a patient data file named `pt_data.csv` located in the R working directory, this will read the CSV file into a data frame titled `pt_data`. Just as we had done previously when constructing a data frame, we need to use the `stringsAsFactors = FALSE` parameter to prevent R from converting all text variables to factors; this step is better left to you, not R, to perform.

If your data reside outside the R working directory, you can specify the path to the CSV file by specifying the full path, for example, `/path/to/mydata.csv` when calling the `read.csv()` function.

By default, R assumes that the CSV file includes a header line listing the names of the features in the dataset. If a CSV file does not have a header, specify the option `header = FALSE` as shown in the following command, and R will assign default feature names in the form `V1`, `V2`, and so on:

```
> mydata <- read.csv("mydata.csv", stringsAsFactors = FALSE,
    header = FALSE)
```

The read.csv() function is a special case of the read.table() function, which can read tabular data in many different forms, including other delimited formats such as **Tab-Separated Value (TSV)**. For more detailed information on the read.table() family of functions, refer to the R help page using the command ?read.table.

To save a data frame to a CSV file, use the write.csv() function. If your data frame is named pt_data, simply enter:

```
> write.csv(pt_data, file = "pt_data.csv")
```

This will write a CSV file with the name pt_data.csv to the R working folder.

# Importing data from SQL databases

If your data is stored in an **ODBC (Open Database Connectivity) SQL (Structured Query Language)** database such as Oracle, MySQL, PostgreSQL, Microsoft SQL, or SQLite, the RODBC package created by *Brian Ripley* can be used to import this data directly into an R data frame.

ODBC is a standard protocol for connecting to databases regardless of operating system or **DBMS (Database Management System)**. If you have previously connected to a database via ODBC, you most likely will have referred to it via its **DSN (Data Source Name)**. You will need the DSN, plus a username and password (if your database requires it) for using RODBC.

> The instructions for configuring an ODBC connection are highly specific to the combination of operating system and DBMS. If you are having trouble setting up an ODBC connection, check with your database administrator. Another way to obtain help is the RODBC package vignette, which you can access in R with the command print(vignette("RODBC")).

If you have not already done so, you will need to install and load the RODBC package:

```
> install.packages("RODBC")
> library(RODBC)
```

Next, we will open a connection called mydb to the database with the DSN my_dsn:

```
> mydb <- odbcConnect("my_dsn")
```

Alternatively, if your ODBC connection requires a username and password, they should be specified when calling the odbcConnect() function:

```
> mydb <- odbcConnect("my_dsn", uid = "my_username"
    pwd = "my_password")
```

Now that we have an open database connection, we can use the `sqlQuery()` function to create an R data frame from the database rows pulled by SQL queries. This function, like many functions that create data frames, allows us to specify `stringsAsFactors = FALSE`, which prevents R from converting character data to factors.

The `sqlQuery()` function uses typical SQL queries as shown in the following command:

```
> patient_query <- "select * from patient_data where alive = 1"
> patient_data <- sqlQuery(channel = mydb, query = patient_query,
    stringsAsFactors = FALSE)
```

The resulting `patient_data` variable will be a data frame containing all of the rows selected using the SQL query stored in `patient_query`.

When you are done using the database, the connection can be closed as shown in the following command:

```
> odbcClose(mydb)
```

This will close the `mydb` connection. Although R will automatically close ODBC connections at the end of an R session, it is better practice to do so explicitly.

# Exploring and understanding data

After collecting data and loading it into R data structures, the next step in the machine learning process involves examining the data in detail. It is during this step that you will begin to explore the data's features and examples, and realize the peculiarities that make your data unique. The better you understand your data, the better you will be able to match a machine learning model to your learning problem.

The best way to understand the process of data exploration is by example. In this section, we will explore the `usedcars.csv` dataset, which contains actual data about used cars recently advertised for sale on a popular U.S. website.

The `usedcars.csv` dataset is available for download on Packt's website. If you are following along with the examples, be sure that this file has been downloaded and saved to your R working directory.

Since the dataset is stored in CSV form, we can use the `read.csv()` function to load the data into an R data frame:

```
usedcars <- read.csv("usedcars.csv", stringsAsFactors = FALSE)
```

Given the `usedcars` data frame, we will now assume the role of a data scientist, who has the task of understanding the used car data. Although data exploration is a fluid process, the steps can be imagined as a sort of investigation in which questions about the data are answered. The exact questions may vary across projects, but the types of questions are always similar. You should be able to adapt the basic steps of this investigation to any dataset you like, large or small.

# Exploring the structure of data

One of the first questions to ask in your investigation should be about how data is organized. If you are fortunate, your source will provide a **data dictionary**, a document that describes the data's features. In our case, the used car data does not come with this documentation, so we'll need to create our own.

The `str()` function provides a method for displaying the structure of a data frame, or any R data structure including vectors and lists. It can be used to create the basic outline for our data dictionary:

```
> str(usedcars)
'data.frame':150 obs. of 6 variables:
 $ year        : int  2011 2011 2011 2011 ...
 $ model       : chr  "SEL" "SEL" "SEL" "SEL" ...
 $ price       : int  21992 20995 19995 17809 ...
 $ mileage     : int  7413 10926 7351 11613 ...
 $ color       : chr  "Yellow" "Gray" "Silver" "Gray" ...
 $ transmission: chr  "AUTO" "AUTO" "AUTO" "AUTO" ...
```

For such a simple command, we learn a wealth of information about the dataset. The statement `150 obs` tells us that the data includes 150 observations, or examples. The number of observations is often simply abbreviated as n. Since we know that the data describes used cars, we can now presume that we have examples of n = 150 automobiles for sale.

The `6 variables` statement refers to the six features that were recorded in the data. These features are listed by name on separate lines. Looking at the line for the feature called `color`, we note some additional details:

```
 $ color       : chr  "Yellow" "Gray" "Silver" "Gray" ...
```

After the variable's name, the `chr` tells us that the feature is character type. In this dataset, three of the variables are character while three are noted as `int`, which indicates integer type. Although this dataset includes only character and integer variables, you are also likely to encounter `num`, or numeric type, when using non-integer data (for example, numbers with decimal places). Any factors would be listed as `Factor` type. Following each variable's type, R presents a sequence of the first few values for the feature. The values `"Yellow" "Gray" "Silver" "Gray"` are the first four values of the `color` feature.

Applying a bit of subject-area knowledge to the feature names and values allows us to make some assumptions about what the variables represent. The variable `year` could refer to the year the vehicle was manufactured, or it could specify the year the advertisement was posted. We will have to investigate this feature in more detail later, since the four example values (`2011 2011 2011 2011`) could be used to argue for either possibility. The variables `model`, `price`, `mileage`, `color`, and `transmission` most likely refer to the characteristics of the car for sale.

Although our data seems to have been given meaningful variable names, this is not always the case. Sometimes, datasets have features with nonsensical names, codes, or simply a number like `V1`. It may be necessary to do additional sleuthing to determine what a feature actually represents. Still, even with helpful feature names, it is always prudent to be skeptical about the labels you have been provided with. Let's investigate further.

# Exploring numeric variables

To investigate the numeric variables in the used car data, we will employ a commonly-used set of measurements for describing values known as **summary statistics**. The `summary()` function displays several common summary statistics. Let's take a look at a single feature, `year`:

```
> summary(usedcars$year)
   Min. 1st Qu.  Median    Mean 3rd Qu.    Max.
   2000    2008    2009    2009    2010    2012
```

Even if you aren't already familiar with summary statistics, you may be able to guess some of them from the heading above the `summary()` output. Ignoring the meaning of the values for now, the fact that we see numbers such as `2000, 2008,` and `2009` could lead us to believe that the `year` variable indicates the year of manufacture rather than the year the advertisement was posted, since we know the vehicles were recently listed for sale.

We can also use the `summary()` function to obtain summary statistics for several numeric variables at the same time:

```
> summary(usedcars[c("price", "mileage")])
     price            mileage
 Min.   : 3800   Min.   :   4867
 1st Qu.:10995   1st Qu.: 27200
 Median :13592   Median : 36385
 Mean   :12962   Mean   : 44261
 3rd Qu.:14904   3rd Qu.: 55125
 Max.   :21992   Max.   :151479
```

The six summary statistics that the `summary()` function provides are simple, yet powerful tools for investigating data. The summary statistics can be divided into two types: measures of center and measures of spread.

# Measuring the central tendency – mean and median

Measures of central tendency are a class of statistics used to identify a value that falls in the middle of a set of data. You are most likely already familiar with one common measure of center: the average. In common use, when something is deemed average, it falls somewhere between the extreme ends of the scale. An average student might have marks falling in the middle of his or her classmates; an average weight is neither unusually light nor heavy. An average item is typical, and not too unlike the others in the group. You might think of it as an exemplar by which all others are judged.

In statistics, the average is also known as the **mean**, a measurement defined as the sum of all values divided by the number of values. For example, to calculate the mean income in a group of three people with incomes of $35,000, $45,000, and $55,000 we could type:

```
> (36000 + 44000 + 56000) / 3
[1] 45333.33
```

R also provides a `mean()` function, which calculates the mean for a vector of numbers:

```
> mean(c(36000, 44000, 56000))
[1] 45333.33
```

The mean income of this group of people is $45,333.33. Conceptually, you can imagine this amount as the income each person would have if the total amount of income was divided equally across every person.

Recall that the preceding `summary()` output listed mean values for the price and mileage variables. The mean price of `12962` and mean mileage of `44261` suggests that the typical used car in this dataset was listed at a price of $12,962 and had an odometer reading of 44,261. What does this tell us about our data? Since the average price is relatively low, we might expect that the data includes economy-class cars. Of course, the data can also include late-model luxury cars with high mileage, but the relatively low mean mileage statistic doesn't provide evidence to support this hypothesis. On the other hand, it doesn't provide evidence to ignore the possibility either. We'll need to keep this in mind as we examine the data further.

Although the mean is by far the most commonly cited statistic for measuring the center of a dataset, it is not always the most appropriate. Another commonly-used measure of central tendency is the **median**, which is the value that occurs halfway through an ordered list of values. As with the mean, R provides a `median()` function, which we can apply to our salary data as shown in the following example:

```
> median(c(36000, 44000, 56000))
[1] 44000
```

Because the middle value is `44000`, the median income is $44,000.

> If a dataset has an even number of values, there is no middle value. In this case, the median is commonly calculated as the average of the two values at the center of the ordered list. For example, the median of the values 1, 2, 3, 4 is 2.5.

At first glance, it seems like the median and mean are very similar measures. Certainly, the mean value of $45,333 and the median value of $44,000 are not very different. Why have two measures of central tendency? The reason is due to the fact that the mean and median are affected differently by values falling at far ends of the range. In particular, the mean is highly sensitive to **outliers**, or values that are atypically high or low relative to the majority of data. Because the mean is sensitive to outliers, it is more likely to be shifted higher or lower by a small number of extreme values.

Recall again the reported median values in the `summary()` output for the used car dataset. Although the mean and median for `price` are fairly similar (differing by approximately 5 percent), there is a much larger difference between the mean and median for `mileage`. For `mileage`, the mean of `44261` is more than 20 percent larger than the median of `36385`. Since the mean is more sensitive to extreme values than the median, the fact that the mean is much higher than the median might lead us to suspect that there are some used cars in the dataset with extremely high mileage values. To investigate this further, we'll need to add additional summary statistics to our analysis.

# Measuring spread – quartiles and the five-number summary

Measuring the mean and median of our data provides one way to quickly summarize the values, but these measures of center tell us little about whether or not there is diversity in the measurements. To measure the diversity, we need to employ another type of summary statistics that are concerned with the **spread** of the data, or how tightly or loosely the values are spaced. Knowing about the spread provides a sense of the data's highs and lows, and whether most values are like or unlike the mean and median.

The **five-number summary** is a set of five statistics that roughly depict the spread of a dataset. All five of the statistics are included in the output of the summary() function. Written in order, they are:

1. Minimum (Min.)
2. First quartile, or Q1 (1st Qu.)
3. Median, or Q2 (Median)
4. Third quartile, or Q3 (3rd Qu.)
5. Maximum (Max.)

As you would expect, the minimum and maximum are the most extreme values found in the dataset, indicating the smallest and largest values respectively. R provides the min() and max() functions to calculate these values on a vector of data.

The span between the minimum and maximum value is known as the **range**. In R, the range() function returns both the minimum and maximum value. Combining range() with the difference function, diff() allows you to examine the range of data with a single command:

```
> range(usedcars$price)
[1]  3800 21992
> diff(range(usedcars$price))
[1] 18192
```

The first and third quartiles, Q1 and Q3, refer to the value below or above which one quarter of the values are found. Along with the median (Q2), the quartiles divide a dataset into four portions, each with the same number of values.

Quartiles are a special case of a type of statistic called **quantiles**, which are numbers that divide data into equally-sized quantities. In addition to quartiles, commonly-used quantiles include tertiles (three parts), quintiles (five parts), deciles (10 parts), and percentiles (100 parts). Percentiles are often used to describe the ranking of a value; for instance, a student whose test score was ranked at the 99th percentile performed better than 99 percent of the other test takers.

The middle 50 percent of data between Q1 and Q3 is of particular interest because it itself is a simple measure of spread. The difference between Q1 and Q3 is known as the **interquartile range (IQR)**, and can be calculated with the IQR() function:

```
> IQR(usedcars$price)
[1] 3909.5
```

We could have also calculated this value by hand from the summary output for the usedcars$price variable by computing *14904 – 10995 = 3909*. The small difference between our calculation and the IQR() output is due to the fact that R automatically rounds the summary() output.

The quantile() function provides a robust tool for identifying quantiles for a set of values. By default, the quantile() function returns the five-number summary. Applying the function to the used car data results in the same statistics as before:

```
> quantile(usedcars$price)
      0%      25%      50%      75%     100%
  3800.0  10995.0  13591.5  14904.5  21992.0
```

When computing quantiles, there are many methods for handling ties among values and datasets with no middle value. The quantile() function allows you to specify among nine different algorithms by specifying the type parameter. If your project requires a precisely-defined quantile, it is important to read the function documentation using the ?quantile command.

If we specify an additional probs parameter using a vector denoting cut points, we can obtain arbitrary quantiles, such as the 1st and 99th percentiles:

```
> quantile(usedcars$price, probs = c(0.01, 0.99))
       1%       99%
  5428.69  20505.00
```

The sequence function `seq()` is used for generating vectors of evenly-spaced values. This makes it easy to obtain other slices of data, such as the quintiles (five groups), as shown in the following command:

```
> quantile(usedcars$price, seq(from = 0, to = 1, by = 0.20))
     0%     20%     40%     60%     80%    100%
 3800.0 10759.4 12993.8 13992.0 14999.0 21992.0
```

Equipped with an understanding of the five-number summary, we can re-examine the used car `summary()` output. On the `price` variable, the minimum was $3,800 and the maximum was $21,992. Interestingly, the difference between the minimum and Q1 is about $7,000, as is the difference between Q3 and the maximum; yet, the difference from Q1 to the median to Q3 is roughly $2,000. This suggests that the lower and upper 25 percent of values are more widely dispersed than the middle 50 percent of values, which seem to be more tightly grouped around the center. We see a similar trend with the `mileage` variable, which is not unsurprising. As you will learn later in this chapter, this pattern of spread is common enough that it has been called a "normal" distribution of data.

The spread of the `mileage` variable also exhibits another interesting property: the difference between Q3 and the maximum is far greater than that between the minimum and Q1. In other words, the larger values are far more spread out than the smaller values.

This finding explains why the mean value is much greater than the median. Because the mean is sensitive to extreme values, it is pulled higher, while the median stays in relatively the same place. This is an important property, which becomes more apparent when the data is presented visually.

# Visualizing numeric variables – boxplots

Visualizing numeric variables can be helpful for diagnosing many problems with data. A common visualization of the five-number summary is a **boxplot** or **box-and-whiskers** plot. The boxplot displays the center and spread of a numeric variable in a format that allows you to quickly obtain a sense of the range and skew of a variable, or compare it to other variables.

Let's take a look at a boxplot for the used car price and mileage data. To obtain a boxplot for a variable, we will use the `boxplot()` function. We will also specify a couple of extra parameters, `main` and `ylab`, to add a title to the figure and label the y axis (the vertical axis), respectively. The commands for creating price and mileage boxplots are:

```
> boxplot(usedcars$price, main="Boxplot of Used Car Prices",
        ylab="Price ($)")
```

```
> boxplot(usedcars$mileage, main="Boxplot of Used Car Mileage",
        ylab="Odometer (mi.)")
```

R will produce figures as follows:

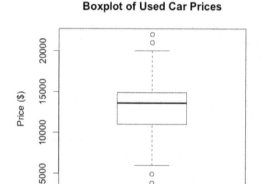 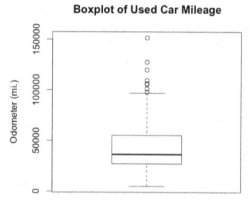

The box-and-whiskers plot depicts the five-number summary values using horizontal lines. The horizontal lines forming the box in the middle of each figure represent Q1, Q2 (the median), and Q3 when reading the plot from bottom-to-top. The median is denoted by the dark line, which lines up with $13,592 on the vertical axis for `price` and 36,385 mi. on the vertical axis for `mileage`.

In simple boxplots such as those in the preceding diagram, the width of the box-and-whiskers is arbitrary and does not illustrate any characteristic of the data. For more sophisticated analyses, it is possible to use the shape and size of the boxes to facilitate comparisons of the data across several groups. To learn more about such features, begin by examining the `notch` and `varwidth` options in the R `boxplot()` documentation by typing the `?boxplot` command.

The minimum and maximum are illustrated using the whiskers that extend below and above the box; however, it is convention to only allow the whiskers to extend to a minimum or maximum of 1.5 times the IQR below Q1 or above Q3. Any values that fall beyond this threshold are considered outliers and are denoted as circles or dots. For example, recall that the IQR for the `price` variable was `3909` with Q1 of `10995` and Q3 of `14904`. An outlier is therefore any value that is less than *10995 - 1.5 * 3905 = 5137.5* or greater than *14904 + 1.5 * 3905 = 20761.5*.

The plot shows two such outliers on both the high and low ends. On the `mileage` boxplot, there are no outliers on the low end and thus the bottom whisker extends to the minimum value, `4867`. On the high end, we see several outliers beyond the 100,000 mile mark. These outliers are responsible for our earlier finding, which noted that the mean value was much greater than the median.

# Visualizing numeric variables – histograms

A **histogram** is another way to graphically depict the spread of a numeric variable. It is similar to a boxplot in that it divides the variable's values into a predefined number of portions, or **bins** that act as containers for values. A boxplot requires that each of four portions of data must contain the same number of values, and widens or narrows the bins as needed. In contrast, a histogram uses any number of bins of identical width, but allows the bins to contain different numbers of values.

We can create a histogram for the used car `price` and `mileage` data using the `hist()` function. As we had done with the boxplot, we will specify a title for the figure using the `main` parameter and label the x axis with the `xlab` parameter. The commands for creating the histograms are:

```
> hist(usedcars$price, main = "Histogram of Used Car Prices",
        xlab = "Price ($)")
> hist(usedcars$mileage, main = "Histogram of Used Car Mileage",
        xlab = "Odometer (mi.)")
```

This produces the following diagram:

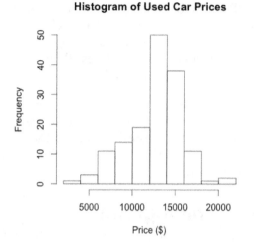

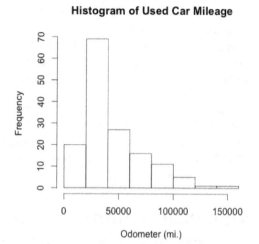

The histogram is composed of a series of bars with heights indicating the count, or **frequency**, of values falling within each of the equally-sized bins partitioning the values. The vertical lines that separate the bars, as labeled on the horizontal axis, indicate the start and end points of the range of values for the bin.

For example, on the `price` histogram, each of the 10 bars spans an interval of $2,000, beginning at $2,000 and ending at $22,000. The tallest bar in the center of the figure covers the range $12,000 to $14,000, and has a frequency of 50. Since we know that our data includes 150 cars, we know that one-third of all the cars are priced from $12,000 to $14,000. Nearly 90 cars—more than half—are priced from $12,000 to $16,000.

The `mileage` histogram includes eight bars indicating bins of 20,000 miles each, beginning at 0 and ending at 160,000 miles. Unlike the `price` histogram, the tallest bar is not in the center of the data, but on the left-hand side of the diagram. The 70 cars contained in this bin have odometer readings from 20,000 to 40,000 miles.

You might also notice that the shape of the two histograms is somewhat different. It seems that the used car prices tend to be evenly divided on both sides of the middle, while the car mileages stretch further to the right. This characteristic is known as **skew**, specifically right skew, because the values on the high end (right side) are far more spread out than the values on the low end (left side). As shown in the following diagram, histograms of skewed data look stretched on one of the sides:

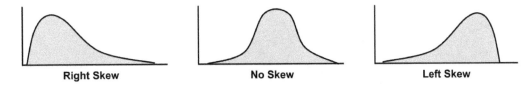

Right Skew        No Skew        Left Skew

The ability to quickly diagnose such patterns in our data is one of the strengths of the histogram as a data exploration tool. This will become even more important as we start examining other patterns of spread in numeric data.

# Understanding numeric data – uniform and normal distributions

Histograms, boxplots, and statistics describing the center and spread all provide ways to examine the distribution of a variable's values. A variable's distribution describes how likely a value is to fall within various ranges.

If all values are equally likely to occur, say for instance, in a dataset recording the values rolled on a fair six-sided die, the distribution is said to be uniform. A uniform distribution is easy to detect with a histogram because the bars are approximately the same height. When visualized with a histogram, it may look something like the following diagram:

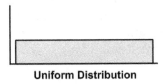

Uniform Distribution

It's important to note that not all random events are uniform. For instance, rolling a weighted six-sided trick die would result in some numbers coming up more often than others. While each roll of the die results in a randomly-selected number, they are not equally likely.

Take, for instance, the used car data. This is clearly not uniform, since some values are seemingly far more likely to occur than others. In fact, on the `price` histogram, it seems that values grow less likely to occur as they are further away from both sides of the center bar, resulting in a bell-shaped distribution of data. This characteristic is so common in real-world data that it is the hallmark of the so-called **normal distribution**. The stereotypical bell-curve is shown in the following diagram:

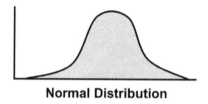

**Normal Distribution**

Although there are numerous types of non-normal distributions, many phenomena generate data that can be described by the normal distribution. Therefore, the normal distribution's properties have been studied in great detail.

## Measuring spread – variance and standard deviation

Distributions allow us to characterize a large number of values using a smaller number of parameters. The normal distribution, which describes many types of real-world data, can be defined with just two: center and spread. The center of the normal distribution is defined by its mean value, which we have used before. The spread is measured by a statistic called the **standard deviation**.

In order to calculate the standard deviation, we must first obtain the **variance**, which is defined as the average of the squared differences between each value and the mean value. In mathematical notation, the variance of a set of $n$ values of $x$ is defined by the following formula. The Greek letter *mu* (similar in appearance to an m) denotes the mean of the values, and the variance itself is denoted by the Greek letter *sigma* squared (similar to a b turned sideways):

$$\text{Var}(X) = \sigma^2 = \frac{1}{n}\sum_{i=1}^{n}\left(x_i - \mu\right)^2$$

The standard deviation is the square root of the variance, and is denoted by *sigma* as shown in the following formula:

$$StdDev(X) = \sigma = \sqrt{\frac{1}{n}\sum_{i=1}^{n}(x_i - \mu)^2}$$

To obtain the variance and standard deviation in R, the `var()` and `sd()` functions can be used. For example, computing the variance and standard deviation on our price and mileage variables, we find:

```
> var(usedcars$price)
[1] 9749892
> sd(usedcars$price)
[1] 3122.482
> var(usedcars$mileage)
[1] 728033954
> sd(usedcars$mileage)
[1] 26982.1
```

When interpreting the variance, larger numbers indicate that the data are spread more widely around the mean. The standard deviation indicates, on average, how much each value differs from the mean.

If you compute these statistics by hand using the formulae in the preceding diagrams, you will obtain a slightly different result than the built-in R functions. This is because the preceding formulae use the population variance (which divides by n), while R uses the sample variance (which divides by n - 1). Except for very small datasets, the distinction is minor.

The standard deviation can be used to quickly estimate how extreme a given value is under the assumption that it came from a normal distribution. The **68-95-99.7 rule** states that 68 percent of values in a normal distribution fall within one standard deviation of the mean, while 95 percent and 99.7 percent of values fall within two and three standard deviations, respectively. This is illustrated in the following diagram:

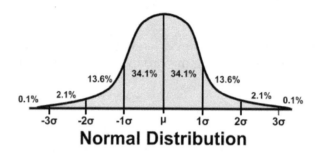

**Normal Distribution**

Applying this information to the used car data, we know that since the mean `price` was $12,962, approximately 68 percent of cars in our data were advertised at prices between $9,840 and $16,804. Although the 68-95-99.7 rule only strictly applies to normal distributions, the basic principle applies to any data; values more than three standard deviations away from the mean are exceedingly rare events.

# Exploring categorical variables

If you recall, the used car dataset had three categorial variables: `model`, `color`, and `transmission`. Because we used the `stringsAsFactors = FALSE` parameter when loading the data, R has left them as character (`chr`) variables rather than automatically converting them into factors. Additionally, we might consider treating `year` as categorical; although it is as a numeric (`int`), each year value is a category that could apply to multiple cars.

In contrast to numeric data, categorical data is examined using tables rather than summary statistics. A table that presents a single categorical variable is known as a **one-way table**. The `table()` function can be used to generate one-way tables for our used car data:

```
> table(usedcars$year)

2000 2001 2002 2003 2004 2005 2006 2007 2008 2009 2010 2011 2012
   3    1    1    1    3    2    6   11   14   42   49   16    1
> table(usedcars$model)
 SE SEL SES
 78  23  49
```

```
> table(usedcars$color)
```

| Black | Blue | Gold | Gray | Green | Red | Silver | White | Yellow |
|-------|------|------|------|-------|-----|--------|-------|--------|
| 35 | 17 | 1 | 16 | 5 | 25 | 32 | 16 | 3 |

The table output lists the categories of the nominal variable and a count of the number of values falling into that category. Since we know that there are 150 used cars in the dataset, we can determine that roughly one-third of all the cars were manufactured in 2010, since 49/150 is about 33 percent.

R can also perform the calculation of table proportions directly by using the `prop.table()` command on a table produced by the `table()` function:

```
> model_table <- table(usedcars$model)
> prop.table(model_table)
```

| SE | SEL | SES |
|----|-----|-----|
| 0.5200000 | 0.1533333 | 0.3266667 |

The proportion of model SE cars is `0.5200000`, so 52 percent of the cars are SE type.

The results of the `prop.table()` can be combined with other R functions to transform the output. Suppose that we would like to display the results in percentages with a single decimal place. We can do this by multiplying the proportions by `100`, then using the `round()` function while specifying `digits = 1`, as shown in the following example:

```
> color_table <- table(usedcars$color)
> color_pct <- prop.table(color_table) * 100
> round(color_pct, digits = 1)
```

| Black | Blue | Gold | Gray | Green | Red | Silver | White | Yellow |
|-------|------|------|------|-------|-----|--------|-------|--------|
| 23.3 | 11.3 | 0.7 | 10.7 | 3.3 | 16.7 | 21.3 | 10.7 | 2.0 |

Although this includes the same information as the default `prop.table()` output, it is a bit easier to read. The results show that black is the most common color, since nearly a quarter (23.3 percent) of all advertised cars are black. Silver is a close second with 21.3 percent and red is third with 16.7 percent.

# Measuring the central tendency – the mode

In statistics terms, the **mode** of a feature is the value occurring most often. Like the mean and median, the mode is another measure of central tendency. It is often used for categorical data, since the mean and median are not defined for nominal variables.

For example, in the used car data, the mode of the `year` variable is `2010`, while the modes for `model` and `color` are `SE` and `Black`, respectively. A variable may have more than one mode; a variable with a single mode is **unimodal**, while a variable with two modes is **bimodal**. Data having multiple modes is more generally called **multimodal**.

 Although you might suspect that you could use the `mode()` function, R uses this to refer to the type of variable (as in numeric, list, and so on) rather than the statistical mode. Instead, to find the statistical mode, simply look at the table output for the category with the greatest number of values.

The mode(s) is/are used in a qualitative sense to gain an understanding of important values in a dataset. Yet, it would be dangerous to place too much emphasis on the mode since the most common value is not necessarily a majority. For instance, although `Black` was the mode of the used car `color` variable, black cars were only about a quarter of all advertised cars.

It is best to think about the modes in relation to the other categories. Is there one category that dominates all others, or are there several? From there, we may ask what the most common values tell us about the variable being measured. If black and silver are common used car colors, we might assume that the data are for luxury cars, which tend to be sold in more conservative colors, or they could also be economy cars, which are sold with fewer color options. We will keep this question in mind as we continue to examine this data.

Thinking about the modes as common values allows us to apply the concept of the statistical mode to numeric data. Strictly speaking, it would be unlikely to have a mode for a continuous variable, since no two values are likely to repeat. Yet if we think about modes as the highest bars on a histogram, we can discuss the modes of variables such as `price` and `mileage`. It can be helpful to consider the mode when exploring numeric data, particularly to examine whether or not the data is multimodal.

# Exploring relationships between variables

So far, we have examined variables one at a time, calculating only **univariate** statistics. During our investigation, we raised questions that we were unable to answer at the time:

- Does the `price` data imply that we are examining only economy-class cars, or are there also luxury cars with high-mileage?
- Do relationships between the `model` and `color` data provide insight into the types of cars we are examining?

These types of questions can be addressed by looking at **bivariate** relationships, which consider the relationship between two variables. Relationships of more than two variables are called **multivariate** relationships Let's begin with the bivariate case.

# Visualizing relationships – scatterplots

A **scatterplot** is a diagram that visualizes a bivariate relationship. It is a two-dimensional figure in which dots are drawn on a coordinate plane using the values of one feature to provide the horizontal *x* coordinates, and the values of another feature to provide the vertical *y* coordinates. Patterns in the placement of dots reveal underlying associations between the two features.

To answer our question about the relationship between `price` and `mileage`, we will examine a scatterplot. We'll use the `plot()` function, along with the `main`, `xlab`, and `ylab` parameters used in previous plots to label the diagram.

To use `plot()`, we need to specify x and y vectors containing the values used to position the dots on the figure. Although the conclusions would be the same regardless of which variable is used to supply the *x* and *y* coordinates, convention dictates that the *y* variable is the one that is presumed to depend on the other (and is thus known as the **dependent** variable). Since an odometer reading cannot be modified by the seller, it is unlikely to be dependent on the car's price. Instead, our hypothesis is that price depends on the odometer mileage. Therefore, we will use `price` as the *y*, or dependent, variable.

The full command for creating our scatterplot is:

```
> plot(x = usedcars$mileage, y = usedcars$price,
    main = "Scatterplot of Price vs. Mileage",
    xlab = "Used Car Odometer (mi.)",
    ylab = "Used Car Price ($)")
```

This results in the following scatterplot:

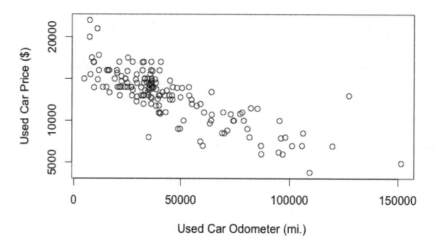

Using the scatterplot, we notice a clear relationship between the price of a used car and the odometer reading. To read the plot, examine how values of the *y* axis variable change as the values on the *x* axis increase. In this case, the values of price tend to be lower as the values of mileage increase, implying that advertised prices are lower for cars with higher mileage. If you have ever sold or shopped for a used car, this is not a profound insight.

Perhaps a more interesting finding is the fact that there are very few cars that have both high price and high mileage, aside from a lone outlier at about 125,000 miles and $14,000. The absence of more points like this provides evidence to support a conclusion that our data is unlikely to include any high mileage luxury cars. All of the most expensive cars in the data, particularly those above $17,500, seem to have extraordinarily low mileage, implying that we could be looking at a type of car retailing for about $20,000, which is new.

The relationship between price and mileage is known as a negative association because it forms a pattern of dots in a line sloping downward. A positive association would appear to form a line sloping upward. A flat line, or a seemingly-random scattering of dots, is evidence that the two variables are not associated at all. The strength of a linear association between two variables is measured by a statistic known as **correlation**. Correlations are discussed in detail in *Chapter 6, Forecasting Numeric Data – Regression Methods*, which covers the use of regression methods for modeling linear relationships.

Keep in mind that not all associations form straight lines. Sometimes the dots form a U-shape or a V-shape; sometimes the pattern seems to be weaker or stronger for increasing values of the x or y variable. Such patterns imply that the relationship between the two variables is not linear.

# Examining relationships – two-way cross-tabulations

To examine a relationship between two nominal variables, a **two-way cross-tabulation** is used (also known as a **crosstab** or a **contingency** table). A cross-tabulation is similar to a scatterplot in that it allows you to examine how the values of one variable vary by the values of another. The format is a table in which the rows are the levels of one variable while the columns are the levels of another. Counts in each of the table's cells indicate the number of values falling into the particular row and column combination.

To answer our question about the relationship between model and color, we will examine a crosstab. There are several functions to produce two-way tables in R, including table(), which we also used for one-way tables. The CrossTable() function in the gmodels package created by *Gregory R. Warnes* is perhaps the most user-friendly because it presents the row, column, and margin percentages in a single table, saving us the trouble of combining this data ourselves. To install the gmodels package, type:

```
> install.packages("gmodels")
```

After the package installs, simply type library(gmodels) to load the package. You will need to load the package during each R session in which you plan on using the CrossTable() function.

Before proceeding with our analysis, let's simplify our project by reducing the number of levels in the color variable. This variable has nine levels, but we don't really need this much detail. What we are really interested in is whether or not the car's color is conservative. Toward this end, we'll divide the nine colors into two groups: the first group will include the conservative colors Black, Gray, Silver, and White; the second group will include Blue, Gold, Green, Red, and Yellow. We will create a binary indicator variable (often called a dummy variable), indicating whether or not the car's color is conservative by our definition. Its value will be 1 if true, 0 otherwise:

```
> usedcars$conservative <-
    usedcars$color %in% c("Black", "Gray", "Silver", "White")
```

You may have noticed a new command here: the `%in%` operator returns TRUE or FALSE for each value in the vector on the left-hand side of the operator, depending on whether the value is found in the vector on the right-hand side. In simple terms, you can translate this line as "is the used car color in the set of black, gray, silver, and white?"

Examining the `table()` output for our newly-created variable, we see that about two-thirds of cars have conservative colors while one-third do not have conservative colors:

```
> table(usedcars$conservative)
```

```
FALSE   TRUE
   51     99
```

Now, let's look at a cross-tabulation to see how the proportion of `conservative` colored cars varies by `model`. Since we're assuming that the model of car dictates the choice of color, we'll treat `conservative` as the dependent (y) variable. The `CrossTable()` command is therefore:

```
> CrossTable(x = usedcars$model, y = usedcars$conservative)
```

Which results in the following table:

```
     Cell Contents
|-------------------------|
|                       N |
|   Chi-square contribution |
|           N / Row Total |
|           N / Col Total |
|         N / Table Total |
|-------------------------|


Total Observations in Table:  150
```

| usedcars$model | usedcars$conservative FALSE | TRUE | Row Total |
|---|---|---|---|
| SE | 27<br>0.009<br>0.346<br>0.529<br>0.180 | 51<br>0.004<br>0.654<br>0.515<br>0.340 | 78<br><br>0.520 |
| SEL | 7<br>0.086<br>0.304<br>0.137<br>0.047 | 16<br>0.044<br>0.696<br>0.162<br>0.107 | 23<br><br>0.153 |
| SES | 17<br>0.007<br>0.347<br>0.333<br>0.113 | 32<br>0.004<br>0.653<br>0.323<br>0.213 | 49<br><br>0.327 |
| Column Total | 51<br>0.340 | 99<br>0.660 | 150 |

There is a wealth of data in the `CrossTable()` output. The legend at the top (labeled `Cell Contents`) indicates how to interpret each value. The rows in the table indicate the three models of used cars: SE, SEL, and SES (plus an additional row for the total across all models). The columns indicate whether or not the car's color is conservative (plus a column totaling across both types of color). The first value in each cell indicates the number of cars with that combination of model and color. The proportions indicate that cell's proportion relative to the Chi-square statistic, the row's total, the columns total, and the table's total.

What we are most interested in is the row proportion for conservative cars for each model. The row proportions tell us that 0.654 (65 percent) of SE cars are colored conservatively, in comparison to 0.696 (70 percent) of SEL cars, and 0.653 (65 percent) of SES. These differences are relatively small, which suggests that there are no substantial differences in the types of colors chosen by model of car.

The Chi-square values refer to the cell's contribution in the **Pearson's Chi-squared test for independence** between two variables. This test measures how likely it is that the difference in cell counts in the table is due to chance alone. If the probability is very low, it provides strong evidence that the two variables are associated.

You can obtain the Chi-squared test results by adding an additional parameter specifying `chisq = TRUE` when calling the `CrossTable()` function. In our case, the probability is about 93 percent, suggesting that it is very likely that the variations in cell count are due to chance alone, and not due to a true association between `model` and `color`.

# Summary

In this chapter, we learned about the basics of managing data in R. We started by taking an in-depth look at the structures used for storing various types of data. The foundational R data structure is the vector, which is extended and combined into more complex data types such as lists and data frames. The data frame is an R data structure that corresponds to the notion of a dataset, having both features and examples.

We also learned about how to get data into R from a variety of sources. R provides functions for reading from and saving to CSV files; SQL databases can be queried with the RODBC package.

Finally, we applied these skills while exploring a real-world dataset containing data on used car prices. We examined numeric variables using common summary statistics of center and spread, and visualized relationships between prices and odometer readings with a scatterplot. We examined nominal variables using tables. In examining the used car data, we followed an exploratory process that can be used to understand any dataset.

Now that we have spent some time understanding the basics of data management with R, you are ready to begin using machine learning to solve real-world problems. In the next chapter, we will tackle our first classification task using **nearest neighbor** methods.

# 3
# Lazy Learning – Classification Using Nearest Neighbors

Recently, I read an article describing a new type of dining experience. Patrons are served in a completely darkened restaurant by waiters who move carefully around memorized routes using only their sense of touch and sound. The allure of these establishments is rooted in the idea that depriving oneself of visual sensory input will enhance the sense of taste and smell, and foods will be experienced in new and exciting ways. Each bite is said to be a small adventure in which the diner discovers the flavors the chef has prepared.

Can you imagine how a diner experiences the unseen food? At first, there might be a rapid phase of data collection: what are the prominent spices, aromas, and textures? Does the food taste savory or sweet? Using this data, the customer might then compare the bite to the food he or she had experienced previously. Briny tastes may evoke images of seafood, while earthy tastes may be linked to past meals involving mushrooms. Personally, I imagine this process of discovery in terms of a slightly modified adage: if it smells like a duck and tastes like a duck, then you are probably eating duck.

This illustrates an idea that can be used for machine learning — as does another maxim involving poultry: "birds of a feather flock together." In other words, things that are alike are likely to have properties that are alike. We can use this principle to classify data by placing it in the category with the most similar, or "nearest" neighbors. This chapter is devoted to classification using this approach. You will learn:

- The key concepts that define nearest neighbor classifiers and why they are considered "lazy" learners

- Methods to measure the similarity of two examples using distance

- How to use an R implementation of the **k-Nearest Neighbors** (kNN) algorithm to diagnose breast cancer

If all this talk about food is making you hungry, you may want to grab a snack. Our first task will be to understand the kNN approach by putting it to use and settling a long-running culinary debate.

# Understanding classification using nearest neighbors

In a single sentence, nearest neighbor classifiers are defined by their characteristic of classifying unlabeled examples by assigning them the class of the most similar labeled examples. Despite the simplicity of this idea, nearest neighbor methods are extremely powerful. They have been used successfully for:

- Computer vision applications, including optical character recognition and facial recognition in both still images and video

- Predicting whether a person enjoys a movie which he/she has been recommended (as in the Netflix challenge)

- Identifying patterns in genetic data, for use in detecting specific proteins or diseases

In general, nearest neighbor classifiers are well-suited for classification tasks where relationships among the features and the target classes are numerous, complicated, or otherwise extremely difficult to understand, yet the items of similar class type tend to be fairly homogeneous. Another way of putting it would be to say that if a concept is difficult to define, but you know it when you see it, then nearest neighbors might be appropriate. On the other hand, if there is not a clear distinction among the groups, the algorithm is by and large not well-suited for identifying the boundary.

# The kNN algorithm

The nearest neighbors approach to classification is utilized by the kNN algorithm. Let us take a look at the strengths and weaknesses of this algorithm:

| Strengths | Weaknesses |
|---|---|
| • Simple and effective<br><br>• Makes no assumptions about the underlying data distribution<br><br>• Fast training phase | • Does not produce a model, which limits the ability to find novel insights in relationships among features<br><br>• Slow classification phase<br><br>• Requires a large amount of memory<br><br>• Nominal features and missing data require additional processing |

The kNN algorithm begins with a training dataset made up of examples that are classified into several categories, as labeled by a nominal variable. Assume that we have a test dataset containing unlabeled examples that otherwise have the same features as the training data. For each record in the test dataset, kNN identifies $k$ records in the training data that are the "nearest" in similarity, where $k$ is an integer specified in advance. The unlabeled test instance is assigned the class of the majority of the $k$ nearest neighbors.

To illustrate this process, let's revisit the blind tasting experience described in the introduction. Suppose that prior to eating the mystery meal we created a taste dataset in which we recorded our impressions of a number of ingredients we tasted previously. To keep things simple, we recorded only two features of each ingredient. The first is a measure from 1 to 10 of how crunchy the ingredient is, and the second is a 1 to 10 score of how sweet the ingredient tastes. We then labeled each ingredient as one of three types of food: fruits, vegetables, or proteins. The first few rows of such a dataset might be structured as follows:

| ingredient | sweetness | crunchiness | food type |
|---|---|---|---|
| apple | 10 | 9 | fruit |
| bacon | 1 | 4 | protein |
| banana | 10 | 1 | fruit |
| carrot | 7 | 10 | vegetable |
| celery | 3 | 10 | vegetable |
| cheese | 1 | 1 | protein |

The kNN algorithm treats the features as coordinates in a multidimensional **feature space**. As our dataset includes only two features, the feature space is two-dimensional. We can plot two-dimensional data on a scatterplot, with the $x$ dimension indicating the ingredient's sweetness and the $y$ dimension indicating the crunchiness. After adding a few more ingredients to the taste dataset, the scatterplot might look like this:

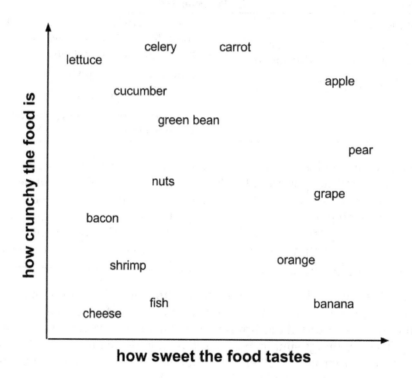

Did you notice the pattern? Similar types of food tend to be grouped closely together. As illustrated in the next figure, vegetables tend to be crunchy but not sweet, fruits tend to be sweet and either crunchy or not crunchy, while proteins tend to be neither crunchy nor sweet:

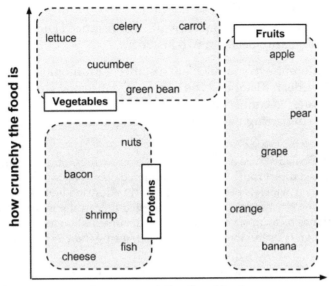

Suppose that after constructing this dataset, we decide to use it to settle the age-old question: is a tomato a fruit or a vegetable? We can use a nearest neighbor approach to determine which class is a better fit as shown in the following figure:

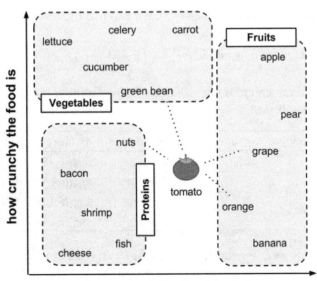

# Calculating distance

Locating the tomato's nearest neighbors requires a **distance function**, or a formula that measures the similarity between two instances.

There are many different ways to calculate distance. Traditionally, the kNN algorithm uses **Euclidean distance**, which is the distance one would measure if you could use a ruler to connect two points, illustrated in the previous figure by the dotted lines connecting the tomato to its neighbors.

> Euclidean distance is measured "as the crow flies," implying the shortest direct route. Another common distance measure is **Manhattan distance**, which is based on the paths a pedestrian would take by walking city blocks. If you are interested in learning more about other distance measures, you can read the documentation for R's distance function (a useful tool in its own right), using the ?dist command.

Euclidean distance is specified by the following formula, where $p$ and $q$ are the examples to be compared, each having $n$ features. The term $p_1$ refers to the value of the first feature of example $p$, while $q_1$ refers to the value of the first feature of example $q$:

$$\text{dist}(p,q) = \sqrt{(p_1 - q_1)^2 + (p_2 - q_2)^2 + ... + (p_n - q_n)^2}$$

The distance formula involves comparing the values of each feature. For example, to calculate the distance between the tomato (sweetness = 6, crunchiness = 4), and the green bean (sweetness = 3, crunchiness = 7), we can use the formula as follows:

$$\text{dist}(tomato, green\ bean) = \sqrt{(6-3)^2 + (4-7)^2} = 4.2$$

In a similar vein, we can calculate the distance between the tomato and several of its closest neighbors as follows:

| ingredient | sweetness | crunchiness | food type | distance to the tomato |
|---|---|---|---|---|
| grape | 8 | 5 | fruit | sqrt((6 - 8)^2 + (4 - 5)^2) = 2.2 |
| green bean | 3 | 7 | vegetable | sqrt((6 - 3)^2 + (4 - 7)^2) = 4.2 |
| nuts | 3 | 6 | protein | sqrt((6 - 3)^2 + (4 - 6)^2) = 3.6 |
| orange | 7 | 3 | fruit | sqrt((6 - 7)^2 + (4 - 3)^2) = 1.4 |

To classify the tomato as a vegetable, protein, or fruit, we'll begin by assigning the tomato, the food type of its single nearest neighbor. This is called 1NN classification because $k = 1$. The orange is the nearest neighbor to the tomato, with a distance of 1.4. As orange is a fruit, the 1NN algorithm would classify tomato as a fruit.

If we use the kNN algorithm with $k = 3$ instead, it performs a vote among the three nearest neighbors: orange, grape, and nuts. Because the majority class among these neighbors is fruit (2 of the 3 votes), the tomato again is classified as a fruit.

## Choosing an appropriate k

Deciding how many neighbors to use for kNN determines how well the model will generalize to future data. The balance between overfitting and underfitting the training data is a problem known as the **bias-variance tradeoff**. Choosing a large $k$ reduces the impact or variance caused by noisy data, but can bias the learner such that it runs the risk of ignoring small, but important patterns.

Suppose we took the extreme stance of setting a very large $k$, equal to the total number of observations in the training data. As every training instance is represented in the final vote, the most common training class always has a majority of the voters. The model would, thus, always predict the majority class, regardless of which neighbors are nearest.

On the opposite extreme, using a single nearest neighbor allows noisy data or outliers, to unduly influence the classification of examples. For example, suppose that some of the training examples were accidentally mislabeled. Any unlabeled example that happens to be nearest to the incorrectly labeled neighbor will be predicted to have the incorrect class, even if the other nine nearest neighbors would have voted differently.

Obviously, the best $k$ value is somewhere between these two extremes.

The following figure illustrates more generally how the decision boundary (depicted by a dashed line) is affected by larger or smaller $k$ values. Smaller values allow more complex decision boundaries that more carefully fit the training data. The problem is that we do not know whether the straight boundary or the curved boundary better represents the true underlying concept to be learned.

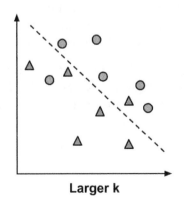

**Larger k**

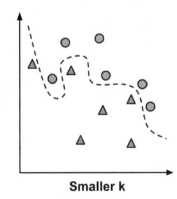

**Smaller k**

In practice, choosing *k* depends on the difficulty of the concept to be learned and the number of records in the training data. Typically, *k* is set somewhere between 3 and 10. One common practice is to set *k* equal to the square root of the number of training examples. In the food classifier we developed previously, we might set *k* = 4, because there were 15 example ingredients in the training data and the square root of 15 is 3.87.

However, such rules may not always result in the single best *k*. An alternative approach is to test several *k* values on a variety of test datasets and choose the one that delivers the best classification performance. On the other hand, unless the data is very noisy, larger and more representative training datasets can make the choice of *k* less important. This is because even subtle concepts will have a sufficiently large pool of examples to vote as nearest neighbors.

A less common, but interesting solution to this problem is to choose a larger *k*, but apply a **weighted voting** process in which the vote of closer neighbors is considered more authoritative than the vote of far away neighbors.

## Preparing data for use with kNN

Features are typically transformed to a standard range prior to applying the kNN algorithm. The rationale for this step is that the distance formula is dependent on how features are measured. In particular, if certain features have much larger values than others, the distance measurements will be strongly dominated by the larger values. This wasn't a problem for us before with the food tasting data, as both sweetness and crunchiness were measured on a scale from 1 to 10.

Suppose that we added an additional feature indicating spiciness, which we measured using the **Scoville** scale. The Scoville scale is a standardized measure of spice heat, ranging from zero (not spicy) to over a million (for the hottest chili peppers). Because the difference between spicy foods and non-spicy foods can be over a million, while the difference between sweet and non-sweet is at most ten, we might find that our distance measures only differentiate foods by their spiciness; the impact of crunchiness and sweetness would be dwarfed by the contribution of spiciness.

What we need is a way of "shrinking" or rescaling the various features such that each one contributes relatively equally to the distance formula. For example, if sweetness and crunchiness are both measured on a scale from 1 to 10, we would also like spiciness to be measured on a scale from 1 to 10. There are several ways to accomplish such scaling.

The traditional method of rescaling features for kNN is **min-max normalization**. This process transforms a feature such that all of its values fall in a range between 0 and 1. The formula for normalizing a feature is as follows. Essentially, the formula subtracts the minimum of feature X from each value and divides by the range of X:

$$X_{new} = \frac{X - \min(X)}{\max(X) - \min(X)}$$

Normalized feature values can be interpreted as indicating how far, from 0 percent to 100 percent, the original value fell along the range between the original minimum and maximum.

Another common transformation is called **z-score standardization**. The following formula subtracts the mean value of feature X and divides by the standard deviation of X:

$$X_{new} = \frac{X - \mu}{\sigma} = \frac{X - \mathrm{Mean}(X)}{\mathrm{StdDev}(X)}$$

This formula, which is based on properties of the normal distribution covered in *Chapter 2, Managing and Understanding Data*, rescales each of a feature's values in terms of how many standard deviations they fall above or below the mean value. The resulting value is called a z-score. The z-scores fall in an unbounded range of negative and positive numbers. Unlike the normalized values, they have no predefined minimum and maximum.

The Euclidean distance formula is not defined for nominal data. Therefore, to calculate the distance between nominal features, we need to convert them into a numeric format. A typical solution utilizes **dummy coding**, where a value of 1 indicates one category, and 0 indicates the other. For instance, dummy coding for a gender variable could be constructed as:

$$\mathrm{male} = \begin{cases} 1 & \text{if } x = \text{male} \\ 0 & \text{otherwise} \end{cases}$$

Notice how dummy coding of the two-category (binary) gender variable results in a single new feature named male. There is no need to construct a separate feature for female; as the two sexes are mutually exclusive, knowing one or the other is enough.

This is true more generally as well. An *n*-category nominal feature can be dummy coded by creating binary indicator variables for (*n* - 1) levels of the feature. For example, dummy coding for a three-category temperature variable (for example, hot, medium, or cold) could be set up as (3 - 1) = 2 features, as shown:

$$hot = \begin{cases} 1 & \text{if } x = hot \\ 0 & \text{otherwise} \end{cases}$$

$$medium = \begin{cases} 1 & \text{if } x = medium \\ 0 & \text{otherwise} \end{cases}$$

Here, knowing that hot and medium are both *0* is enough to know that the temperature is cold. We, therefore, do not need a third feature for the cold attribute.

A convenient aspect of dummy coding is that the distance between dummy coded features is always one or zero, and thus, the values fall on the same scale as normalized numeric data. No additional transformation is necessary.

If your nominal feature is ordinal, (one could make such an argument for the temperature variable that we just saw) an alternative to dummy coding would be to number the categories and apply normalization. For instance, cold, warm, and hot could be numbered as 1, 2, and 3, which normalizes to 0, 0.5, and 1. A caveat to this approach is that it should only be used if you believe that the steps between categories are equivalent. For instance, you could argue that although, poor, middle class, and wealthy are ordered, the difference between poor and middle class is greater (or lesser) than the difference between middle class and wealthy. In this case, dummy coding is a safer approach.

# Why is the kNN algorithm lazy?

Classification algorithms based on nearest neighbor methods are considered lazy learning algorithms because, technically speaking, no abstraction occurs. The abstraction and generalization processes are skipped altogether, which undermines the definition of learning presented in *Chapter 1, Introducing Machine Learning*.

Using the strict definition of learning, a lazy learner is not really learning anything. Instead, it merely stores the training data verbatim. This allows the training phase to occur very rapidly, with a potential downside being that the process of making predictions tends to be relatively slow. Due to the heavy reliance on the training instances, lazy learning is also known as **instance-based learning** or **rote learning**.

As instance-based learners do not build a model, the method is said to be in a class of **non-parametric** learning methods—no parameters are learned about the data. Without generating theories about the underlying data, non-parametric methods limit our ability to understand how the classifier is using the data. On the other hand, this allows the learner to find natural patterns rather than trying to fit the data into a preconceived form.

Although kNN classifiers may be considered lazy, they are still quite powerful. As you will soon see, the simple principles of kNN can be used to automate the process of screening for cancer.

# Diagnosing breast cancer with the kNN algorithm

Routine breast cancer screening allows the disease to be diagnosed and treated prior to it causing noticeable symptoms. The process of early detection involves examining the breast tissue for abnormal lumps or masses. If a lump is found, a fine-needle aspiration biopsy is performed, which utilizes a hollow needle to extract a small portion of cells from the mass. A clinician then examines the cells under a microscope to determine whether the mass is likely to be malignant or benign.

If machine learning could automate the identification of cancerous cells, it would provide considerable benefit to the health system. Automated processes are likely to improve the efficiency of the detection process, allowing physicians to spend less time diagnosing and more time treating the disease. An automated screening system might also provide greater detection accuracy by removing the inherently subjective human component from the process.

We will investigate the utility of machine learning for detecting cancer by applying the kNN algorithm to measurements of biopsied cells from women with abnormal breast masses.

# Step 1 – collecting data

We will utilize the "Breast Cancer Wisconsin Diagnostic" dataset from the *UCI Machine Learning Repository*, which is available at `http://archive.ics.uci.edu/ml`. This data was donated by researchers of the University of Wisconsin and includes measurements from digitized images of fine-needle aspirate of a breast mass. The values represent characteristics of the cell nuclei present in the digital image.

 To read more about the Wisconsin breast cancer data, refer to the authors' publication: *Nuclear feature extraction for breast tumor diagnosis. IS&T/SPIE 1993 International Symposium on Electronic Imaging: Science and Technology, volume 1905*, pp 861-870 by *W.N. Street, W.H. Wolberg, and O.L. Mangasarian*, 1993.

The breast cancer data includes 569 examples of cancer biopsies, each with 32 features. One feature is an identification number, another is the cancer diagnosis, and 30 are numeric-valued laboratory measurements. The diagnosis is coded as M to indicate malignant or B to indicate benign.

The 30 numeric measurements comprise the mean, standard error, and worst (that is, largest) value for 10 different characteristics of the digitized cell nuclei. These include:

- Radius
- Texture
- Perimeter
- Area
- Smoothness
- Compactness
- Concavity
- Concave points
- Symmetry
- Fractal dimension

Based on their names, all of the features seem to relate to the shape and size of the cell nuclei. Unless you are an oncologist, you are unlikely to know how each relates to benign or malignant masses. These patterns will be revealed as we continue in the machine learning process.

# Step 2 – exploring and preparing the data

Let's explore the data and see if we can shine some light on the relationships. At the same time, we will prepare the data for use with the kNN learning method.

 If you plan on following along, download the wisc_bc_data.csv file from the Packt website and save it to your R working directory. The dataset was modified very slightly for this book. In particular, a header line was added and the rows of data were randomly ordered.

We'll begin by importing the CSV data file as we have done previously, saving the Wisconsin breast cancer data to the wbcd data frame:

```
> wbcd <- read.csv("wisc_bc_data.csv", stringsAsFactors = FALSE)
```

Using the command str(wbcd), we can confirm that the data is structured with 569 examples and 32 features as we expected. The first several lines of output are as follows:

```
'data.frame':   569 obs. of   32 variables:
 $ id                : int   87139402 8910251 905520 ...
 $ diagnosis         : chr   "B" "B" "B" "B" ...
 $ radius_mean       : num   12.3 10.6 11 11.3 15.2 ...
 $ texture_mean      : num   12.4 18.9 16.8 13.4 13.2 ...
 $ perimeter_mean    : num   78.8 69.3 70.9 73 97.7 ...
 $ area_mean         : num   464 346 373 385 712 ...
```

The first variable is an integer variable named id. As this is simply a unique identifier (ID) for each patient in the data, it does not provide useful information and we will need to exclude it from the model.

 Regardless of the machine learning method, ID variables should always be excluded. Neglecting to do so can lead to erroneous findings because the ID can be used to uniquely "predict" each example. Therefore, a model that includes an identifier will most likely suffer from overfitting, and is not likely to generalize well to other data.

Let's drop the id feature altogether. As it is located in the first column, we can exclude it by making a copy of the wbcd data frame without column 1:

```
> wbcd <- wbcd[-1]
```

The next variable, `diagnosis`, is of particular interest, as it is the outcome we hope to predict. This feature indicates whether the example is from a benign or malignant mass. The `table()` output indicates that 357 masses are benign while 212 are malignant:

```
> table(wbcd$diagnosis)

  B   M
357 212
```

Many R machine learning classifiers require that the target feature is coded as a factor, so we will need to recode the `diagnosis` variable. We will also take this opportunity to give the B and M values more informative labels using the `labels` parameter:

```
> wbcd$diagnosis <- factor(wbcd$diagnosis, levels = c("B", "M"),
                   labels = c("Benign", "Malignant"))
```

Now, when we look at the `prop.table()` output, we notice that the values have been labeled Benign and Malignant, with 62.7 percent and 37.3 percent of the masses, respectively:

```
> round(prop.table(table(wbcd$diagnosis)) * 100, digits = 1)

   Benign Malignant
     62.7      37.3
```

The remaining 30 features are all numeric, and as expected, consist of three different measurements of ten characteristics. For illustrative purposes, we will only take a closer look at three of the features:

```
> summary(wbcd[c("radius_mean", "area_mean", "smoothness_mean")])
  radius_mean        area_mean       smoothness_mean
 Min.   : 6.981   Min.   : 143.5   Min.   :0.05263
 1st Qu.:11.700   1st Qu.: 420.3   1st Qu.:0.08637
 Median :13.370   Median : 551.1   Median :0.09587
 Mean   :14.127   Mean   : 654.9   Mean   :0.09636
 3rd Qu.:15.780   3rd Qu.: 782.7   3rd Qu.:0.10530
 Max.   :28.110   Max.   :2501.0   Max.   :0.16340
```

Looking at the features side-by-side, do you notice anything problematic about the values? Recall that the distance calculation for kNN is heavily dependent upon the measurement scale of the input features. As `smoothness_mean` ranges from 0.05 to 0.16, while `area_mean` ranges from 143.5 to 2501.0, the impact of area is going to be much larger than smoothness in the distance calculation. This could potentially cause problems for our classifier, so let's apply normalization to rescale the features to a standard range of values.

# Transformation – normalizing numeric data

To normalize these features, we need to create a `normalize()` function in R. This function takes a vector x of numeric values, and for each value in x, subtract the minimum value in x and divide by the range of values in x. Finally, the resulting vector is returned. The code for the function is as follows:

```
> normalize <- function(x) {
    return ((x - min(x)) / (max(x) - min(x)))
  }
```

After executing the previous code, the `normalize()` function is available for use. Let's test the function on a couple of vectors:

```
> normalize(c(1, 2, 3, 4, 5))
[1] 0.00 0.25 0.50 0.75 1.00
> normalize(c(10, 20, 30, 40, 50))
[1] 0.00 0.25 0.50 0.75 1.00
```

The function appears to be working correctly. Despite the fact that the values in the second vector are 10 times larger than the first vector, after normalization, they both appear exactly the same.

We can now apply the `normalize()` function to the numeric features in our data frame. Rather than normalizing each of the 30 numeric variables individually, we will use one of R's functions to automate the process.

The `lapply()` function of R takes a list and applies a function to each element of the list. As a data frame is a list of equal-length vectors, we can use `lapply()` to apply `normalize()` to each feature in the data frame. The final step is to convert the list returned by `lapply()` to a data frame using the `as.data.frame()` function. The full process looks like this:

```
> wbcd_n <- as.data.frame(lapply(wbcd[2:31], normalize))
```

In plain English, this command applies the `normalize()` function to columns 2 through 31 in the `wbcd` data frame, converts the resulting list to a data frame, and assigns it the name `wbcd_n`. The _n suffix is used here as a reminder that the values in `wbcd` have been normalized.

To confirm that the transformation was applied correctly, let's look at one variable's summary statistics:

```
> summary(wbcd_n$area_mean)
   Min. 1st Qu.  Median    Mean 3rd Qu.    Max.
 0.0000  0.1174  0.1729  0.2169  0.2711  1.0000
```

As expected, the `area_mean` variable, which originally ranged from 143.5 to 2501.0, now ranges from 0 to 1.

# Data preparation – creating training and test datasets

Although all 569 biopsies are labeled with a benign or malignant status, it is not very interesting to predict what we already know. Additionally, any performance measures we obtain during training may be misleading, as we do not know the extent to which cases has been overfitted, or how well it will generalize to unseen cases. A more interesting question is how well our learner performs on a dataset of unlabeled data. If we had access to a laboratory, we could apply our learner to measurements taken from the next 100 masses of unknown cancer status and see how well the machine learner's predictions compare to diagnoses obtained using conventional methods.

In the absence of such data, we can simulate this scenario by dividing our data into two portions: a training dataset that will be used to build the kNN model and a test dataset that will be used to estimate the predictive accuracy of the model. We will use the first 469 records for the training dataset and the remaining 100 to simulate new patients.

Using the data extraction methods presented in *Chapter 2, Managing and Understanding Data*, we will split the `wcbd_n` data frame into the `wbcd_train` and `wbcd_test` data frames:

```
> wbcd_train <- wbcd_n[1:469, ]
> wbcd_test <- wbcd_n[470:569, ]
```

If the previous code is confusing, remember that data is extracted from data frames using the `[row, column]` syntax. A blank value for the row or column value indicates that all rows or columns should be included. Hence, the first line of code takes rows 1 to 469 and all columns, and the second line takes 100 rows from 470 to 569 and all columns.

When constructing training and test datasets, it is important that each dataset is a representative subset of the full set of data. In the case that we just saw, the records were already sorted in a random order, so we could simply extract 100 consecutive records to create a test dataset. This would not be an appropriate method if the data was ordered in a non-random pattern such as chronologically, or in groups of similar values. In these cases, random sampling methods would be needed.

When we constructed our training and test data, we excluded the target variable, diagnosis. For training the kNN model, we will need to store these class labels in factor vectors, divided to the training and test datasets:

```
> wbcd_train_labels <- wbcd[1:469, 1]
> wbcd_test_labels <- wbcd[470:569, 1]
```

This code takes the diagnosis factor in column 1 of the wbcd data frame and creates the vectors, wbcd_train_labels and wbcd_test_labels. We will use these in the next steps of training and evaluating our classifier.

# Step 3 – training a model on the data

Equipped with our training data and labels vector, we are now ready to classify our unknown records. For the kNN algorithm, the training phase actually involves no model building—the process of training a lazy learner like kNN simply involves storing the input data in a structured format.

To classify our test instances, we will use a kNN implementation from the class package, which provides a set of basic R functions for classification. If this package is not already installed on your system, you can install it by typing:

```
> install.packages("class")
```

To load the package during any session in which you wish to use the functions, simply enter the command library(class).

The knn() function in the class package provides a standard, classic implementation of the kNN algorithm. For each instance in the test data, the function will identify the *k*-nearest neighbors, using Euclidean distance, where *k* is a user-specified number. The test instance is classified by taking a "vote" among the *k*-Nearest Neighbors—specifically, this involves assigning the class of the majority of the *k* neighbors. A tie vote is broken at random.

There are several other kNN functions in other R packages, providing more sophisticated or more efficient implementations. If you run into limits with knn(), take a look at the **Comprehensive R Archive Network (CRAN)** to see what else is out there. With that said, you may be surprised how well the basic knn() function works out of the box.

Training and classification using the knn() function is performed in a single function call, using four parameters as shown in the following table:

| **kNN classification syntax** |
| --- |
| using the knn() function in the class package |
| **Building the classifier and making predictions:**<br><br>p <- knn(train, test, class, k)<br><br>  • train is a data frame containing numeric training data<br>  • test is a data frame containing numeric test data<br>  • class is a factor vector with the class for each row in the training data<br>  • k is an integer indicating the number of nearest neighbors<br><br>The function returns a factor vector of predicted classes for each row in the test data frame.<br><br>**Example:**<br><br>wbcd_pred <- knn(train = wbcd_train, test = wbcd_test,<br>        cl = wbcd_train_labels, k = 3) |

We already have nearly everything that we need to apply the kNN algorithm to this data. We split our data into training and test datasets, each with exactly the same numeric features. The labels for the training data are stored in a separate factor vector. The only remaining parameter is k, which specifies the number of neighbors to include in the vote.

As our training data includes 469 instances, we might try k = 21, an odd number roughly equal to the square root of 469. Using an odd number will reduce the chance of ending with a tie vote.

Now we can use the knn() function to classify the test data:

```
> wbcd_test_pred <- knn(train = wbcd_train, test = wbcd_test,
                        cl = wbcd_train_labels, k=21)
```

The knn() function returns a factor vector of predicted labels for each of the examples in the test dataset, which we have assigned to wbcd_test_pred.

# Step 4 – evaluating model performance

The next step of the process is to evaluate how well the predicted classes in the wbcd_test_pred vector match up with the known values in the wbcd_test_labels vector. To do this, we can use the CrossTable() function in the gmodels package, which was introduced in *Chapter 2, Managing and Understanding Data*. If you haven't done so already, please install this package using the command install.packages("gmodels").

After loading the package with the library(gmodels) command, we can create a cross tabulation indicating the agreement between the two vectors. Specifying prop.chisq = FALSE will remove the **chi-square** values that are not needed, from the output:

```
> CrossTable(x = wbcd_test_labels, y = wbcd_test_pred,
            prop.chisq=FALSE)
```

The resulting table looks like this:

```
   Cell Contents
|-------------------------|
|                       N |
|           N / Row Total |
|           N / Col Total |
|         N / Table Total |
|-------------------------|


Total Observations in Table:   100


                 | wbcd_test_pred
wbcd_test_labels |    Benign |  Malignant | Row Total |
-----------------|-----------|------------|-----------|
          Benign |        61 |          0 |        61 |
                 |     1.000 |      0.000 |     0.610 |
                 |     0.968 |      0.000 |           |
                 |     0.610 |      0.000 |           |
-----------------|-----------|------------|-----------|
       Malignant |         2 |         37 |        39 |
                 |     0.051 |      0.949 |     0.390 |
                 |     0.032 |      1.000 |           |
                 |     0.020 |      0.370 |           |
-----------------|-----------|------------|-----------|
    Column Total |        63 |         37 |       100 |
                 |     0.630 |      0.370 |           |
-----------------|-----------|------------|-----------|
```

The cell percentages in the table indicate the proportion of values that fall into four categories. In the top-left cell (labeled **TN**), are the true negative results. These 61 of 100 values indicate cases where the mass was benign, and the kNN algorithm correctly identified it as such. The bottom-right cell (labeled **TP**), indicates the true positive results, where the classifier and the clinically determined label agree that the mass is malignant. A total of 37 of 100 predictions were true positives.

The cells falling on the other diagonal contain counts of examples where the kNN approach disagreed with the true label. The 2 examples in the lower-left **FN** cell are false negative results; in this case, the predicted value was benign but the tumor was actually malignant. Errors in this direction could be extremely costly, as they might lead a patient to believe that she is cancer-free, when in reality the disease may continue to spread. The cell labeled **FP** would contain the false positive results, if there were any. These values occur when the model classifies a mass as **malignant** when in reality it was benign. Although such errors are less dangerous than a false negative result, they should also be avoided as they could lead to additional financial burden on the health care system, or additional stress for the patient, as additional tests or treatment may have to be provided.

If we desired, we could totally eliminate false negatives by classifying every mass as malignant. Obviously, this is not a realistic strategy. Still, it illustrates the fact that prediction involves striking a balance between the false positive rate and the false negative rate. In *Chapter 10, Evaluating Model Performance,* you will learn more sophisticated methods for measuring predictive accuracy that can be used to identify places where the error rate can be optimized depending on the costs of each type of error.

A total of 2 percent, that is, 2 out of 100 masses were incorrectly classified by the kNN approach. While 98 percent accuracy seems impressive for a few lines of R code, we might try another iteration of the model to see if we can improve the performance and reduce the number of values that have been incorrectly classified, particularly, as the errors were dangerous false negatives.

# Step 5 – improving model performance

We will attempt two simple variations on our previous classifier. First, we will employ an alternative method for rescaling our numeric features. Second, we will try several different values for *k*.

## Transformation – z-score standardization

Although normalization is traditionally used for kNN classification, it may not always be the most appropriate way to rescale features. Because z-score standardized values have no predefined minimum and maximum, extreme values are not compressed towards the center. One might suspect that with a malignant tumor, we might see some very extreme outliers, as the tumors grow uncontrollably. It might, therefore, be reasonable to allow the outliers to be weighted more heavily in the distance calculation. Let's see whether z-score standardization can improve our predictive accuracy.

To standardize a vector, we can use R's built in `scale()` function, which by default rescales values using the z-score standardization. The `scale()` function offers the additional benefit that it can be applied directly to a data frame, so we can avoid use of the `lapply()` function. To create a z-score standardized version of the `wbcd` data, we can use the following command, which rescales all features with the exception of `diagnosis`, and stores the result as a data frame in the `wbcd_z` variable. The `_z` suffix is a reminder that the values were z-score transformed.

```
> wbcd_z <- as.data.frame(scale(wbcd[-1]))
```

To confirm that the transformation was applied correctly, we can look at the summary statistics:

```
> summary(wbcd_z$area_mean)
   Min. 1st Qu.  Median    Mean 3rd Qu.    Max.
-1.4530 -0.6666 -0.2949  0.0000  0.3632  5.2460
```

The mean of a z-score standardized variable should always be zero, and the range should be fairly compact. A z-score greater than 3 or less than -3 indicates an extremely rare value. The previous summary seems reasonable.

As we had done before, we need to divide the data into training and test sets, then classify the test instances using the `knn()` function. We'll then compare the predicted labels to the actual labels using `CrossTable()`:

```
> wbcd_train <- wbcd_z[1:469, ]
> wbcd_test <- wbcd_z[470:569, ]
> wbcd_train_labels <- wbcd[1:469, 1]
> wbcd_test_labels <- wbcd[470:569, 1]
> wbcd_test_pred <- knn(train = wbcd_train, test = wbcd_test,
                        cl = wbcd_train_labels, k=21)
> CrossTable(x = wbcd_test_labels, y = wbcd_test_pred,
            prop.chisq=FALSE)
```

Unfortunately, in the following table, the results of our new transformation show a slight decline in accuracy. The instances where we had correctly classified 98 percent of examples previously, we classified only 95 percent correctly this time. Making matters worse, we did no better at classifying the dangerous false negatives.

```
                        | wbcd_test_pred
  wbcd_test_labels      |   Benign | Malignant | Row Total
 ---------------------- | -------- | --------- | ---------
            Benign      |       61 |         0 |        61
                        |    1.000 |     0.000 |     0.610
                        |    0.924 |     0.000 |
                        |    0.610 |     0.000 |
 ---------------------- | -------- | --------- | ---------
            Malignant   |        5 |        34 |        39
                        |    0.128 |     0.872 |     0.390
                        |    0.076 |     1.000 |
                        |    0.050 |     0.340 |
 ---------------------- | -------- | --------- | ---------
          Column Total  |       66 |        34 |       100
                        |    0.660 |     0.340 |
 ---------------------- | -------- | --------- | ---------
```

# Testing alternative values of k

We may be able do even better by examining performance across various values of k. Using the normalized training and test datasets, the same 100 records were classified using several different *k* values. The number of false negatives and false positives are shown for each iteration:

| k value | # false negatives | # false positives | Percent classified Incorrectly |
|---------|-------------------|-------------------|--------------------------------|
| 1 | 1 | 3 | 4 percent |
| 5 | 2 | 0 | 2 percent |
| 11 | 3 | 0 | 3 percent |
| 15 | 3 | 0 | 3 percent |
| 21 | 2 | 0 | 2 percent |
| 27 | 4 | 0 | 4 percent |

Although the classifier was never perfect, the 1NN approach was able to avoid some of the false negatives at the expense of adding false positives. It is important to keep in mind, however, that it would be unwise to tailor our approach too closely to our test data; after all, a different set of 100 patient records is likely to be somewhat different from those used to measure our performance.

If you need to be certain that a learner will generalize to future data, you might create several sets of 100 patients at random and repeatedly retest the result. Methods to carefully evaluate the performance of machine learning models are discussed further in *Chapter 10, Evaluating Model Performance.*

# Summary

In this chapter, we learned about classification using k-nearest neighbors. Unlike many classification algorithms, kNN does not do any learning. It simply stores the training data verbatim. Unlabeled test examples are then matched to the most similar records in the training set using a distance function, and the unlabeled example is assigned the label of its neighbors.

In spite of the fact that kNN is a simple algorithm, it is capable of tackling extremely complex tasks, such as identifying cancerous masses. In a few simple lines of R code, we were able to correctly identify whether a mass was malignant or benign 98 percent of the time.

In the next chapter, we will examine a classification method that uses probability to estimate the likelihood that an observation falls into certain categories. It will be interesting to compare how this approach differs from kNN. Later on, in *Chapter 9, Finding Groups of Data – Clustering with k-means*, we will learn about a close relative to kNN, which uses distance measures for a completely different learning task.

# Summary

# 4
# Probabilistic Learning – Classification Using Naive Bayes

When a meteorologist provides a weather forecast, precipitation is typically predicted using terms such as "70 percent chance of rain." These forecasts are known as probability of precipitation reports. Have you ever considered how they are calculated? It is a puzzling question, because in reality, it will either rain or it will not.

These estimates are based on probabilistic methods, or methods concerned with describing uncertainty. They use data on past events to extrapolate future events. In the case of weather, the chance of rain describes the proportion of prior days with similar measurable atmospheric conditions in which precipitation occurred. A 70 percent chance of rain therefore implies that in 7 out of 10 past cases with similar weather patterns, precipitation occurred somewhere in the area.

This chapter covers a machine learning algorithm called **naive Bayes**, which also uses principles of probability for classification. Just as meteorologists forecast weather, naive Bayes uses data about prior events to estimate the probability of future events. For instance, a common application of naive Bayes uses the frequency of words in past junk email messages to identify new junk mail. While studying how this works, you will learn:

- Basic principles of probability that are utilized for naive Bayes
- Specialized methods, visualizations, and data structures used for analyzing text data with R
- How to employ an R implementation of naive Bayes classifier to build an SMS message filter

If you've taken a statistics class before, some of the material in this chapter may seem like a bit of a review of the subject. Even so, it may be helpful to refresh your knowledge of probability, as these principles are the basis of how naive Bayes got such a strange name.

# Understanding naive Bayes

The basic statistical ideas necessary to understand the naive Bayes algorithm have been around for centuries. The technique descended from the work of the 18th century mathematician *Thomas Bayes*, who developed foundational mathematical principles (now known as **Bayesian methods**) for describing the probability of events, and how probabilities should be revised in light of additional information.

We'll go more in depth later, but for now it suffices to say that the probability of an event is a number between 0 percent and 100 percent that captures the chance that the event will occur given the available evidence. The lower the probability, the less likely the event is to occur. A probability of 0 percent indicates that the event definitely will not occur, while a probability of 100 percent indicates that the event certainly will occur.

Classifiers based on Bayesian methods utilize training data to calculate an observed probability of each class based on feature values. When the classifier is used later on unlabeled data, it uses the observed probabilities to predict the most likely class for the new features. It's a simple idea, but it results in a method that often has results on par with more sophisticated algorithms. In fact, Bayesian classifiers have been used for:

- Text classification, such as junk email (spam) filtering, author identification, or topic categorization
- Intrusion detection or anomaly detection in computer networks
- Diagnosing medical conditions, when given a set of observed symptoms

Typically, Bayesian classifiers are best applied to problems in which the information from numerous attributes should be considered simultaneously in order to estimate the probability of an outcome. While many algorithms ignore features that have weak effects, Bayesian methods utilize all available evidence to subtly change the predictions. If a large number of features have relatively minor effects, taken together their combined impact could be quite large.

# Basic concepts of Bayesian methods

Before jumping into the naive Bayes algorithm, it's worth spending some time defining the concepts that are used across Bayesian methods. Summarized in a single sentence, Bayesian probability theory is rooted in the idea that the estimated likelihood of an event should be based on the evidence at hand. **Events** are possible outcomes, such as sunny and rainy weather, a heads or tails result in a coin flip, or spam and not spam email messages. A **trial** is a single opportunity for the event to occur, such as a day's weather, a coin flip, or an email message.

# Probability

The probability of an event can be estimated from observed data by dividing the number of trials in which an event occurred by the total number of trials. For instance, if it rained 3 out of 10 days, the probability of rain can be estimated as 30 percent. Similarly, if 10 out of 50 email messages are spam, then the probability of spam can be estimated as 20 percent. The notation $P(A)$ is used to denote the probability of event $A$, as in $P(spam) = 0.20$.

The total probability of all possible outcomes of a trial must always be 100 percent. Thus, if the trial only has two outcomes that cannot occur simultaneously, such as heads or tails, or spam and ham (non-spam), then knowing the probability of either outcome reveals the probability of the other. For example, given the value $P(spam) = 0.20$, we are able to calculate $P(ham) = 1 - 0.20 = 0.80$. This works because the events spam and ham are **mutually exclusive** and **exhaustive**. This means that the events cannot occur at the same time and are the only two possible outcomes. As shorthand, the notation $P(\neg A)$ can be used to denote the probability of event $A$ not occurring, as in $P(\neg spam) = 0.80$.

For illustrative purposes, it is often helpful to imagine probability as a two-dimensional space that is partitioned into event probabilities for events. In the following diagram, the rectangle represents the set of all possible outcomes for an email message. The circle represents the probability that the message is spam. The remaining 80 percent represents the messages that are not spam:

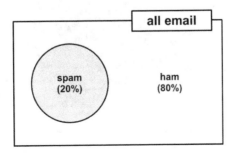

# Joint probability

Often, we are interested in monitoring several non-mutually exclusive events for the same trial. If some events occur with the event of interest, we may be able to use them to make predictions. Consider, for instance, a second event based on the outcome that the email message contains the word Viagra. For most people, this word is only likely to appear in a spam message; its presence in a message is therefore a very strong piece of evidence that the email is spam. The preceding diagram, updated for this second event, might appear as shown in the following diagram:

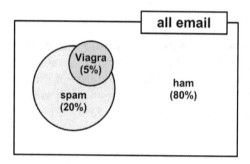

Notice in the diagram that the Viagra circle does not completely fill the spam circle, nor is it completely contained by the spam circle. This implies that not all spam messages contain the word Viagra, and not every email with the word Viagra is spam.

To zoom in for a closer look at the overlap between the spam and Viagra circles, we'll employ a visualization known as a **Venn diagram**. First used in the late 19th century by *John Venn*, the diagram uses circles to illustrate the overlap between sets of items. In most Venn diagrams such as the following one, the size of the circles and the degree of the overlap is not important. Instead, it is used as a way to remind you to allocate probability to all possible combinations of events.

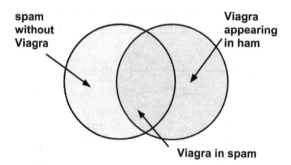

We know that 20 percent of all messages were spam (the left circle), and 5 percent of all messages contained spam (the right circle). Our job is to quantify the degree of overlap between these two proportions. In other words, we hope to estimate the probability of both *P(spam)* and *P(Viagra)* occurring, which can be written as *P(spam ∩ Viagra)*.

Calculating *P(spam ∩ Viagra)* depends on the **joint probability** of the two events, or how the probability of one event is related to the probability of the other. If the two events are totally unrelated, they are called **independent events**. For instance, the outcome of a coin flip is independent from whether the weather is rainy or sunny.

If all events were independent, it would be impossible to predict any event using the data obtained by another. On the other hand, **dependent events** are the basis of predictive modeling. For instance, the presence of clouds is likely to be predictive of a rainy day, and the appearance of the word Viagra is predictive of a spam email.

With the knowledge that *P(spam)* and *P(Viagra)* were independent, we could then easily calculate *P(spam ∩ Viagra)*; the probability of both events happening at the same time. Because 20 percent of all messages are spam, and 5 percent of all emails contain the word Viagra, we could assume that 5 percent of 20 percent *(0.05 * 0.20 = 0.01)*, or 1 percent of all messages are spam containing the word Viagra. More generally, for independent events *A* and *B*, the probability of both happening is *P(A ∩ B) = P(A) * P(B)*.

In reality, it is far more likely that *P(spam)* and *P(Viagra)* are highly dependent, which means that this calculation is incorrect. We need to use a more careful formulation of the relationship between these two events.

# Conditional probability with Bayes' theorem

The relationships between dependent events can be described using **Bayes' theorem**, as shown in the following formula. The notation *P(A | B)* can be read as the probability of event A given that event B occurred. This is known as **conditional probability**, since the probability of *A* is dependent (that is, conditional) on what happened with event *B*.

$$P(A \mid B) = \frac{P(B \mid A)P(A)}{P(B)} = \frac{P(A \cap B)}{P(B)}$$

To understand how Bayes' theorem works in practice, suppose that you were tasked with guessing the probability that an incoming email was spam. Without any additional evidence, the most reasonable guess would be the probability that any prior message was spam (that is, 20 percent in the preceding example). This estimate is known as the **prior probability**.

Now, also suppose that you obtained an additional piece of evidence; you were told that the incoming message used the term Viagra. The probability that the word Viagra was used in previous spam messages is called the **likelihood** and the probability that Viagra appeared in any message at all is known as the **marginal likelihood**.

By applying Bayes' theorem to this evidence, we can compute a **posterior probability** that measures how likely the message is to be spam. If the posterior probability is greater than 50 percent, the message is more likely to be spam than ham, and it should be filtered. The following formula is the Bayes' theorem for the given evidence:

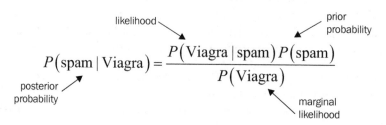

To calculate the components of Bayes' theorem, we must construct a **frequency table** (shown on the left in the following diagram) that records the number of times Viagra appeared in spam and ham messages. Just like a two-way cross-tabulation, one dimension of the table indicates levels of the class variable (spam or ham), while the other dimension indicates levels for features (Viagra: yes or no). The cells then indicate the number of instances having the particular combination of class value and feature value. The frequency table can then be used to construct a **likelihood table**, as shown on right in the following diagram:

| Frequency | Viagra | | |
|---|---|---|---|
| | Yes | No | Total |
| spam | 4 | 16 | 20 |
| ham | 1 | 79 | 80 |
| Total | 5 | 95 | 100 |

| Likelihood | Viagra | | |
|---|---|---|---|
| | Yes | No | Total |
| spam | 4 / 20 | 16 / 20 | 20 |
| ham | 1 / 80 | 79 / 80 | 80 |
| Total | 5 / 100 | 95 / 100 | 100 |

The likelihood table reveals that $P(Viagra \mid spam) = 4/20 = 0.20$, indicating that the probability is 20 percent that a spam message contains the term Viagra. Additionally, since the theorem says that $P(B \mid A) * P(A) = P(A \cap B)$, we can calculate $P(spam \cap Viagra)$ as $P(Viagra \mid spam) * P(spam) = (4/20) * (20/100) = 0.04$. This is four times greater than the previous estimate under the faulty independence assumption illustrating the importance of Bayes' theorem when calculating joint probability.

To compute the posterior probability, *P(spam | Viagra)*, we simply take
*P(Viagra | spam) * P(spam) / P(Viagra)*, or *(4/20) * (20/100) / (5/100) = 0.80*. Therefore,
the probability is 80 percent that a message is spam, given that it contains the word
Viagra. Therefore, any message containing this term should be filtered.

This is very much how commercial spam filters work, although they consider a
much larger number of words simultaneously when computing the frequency and
likelihood tables. In the next section, we'll see how this concept is put to use when
additional features are involved.

# The naive Bayes algorithm

The **naive Bayes** (**NB**) algorithm describes a simple application using Bayes' theorem
for classification. Although it is not the only machine learning method utilizing
Bayesian methods, it is the most common, particularly for text classification where
it has become the de facto standard. Strengths and weaknesses of this algorithm are
as follows:

| Strengths | Weaknesses |
|---|---|
| <ul><li>Simple, fast, and very effective</li><li>Does well with noisy and missing data</li><li>Requires relatively few examples for training, but also works well with very large numbers of examples</li><li>Easy to obtain the estimated probability for a prediction</li></ul> | <ul><li>Relies on an often-faulty assumption of equally important and independent features</li><li>Not ideal for datasets with large numbers of numeric features</li><li>Estimated probabilities are less reliable than the predicted classes</li></ul> |

The naive Bayes algorithm is named as such because it makes a couple of "naive"
assumptions about the data. In particular, naive Bayes assumes that all of the
features in the dataset are equally important and independent. These assumptions
are rarely true in most of the real-world applications.

For example, if you were attempting to identify spam by monitoring email messages,
it is almost certainly true that some features will be more important than others.
For example, the sender of the email may be a more important indicator of spam
than the message text. Additionally, the words that appear in the message body are
not independent from one another, since the appearance of some words is a very
good indication that other words are also likely to appear. A message with the word
Viagra is probably likely to also contain the words prescription or drugs.

However, in most cases when these assumptions are violated, naive Bayes still performs fairly well. This is true even in extreme circumstances where strong dependencies are found among the features. Due to the algorithm's versatility and accuracy across many types of conditions, naive Bayes is often a strong first candidate for classification learning tasks.

The exact reason why naive Bayes works well in spite of its faulty assumptions has been the subject of much speculation. One explanation is that it is not important to obtain a careful estimate of probability so long as the predicted class values are true. For instance, if a spam filter correctly identifies spam, does it matter that it was 51 percent or 99 percent confident in its prediction? For more information on this topic, refer to *On the optimality of the simple Bayesian classifier under zero-one loss* in Machine Learning, by *Pedro Domingos* and *Michael Pazzani* (1997).

## The naive Bayes classification

Let's extend our spam filter by adding a few additional terms to be monitored: money, groceries, and unsubscribe. The naive Bayes learner is trained by constructing a likelihood table for the appearance of these four words (W**1**, W**2**, W**3**, and W**4**), as shown in the following diagram for 100 emails:

| Likelihood | Viagra ($W_1$) | | Money ($W_2$) | | Groceries ($W_3$) | | Unsubscribe ($W_4$) | | Total |
|---|---|---|---|---|---|---|---|---|---|
| | Yes | No | Yes | No | Yes | No | Yes | No | |
| spam | 4 / 20 | 16 / 20 | 10 / 20 | 10 / 20 | 0 / 20 | 20 / 20 | 12 / 20 | 8 / 20 | 20 |
| ham | 1 / 80 | 79 / 80 | 14 / 80 | 66 / 80 | 8 / 80 | 71 / 80 | 23 / 80 | 57 / 80 | 80 |
| Total | 5 / 100 | 95 / 100 | 24 / 100 | 76 / 100 | 8 / 100 | 91 / 100 | 35 / 100 | 65 / 100 | 100 |

As new messages are received, the posterior probability must be calculated to determine whether they are more likely spam or ham, given the likelihood of the words found in the message text. For example, suppose that a message contains the terms Viagra and Unsubscribe, but does not contain either Money or Groceries.

Using Bayes' theorem, we can define the problem as shown in the following formula, which captures the probability that a message is spam, given that Viagra = Yes, Money = No, Groceries = No, and Unsubscribe = Yes:

$$P\left(\text{Spam} \mid W_1 \cap \neg W_2 \cap \neg W_3 \cap W_4\right) = \frac{P\left(W_1 \cap \neg W_2 \cap \neg W_3 \cap W_4 \mid \text{spam}\right) P\left(\text{spam}\right)}{P\left(W_1 \cap \neg W_2 \cap \neg W_3 \cap W_4\right)}$$

For a number of reasons, this formula is computationally difficult to solve. As additional features are added, tremendous amounts of memory are needed to store probabilities for all of the possible intersecting events; imagine the complexity of a Venn diagram for the events for four words, let alone for hundreds or more. Enormous training datasets would be required to ensure that enough data is available to model all of the possible interactions.

The work becomes much easier if we can exploit the fact that naive Bayes assumes independence among events. Specifically, naive Bayes assumes **class-conditional independence**, which means that events are independent so long as they are conditioned on the same class value. Assuming conditional independence allows us to simplify the formula using the probability rule for independent events, which you may recall is $P(A \cap B) = P(A) * P(B)$. This results in a much easier-to-compute formulation, shown as follows:

$$P\left(\text{Spam} \mid W_1 \cap \neg W_2 \cap \neg W_3 \cap W_4\right) = \frac{P\left(W_1 \mid \text{spam}\right) P\left(\neg W_2 \mid \text{spam}\right) P\left(\neg W_3 \mid \text{spam}\right) P\left(W_4 \mid \text{spam}\right) P\left(\text{spam}\right)}{P\left(W_1\right) P\left(\neg W_2\right) P\left(\neg W_3\right) P\left(W_4\right)}$$

The result of this formula should be compared to the probability that the message is ham:

$$P\left(\text{ham} \mid W_1 \cap \neg W_2 \cap \neg W_3 \cap W_4\right) = \frac{P\left(W_1 \mid \text{ham}\right) P\left(\neg W_2 \mid \text{ham}\right) P\left(\neg W_3 \mid \text{ham}\right) P\left(W_4 \mid \text{ham}\right) P\left(\text{ham}\right)}{P\left(W_1\right) P\left(\neg W_2\right) P\left(\neg W_3\right) P\left(W_4\right)}$$

Using the values in the likelihood table, we can start filling numbers in these equations. Because the denominator is the same in both cases, it can be ignored for now. The overall likelihood of spam is then:

$$(4/20) * (10/20) * (20/20) * (12/20) * (20/100) = 0.012$$

While the likelihood of ham given this pattern of words is:

$$(1/80) * (66/80) * (71/80) * (23/80) * (80/100) = 0.002$$

Because *0.012 / 0.002 = 6*, we can say that this message is six times more likely to be spam than ham. However, to convert these numbers to probabilities, we need one last step.

The probability of spam is equal to the likelihood that the message is spam divided by the likelihood that the message is either spam or ham:

$$0.012 / (0.012 + 0.002) = 0.857$$

Similarly, the probability of ham is equal to the likelihood that the message is ham divided by the likelihood that the message is either spam or ham:

$$0.002 / (0.012 + 0.002) = 0.143$$

Given the pattern of words in the message, we expect that the message is spam with 85.7 percent probability, and ham with 14.3 percent probability. Because these are mutually exclusive and exhaustive events, the probabilities sum up to one.

The naive Bayes classification algorithm we used in the preceding example can be summarized by the following formula. Essentially, the probability of level $L$ for class $C$, given the evidence provided by features $F_1$ through $F_n$, is equal to the product of the probabilities of each piece of evidence conditioned on the class level, the prior probability of the class level, and a scaling factor $1 / Z$, which converts the result to a probability:

$$P\left(C_L \mid F_1, \dots, F_n\right) = \frac{1}{Z} p\left(C_L\right) \prod_{i=1}^{n} p\left(F_i \mid C_L\right)$$

## The Laplace estimator

Let's look at one more example. Suppose we received another message, this time containing the terms: Viagra, Groceries, Money, and Unsubscribe. Using the naive Bayes algorithm as before, we can compute the likelihood of spam as:

$$(4/20) * (10/20) * (0/20) * (12/20) * (20/100) = 0$$

And the likelihood of ham is:

$$(1/80) * (14/80) * (8/80) * (23/80) * (80/100) = 0.00005$$

Therefore, the probability of spam is:

$$0 / (0 + 0.0099) = 0$$

And the probability of ham is:

$$0.00005 / (0 + 0.\,0.00005) = 1$$

These results suggest that the message is spam with 0 percent probability and ham with 100 percent probability. Does this prediction make sense? Probably not. The message contains several words usually associated with spam, including Viagra, which is very rarely used in legitimate messages. It is therefore very likely that the message has been incorrectly classified.

This problem might arise if an event never occurs for one or more levels of the class. For instance, the term Groceries had never previously appeared in a spam message. Consequently, *P(spam | groceries) = 0%*.

Because probabilities in naive Bayes are multiplied, this 0 percent value causes the posterior probability of spam to be zero, giving the word Groceries the ability to effectively nullify and overrule all of the other evidence. Even if the email was otherwise overwhelmingly expected to be spam, the absence of the word Groceries will always result in a probability of spam being zero.

A solution to this problem involves using something called the **Laplace estimator**, which is named after the French mathematician *Pierre-Simon Laplace*. The Laplace estimator essentially adds a small number to each of the counts in the frequency table, which ensures that each feature has a nonzero probability of occurring with each class. Typically, the Laplace estimator is set to 1, which ensures that each class-feature combination is found in the data at least once.

The Laplace estimator can be set to any value, and does not necessarily even have to be the same for each of the features. If you were a devoted Bayesian, you could use a Laplace estimator to reflect a presumed prior probability of how the feature relates to the class. In practice, given a large enough training dataset, this step is unnecessary, and the value of 1 is almost always used.

Let's see how this affects our prediction for this message. Using a Laplace value of 1, we add one to each numerator in the likelihood function. The total number of 1s must also be added to each denominator. The likelihood of spam is therefore:

$$(5/24) * (11/24) * (1/24) * (13/24) * (20/100) = 0.0004$$

And the likelihood of ham is:

$$(2/84) * (15/84) * (9/84) * (24/84) * (80/100) = 0.0001$$

This means that the probability of spam is 80 percent and the probability of ham is 20 percent; a more plausible result than the one obtained when Groceries alone determined the result.

# Using numeric features with naive Bayes

Because naive Bayes uses frequency tables for learning the data, each feature must be categorical in order to create the combinations of class and feature values comprising the matrix. Since numeric features do not have categories of values, the preceding algorithm does not work directly with numeric data. There are, however, ways that this can be addressed.

One easy and effective solution is to **discretize** numeric features, which simply means that the numbers are put into categories known as **bins**. For this reason, discretization is also sometimes called **binning**. This method is ideal when there are large amounts of training data, a common condition when working with naive Bayes.

There are several different ways to discretize a numeric feature. Perhaps the most common is to explore the data for natural categories or **cut points** in the distribution of data. For example, suppose that you added a feature to the spam dataset that recorded the time of night or day the email was sent, from 0 to 24 hours past midnight.

Depicted using a histogram, the time data might look something like the following diagram. In the early hours of morning, message frequency is low. Activity picks up during business hours, and tapers off in the evening. This seems to create four natural bins of activity, as partitioned by the dashed lines indicating places where the numeric data are divided into levels of a new nominal feature, which could then be used with naive Bayes:

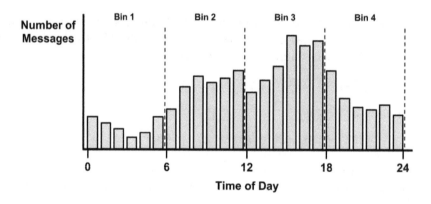

Keep in mind that the choice of four bins was somewhat arbitrary, based on the natural distribution of data and a hunch about how the proportion of spam might change throughout the day. We might expect that spammers operate in the late hours of the night, or they may operate during the day, when people are likely to check their email. That said, to capture these trends, we could have just as easily used three bins or twelve.

If there are no obvious cut points, one option is to discretize the feature using quantiles. You could divide the data into three bins with tertiles, four bins with quartiles, or five bins with quintiles.

One thing to keep in mind is that discretizing a numeric feature always results in a reduction of information, as the feature's original granularity is reduced to a smaller number of categories. It is important to strike a balance, since too few bins can result in important trends being obscured, while too many bins can result in small counts in the naive Bayes frequency table.

# Example – filtering mobile phone spam with the naive Bayes algorithm

As worldwide use of mobile phones has grown, a new avenue for electronic junk mail has been opened for disreputable marketers. These advertisers utilize **Short Message Service (SMS)** text messages to target potential consumers with unwanted advertising known as SMS spam. This type of spam is particularly troublesome because, unlike email spam, many cellular phone users pay a fee per SMS received. Developing a classification algorithm that could filter SMS spam would provide a useful tool for cellular phone providers.

Since naive Bayes has been used successfully for email spam filtering, it seems likely that it could also be applied to SMS spam. However, relative to email spam, SMS spam poses additional challenges for automated filters. SMS messages are often limited to 160 characters, reducing the amount of text that can be used to identify whether a message is junk. The limit, combined with small mobile phone keyboards, has led many to adopt a form of SMS shorthand lingo, which further blurs the line between legitimate messages and spam. Let's see how well a simple naive Bayes classifier handles these challenges.

# Step 1 – collecting data

To develop the naive Bayes classifier, we will use data adapted from the SMS Spam Collection at `http://www.dt.fee.unicamp.br/~tiago/smsspamcollection/`.

 To read more about the SMS Spam Collection, refer to the authors' full publication: *On the Validity of a New SMS Spam Collection* by *J.M. Gómez Hidalgo, T.A. Almeida*, and *A. Yamakami* in *Proceedings of the 11th IEEE International Conference on Machine Learning and Applications*, (2012.)

This dataset includes the text of SMS messages along with a label indicating whether the message is unwanted. Junk messages are labeled spam, while legitimate messages are labeled ham. Some examples of spam and ham are shown in the following example:

The following is a sample ham messages:

**Better. Made up for Friday and stuffed myself like a pig yesterday. Now I feel bleh. But at least its not writhing pain kind of bleh.**

**If he started searching he will get job in few days. He have great potential and talent.**

**I got another job! The one at the hospital doing data analysis or something, starts on monday! Not sure when my thesis will got finished**

The following is a sample spam messages:

**Congratulations ur awarded 500 of CD vouchers or 125gift guaranteed & Free entry 2 100 wkly draw txt MUSIC to 87066**

**December only! Had your mobile 11mths+? You are entitled to update to the latest colour camera mobile for Free! Call The Mobile Update Co FREE on 08002986906**

**Valentines Day Special! Win over £1000 in our quiz and take your partner on the trip of a lifetime! Send GO to 83600 now. 150p/msg rcvd.**

Looking at the preceding sample messages, do you notice any distinguishing characteristics of spam? One notable characteristic is that two of the three spam messages use the word "free", yet the word does not appear in any of the ham messages. On the other hand, two of the ham messages cite specific days of week, when compared to zero spam messages.

Our naive Bayes classifier will take advantage of such patterns in the word frequency to determine whether the SMS messages seem to better fit the profile of spam or ham. While it's not inconceivable that the word "free" would appear outside of a spam SMS, a legitimate message is likely to provide additional words providing context. For instance, a ham message might state "are you free on Sunday?", whereas a spam message might use the phrase "free ringtones." The classifier will compute the probability of spam and ham given the evidence provided by all the words in the message.

# Step 2 – exploring and preparing the data

The first step towards constructing our classifier involves processing the raw data for analysis. Text data are challenging to prepare because it is necessary to transform the words and sentences into a form that a computer can understand. We will transform our data into a representation known as **bag-of-words**, which ignores the order that words appear in and simply provides a variable indicating whether the word appears at all.

 The data used here have been modified slightly from the original in order to make it easier to work with in R. If you plan on following along with the example, download the sms_spam.csv file from the Packt Publishing's website and save it to your R working directory.

We'll begin by importing the CSV data using the read.csv() function and saving it to a data frame titled sms_raw:

```
> sms_raw <- read.csv("sms_spam.csv", stringsAsFactors = FALSE)
```

Using the structure function str(), we see that the sms_raw data frame includes 5,559 total SMS messages with two features: type and text. The SMS type has been coded as either ham or spam, and the text variable stores the full raw SMS message text.

```
> str(sms_raw)
'data.frame': 5559 obs. of  2 variables:
 $ type: chr  "ham" "ham" "ham" "spam" ...
 $ text: chr  "Hope you are having a good week. Just checking in" "K..
give back my thanks." "Am also doing in cbe only. But have to pay."
"complimentary 4 STAR Ibiza Holiday or £10,000 cash needs your URGENT
collection. 09066364349 NOW from Landline not to lose out"| __truncated__
...
```

The `type` variable is currently a character vector. Since this is a categorical variable, it would be better to convert it to a factor, as shown in the following code:

```
> sms_raw$type <- factor(sms_raw$type)
```

Examining the `type` variable with the `str()` and `table()` functions, we see that the variable has now been appropriately recoded as a factor. Additionally, we see that 747 (or about 13 percent) of SMS messages in our data were labeled `spam`, while the remainder were labeled `ham`:

```
> str(sms_raw$type)
 Factor w/ 2 levels "ham","spam": 1 1 1 2 2 1 1 1 2 1 ...
> table(sms_raw$type)

 ham spam

4812  747
```

For now, we will leave the `text` variable alone. As you will learn in the next section, processing the raw SMS messages will require the use of a new set of powerful tools designed specifically for processing text data.

# Data preparation – processing text data for analysis

SMS messages are strings of text composed of words, spaces, numbers, and punctuation. Handling this type of complex data takes a large amount of thought and effort. One needs to consider how to remove numbers, punctuation, handle uninteresting words such as **and**, **but**, and **or**, and how to break apart sentences into individual words. Thankfully, this functionality has been provided by members of the R community in a text mining package titled `tm`.

> The `tm` package was originally created by *Ingo Feinerer* as a dissertation project at the Vienna University of Economics and Business. To learn more, visit http://tm.r-forge.r-project.org/.

The `tm` text mining package can be installed via the `install.packages("tm")` command and loaded with `library(tm)`.

The first step in processing text data involves creating a **corpus**, which refers to a collection of text documents. In our project, a text document refers to a single SMS message. We'll build a corpus containing the SMS messages in the training data using the following command:

```
> sms_corpus <- Corpus(VectorSource(sms_raw$text))
```

This command uses two functions. First, the `Corpus()` function creates an R object to store text documents. This function takes a parameter specifying the format of the text documents to be loaded. Since we have already read the SMS messages and stored them in an R vector, we specify `VectorSource()`, which tells `Corpus()` to use the messages in the vector `sms_train$text`. The `Corpus()` function stores the result in an object named `sms_corpus`.

> The `Corpus()` function is extremely flexible and can read documents from many different sources such as PDFs and Microsoft Word documents. To learn more, examine the *Data Import* section in the `tm` package vignette using the command: `print(vignette("tm"))`

If we `print()` the corpus we just created, we will see that it contains documents for each of the 5,559 SMS messages in the training data:

```
> print(sms_corpus)
A corpus with 5559 text documents
```

To look at the contents of the corpus, we can use the `inspect()` function. By combining this with methods for accessing vectors, we can view specific SMS messages. The following command will view the first, second, and third SMS messages:

```
> inspect(sms_corpus[1:3])
[[1]]
Hope you are having a good week. Just checking in
[[2]]
K..give back my thanks.
[[3]]
Am also doing in cbe only. But have to pay.
```

The corpus now contains the raw text of 5,559 text messages. Before splitting the text into words, we will need to perform some common cleaning steps in order to remove punctuation and other characters that may clutter the result. For example, we would like to count `hello!`, `HELLO...`, and `Hello` as instances of the word hello.

The function `tm_map()` provides a method for transforming (that is, mapping) a tm corpus. We will use this to clean up our corpus using a series of transformation functions, and save the result in a new object called `corpus_clean`.

First, we will convert all of the SMS messages to lowercase and remove any numbers:

```
> corpus_clean <- tm_map(sms_corpus, tolower)
> corpus_clean <- tm_map(corpus_clean, removeNumbers)
```

A common practice when analyzing text data is to remove filler words such as **to**, **and**, **but**, and **or**. These are known as **stop words**. Rather than define a list of stop words ourselves, we will use the `stopwords()` function provided by the tm package. It contains a set of numerous stop words. To see them all, type `stopwords()` at the command line. As we did before, we'll use the `tm_map()` function to apply this function to the data:

```
> corpus_clean <- tm_map(corpus_clean, removeWords, stopwords())
```

We'll also remove punctuation:

```
> corpus_clean <- tm_map(corpus_clean, removePunctuation)
```

Now that we have removed numbers, stop words, and punctuation, the text messages are left with blank spaces where these characters used to be. The last step then is to remove additional whitespace, leaving only a single space between words.

```
> corpus_clean <- tm_map(corpus_clean, stripWhitespace)
```

The following table shows the first three messages in SMS corpus before and after the cleaning process. The messages have been limited to the most interesting words and punctuation and capitalization have been removed:

| SMS messages before cleaning | SMS messages after cleaning |
| --- | --- |
| `> inspect(sms_corpus[1:3])`<br>`[[1]]`<br><br>`Hope you are having a good week.`<br>`Just checking in`<br>`[[2]]`<br><br>`K..give back my thanks.`<br>`[[3]]`<br><br>`Am also doing in cbe only. But have`<br>`to pay.` | `> inspect(corpus_clean[1:3])`<br>`[[1]]`<br><br>`hope good week just checking`<br>`[[2]]`<br><br>`kgive back thanks`<br>`[[3]]`<br><br>`also cbe pay` |

Now that the data are processed to our liking, the final step is to split the messages into individual components through a process called **tokenization**. A token is a single element of a text string; in this case, the tokens are words.

The example here was tested using R 2.15.3 on Microsoft Windows 7, with tm package Version 0.5-9.1. Because these projects are ever-changing the results may differ slightly if you are using another version or another platform.

As you might assume, the tm package provides functionality to tokenize the SMS message corpus. The DocumentTermMatrix() function will take a corpus and create a data structure called a **sparse matrix**, in which the rows of the matrix indicate documents (that is, SMS messages) and the columns indicate terms (that is, words). Each cell in the matrix stores a number indicating a count of the times the word indicated by the column appears in the document indicated by the row. The following screenshot illustrates a small portion of the document term matrix for the SMS corpus, as the complete matrix has 5,559 rows and over 7,000 columns:

| A | B | C | D | E | F | G |
|---|---|---|---|---|---|---|
|   | balloon | balls | bam | bambling | band | bandages |
| 1 | 0 | 0 | 0 | 0 | 0 | 0 |
| 2 | 0 | 0 | 0 | 0 | 0 | 0 |
| 3 | 0 | 0 | 0 | 0 | 0 | 0 |
| 4 | 0 | 0 | 0 | 0 | 0 | 0 |
| 5 | 0 | 0 | 0 | 0 | 0 | 0 |

The fact that each cell in the table is zero implies that none of the words listed at the top of the columns appears in any of the first five messages in the corpus. This highlights the reason why this data structure is called a sparse matrix; the vast majority of cells in the matrix are filled with zeros. Although each message contains some words, the probability of any specific word appearing in a given message is small.

Creating a sparse matrix given a tm corpus involves a single command:

```
> sms_dtm <- DocumentTermMatrix(corpus_clean)
```

This will tokenize the corpus and return the sparse matrix with the name sms_dtm. From here, we'll be able to perform analyses involving word frequency.

# Data preparation – creating training and test datasets

Since our data have been prepared for analysis, we now need to split the data into a training dataset and test dataset so that the spam classifier can be evaluated on data it had not seen previously. We'll divide the data into two portions: 75 percent for training and 25 percent for testing. Since the SMS messages are sorted in a random order, we can simply take the first 4,169 for training and leave the remaining 1,390 for testing.

We'll begin by splitting the raw data frame:

```
> sms_raw_train <- sms_raw[1:4169, ]
> sms_raw_test  <- sms_raw[4170:5559, ]
```

Then the document-term matrix:

```
> sms_dtm_train <- sms_dtm[1:4169, ]
> sms_dtm_test  <- sms_dtm[4170:5559, ]
```

And finally, the corpus:

```
> sms_corpus_train <- corpus_clean[1:4169]
> sms_corpus_test  <- corpus_clean[4170:5559]
```

To confirm that the subsets are representative of the complete set of SMS data, let's compare the proportion of spam in the training and test data frames:

```
> prop.table(table(sms_raw_train$type))
      ham       spam
0.8647158 0.1352842
> prop.table(table(sms_raw_test$type))
      ham       spam
0.8683453 0.1316547
```

Both the training data and test data contain about 13 percent spam. This suggests that the spam messages were divided evenly between the two datasets.

# Visualizing text data – word clouds

A **word cloud** is a way to visually depict the frequency at which words appear in text data. The cloud is made up of words scattered somewhat randomly around the figure. Words appearing more often in the text are shown in a larger font, while less common terms are shown in smaller fonts. This type of figure has grown in popularity recently since it provides a way to observe trending topics on social media websites.

The wordcloud package provides a simple R function to create this type of diagram. We'll use it to visualize the types of words in SMS messages. Comparing the word clouds for spam and ham messages will help us gauge whether our naive Bayes spam filter is likely to be successful. If you haven't already done so, install the package by typing install.packages("wordcloud") and load the package by typing library(wordcloud) at the R command line.

> The wordcloud package was written by *Ian Fellows*, a professional statistician out of the University of California, Los Angeles. For more information about this package, visit http://cran.r-project.org/web/packages/wordcloud/index.html.

A word cloud can be created directly from a tm corpus object using the syntax:

```
> wordcloud(sms_corpus_train, min.freq = 40, random.order = FALSE)
```

This will create a word cloud from sms_corpus_train corpus. Since we specified random.order = FALSE, the cloud will be arranged in non-random order, with the higher-frequency words placed closer to the center. If we do not specify random.order, the cloud would be arranged randomly by default. The min.freq parameter specifies the number of times a word must appear in the corpus before it will be displayed in the cloud. A general rule is to begin by setting min.freq to a number roughly 10 percent of the number of documents in the corpus; in this case 10 percent is about 40. Therefore, words in the cloud must appear in at least 40 SMS messages.

> You might get a warning message noting that R was unable to fit all of the words on the figure. If so, try adjusting the min.freq value up, reduce the number of words in the cloud. It may also help to use the scale parameter to reduce the font size.

The resulting word cloud is as follows:

Another interesting visualization involves comparing the clouds for SMS spam and ham. Since we did not construct separate corpora for spam and ham, this is an appropriate time to note a very helpful feature of the wordcloud() function. Given raw text, it will automatically apply text transformation processes before building a corpus and displaying the cloud.

Let's use R's subset() function to take a subset of the sms_raw_train data by SMS type. First, we'll create a subset where type is equal to spam:

```
> spam <- subset(sms_raw_train, type == "spam")
```

Next, we'll do the same thing for the ham subset:

```
> ham <- subset(sms_raw_train, type == "ham")
```

Be careful to note the double equal sign. Like many programming languages, R uses == to test equality. If you accidently use a single equal sign, you'll end up with a subset much larger than you expected!

We now have two data frames, spam and ham, each with a text feature containing the raw text strings for SMS messages. Creating word clouds is as simple as before. This time, we'll use the max.words parameter to look at the 40 most common words in each of the two sets. The scale parameter allows us to adjust the maximum and minimum font size for words in the cloud. Feel free to adjust these parameters as you see fit. This is illustrated in the following code:

```
> wordcloud(spam$text, max.words = 40, scale = c(3, 0.5))
> wordcloud(ham$text, max.words = 40, scale = c(3, 0.5))
```

The resulting word clouds are shown in the following diagram. Do you have a hunch which one is the spam cloud and which represents ham?

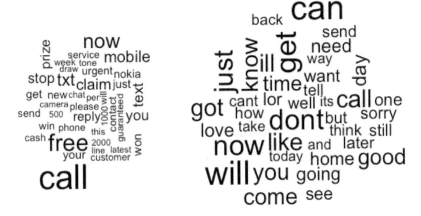

Because of the randomization process, each word cloud may look slightly different. Running the wordcloud() function several times allows you to choose the cloud that is the most visually appealing for presentation purposes.

If you hadn't already guessed, the spam cloud is on the left. Spam SMS messages include words such as **urgent, free, mobile, call, claim,** and **stop**; these terms do not appear in the ham cloud at all. Instead, ham messages use words such as **can, sorry, need,** and **time**. These stark differences suggest that our naive Bayes model will have some strong key words to differentiate between the classes.

# Data preparation – creating indicator features for frequent words

The final step in the data preparation process is to transform the sparse matrix into a data structure that can be used to train a naive Bayes classifier. Currently, the sparse matrix includes over 7,000 features a feature for every word that appears in at least one SMS message. It's unlikely that all of these are useful for classification. To reduce the number of features, we will eliminate any words that appear in less than five SMS messages, or less than about 0.1 percent of records in the training data.

Finding frequent words requires use of the `findFreqTerms()` function in the `tm` package. This function takes a document term matrix and returns a character vector containing the words appearing at least a specified number of times. For instance, the following command will display a character vector of the words appearing at least 5 times in the `sms_dtm_train` matrix:

```
> findFreqTerms(sms_dtm_train, 5)
```

To save this list of frequent terms for use later, we'll use the `Dictionary()` function:

```
> sms_dict <- Dictionary(findFreqTerms(sms_dtm_train, 5))
```

A dictionary is a data structure allowing us to specify which words should appear in a document term matrix. To limit our training and test matrixes to only the words in the preceding dictionary, use the following commands:

```
> sms_train <- DocumentTermMatrix(sms_corpus_train,
    list(dictionary = sms_dict))
> sms_test  <- DocumentTermMatrix(sms_corpus_test,
    list(dictionary = sms_dict))
```

The training and test data now includes roughly 1,200 features corresponding only to words appearing in at least five messages.

The naive Bayes classifier is typically trained on data with categorical features. This poses a problem since the cells in the sparse matrix indicate a count of the times a word appears in a message. We should change this to a factor variable that simply indicates yes or no depending on whether the word appears at all.

The following code defines a `convert_counts()` function to convert counts to factors:

```
> convert_counts <- function(x) {
    x <- ifelse(x > 0, 1, 0)
    x <- factor(x, levels = c(0, 1), labels = c(""No"", ""Yes""))
    return(x)
  }
```

By now, some of the pieces of the preceding function should look familiar. The first line defines the function. The statement `ifelse(x > 0, 1, 0)` will transform the values in x so that if the value is greater than 0, then it will be replaced with 1, otherwise it will remain at 0. The `factor` command simply transforms the 1 and 0 values to a factor with labels `No` and `Yes`. Finally, the newly-transformed vector x is returned.

Now, we just need to apply `convert_counts` to each of the columns in our sparse matrix. You may be able to guess the R function can do exactly that; it's stated in the preceding sentence. The function is simply called `apply()`.

The `apply()` function is part of a family of functions including `lapply()` and `sapply()` that perform operations on each element of an R data structure. These functions are one of the key idioms of the R language. Experienced R coders use these functions rather than using loops such as `for` or `while` as you would in other programming languages because they result in more readable (and sometimes more efficient) code.

The `apply()` function allows a function to be used on each of the rows or columns in a matrix. It uses a MARGIN parameter to specify either rows or columns. Here, we'll use MARGIN = 2 since we're interested in the columns (MARGIN = 1 is used for rows). The full commands to convert the training and test matrixes are as follows:

```
> sms_train <- apply(sms_train, MARGIN = 2, convert_counts)
> sms_test  <- apply(sms_test, MARGIN = 2, convert_counts)
```

The result will be two matrixes, each with factor type columns indicating `Yes` or `No` for whether each column's word appears in the messages comprising the rows.

# Step 3 – training a model on the data

Now that we have transformed the raw SMS messages into a format that can be represented by a statistical model, it is time to apply the naive Bayes algorithm. The algorithm will use the presence or absence of words to estimate the probability that a given SMS message is spam.

The naive Bayes implementation we will employ is in the `e1071` package. This package was developed at the statistics department at the Vienna University of Technology (TU Wien), and includes a variety of functions for machine learning. If you have not done so already, be sure to prepare the package using the commands, `install.packages("e1071")` and `library(e1071)` before continuing.

Many machine learning approaches are implemented in more than one R package, and naive Bayes is no exception. Another commonly-cited naive Bayes function is `NaiveBayes()` in the klaR package, which is nearly identical to the one described in this text. Feel free to use whichever you prefer.

Unlike the kNN algorithm we used for classification in the previous chapter, training a naive Bayes learner and using it for classification occur in separate stages. Still, as shown in the following table, classification is fairly straightforward:

---

**Naive Bayes classification syntax**

using the `naiveBayes()` function in the e1071 package

**Building the classifier:**

```
m <- naiveBayes(train, class, laplace = 0)
```

- `train` is a data frame or matrix containing training data
- `class` is a factor vector with the class for each row in the training data
- `laplace` is a number to control the Laplace estimator (by default, 0)

The function will return a naive Bayes model object that can be used to make predictions.

**Making predictions:**

```
p <- predict(m, test, type = "class")
```

- `m` is a model trained by the `naiveBayes()` function
- `test` is a data frame or matrix containing test data with the same features as the training data used to build the classifier
- `type` is either `"class"` or `"raw"` and specifies whether the predictions should be the most likely class value or the raw predicted probabilities

The function will return a vector of predicted class values or raw predicted probabilities depending upon the value of the `type` parameter.

**Example:**

```
sms_classifier <- naiveBayes(sms_train, sms_type)
sms_predictions <- predict(sms_classifier, sms_test)
```

---

To build our model on the `sms_train` matrix, we'll use the following command:

```
> sms_classifier <- naiveBayes(sms_train, sms_raw_train$type)
```

The `sms_classifier` variable now contains a `naiveBayes` classifier object that can be used to make predictions.

# Step 4 – evaluating model performance

To evaluate the SMS message classifier, we need to test its predictions on the unseen messages in the test data. Recall that the unseen message features are stored in a matrix named sms_test, while the class labels spam or ham are stored in a vector named type in the sms_raw_test data frame. The classifier that we trained has been named sms_classifier. We will use this to generate predictions, and we will compare the predictions to the true values.

The predict() function is used to make the predictions. We will store these in a vector named sms_test_pred:

```
> sms_test_pred <- predict(sms_classifier, sms_test)
```

To compare the predicted values to the actual values, we'll use the CrossTable() function in the gmodels package, which we have used previously. This time, we'll add some additional parameters to eliminate unnecessary cell proportions, and use the dnn parameter (dimension names) to relabel the rows and columns, as shown in the following code:

```
> library(gmodels)
> CrossTable(sms_test_pred, sms_raw_test$type,
    prop.chisq = FALSE, prop.t = FALSE,
    dnn = c('predicted', 'actual'))
```

This produces the following table:

```
      Total Observations in Table:  1390

               | actual
     predicted |       ham |      spam | Row Total |
   ------------|-----------|-----------|-----------|
           ham |      1203 |        32 |      1235 |
               |     0.997 |     0.175 |           |
   ------------|-----------|-----------|-----------|
          spam |         4 |       151 |       155 |
               |     0.003 |     0.825 |           |
   ------------|-----------|-----------|-----------|
  Column Total |      1207 |       183 |      1390 |
               |     0.868 |     0.132 |           |
   ------------|-----------|-----------|-----------|
```

Looking at the table, we can see that 4 of 1207 ham messages (0.3 percent) were incorrectly classified as spam, while 32 of 183 spam messages (17.5 percent) were incorrectly classified as ham. Considering the little effort we put into the project, this level of performance seems quite impressive. This case study exemplifies the reason why naive Bayes is the standard for text classification; directly out of the box, it performs surprisingly well.

On the other hand, the four legitimate messages that were incorrectly classified as spam could cause significant problems for the deployment of our filtering algorithm. If the filter caused a person to miss an important text message for an appointment or emergency, they would quickly abandon the product. We should investigate the incorrectly classified SMS messages to see where things went wrong.

# Step 5 – improving model performance

You may have noticed that we didn't set a value for the Laplace estimator when training our model. This allows words that appeared in zero spam or zero ham messages to have an indisputable say in the classification process. Just because the word "ringtone" only appeared in spam messages in the training data, it does not mean that every message with that word should be classified as spam.

We'll build a naive Bayes model as before, but this time set `laplace = 1`:

```
> sms_classifier2 <- naiveBayes(sms_train, sms_raw_train$type,
    laplace = 1)
```

Next, we'll make predictions:

```
> sms_test_pred2 <- predict(sms_classifier2, sms_test)
```

Finally, we'll compare the predicted classes to the actual classifications using a cross tabulation:

```
> CrossTable(sms_test_pred2, sms_raw_test$type,
    prop.chisq = FALSE, prop.t = FALSE, prop.r = FALSE,
    dnn = c('predicted', 'actual'))
```

This results in the following table:

```
         Total Observations in Table:  1390
```

| predicted | actual ham | spam | Row Total |
|---|---|---|---|
| ham | 1204 0.998 | 31 0.169 | 1235 |
| spam | 3 0.002 | 152 0.831 | 155 |
| Column Total | 1207 0.868 | 183 0.132 | 1390 |

In spite of reducing the number of false positives (ham messages erroneously classified as spam) from four to three, we also reduced the number of false negatives from 32 to 31. Although this seems like a small improvement, we must also be aware of the potential for important messages to be missed if we are too aggressive at filtering spam.

# Summary

In this chapter, we learned about classification using naive Bayes. This algorithm constructs tables of probabilities that are used to estimate the likelihood that new examples belong to various classes. The probabilities are calculated using a formula known as Bayes' theorem, which specifies how dependent events are related. Although Bayes' theorem can be computationally expensive to process, a simplified version that makes so-called "naive" assumptions about the independence of features is capable of being used with extremely large datasets.

The naive Bayes classifier is often used for text classification. To illustrate its effectiveness, we employed naive Bayes on a classification task involving filtering spam SMS messages. Preparing the text data for analysis required the use of specialized R packages for text processing and visualization. Ultimately, the model was able to classify nearly 98 percent of all SMS messages correctly as spam or ham.

In the next chapter, we will examine a set of two more machine learning methods. Each performs classification by partitioning data into groups of similar values.

# 5
# Divide and Conquer – Classification Using Decision Trees and Rules

To make a difficult decision, some people weigh their options by making lists of pros and cons for each possibility. Suppose a job seeker was deciding between several offers, some closer or further from home, with various levels of pay and benefits. He or she might create a list with the features of each position. Based on these features, rules can be created to eliminate some options. For instance, "if I have a commute longer than an hour, then I will be unhappy", or "if I make less than $50k, I won't be able to support my family." The difficult decision of predicting future happiness can be reduced to a series of small, but increasingly specific choices.

This chapter covers decision trees and rule learners—two machine learning methods that apply a similar strategy of dividing data into smaller and smaller portions to identify patterns that can be used for prediction. The knowledge is then presented in the form of logical structures that can be understood without any statistical knowledge. This aspect makes these models particularly useful for business strategy and process improvement.

By the end of this chapter, you will learn:

- The strategy each method employs to tackle the problem of partitioning data into interesting segments
- Several implementations of decision trees and classification rule learners, including the C5.0, 1R, and RIPPER algorithms

- How to use these algorithms for performing real-world classification tasks such as identifying risky bank loans and poisonous mushrooms

We will begin by examining decision trees and follow with a look at classification rules. Lastly, we'll wrap up with a summary of what we learned and preview later chapters, which discuss methods that use trees and rules as a foundation for other advanced machine learning techniques.

# Understanding decision trees

As you might intuit from the name, decision tree learners build a model in the form of a **tree structure**. The model itself comprises a series of logical decisions, similar to a flowchart, with **decision nodes** that indicate a decision to be made on an attribute. These split into **branches** that indicate the decision's choices. The tree is terminated by **leaf nodes** (also known as terminal nodes) that denote the result of following a combination of decisions.

Data that is to be classified begin at the **root node** where it is passed through the various decisions in the tree according to the values of its features. The path that the data takes funnels each record into a leaf node, which assigns it a predicted class.

As the decision tree is essentially a flowchart, it is particularly appropriate for applications in which the classification mechanism needs to be transparent for legal reasons or the results need to be shared in order to facilitate decision making. Some potential uses include:

- Credit scoring models in which the criteria that causes an applicant to be rejected need to be well-specified
- Marketing studies of customer churn or customer satisfaction that will be shared with management or advertising agencies
- Diagnosis of medical conditions based on laboratory measurements, symptoms, or rate of disease progression

Although the previous applications illustrate the value of trees for informing decision processes, that is not to suggest that their utility ends there. In fact, decision trees are perhaps the single most widely used machine learning technique, and can be applied for modeling almost any type of data—often with unparalleled performance.

In spite of their wide applicability, it is worth noting some scenarios where trees may not be an ideal fit. One such case might be a task where the data has a large number of nominal features with many levels or if the data has a large number of numeric features. These cases may result in a very large number of decisions and an overly complex tree.

# Divide and conquer

Decision trees are built using a heuristic called **recursive partitioning**. This approach is generally known as **divide and conquer** because it uses the feature values to split the data into smaller and smaller subsets of similar classes.

Beginning at the root node, which represents the entire dataset, the algorithm chooses a feature that is the most predictive of the target class. The examples are then partitioned into groups of distinct values of this feature; this decision forms the first set of tree branches. The algorithm continues to divide-and-conquer the nodes, choosing the best candidate feature each time until a stopping criterion is reached. This might occur at a node if:

- All (or nearly all) of the examples at the node have the same class
- There are no remaining features to distinguish among examples
- The tree has grown to a predefined size limit

To illustrate the tree building process, let's consider a simple example. Imagine that you are working for a Hollywood film studio, and your desk is piled high with screenplays. Rather than read each one cover-to-cover, you decide to develop a decision tree algorithm to predict whether a potential movie would fall into one of three categories: mainstream hit, critic's choice, or box office bust.

To gather data for your model, you turn to the studio archives to examine the previous ten years of movie releases. After reviewing the data for 30 different movie scripts, a pattern emerges. There seems to be a relationship between the film's proposed shooting budget, the number of A-list celebrities lined up for starring roles, and the categories of success. A scatter plot of this data might look something like the following diagram:

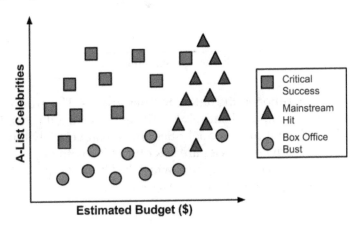

To build a simple decision tree using this data, we can apply a divide-and-conquer strategy. Let's first split the feature indicating the number of celebrities, partitioning the movies into groups with and without a low number of A-list stars:

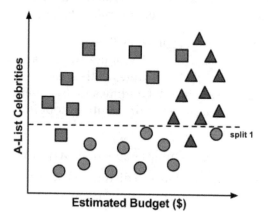

Next, among the group of movies with a larger number of celebrities, we can make another split between movies with and without a high budget:

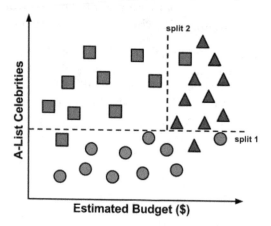

At this point we have partitioned the data into three groups. The group at the top-left corner of the diagram is composed entirely of critically-acclaimed films. This group is distinguished by a high number of celebrities and a relatively low budget. At the top-right corner, the majority of movies are box office hits, with high budgets and a large number of celebrities. The final group, which has little star power but budgets ranging from small to large, contains the flops.

If we wanted, we could continue to divide the data by splitting it based on increasingly specific ranges of budget and celebrity counts until each of the incorrectly classified values resides in its own, perhaps tiny partition. Since the data can continue to be split until there are no distinguishing features within a partition, a decision tree can be prone to be overfitting for the training data with overly-specific decisions. We'll avoid this by stopping the algorithm here since more than 80 percent of the examples in each group are from a single class.

You might have noticed that diagonal lines could have split the data even more cleanly. This is one limitation of the decision tree's knowledge representation, which uses **axis-parallel splits**. The fact that each split considers one feature at a time prevents the decision tree from forming more complex decisions such as "if the number of celebrities is greater than the estimated budget, then it will be a critical success".

Our model for predicting the future success of movies can be represented in a simple tree as shown in the following diagram. To evaluate a script, follow the branches through each decision until its success or failure has been predicted. In no time, you will be able to classify the backlog of scripts and get back to more important work such as writing an awards acceptance speech.

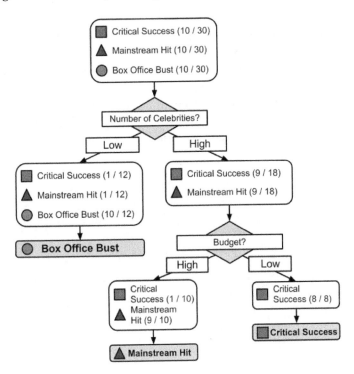

Since real-world data contains more than two features, decision trees quickly become far more complex than this, with many more nodes, branches, and leaves. In the next section you will learn about a popular algorithm for building decision tree models automatically.

# The C5.0 decision tree algorithm

There are numerous implementations of decision trees, but one of the most well-known is the **C5.0 algorithm**. This algorithm was developed by computer scientist *J. Ross Quinlan* as an improved version of his prior algorithm, C4.5, which itself is an improvement over his ID3 (Iterative Dichotomiser 3) algorithm. Although *Quinlan* markets C5.0 to commercial clients (see http://www.rulequest.com/ for details), the source code for a single-threaded version of the algorithm was made publically available, and has therefore been incorporated into programs such as R.

> To further confuse matters, a popular Java-based open-source alternative to C4.5, titled J48, is included in the RWeka package. Because the differences among C5.0, C4.5, and J48 are minor, the principles in this chapter will apply to any of these three methods and the algorithms should be considered synonymous.

The C5.0 algorithm has become the industry standard for producing decision trees, because it does well for most types of problems directly out of the box. Compared to other advanced machine learning models (such as those described in *Chapter 7, Black Box Methods – Neural Networks and Support Vector Machines*) the decision trees built by C5.0 generally perform nearly as well but are much easier to understand and deploy. Additionally, as shown in the following table, the algorithm's weaknesses are relatively minor and can be largely avoided.

| Strengths | Weaknesses |
|---|---|
| • An all-purpose classifier that does well on most problems | • Decision tree models are often biased toward splits on features having a large number of levels |
| • Highly-automatic learning process can handle numeric or nominal features, missing data | • It is easy to overfit or underfit the model |
| • Uses only the most important features | • Can have trouble modeling some relationships due to reliance on axis-parallel splits |
| • Can be used on data with relatively few training examples or a very large number | • Small changes in training data can result in large changes to decision logic |
| • Results in a model that can be interpreted without a mathematical background (for relatively small trees) | • Large trees can be difficult to interpret and the decisions they make may seem counterintuitive |
| • More efficient than other complex models | |

Earlier in this chapter, we followed a simple example illustrating how a decision tree models data using a divide-and-conquer strategy. Let's explore this in more detail to examine how this heuristic works in practice.

## Choosing the best split

The first challenge that a decision tree will face is to identify which feature to split upon. In the previous example, we looked for feature values that split the data in such a way that partitions contained examples primarily of a single class. If the segments of data contain only a single class, they are considered **pure**. There are many different measurements of purity for identifying splitting criteria.

C5.0 uses **entropy** for measuring purity. The entropy of a sample of data indicates how mixed the class values are; the minimum value of 0 indicates that the sample is completely homogenous, while 1 indicates the maximum amount of disorder. The definition of entropy is specified by:

$$\text{Entropy}(S) = \sum_{i=1}^{c} -p_i \, log_2(p_i)$$

In the entropy formula, for a given segment of data ($S$), the term $c$ refers to the number of different class levels, and $p_i$ refers to the proportion of values falling into class level $i$. For example, suppose we have a partition of data with two classes: red (60 percent), and white (40 percent). We can calculate the entropy as:

```
> -0.60 * log2(0.60) - 0.40 * log2(0.40)
[1] 0.9709506
```

We can examine the entropy for all possible two-class arrangements. If we know the proportion of examples in one class is x, then the proportion in the other class is 1 - x. Using the `curve()` function, we can then plot the entropy for all possible values of x:

```
> curve(-x * log2(x) - (1 - x) * log2(1 - x),
      col="red", xlab = "x", ylab = "Entropy", lwd=4)
```

This results in the following figure:

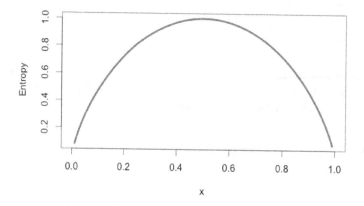

As illustrated by the peak in entropy at x = 0.50, a 50-50 split results in the maximum entropy. As one class increasingly dominates the other, the entropy reduces to zero.

Given this measure of purity, the algorithm must still decide which feature to split upon. For this, the algorithm uses entropy to calculate the change in homogeneity resulting from a split on each possible feature. The calculation is known as **information gain**. The information gain for a feature $F$ is calculated as the difference between the entropy in the segment before the split ($S_1$), and the partitions resulting from the split ($S_2$):

$$\text{InfoGain}(F) = \text{Entropy}(S_1) - \text{Entropy}(S_2)$$

The one complication is that after a split, the data is divided into more than one partition. Therefore, the function to calculate *Entropy(S₂)* needs to consider the total entropy across all of the partitions. It does this by weighing each partition's entropy by the proportion of records falling into that partition. This can be stated in a formula as:

$$\text{Entropy}\left(S\right) = \sum_{i=1}^{n} w_i \, \text{Entropy}\left(P_i\right)$$

In simple terms, the total entropy resulting from a split is the sum of entropy of each of the *n* partitions weighted by the proportion of examples falling in that partition ($w_i$).

The higher the information gain, the better a feature is at creating homogeneous groups after a split on that feature. If the information gain is zero, there is no reduction in entropy for splitting on this feature. On the other hand, the maximum information gain is equal to the entropy prior to the split. This would imply the entropy after the split is zero, which means that the decision results in completely homogeneous groups.

The previous formulae assume nominal features, but decision trees use information gain for splitting on numeric features as well. A common practice is testing various splits that divide the values into groups greater than or less than a threshold. This reduces the numeric feature into a two-level categorical feature and information gain can be calculated easily. The numeric threshold yielding the largest information gain is chosen for the split.

 Though it is used by C5.0, information gain is not the only splitting criterion that can be used to build decision trees. Other commonly used criteria are **Gini index**, **Chi-Squared statistic**, and **gain ratio**. For a review of these (and many more) criteria, refer to: *An Empirical Comparison of Selection Measures for Decision-Tree Induction, Machine Learning, Vol. 3,* pp. 319-342, by *J. Mingers* (1989).

# Pruning the decision tree

A decision tree can continue to grow indefinitely, choosing splitting features and dividing into smaller and smaller partitions until each example is perfectly classified or the algorithm runs out of features to split on. However, if the tree grows overly large, many of the decisions it makes will be overly specific and the model will have been overfitted to the training data. The process of **pruning** a decision tree involves reducing its size such that it generalizes better to unseen data.

One solution to this problem is to stop the tree from growing once it reaches a certain number of decisions or if the decision nodes contain only a small number of examples. This is called early stopping or **pre-pruning** the decision tree. As the tree avoids doing needless work, this is an appealing strategy. However, one downside is that there is no way to know whether the tree will miss subtle, but important patterns that it would have learned had it grown to a larger size.

An alternative, called **post-pruning** involves growing a tree that is too large, then using pruning criteria based on the error rates at the nodes to reduce the size of the tree to a more appropriate level. This is often a more effective approach than pre-pruning because it is quite difficult to determine the optimal depth of a decision tree without growing it first. Pruning the tree later on allows the algorithm to be certain that all important data structures were discovered.

The implementation details of pruning operations are very technical and beyond the scope of this book. For a comparison of some of the available methods, see: *A comparative analysis of methods for pruning decision trees. IEEE Transactions on Pattern Analysis and Machine Intelligence, Vol. 19, pp. 476-491, by F. Esposito, D. Malerba, and G. Semeraro (1997)*.

One of the benefits of the C5.0 algorithm is that it is opinionated about pruning – it takes care of many of the decisions, automatically using fairly reasonable defaults. Its overall strategy is to postprune the tree. It first grows a large tree that overfits the training data. Later, nodes and branches that have little effect on the classification errors are removed. In some cases, entire branches are moved further up the tree or replaced by simpler decisions. These processes of grafting branches are known as **subtree raising** and **subtree replacement**, respectively.

Balancing overfitting and underfitting a decision tree is a bit of an art, but if model accuracy is vital it may be worth investing some time with various pruning options to see if it improves performance on the test data. As you will soon see, one of the strengths of the C5.0 algorithm is that it is very easy to adjust the training options.

# Example – identifying risky bank loans using C5.0 decision trees

The global financial crisis of 2007-2008 has highlighted the importance of transparency and rigor in banking practices. As the availability of credit has been limited, banks are increasingly tightening their lending systems and turning to machine learning to more accurately identify risky loans.

Decision trees are widely used in the banking industry due to their high accuracy and ability to formulate a statistical model in plain language. Since government organizations in many countries carefully monitor lending practices, executives must be able to explain why one applicant was rejected for a loan while others were approved. This information is also useful for customers hoping to determine why their credit rating is unsatisfactory.

It is likely that automated credit scoring models are employed for instantly approving credit applications on the telephone and the web. In this section, we will develop a simple credit approval model using C5.0 decision trees. We will also see how the results of the model can be tuned to minimize errors that result in a financial loss for the institution.

# Step 1 – collecting data

The idea behind our credit model is to identify factors that make an applicant at higher risk of default. Therefore, we need to obtain data on a large number of past bank loans and whether the loan went into default, as well as information about the applicant.

Data with these characteristics are available in a dataset donated to the UCI Machine Learning Data Repository (http://archive.ics.uci.edu/ml) by *Hans Hofmann* of the University of Hamburg. They represent loans obtained from a credit agency in Germany.

The data presented in this chapter has been modified slightly from the original one for eliminating some preprocessing steps. To follow along with the examples, download the credit.csv file from Packt Publishing's website and save it to your R working directory.

The credit dataset includes 1,000 examples of loans, plus a combination of numeric and nominal features indicating characteristics of the loan and the loan applicant. A class variable indicates whether the loan went into default. Let's see if we can determine any patterns that predict this outcome.

# Step 2 – exploring and preparing the data

As we have done previously, we will import the data using the `read.csv()` function. We will ignore the `stringsAsFactors` option (and therefore use the default value, TRUE) as the majority of features in the data are nominal. We'll also look at the structure of the credit data frame we created:

```
> credit <- read.csv("credit.csv")
> str(credit)
```

The first several lines of output from the `str()` function are as follows:

```
'data.frame':1000 obs. of  17 variables:
 $ checking_balance : Factor w/ 4 levels "< 0 DM","> 200 DM",..
 $ months_loan_duration: int  6 48 12 ...
 $ credit_history      : Factor w/ 5 levels "critical","good",..
 $ purpose             : Factor w/ 6 levels "business","car",..
 $ amount              : int  1169 5951 2096 ...
```

We see the expected 1,000 observations and 17 features, which are a combination of factor and integer data types.

Let's take a look at some of the `table()` output for a couple of features of loans that seem likely to predict a default. The `checking_balance` and `savings_balance` features indicate the applicant's checking and savings account balance, and are recorded as categorical variables:

```
> table(credit$checking_balance)

    < 0 DM    > 200 DM 1 - 200 DM     unknown
       274          63         269         394
> table(credit$savings_balance)
    < 100 DM > 1000 DM  100 - 500 DM 500 - 1000 DM     unknown
         603        48           103            63         183
```

Since the loan data was obtained from Germany, the currency is recorded in Deutsche Marks (DM). It seems like a safe assumption that larger checking and savings account balances should be related to a reduced chance of loan default.

Some of the loan's features are numeric, such as its term (`months_loan_duration`), and the amount of credit requested (`amount`).

```
> summary(credit$months_loan_duration)
   Min. 1st Qu.  Median    Mean 3rd Qu.    Max.
    4.0    12.0    18.0    20.9    24.0    72.0
> summary(credit$amount)
   Min. 1st Qu.  Median    Mean 3rd Qu.    Max.
    250    1366    2320    3271    3972   18420
```

The loan amounts ranged from 250 DM to 18,420 DM across terms of 4 to 72 months, with a median duration of 18 months and amount of 2,320 DM.

The `default` variable indicates whether the loan applicant was unable to meet the agreed payment terms and went into default. A total of 30 percent of the loans went into default:

```
> table(credit$default)

 no yes

700 300
```

A high rate of `default` is undesirable for a bank because it means that the bank is unlikely to fully recover its investment. If we are successful, our model will identify applicants that are likely to default, so that this number can be reduced.

# Data preparation – creating random training and test datasets

As we have done in previous chapters, we will split our data into two portions: a training dataset to build the decision tree and a test dataset to evaluate the performance of the model on new data. We will use 90 percent of the data for training and 10 percent for testing, which will provide us with 100 records to simulate new applicants.

As prior chapters used data that had been sorted in a random order, we simply divided the dataset into two portions by taking the first 90 percent of records for training, and the remaining 10 percent for testing. In contrast, our data here is not randomly ordered. Suppose that the bank had sorted the data by the loan amount, with the largest loans at the end of the file. If we use the first 90 percent for training and the remaining 10 percent for testing, we would be building a model on only the small loans and testing the model on the big loans. Obviously, this could be problematic.

We'll solve this problem by randomly ordering our credit data frame prior to splitting. The order () function is used to rearrange a list of items in ascending or descending order. If we combine this with a function to generate a list of random numbers, we can generate a randomly-ordered list. For random number generation, we'll use the runif () function, which by default generates a sequence of random numbers between 0 and 1.

> If you're trying to figure out where the runif () function gets its name, the answer is due to the fact that it chooses numbers from a uniform distribution, which we learned about in *Chapter 2, Managing and Understanding Data*.

The following command creates a randomly-ordered credit data frame. The set.seed() function is used to generate random numbers in a predefined sequence, starting from a position known as a **seed** (set here to the arbitrary value 12345). It may seem that this defeats the purpose of generating random numbers, but there is a good reason for doing it this way. The set.seed() function ensures that if the analysis is repeated, an identical result is obtained.

```
> set.seed(12345)
> credit_rand <- credit[order(runif(1000)), ]
```

The runif(1000) command generates a list of 1,000 random numbers. We need exactly 1,000 random numbers because there are 1,000 records in the credit data frame. The order () function then returns a vector of numbers indicating the sorted position of the 1,000 random numbers. We then use these positions to select rows in the credit data frame and store in a new data frame named credit_rand.

> To better understand how this function works, note that order(c(0.5, 0.25, 0.75, 0.1)) returns the sequence 4 1 2 3 because the smallest number (0.1) appears fourth, the second smallest (0.25) appears first, and so on.

To confirm that we have the same data frame sorted differently, we'll compare values on the amount feature across the two data frames. The following code shows the summary statistics:

```
> summary(credit$amount)
   Min. 1st Qu.  Median    Mean 3rd Qu.    Max.
    250    1366    2320    3271    3972   18420
> summary(credit_rand$amount)
   Min. 1st Qu.  Median    Mean 3rd Qu.    Max.
    250    1366    2320    3271    3972   18420
```

We can use the `head()` function to examine the first few values in each data frame:

```
> head(credit$amount)
[1] 1169 5951 2096 7882 4870 9055
> head(credit_rand$amount)
[1] 1199 2576 1103 4020 1501 1568
```

Since the summary statistics are identical while the first few values are different, this suggests that our random shuffle worked correctly.

 If your results do not match exactly with the previous ones, ensure that you run the command `set.seed(214805)` immediately prior to creating the `credit_rand` data frame.

Now, we can split into training (90 percent or 900 records), and test data (10 percent or 100 records) as we have done in previous analyses:

```
> credit_train <- credit_rand[1:900, ]
> credit_test  <- credit_rand[901:1000, ]
```

If all went well, we should have about 30 percent of defaulted loans in each of the datasets.

```
> prop.table(table(credit_train$default))

      no       yes
0.7022222 0.2977778
> prop.table(table(credit_test$default))

  no  yes
0.68 0.32
```

This appears to be a fairly equal split, so we can now build our decision tree.

# Step 3 – training a model on the data

We will use the C5.0 algorithm in the `C50` package for training our decision tree model. If you have not done so already, install the package with `install.packages("C50")` and load it to your R session using `library(C50)`.

The following syntax box lists some of the most commonly used commands for building decision trees. Compared to the machine learning approaches we have used previously, the C5.0 algorithm offers many more ways to tailor the model to a particular learning problem, but even more options are available. The `?C5.0Control` command displays the help page for more details on how to finely-tune the algorithm.

---

**C5.0 decision tree syntax**

using the `C5.0()` function in the C50 package

**Building the classifier:**

```
m <- C5.0(train, class, trials = 1, costs = NULL)
```

- **train** is a data frame containing training data
- **class** is a factor vector with the class for each row in the training data
- **trials** is an optional number to control the number of boosting iterations (by default, 1)
- **costs** is an optional matrix specifying costs associated with types of errors

The function will return a C5.0 model object that can be used to make predictions.

**Making predictions:**

```
p <- predict(m, test, type = "class")
```

- **m** is a model trained by the `C5.0()` function
- **test** is a data frame containing test data with the same features as the training data used to build the classifier.
- **type** is either **"class"** or **"prob"** and specifies whether the predictions should be the most likely class value or the raw predicted probabilities

The function will return a vector of predicted class values or raw predicted probabilities depending upon the value of the **type** parameter.

**Example:**

```
credit_model <- C5.0(credit_train, loan_default)
credit_prediction <- predict(credit_model, credit_test)
```

---

For the first iteration of our credit approval model, we'll use the default `C5.0` configuration, as shown in the following code. The 17th column in `credit_train` is the class variable, `default`, so we need to exclude it from the training data frame as an independent variable, but supply it as the target factor vector for classification:

```
> credit_model <- C5.0(credit_train[-17], credit_train$default)
```

The `credit_model` object now contains a `C5.0` decision tree object. We can see some basic data about the tree by typing its name:

```
> credit_model
```

```
Call:
C5.0.default(x = credit_train[-17], y = credit_train$default)
```

```
Classification Tree
Number of samples: 900
Number of predictors: 16
```

```
Tree size: 67
```

The preceding text shows some simple facts about the tree, including the function call that generated it, the number of features (that is, `predictors`), and examples (that is, `samples`) used to grow the tree. Also listed is the tree size of 67, which indicates that the tree is 67 decisions deep – quite a bit larger than the trees we've looked at so far!

To see the decisions, we can call the `summary()` function on the model:

```
> summary(credit_model)
```

This results in the following output:

```
C5.0 [Release 2.07 GPL Edition]
-------------------------------

Class specified by attribute `outcome'

Read 900 cases (17 attributes) from undefined.data

Decision tree:

checking_balance = unknown: no (358/44)
checking_balance in {< 0 DM,> 200 DM,1 - 200 DM}:
:...credit_history in {perfect,very good}:
    :...dependents > 1: yes (10/1)
    :   dependents <= 1:
    :   :...savings_balance = < 100 DM: yes (39/11)
    :       savings_balance in {> 1000 DM,500 - 1000 DM,unknown}: no (8/1)
    :       savings_balance = 100 - 500 DM:
    :       :...checking_balance = < 0 DM: no (1)
    :           checking_balance in {> 200 DM,1 - 200 DM}: yes (5/1)
```

The preceding output shows some of the first branches in the decision tree. The first four lines could be represented in plain language as:

1. If the checking account balance is unknown, then classify as **not likely to default**.

2. Otherwise, if the checking account balance is less than zero DM, between one and 200 DM, or greater than 200 DM and...

3. The credit history is very good or perfect, and...

4. There is more than one dependent, then classify as **likely to default**.

The numbers in parentheses indicate the number of examples meeting the criteria for that decision, and the number incorrectly classified by the decision. For instance, on the first line, (358/44) indicates that of the 358 examples reaching the decision, 44 were incorrectly classified as no, that is, not likely to default. In other words, 44 applicants actually defaulted in spite of the model's prediction to the contrary.

> Some of the tree's decisions do not seem to make logical sense. Why would an applicant whose credit history is very good be likely to default, while those whose checking balance is unknown are not likely to default? Contradictory rules like this occur sometimes. They might reflect a real pattern in the data, or they may be a statistical anomaly.

After the tree output, the summary(credit_model) displays a confusion matrix, which is a cross-tabulation that indicates the model's incorrectly classified records in the training data:

```
Evaluation on training data (900 cases):


    Decision Tree

    ----------------

   Size        Errors
    66    125(13.9%)    <<


   (a)     (b)      <-classified as
   ----    ----
    609     23      (a): class no
    102    166      (b): class yes
```

The `Errors` field notes that the model correctly classified all but 125 of the 900 training instances for an error rate of 13.9 percent. A total of 23 actual `no` values were incorrectly classified as `yes` (false positives), while 102 `yes` values were misclassified as `no` (false negatives).

Decision trees are known for having a tendency to overfit the model to the training data. For this reason, the error rate reported on training data may be overly optimistic, and it is especially important to evaluate decision trees on a test dataset.

# Step 4 – evaluating model performance

To apply our decision tree to the test dataset, we use the `predict()` function as shown in the following line of code:

```
> credit_pred <- predict(credit_model, credit_test)
```

This creates a vector of predicted class values, which we can compare to the actual class values using the `CrossTable()` function in the gmodels package. Setting the `prop.c` and `prop.r` parameters to `FALSE` removes the column and row percentages from the table. The remaining percentage (`prop.t`) indicates the proportion of records in the cell out of the total number of records.

```
> library(gmodels)
> CrossTable(credit_test$default, credit_pred,
            prop.chisq = FALSE, prop.c = FALSE, prop.r = FALSE,
            dnn = c('actual default', 'predicted default'))
```

This results in the following table:

| actual default | predicted default no | yes | Row Total |
|---|---|---|---|
| no | 57<br>0.570 | 11<br>0.110 | 68 |
| yes | 16<br>0.160 | 16<br>0.160 | 32 |
| Column Total | 73 | 27 | 100 |

Out of the 100 test loan application records, our model correctly predicted that 57 did not default and 16 did default, resulting in an accuracy of 73 percent and an error rate of 27 percent. This is somewhat worse than its performance on the training data, but not unexpected, given that a model's performance is often worse on unseen data. Also note that the model only correctly predicted 50 percent of the 32 loan defaults in the test data. Unfortunately, this type of error is a potentially very costly mistake. Let's see if we can improve the result with a bit more effort.

# Step 5 – improving model performance

Our model's error rate is likely to be too high to deploy it in a real-time credit scoring application. In fact, if the model had predicted "no default" for every test case, it would have been correct 68 percent of the time—a result not much worse than our model, but requiring much less effort! Predicting loan defaults from 900 examples seems to be a challenging problem.

Making matters even worse, our model performed especially poorly at identifying applicants who default. Luckily, there are a couple of simple ways to adjust the C5.0 algorithm that may help to improve the performance of the model, both overall and for the more costly mistakes.

## Boosting the accuracy of decision trees

One way the C5.0 algorithm improved upon the C4.5 algorithm was by adding **adaptive boosting**. This is a process in which many decision trees are built, and the trees vote on the best class for each example.

> The idea of boosting is based largely upon research by *Rob Schapire* and *Yoav Freund*. For more information, try searching the web for their publications or their recent textbook: *Boosting: Foundations and Algorithms Understanding Rule Learners* (The MIT Press, 2012).

As boosting can be applied more generally to any machine learning algorithm, it is covered in more detail later in this book in *Chapter 11, Improving Model Performance*. For now, it suffices to say that boosting is rooted in the notion that by combining a number of weak performing learners, you can create a team that is much stronger than any one of the learners alone. Each of the models has a unique set of strengths and weaknesses, and may be better or worse at certain problems. Using a combination of several learners with complementary strengths and weaknesses can therefore dramatically improve the accuracy of a classifier.

The `C5.0()` function makes it easy to add boosting to our C5.0 decision tree. We simply need to add an additional `trials` parameter indicating the number of separate decision trees to use in the boosted team. The `trials` parameter sets an upper limit; the algorithm will stop adding trees if it recognizes that additional trials do not seem to be improving the accuracy. We'll start with 10 trials—a number that has become the de facto standard, as research suggests that this reduces error rates on test data by about 25 percent.

```
> credit_boost10 <- C5.0(credit_train[-17], credit_train$default,
                         trials = 10)
```

While examining the resulting model, we can see that some additional lines have been added indicating the changes:

```
> credit_boost10
Number of boosting iterations: 10
Average tree size: 56
```

Across the 10 iterations, our tree size shrunk. If you would like, you can see all 10 trees by typing `summary(credit_boost10)` at the command prompt.

Let's take a look at the performance on our training data:

```
> summary(credit_boost10)


     (a)    (b)      <-classified as

    ----   ----

     626     6      (a): class no
      25    243     (b): class yes
```

The classifier made 31 mistakes on 900 training examples for an error rate of 3.4 percent. This is quite an improvement over the 13.9 percent training error rate we noted before adding boosting! However, it remains to be seen whether we see a similar improvement on the test data. Let's take a look:

```
> credit_boost_pred10 <- predict(credit_boost10, credit_test)
> CrossTable(credit_test$default, credit_boost_pred10,
             prop.chisq = FALSE, prop.c = FALSE, prop.r = FALSE,
             dnn = c('actual default', 'predicted default'))
```

The resulting table is as follows:

```
                   | predicted default
actual default     |       no      |      yes   | Row Total |
-------------------|---------------|------------|-----------|
             no    |       60      |        8   |       68  |
                   |     0.600     |     0.080  |           |
-------------------|---------------|------------|-----------|
            yes    |       15      |       17   |       32  |
                   |     0.150     |     0.170  |           |
-------------------|---------------|------------|-----------|
    Column Total   |       75      |       25   |      100  |
-------------------|---------------|------------|-----------|
```

Here, we reduced the total error rate from 27 percent prior to boosting down to 23 percent in the boosted model. It does not seem like a large gain, but it is reasonably close to the 25 percent reduction we hoped for. On the other hand, the model is still not doing well at predicting defaults, getting $15/32 = 47\%$ wrong. The lack of an even greater improvement may be a function of our relatively small training dataset, or it may just be a very difficult problem to solve.

That said, if boosting can be added this easily, why not apply it by default to every decision tree? The reason is twofold. First, if building a decision tree once takes a great deal of computation time, building many trees may be computationally impractical. Secondly, if the training data is very noisy, then boosting might not result in an improvement at all. Still, if greater accuracy is needed, it's worth giving it a try.

## Making some mistakes more costly than others

Giving a loan out to an applicant who is likely to default can be an expensive mistake. One solution to reduce the number of false negatives may be to reject a larger number of borderline applicants. The few years' worth of interest that the bank would earn from a risky loan is far outweighed by the massive loss it would take if the money was never paid back at all.

The C5.0 algorithm allows us to assign a penalty to different types of errors in order to discourage a tree from making more costly mistakes. The penalties are designated in a **cost matrix**, which specifies how many times more costly each error is, relative to any other. Suppose we believe that a loan default costs the bank four times as much as a missed opportunity. Our cost matrix then could be defined as:

```
> error_cost <- matrix(c(0, 1, 4, 0), nrow = 2)
```

This creates a matrix with two rows and two columns, arranged somewhat differently than the confusion matrixes we have been working with. The value 1 indicates no and the value 2 indicates yes. Rows are for predicted values and columns are for actual values:

```
> error_cost
     [,1]  [,2]
[1,]   0    4
[2,]   1    0
```

As defined by this matrix, there is no cost assigned when the algorithm classifies a no or yes correctly, but a false negative has a cost of 4 versus a false positive's cost of 1. To see how this impacts classification, let's apply it to our decision tree using the costs parameter of the C5.0() function. We'll otherwise use the same steps as before:

```
> credit_cost <- C5.0(credit_train[-17], credit_train$default,
                     costs = error_cost)
> credit_cost_pred <- predict(credit_cost, credit_test)
> CrossTable(credit_test$default, credit_cost_pred,
           prop.chisq = FALSE, prop.c = FALSE, prop.r = FALSE,
           dnn = c('actual default', 'predicted default'))
```

This produces the following confusion matrix:

| actual default | predicted default no | yes | Row Total |
|---|---|---|---|
| no | 42<br>0.420 | 26<br>0.260 | 68 |
| yes | 6<br>0.060 | 26<br>0.260 | 32 |
| Column Total | 48 | 52 | 100 |

Compared to our best boosted model, this version makes more mistakes overall: 32 percent here versus 23 percent in the boosted case. However, the types of mistakes vary dramatically. Where the previous models incorrectly classiifed nearly half of the defaults incorrectly, in this model, only 25 percent of the defaults were predicted to be non-defaults. This trade resulting in a reduction of false negatives at the expense of increasing false positives may be acceptable if our cost estimates were accurate.

# Understanding classification rules

Classification rules represent knowledge in the form of logical `if-else` statements that assign a class to unlabeled examples. They are specified in terms of an **antecedent** and a **consequent**; these form a hypothesis stating that "if this happens, then that happens." A simple rule might state that "if the hard drive is making a clicking sound, then it is about to fail." The antecedent comprises certain combinations of feature values, while the consequent specifies the class value to assign if the rule's conditions are met.

Rule learners are often used in a manner similar to decision tree learners. Like decision trees, they can be used for applications that generate knowledge for future action, such as:

- Identifying conditions that lead to a hardware failure in mechanical devices
- Describing the defining characteristics of groups of people for customer segmentation
- Finding conditions that precede large drops or increases in the prices of shares on the stock market

On the other hand, rule learners offer some distinct advantages over trees for some tasks. Unlike a tree, which must be applied from top-to-bottom, rules are facts that stand alone. The result of a rule learner is often more parsimonious, direct, and easier to understand than a decision tree built on the same data.

 As you will see later in this chapter, rules can be generated using decision trees. So, why bother with a separate group of rule learning algorithms? The reason is that decision trees bring a particular set of biases to the task that a rule learner avoids by identifying the rules directly.

Rule learners are generally applied to problems where the features are primarily or entirely nominal. They do well at identifying rare events, even if the rare event occurs only for a very specific interaction among features.

# Separate and conquer

Classification rule learning algorithms utilize a heuristic known as **separate and conquer**. The process involves identifying a rule that covers a subset of examples in the training data, and then separating this partition from the remaining data. As rules are added, additional subsets of data are separated until the entire dataset has been covered and no more examples remain.

The difference between divide and conquer and separate and conquer is subtle. Perhaps the best way to distinguish the two is by considering that each decision node in a tree is affected by the history of past decisions. There is no such lineage for rule learners; once the algorithm separates a set of examples, the next set might split on entirely different features, in an entirely different order.

One way to imagine the rule learning process is to think about drilling down into data by creating increasingly specific rules for identifying class values. Suppose you were tasked with creating rules for identifying whether or not an animal is a mammal. You could depict the set of all animals as a large space, as shown in the following diagram:

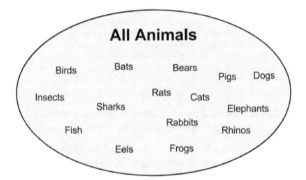

A rule learner begins by using the available features to find homogeneous groups. For example, using a feature that measured whether the species travels via land, sea, or air, the first rule might suggest that any land-based animals are mammals:

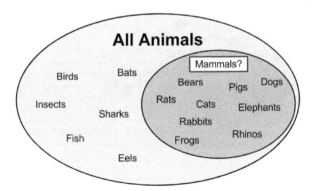

Do you notice any problems with this rule? If you look carefully, you might note that frogs are amphibians, not mammals. Therefore, our rule needs to be a bit more specific. Let's drill down further by suggesting that mammals walk on land and have a tail:

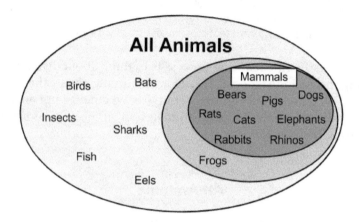

As shown in the previous figure, our more specific rule results in a subset of animals that are entirely mammals. Thus, this subset can be separated from the other data and additional rules can be defined to identify the remaining mammal bats. A potential feature distinguishing bats from the other remaining animals would be the presence of fur. Using a rule built around this feature, we have then correctly identified all the animals:

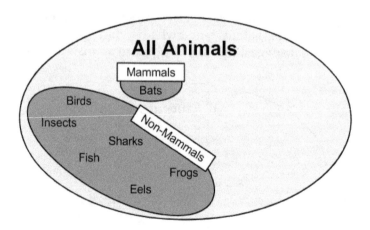

At this point, since all of the training instances have been classified, the rule learning process would stop. We learned a total of three rules:

- Animals that walk on land and have tails are mammals
- If the animal has fur, it is a mammal
- Otherwise, the animal is not a mammal

The previous example illustrates how rules gradually consume larger and larger segments of data to eventually classify all instances. Divide-and-conquer and separate-and-conquer algorithms are known as greedy learners because data is used on a first-come, first-served basis.

 Greedy algorithms are generally more efficient, but are not guaranteed to generate the best rules or minimum number of rules for a particular dataset.

As the rules seem to cover portions of the data, separate-and-conquer algorithms are also known as **covering algorithms**, and the rules are called covering rules. In the next section, we will learn how covering rules are applied in practice by examining a simple rule-learning algorithm. We will then examine a more complex rule learner, and apply both to a real-world problem.

# The One Rule algorithm

Suppose that as part of a television game show, there was a wheel with ten evenly-sized colored slices. Three of the segments were colored red, three were blue, and four were white. Prior to spinning the wheel, you are asked to choose one of these colors. When the wheel stops spinning, if the color shown matches your prediction, you win a large cash prize. What color should you pick?

If you choose white, you are of course more likely to win the prize—this is the most common color on the wheel. Obviously, this game show is a bit ridiculous, but it demonstrates the simplest classifier, **ZeroR**, a rule learner that literally learns no rules (hence the name). For every unlabeled example, regardless of the values of its features, it predicts the most common class.

The **One Rule algorithm** (1R or OneR), improves over ZeroR by selecting a single rule. Although this may seem overly simplistic, it tends to perform better than you might expect. As *Robert C. Holte* showed in a 1993 paper, *Very Simple Classification Rules Perform Well on Most Commonly Used Datasets (in Machine Learning, Vol. 11,* pp. 63-91), the accuracy of this algorithm can approach that of much more sophisticated algorithms for many real-world tasks. The strengths and weaknesses of this algorithm are shown in the following table:

| Strengths | Weaknesses |
|---|---|
| • Generates a single, easy-to-understand, human-readable rule-of-thumb<br><br>• Often performs surprisingly well<br><br>• Can serve as a benchmark for more complex algorithms | • Uses only a single feature<br><br>• Probably overly simplistic |

The way this algorithm works is simple. For each feature, 1R divides the data into groups based on similar values of the feature. Then, for each segment, the algorithm predicts the majority class. The error rate for the rule based on each feature is calculated, and the rule with the fewest errors is chosen as the one rule.

The following tables show how this would work for the animal data we looked at earlier in this section:

| Animal | Travels By | Has Fur | Mammal |
|---|---|---|---|
| Bats | Air | Yes | Yes |
| Bears | Land | Yes | Yes |
| Birds | Air | No | No |
| Cats | Land | Yes | Yes |
| Dogs | Land | Yes | Yes |
| Eels | Sea | No | No |
| Elephants | Land | No | Yes |
| Fish | Sea | No | No |
| Frogs | Land | No | No |
| Insects | Air | No | No |
| Pigs | Land | No | Yes |
| Rabbits | Land | Yes | Yes |
| Rats | Land | Yes | Yes |
| Rhinos | Land | No | Yes |
| Sharks | Sea | No | No |

| Travels By | Predicted | Actual | |
|---|---|---|---|
| Air | No | Yes | × |
| Air | No | No | |
| Air | No | No | |
| Land | Yes | Yes | |
| Land | Yes | Yes | |
| Land | Yes | Yes | |
| Land | Yes | Yes | |
| Land | Yes | No | × |
| Land | Yes | Yes | |
| Land | Yes | Yes | |
| Land | Yes | Yes | |
| Sea | No | No | |
| Sea | No | No | |
| Sea | No | No | |

**Rule for Travels By:**
**Errors = 2 / 15**

| Has Fur | Predicted | Actual | |
|---|---|---|---|
| No | No | No | |
| No | No | No | |
| No | No | Yes | × |
| No | No | No | |
| No | No | No | |
| No | No | No | |
| No | No | Yes | × |
| No | No | Yes | × |
| No | No | No | |
| Yes | Yes | Yes | |
| Yes | Yes | Yes | |
| Yes | Yes | Yes | |
| Yes | Yes | Yes | |
| Yes | Yes | Yes | |

**Rule for Has Fur:**
**Errors = 3 / 15**

For the **Travels By** feature, the data was divided into three groups: **Air**, **Land**, and **Sea**. Animals in the **Air** and **Sea** groups were predicted to be non-mammal, while animals in the **Land** group were predicted to be mammals. This resulted in two errors: bats and frogs. The **Has Fur** feature divided animals into two groups. Those with fur were predicted to be mammals, while those without were not. Three errors were counted: pigs, elephants, and rhinos. As the **Travels By** feature resulted in fewer errors, the 1R algorithm would return the following "one rule" based on **Travels By**:

- If the animal travels by air, it is not a mammal
- If the animal travels by land, it is a mammal
- If the animal travels by sea, it is not a mammal

The algorithm stops here, having found the single most important rule.

Obviously, this rule learning algorithm may be too basic for some tasks. Would you want a medical diagnosis system to consider only a single symptom, or an automated driving system to stop or accelerate your car based on only a single factor? For these types of tasks a more sophisticated rule learner might be useful. We'll learn about one in the following section.

# The RIPPER algorithm

Early rule-learning algorithms were plagued by a couple of problems. First, they were notorious for being slow, making them ineffective for the increasing number of Big Data problems. Secondly, they were often prone to being inaccurate on noisy data.

A first step toward solving these problems was proposed in a 1994 paper by *Johannes Furnkranz* and *Gerhard Widmer*, *Incremental Reduced Error Pruning* (in *Proceedings of the 11th International Conference on Machine Learning*, pp. 70-77). The **Incremental Reduced Error Pruning algorithm** (IREP) uses a combination of pre-pruning and post-pruning methods that grow very complex rules and prune them before separating the instances from the full dataset. Although this strategy helped the performance of rule learners, decision trees often still performed better.

Rule learners took another step forward in 1995 with the publication of a landmark paper by *William W. Cohen*, *Fast Effective Rule Induction* (in *Proceedings of the 12th International Conference on Machine Learning*, pp. 115-123). This paper introduced the **RIPPER** algorithm (Repeated Incremental Pruning to Produce Error Reduction), which improved upon IREP to generate rules that match or exceed the performance of decision trees.

The evolution of classification rule learners didn't stop here. New rule-learning algorithms are being proposed rapidly. A survey of literature shows algorithms called IREP++, SLIPPER, TRIPPER, among many others.

As outlined in the following table, the strengths and weaknesses of RIPPER rule learners are generally comparable to decision trees. The chief benefit is that they may result in a slightly more parsimonious model.

| Strengths | Weaknesses |
|---|---|
| • Generates easy-to-understand, human-readable rules <br> • Efficient on large and noisy datasets <br> • Generally produces a simpler model than a comparable decision tree | • May result in rules that seem to defy common sense or expert knowledge <br> • Not ideal for working with numeric data <br> • Might not perform as well as more complex models |

Having evolved from several iterations of rule-learning algorithms, the RIPPER algorithm is a patchwork of efficient heuristics for rule learning. Due to its complexity, a discussion of the technical implementation details is beyond the scope of this book. However, it can be understood in general terms as a three-step process:

1. Grow
2. Prune
3. Optimize

The growing process uses separate-and-conquer technique to greedily add conditions to a rule until it perfectly classifies a subset of data or runs out of attributes for splitting. Similar to decision trees, the information gain criterion is used to identify the next splitting attribute. When increasing a rule's specificity no longer reduces entropy, the rule is immediately pruned. Steps one and two are repeated until reaching a stopping criterion, at which point the entire set of rules are optimized using a variety of heuristics.

The rules from RIPPER can be more complex than 1R, with multiple antecedents. This means that it can consider multiple attributes like "if an animal flies and has fur, then it is a mammal." This improves the algorithm's ability to model complex data, but just like decision trees, it means that the rules can quickly become more difficult to comprehend.

# Rules from decision trees

Classification rules can also be obtained directly from decision trees. Beginning at a leaf node and following the branches back to the root, you will have obtained a series of decisions. These can be combined into a single rule. The following figure shows how rules could be constructed from the decision tree for predicting movie success:

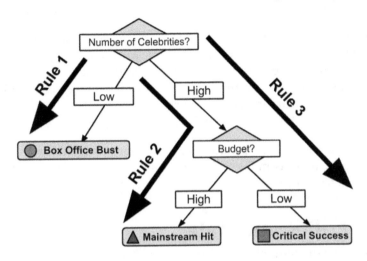

Following the paths from the root to each leaf, the rules would be:

1. If the number of celebrities is low, then the movie will be a Box Office Bust.

2. If the number of celebrities is high and the budget is high, then the movie will be a **Mainstream Hit**.

3. If the number of celebrities is high and the budget is low, then the movie will be a **Critical Success**.

The chief downside to using a decision tree to generate rules is that the resulting rules are often more complex than those learned by a rule-learning algorithm. The divide-and-conquer strategy employed by decision trees biases the results differently than that of a rule learner. On the other hand, it is sometimes more computationally efficient to generate rules from trees.

 The C5.0() function will generate a model using classification rules if you specify rules = TRUE when training the model.

# Example – identifying poisonous mushrooms with rule learners

Each year, many people fall ill and sometimes even die from ingesting poisonous, wild mushrooms. Since many mushrooms are very similar to each other in appearance, occasionally even experienced mushroom gatherers are poisoned.

Unlike the identification of harmful plants such as a poison oak or poison ivy, there are no clear rules like "leaves of three, let them be" for identifying whether a wild mushroom is poisonous or edible. Complicating matters, many traditional rules such as "poisonous mushrooms are brightly colored" provide dangerous or misleading information. If simple, clear, and consistent rules were available for identifying poisonous mushrooms, they could save the lives of foragers.

As one of the strengths of rule-learning algorithms is the fact that they generate easy to understand rules, they seem like an appropriate fit for this classification task. However, the rules will only be as useful as they are accurate.

## Step 1 – collecting data

To identify rules for distinguishing poisonous mushrooms, we will utilize the Mushroom dataset donated by *Jeff Schlimmer* of Carnegie Mellon University to the UCI Machine Learning Repository. The raw data is available at `http://archive.ics.uci.edu/ml/datasets/Mushroom`.

The dataset includes information on 8,124 mushroom samples from 23 species of gilled mushrooms listed in the *Audubon Society Field Guide to North American Mushrooms* (1981). In the Field Guide, each of mushroom species is identified as "definitely edible", "definitely poisonous", "likely poisonous, and not recommended to be eaten". For the purposes of this dataset, the latter group was combined with the definitely poisonous group to make two classes: poisonous and non-poisonous. The data dictionary available on the UCI website describes the 22 features of the mushroom samples, including characteristics such as cap shape, cap color, odor, gill size and color, stalk shape, and habitat.

> This chapter uses a slightly-modified version of the mushroom data. If you plan on following along with the example, download the `mushrooms.csv` file from the Packt Publishing's website and save to your R working directory.

# Step 2 – exploring and preparing the data

We begin by using `read.csv()`, to import the data for our analysis. Since all 22 features and the target class are nominal, in this case we will set `stringsAsFactors = TRUE` and take advantage of the automatic factor conversion:

```
> mushrooms <- read.csv("mushrooms.csv", stringsAsFactors = TRUE)
```

The output of the `str(mushrooms)` command notes that the data contain 8124 observations of 23 variables as the data dictionary had described. While most of the `str()` output is unremarkable, one feature is worth mentioning. Do you notice anything peculiar about the `veil_type` variable in the following line?

```
$ veil_type : Factor w/ 1 level "partial": 1 1 1 1 1 1 ...
```

If you think it is odd that a factor variable has only one level, you are correct. The data dictionary lists two levels for this feature: `partial` and `universal`, however all examples in our data are classified as partial. It is likely that this variable was somehow coded incorrectly. In any case, since `veil_type` does not vary across samples, it does not provide any useful information for prediction. We will drop this variable from our analysis using the following command:

```
> mushrooms$veil_type <- NULL
```

By assigning `NULL` to `veil_type`, R eliminates the feature from the mushrooms data frame.

Before going much further, we should take a quick look at the distribution of the class variable in our dataset, mushroom type. If the class levels are distributed very unevenly—meaning they are heavily imbalanced—some models, such as rule learners, can have trouble predicting the minority class:

```
> table(mushrooms$type)
   edible poisonous
     4208      3916
```

About 52 percent of the mushroom samples (N = 4,208) are edible, while 48 percent (N = 3,916) are poisonous. As the class levels are split into about 50/50, we do not need to worry about imbalanced data.

For the purposes of this experiment, we will consider the 8,214 samples in the mushroom data to be an exhaustive set of all the possible wild mushrooms. This is an important assumption because it means that we do not need to hold some samples out of the training data for testing purposes. We are not trying to develop rules that cover unforeseen types of mushrooms; we are merely trying to find rules that accurately depict the complete set of known mushroom types. Therefore, we can build and test the model on the same data.

# Step 3 – training a model on the data

If we trained a hypothetical ZeroR classifier on this data, what would it predict? Since ZeroR ignores all of the features and simply predicts the target's mode, in plain language its rule would state that "all mushrooms are edible." Obviously, this is not a very helpful classifier because it would leave a mushroom gatherer sick or dead for nearly half of the mushroom samples. Our rules will need to do much better than this benchmark in order to provide safe advice that can be published. At the same time, we need simple rules that are easy to remember.

Since simple rules can often be extremely predictive, let's see how a very simple rule learner performs on the mushroom data. Toward this end, we will apply the 1R classifier, which identifies the single feature that is the most predictive of the target class and uses this feature to construct a set of rules.

We will use the 1R implementation in the RWeka package, called OneR(). You may recall that we had installed RWeka in *Chapter 1, Introducing Machine Learning*, as part of the tutorial on installing and loading packages. If you haven't installed the package per those instructions, you will need to use the command install.packages("RWeka"), and have Java installed on your system (refer to the installation instructions for more details). With those steps complete, load the package by typing library(RWeka).

---

**1R classification rule syntax**

using the OneR() function in the RWeka package

**Building the classifier:**

```
m <- OneR(class ~ predictors, data = mydata)
```

- class is the column in the mydata data frame to be predicted
- predictors is an R formula specifying the features in the mydata data frame to use for prediction
- data is the data frame in which class and predictors can be found

The function will return a 1R model object that can be used to make predictions.

**Making predictions:**

```
p <- predict(m, test)
```

- m is a model trained by the OneR() function
- test is a data frame containing test data with the same features as the training data used to build the classifier.

The function will return a vector of predicted class values.

**Example:**

```
mushroom_classifier <- OneR(type ~ odor + cap_color,
                            data = mushroom_train)
mushroom_prediction <- predict(mushroom_classifier,
                               mushroom_test)
```

---

OneR() uses the R formula syntax for specifying the model to be trained. The formula syntax uses the ~ operator (known as the tilde), to express the relationship between a target variable and its predictors. The class variable to be learned goes to the left of the tilde, and the predictor features are written on the right, separated by + operators. I you would like to model the relationship between the class y and predictors x1 and x2, you would write the formula as: y ~ x1 + x2. If you would like to include all variables in the model, the special term '.' is used. For example, y ~ . specifies the relationship between y and all other features in the dataset.

The R formula syntax is used across many R functions and offers some powerful features to describe the relationships among predictor variables. We will explore some of these features in later chapters. However, if you're eager for a sneak peak, feel free to read the documentation using the ?formula command.

Using the formula type ~ ., we will allow our first OneR() rule learner to consider all possible features in the mushroom data when constructing its rules to predict type:

```
> mushroom_1R <- OneR(type ~ ., data = mushrooms)
```

To examine the rules it created, we can type the name of the classifier object, in this case mushroom_1R:

```
> mushroom_1R
```

```
odor:
  almond   -> edible
  anise    -> edible
  creosote -> poisonous
  fishy    -> poisonous
  foul     -> poisonous
  musty    -> poisonous
  none     -> edible
  pungent  -> poisonous
  spicy    -> poisonous
(8004/8124 instances correct)
```

On the first line of the output, we see that the odor feature was selected for rule generation. The categories of odor, such as almond, anise, and so on, specify rules for whether the mushroom is likely to edible or poisonous. For instance, if the mushroom smells fishy, foul, musty, pungent, spicy, or like creosote, the mushroom is likely to be poisonous. On the other hand, more pleasant smells like almond and anise (or none, that is, no smell at all), indicate edible mushrooms. For the purposes of a field guide for mushroom gathering, these rules could be summarized in a single, simple rule-of-thumb: "if the mushroom smells unappetizing, then it is likely to be poisonous."

# Step 4 – evaluating model performance

The last line of the output notes that the rules correctly specify 8,004 of the 8,124 mushroom samples, or nearly 99 percent. We can obtain additional details about the classifier using the summary() function, as shown in the following example:

```
> summary(mushroom_1R)
```

```
=== Summary ===
Correctly Classified Instances          8004   98.5229 %
Incorrectly Classified Instances         120    1.4771 %
Kappa statistic                                0.9704
Mean absolute error                            0.0148
Root mean squared error                        0.1215
Relative absolute error                        2.958  %
Root relative squared error                   24.323  %
Coverage of cases (0.95 level)                98.5229 %
Mean rel. region size (0.95 level)         50         %
Total Number of Instances                   8124
```

```
=== Confusion Matrix ===
    a    b    <-- classified as
 4208    0 |    a = edible
  120 3796 |    b = poisonous
```

The section labeled Summary lists a number of different ways to measure the performance of our 1R classifier. We will cover many of these statistics later on in *Chapter 10, Evaluating Model Performance*, so we will ignore them for now.

The section labeled `Confusion Matrix` is similar to those used before. Here, we can see where our rules went wrong. The columns in the table indicate the true class of the mushroom while the rows in the table indicate the predicted values. The key is displayed on the right, with `a = edible` and `b = poisonous`. The 120 values in the lower-left corner indicate mushrooms that are actually edible but were classified as poisonous. On the other hand, there were zero mushrooms that were poisonous but erroneously classified as edible.

Based on this information, it seems that our 1R rule actually plays it safe—if you avoid unappetizing smells when foraging for mushrooms, you will avoid eating any poisonous mushrooms. However, you might pass up some mushrooms that are actually edible. Considering that the learner utilized only a single feature, we did quite well; the publisher of the next field guide to mushrooms should be very happy. Still, let's see if we can add a few more rules and develop an even better classifier.

# Step 5 – improving model performance

For a more sophisticated rule learner, we will use `JRip()`, a Java-based implementation of the RIPPER rule learning algorithm. As with the 1R implementation we used previously, `JRip()` is included in the `RWeka` package. If you have not done so yet, be sure to load the package using the `library(RWeka)` command.

---

**RIPPER classification rule syntax**

using the `JRip()` function in the `RWeka` package

**Building the classifier:**

```
m <- JRip(class ~ predictors, data = mydata)
```

- `class` is the column in the `mydata` data frame to be predicted
- `predictors` is an R formula specifying the features in the `mydata` data frame to use for prediction
- `data` is the data frame in which `class` and `predictors` can be found

The function will return a RIPPER model object that can be used to make predictions.

**Making predictions:**

```
p <- predict(m, test)
```

- `m` is a model trained by the `JRip()` function
- `test` is a data frame containing test data with the same features as the training data used to build the classifier.

The function will return a vector of predicted class values.

**Example:**

```
mushroom_classifier <- JRip(type ~ odor + cap_color,
                            data = mushroom_train)

mushroom_prediction <- predict(mushroom_classifier,
                               mushroom_test)
```

---

As shown in the syntax box, the process of training a `JRip()` model is very similar to how we previously trained a `OneR()` model. This is one of the pleasant benefits of the functions in the `RWeka` package; the syntax is consistent across algorithms, which makes the process of comparing a number of different models very simple.

Let's train the `JRip()` rule learner as we had done with `OneR()`, allowing it to choose rules from all available features:

```
> mushroom_JRip <- JRip(type ~ ., data = mushrooms)
```

To examine the rules, type the name of the classifier:

```
> mushroom_JRip
```

```
JRIP rules:
===========
(odor = foul) => type=poisonous (2160.0/0.0)
(gill_size = narrow) and (gill_color = buff) => type=poisonous
(1152.0/0.0)
(gill_size = narrow) and (odor = pungent) => type=poisonous (256.0/0.0)
(odor = creosote) => type=poisonous (192.0/0.0)
(spore_print_color = green) => type=poisonous (72.0/0.0)
(stalk_surface_below_ring = scaly) and (stalk_surface_above_ring = silky)
=> type=poisonous (68.0/0.0)
(habitat = leaves) and (cap_color = white) => type=poisonous (8.0/0.0)
(stalk_color_above_ring = yellow) => type=poisonous (8.0/0.0)
 => type=edible (4208.0/0.0)
Number of Rules : 9
```

The `JRip()` classifier learned a total of nine rules from the `mushroom` data. An easy way to read these rules is to think of them as a list of `if-else` statements similar to programming logic. The first three rules could be expressed as:

- If the odor is foul, then the mushroom type is poisonous
- If the gill size is narrow and the gill color is buff, then the mushroom type is poisonous
- If the gill size is narrow and the odor is pungent, then the mushroom type is poisonous

Finally, the ninth rule implies that any mushroom sample that was not covered by the preceding eight rules is edible. Following the example of our programming logic, this can be read as:

- Else, the mushroom is edible

The numbers next to each rule indicate the number of instances covered by the rule and a count of misclassified instances. Notably, there were no misclassified mushroom samples using these nine rules. As a result, the number of instances covered by the last rule is exactly equal to the number of edible mushrooms in the data (N = 4,208).

The following figure provides a rough illustration of how the rules are applied to the mushroom data. If you imagine everything within the oval as all species of mushroom, the rule learner identified features, or sets of features, which create homogeneous segments within the larger group. First, the algorithm found a large group of poisonous mushrooms uniquely distinguished by their foul odor. Next, it found smaller and more specific groups of poisonous mushrooms. By identifying covering rules for each of the varieties of poisonous mushrooms, all of the remaining mushrooms were edible. Thanks to Mother Nature, each variety of mushrooms was unique enough that the classifier was able to achieve 100 percent accuracy.

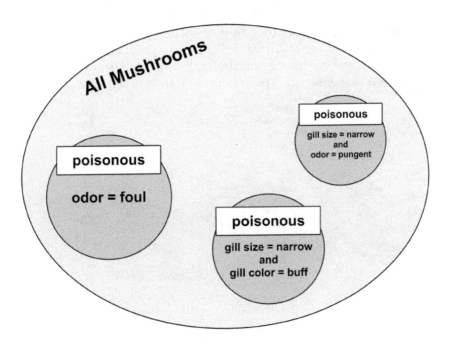

# Summary

This chapter covered two classification methods that partition the data according to values of the features. Decision trees use a divide-and-conquer strategy to create flowcharts, while rule learners separate-and-conquer data to identify logical `if-else` rules. Both methods produce models that can be understood without a statistical background.

One popular and highly-configurable decision tree algorithm is C5.0. We used the C5.0 algorithm to create a tree to predict whether a loan applicant will default. Using options for boosting and cost-sensitive errors, we were able to improve our accuracy and avoid risky loans that cost the bank more money.

We also used two rule learners, 1R and RIPPER, to develop rules for identifying poisonous mushrooms. The 1R algorithm used a single feature to achieve 99 percent accuracy in identifying potentially-fatal mushroom samples. On the other hand, the set of nine rules generated by the more sophisticated RIPPER algorithm correctly identified the edibility of every mushroom.

This chapter merely scratched the surface of how trees and rules can be used. *Chapter 6, Forecasting Numeric Data – Regression Methods*, describes techniques known as regression trees and model trees, which use decision trees for numeric prediction. In *Chapter 11, Improving Model Performance*, we will discover how the performance of decision trees can be improved by grouping them together in a model known as a random forest. And in *Chapter 8, Finding Patterns – Market Basket Analysis Using Association Rules*, we will see how association rules—a relative of classification rules—can be used to identify groups of items in transactional data.

# 6
# Forecasting Numeric Data – Regression Methods

Mathematical relationships describe many aspects of everyday life. For example, a person's body weight can be described in terms of his or her calorie intake; one's income can be related to years of education and job experience; and the president's odds of being re-elected can be estimated by popular opinion poll numbers.

In each of these cases, numbers specify precisely how the data elements are related. An additional 250 kilocalories consumed daily is likely to result in nearly a kilogram of weight gain per month. Each year of job experience may be worth an additional $1,000 in yearly salary while years of education might be worth $2,500. A president is more likely to be re-elected with a high approval rating. Obviously, these types of equations do not perfectly model every case, but on average, the rules might work fairly well.

A large body of work in the field of statistics describes techniques for estimating such numeric relationships among data elements, a field of study known as regression analysis. These methods can be used for forecasting numeric data and quantifying the size and strength of a relationship between an outcome and its predictors.

By the end of this chapter, you will have learned how to apply regression methods to your own data. Along the way, you will learn:

- The basic statistical principles that linear regression methods use to fit equations to data, and how they describe relationships among data elements
- How to use R to prepare data for regression analysis, define a linear equation, and estimate the regression model
- How to use hybrid models known as regression trees and model trees, which allow decision trees to be used for numeric prediction

Until now, we have only looked at machine learning methods suitable for classification. The methods in this chapter will allow you to tackle an entirely new set of learning tasks. With that in mind, let's get started.

# Understanding regression

Regression is concerned with specifying the relationship between a single numeric **dependent variable** (the value to be predicted) and one or more numeric **independent variables** (the predictors). We'll begin by assuming that the relationship between the independent and dependent variables follows a straight line.

> The origin of the term "regression" to describe the process of fitting lines to data is rooted in a study of genetics by *Sir Francis Galton* in the late 19th century. Galton discovered that fathers that were extremely short or extremely tall tended to have sons whose heights were closer to average. He called this phenomenon "regression to the mean".

You might recall from algebra that lines can be defined in a slope-intercept form similar to $y = a + bx$, where $y$ is the dependent variable and $x$ is the independent variable. In this formula, the **slope** $b$ indicates how much the line rises for each increase in $x$. The variable $a$ indicates the value of $y$ when $x = 0$. It is known as the intercept because it specifies where the line crosses the vertical axis.

Regression equations model data using a similar slope-intercept format. The machine's job is to identify values of $a$ and $b$ such that the specified line is best able to relate the supplied $x$ values to the values of $y$. It might not be a perfect match, so the machine should also have some way to quantify the margin of error. We'll discuss this in depth shortly.

Regression analysis is commonly used for modeling complex relationships among data elements, estimating the impact of a treatment on an outcome, and extrapolating into the future. Some specific use cases include:

- Examining how populations and individuals vary by their measured characteristics, for scientific research across fields as diverse as economics, sociology, psychology, physics, and ecology

- Quantifying the causal relationship between an event and the response, such as those in clinical drug trials, engineering safety tests, or marketing research

- Identifying patterns that can be used to forecast future behavior given known criteria, such as for predicting insurance claims, natural disaster damage, election results, and crime rates

Regression methods are also used for hypothesis testing, which involves determining whether data indicate that a presupposition is more likely to be true or false. The regression model's estimates of the strength and consistency of a relationship provide information that can be used to assess whether the findings are due to chance alone.

 Because hypothesis testing is technically not a learning task, we will not cover it in depth. If you are interested in this topic, an introductory statistics textbook is a good place to get started.

Unlike the other machine learning methods we've covered thus far, regression analysis is not synonymous with a single algorithm. Rather, it is an umbrella for a large number of methods that can be adapted to nearly any machine learning task. If you were limited to choosing only a single analysis method, regression would be a good choice. You could devote an entire career to nothing else and perhaps still have much to learn.

In this chapter, we'll focus only on the most basic regression models—those that use straight lines. This is called **linear regression**. If there is only a single independent variable, this is known as **simple linear regression**, otherwise it is known as **multiple regression**. Both of these models assume that the dependent variable is continuous.

It is possible to use regression for other types of dependent variables and even for classification tasks. For instance, **logistic regression** can be used to model a binary categorical outcome, while **Poisson regression**—named after the French mathematician *Siméon Poisson*—models integer count data. The same basic principles apply to all regression methods, so once you understand the linear case, you can move on to the others.

 Linear regression, logistic regression, Poisson regression, and many others fall in a class of models known as **generalized linear models** (GLM), which allow regression to be applied to many types of data. Linear models are generalized via the use of a **link function**, which specifies the mathematical relationship between $x$ and $y$.

Despite the name, simple linear regression is not too simple to solve complex problems. In the next section, we'll see how the use of a simple linear regression model might have averted a tragic engineering disaster.

# Simple linear regression

On January 28, 1986, seven crewmembers of the United States space shuttle Challenger were killed when O-rings responsible for sealing the joints of the rocket booster failed and caused a catastrophic explosion.

The night prior, there had been a lengthy discussion about how the low temperature forecast might affect the safety of the launch. The shuttle components had never been tested in such cold weather; therefore, it was unclear whether the equipment could withstand the strain from freezing temperatures. The rocket engineers believed that cold temperatures could make the components more brittle and less able to seal properly, which would result in a higher chance of a dangerous fuel leak. However, given the political pressure to continue with the launch, they needed data to support their hypothesis.

 This section's analysis is based on data presented in *Risk analysis of the space shuttle: pre-Challenger prediction of failure, Journal of the American Statistical Association, Vol. 84*, pp. 945-957, by S.R. Dalal, E.B. Fowlkes, and B. Hoadley, (1989).

The scientists' discussion turned to data from 23 previous successful shuttle launches which recorded the number of O-ring failures versus the launch temperature. Since the shuttle has a total of six O-rings, each additional failure increases the odds of a catastrophic leak. The following scatterplot shows this data:

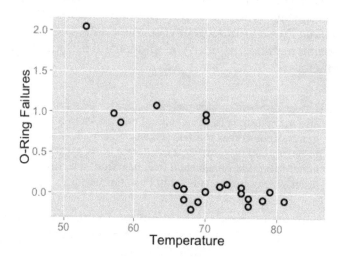

Examining the plot, there is an apparent trend between temperature and number of failures. Launches occurring at higher temperatures tend to have fewer O-ring failures. Additionally, the coldest launch (62 degrees F) had two rings fail, the most of any launch. The fact that the Challenger was scheduled to launch at a temperature about 30 degrees colder seems concerning. To put this risk in quantitative terms, we can turn to simple linear regression.

Simple linear regression defines the relationship between a dependent variable and a single independent predictor variable using a line denoted by an equation in the following form:

$$y = \alpha + \beta x$$

Don't be alarmed by the Greek characters; this equation can still be understood using the slope-intercept form described previously. The intercept, $a$ (alpha), describes where the line crosses the y axis, while the slope, $\beta$ (beta), describes the change in $y$ given an increase of $x$. For the shuttle launch data, the slope would tell us the expected reduction in number of O-ring failures for each degree the launch temperature increases.

Greek characters are often used in the field of statistics to indicate variables that are parameters of a statistical function. Therefore, performing a regression analysis involves finding **parameter estimates** for $a$ and $\beta$. The parameter estimates for alpha and beta are typically denoted using $a$ and $b$, although you may find that some of this terminology and notation is used interchangeably.

Suppose we know that the estimated regression parameters in the equation for the shuttle launch data are:

- $a = 4.30$
- $b = -0.057$

Hence, the full linear equation is $y = 4.30 - 0.057x$. Ignoring for a moment how these numbers were obtained, we can plot the line on the scatterplot:

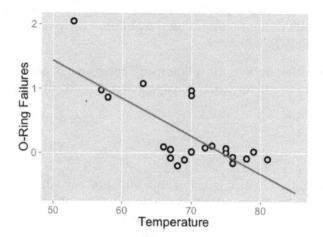

As the line shows, at 60 degrees Fahrenheit, we predict just under one O-ring failure. At 70 degrees Fahrenheit, we expect around 0.3 failures. If we extrapolate our model all the way out to 31 degrees—the forecasted temperature for the Challenger launch—we would expect about $4.30 - 0.057 * 31 = 2.53$ O-ring failures. Assuming that each O-ring failure is equally likely to cause a catastrophic fuel leak, this means that the Challenger launch was about three times more risky than the typical launch at 60 degrees, and over eight times more risky than a launch at 70 degrees.

Notice that the line doesn't predict the data exactly. Instead, it cuts through the data somewhat evenly, with some predictions lower than expected and some higher. In the next section, we will learn about why this particular line was chosen.

# Ordinary least squares estimation

In order to determine the optimal estimates of $a$ and $\beta$, an estimation method known as **ordinary least squares (OLS)** was used. In OLS regression, the slope and intercept are chosen such that they minimize the sum of the squared errors, that is, the vertical distance between the predicted $y$ value and the actual $y$ value. These errors are known as **residuals**, and are illustrated for several points in the preceding diagram:

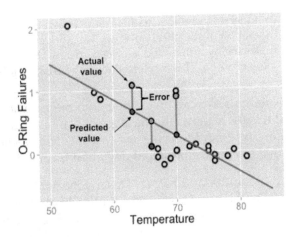

In mathematical terms, the goal of OLS regression can be expressed as the task of minimizing the following equation:

$$\sum(y_i - \hat{y}_i)^2 = \sum e_i^2$$

In plain language, this equation defines e (the error) as the difference between the actual y value and the predicted y value. The error values are squared and summed across all points in the data.

 The caret character (^) above the y term is a commonly used feature of statistical notation. It indicates that the term is an estimate for the true y value. This is referred to as the y-hat.

Though the proof is beyond the scope of this book, it can be shown using calculus that the value of b that results in the minimum squared error is:

$$b = \frac{\sum(x_i - \overline{x})(y_i - \overline{y})}{\sum(x_i - \overline{x})^2}$$

While the optimal value of a is:

$$a = \overline{y} - b\overline{x}$$

To understand these equations, you'll need to know another bit of statistical notation. The horizontal bar appearing over the *x* and *y* terms indicates the mean value of *x* or *y*. This is referred to as the *x*-bar or *y*-bar.

To understand these equations, we can break them into pieces. The denominator for *b* should look familiar; it is the same as the variance of *x*, which can be denoted as *Var(x)*. As we learned in *Chapter 2, Managing and Understanding Data*, calculating the variance involves finding the average squared deviation from the mean of *x*.

We have not computed the numerator before. This involves taking the sum of each data point's deviation from the mean *x* value multiplied by that point's deviation away from the mean *y* value. This is known as the **covariance** of *x* and *y*, denoted as *Cov(x, y)*. With this in mind, we can re-write the formula for *b* as:

$$b = \frac{Cov(x, y)}{Var(x)}$$

 If you would like to follow along with these examples, download the `challenger.csv` file from the Packt Publishing's website and load to a data frame using the command `launch <- read.csv("challenger.csv")`.

Given this formula, it is easy to calculate the value of *b* using R functions. Assume that our shuttle launch data are stored in a data frame named `launch`, the independent variable *x* is `temperature`, and the dependent variable *y* is `distress_ct`. We can then use R's built-in `cov()` and `var()` functions to estimate *b*:

```
> b <- cov(launch$temperature, launch$distress_ct) /
          var(launch$temperature)
> b
[1] -0.05746032
```

From here, we can estimate *a* using the `mean()` function:

```
> a <- mean(launch$distress_ct) - b * mean(launch$temperature)
> a
[1] 4.301587
```

Estimating the regression equation in this way is not ideal, so R of course provides functions for doing this automatically. We will look at those shortly. First, we will expand our understanding of regression by learning a method for measuring the strength of a linear relationship and then see how linear regression can be applied to data having more than one independent variable.

# Correlations

The **correlation** between two variables is a number that indicates how closely their relationship follows a straight line. Without additional qualification, correlation refers to Pearson's correlation coefficient, which was developed by the 20th century mathematician *Karl Pearson*. The correlation ranges between -1 and +1. The extreme values indicate a perfectly linear relationship, while a correlation close to zero indicates the absence of a linear relationship.

The following formula defines Pearson's correlation:

$$\rho_{x,y} = Corr(x, y) = \frac{Cov(x, y)}{\sigma_x \sigma_y}$$

Some more Greek notation has been introduced here: the first symbol (looks like a lowercase 'p') is *rho*, and it is used to denote the Pearson correlation statistic. The characters that look like 'q' turned sideways are *sigma*, and they indicate the standard deviation of *x* or *y*.

Using this formula, we can calculate the correlation between the launch temperature and the number of O-ring failures. Recall that the covariance function is cov() and the standard deviation function is sd(). We'll store the result in r, a letter that is commonly used to indicate the estimated correlation:

```
> r <- cov(launch$temperature, launch$distress_ct) /
        (sd(launch$temperature) * sd(launch$distress_ct))
> r
[1] -0.725671
```

Alternatively, we can use the built in correlation function, cor():

```
> cor(launch$temperature, launch$distress_ct)
[1] -0.725671
```

Since the correlation is about -0.73, this implies that there is a fairly strong negative linear association between the temperature and the number of distressed O-rings. The negative association implies that an increase in temperature is correlated with fewer distressed O-rings. To the NASA engineers studying the O-ring data, this might have been a very clear indicator that a low-temperature launch could be problematic.

There are various rules-of-thumb used to interpret correlations. One method assigns a weak correlation to values between 0.1 and 0.3, moderate for 0.3 to 0.5, and strong for values above 0.5 (these also apply to similar ranges of negative correlations). However, these thresholds may be too lax for some purposes. Often, the correlation must be interpreted in context. For data involving human beings, a correlation of 0.5 may be considered extremely high; for data generated by mechanical processes, a correlation of 0.5 may be weak.

You have probably heard the expression "correlation does not imply causation". This is rooted in the fact that a correlation only describes the association between a pair of variables, yet there could be other explanations. For example, there may be a strong association between life expectancy and time per day spent watching movies, but before doctors start recommending that we all watch more movies, we need to rule out another explanation: older people watch fewer movies and are more likely to die.

Measuring the correlation between two variables gives us a way to quickly gauge relationships among independent variables and the dependent variable. This will be increasingly important as we start defining regression models with a larger number of predictors.

# Multiple linear regression

Most real-world analyses have more than one independent variable. Therefore, it is likely that you will be using **multiple linear regression** most of the time you use regression for a numeric prediction task. The strengths and weaknesses of multiple linear regression are shown in the following table:

| Strengths | Weaknesses |
|---|---|
| • By far the most common approach for modeling numeric data<br><br>• Can be adapted to model almost any data<br><br>• Provides estimates of the strength and size of the relationships among features and the outcome | • Makes strong assumptions about the data<br><br>• The model's form must be specified by the user in advance<br><br>• Does not do well with missing data<br><br>• Only works with numeric features, so categorical data require extra processing<br><br>• Requires some knowledge of statistics to understand the model |

We can understand multiple regression as an extension of simple linear regression. The goal in both cases is similar: find values of beta coefficients that minimize the prediction error of a linear equation. The key difference is that there are additional terms for the additional independent variables.

Multiple regression equations generally follow the form of the following equation. The dependent variable $y$ is specified as the sum of an intercept term plus the product of the estimated $\beta$ value and the $x$ value for each of $i$ features. An error term (denoted by the Greek letter epsilon) has been added here as a reminder that the predictions are not perfect. This is the residual term noted previously.

$$y = \alpha + \beta_1 x_1 + \beta_2 x_2 + \ldots + \beta_i x_i + \varepsilon$$

Let's consider for a moment the interpretation of the estimated regression parameters. You will note that in the preceding equation, a coefficient is estimated for each feature. This allows each feature to have a separate estimated effect on the value of $y$. In other words, $y$ changes by the amount $\beta_i$ for each unit increase in $x_i$. The intercept is then the expected value of $y$ when the independent variables are all zero.

Since the intercept is really no different than any other regression parameter, it can also be denoted as $\beta_0$ (pronounced beta-naught) as shown in the following equation:

$$y = \beta_0 + \beta_1 x_1 + \beta_2 x_2 + \ldots + \beta_i x_i + \varepsilon$$

This can be re-expressed using a condensed formulation:

$$Y = X\beta + \varepsilon$$

Even though this looks familiar, there are a few subtle changes. The dependent variable is now a vector, $Y$, with a row for every example. The independent variables have been combined into a matrix, $X$, with a column for each feature plus an additional column of '1' values for the intercept term. The regression coefficients $\beta$ and errors $\varepsilon$ are also now vectors.

The following figure illustrates these changes:

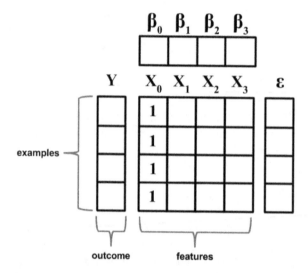

The goal now is to solve for the vector $\beta$ that minimizes the sum of the squared errors between the predicted and actual $y$ values. Finding the optimal solution requires the use of matrix algebra; therefore, the derivation deserves more careful attention than can be provided in this text. However, if you're willing to trust the work of others, the best estimate of the vector $\beta$ can be computed as:

$$\hat{\beta} = \left(X^T X\right)^{-1} X^T Y$$

This solution uses a pair of matrix operations: the $T$ indicates the transpose of matrix $X$, while the negative exponent indicates the matrix inverse. Using built-in R matrix operations, we can thus implement a simple multiple regression learner. Let's see if we can apply this formula to the Challenger launch data.

If you are unfamiliar with the preceding matrix operations, the Wikipedia pages for **transpose** and **matrix inverse** provide a thorough introduction and are quite understandable, even without a strong mathematics background.

Using the following code, we can create a simple regression function named `reg` which takes a parameter `y` and a parameter `x` and returns a matrix of estimated beta coefficients.

```
> reg <- function(y, x) {
    x <- as.matrix(x)
    x <- cbind(Intercept = 1, x)
    solve(t(x) %*% x) %*% t(x) %*% y
  }
```

This function uses several R commands we have not used previously. First, since we will be using the function with sets of columns from a data frame, the `as.matrix()` function is used to coerce the data into matrix form. Next, the `cbind()` function is used to bind an additional column onto the x matrix; the command `Intercept = 1` instructs R to name the new column `Intercept` and to fill the column with repeating `1` values. Finally, a number of matrix operations are performed on the x and y objects:

- `solve()` takes the inverse of a matrix
- `t()` is used to transpose a matrix
- `%*%` multiplies two matrices

By combining these as shown in the formula for the estimated beta vector, our function will return estimated parameters for the linear model relating x to y.

Let's apply our `reg()` function to the shuttle launch data. As shown in the following code, the data include four features and the outcome of interest, `distress_ct` (the number of O-ring failures):

```
> str(launch)
'data.frame': 23 obs. of  5 variables:
 $ o_ring_ct  : int  6 6 6 6 6 6 6 6 6 6 ...
 $ distress_ct: int  0 1 0 0 0 0 0 0 1 1 ...
 $ temperature: int  66 70 69 68 67 72 73 70 57 63 ...
 $ pressure   : int  50 50 50 50 50 50 100 100 200 200 ...
 $ launch_id  : int  1 2 3 4 5 6 7 8 9 10 ...
```

We can confirm that our function is working correctly by comparing its result to the simple linear regression model of O-ring failures versus temperature, which we found earlier to have parameters `a = 4.30` and `b = -0.057`. Since `temperature` is the third column of the `launch` data, we can run the `reg()` function as follows:

```
> reg(y = launch$distress_ct, x = launch[3])
                 [,1]
Intercept    4.30158730
temperature -0.05746032
```

These values exactly match our prior result, so let's use the function to build a multiple regression model. We'll apply it just as before, but this time specifying three columns of data instead of just one:

```
> reg(y = launch$distress_ct, x = launch[3:5])
                      [,1]
Intercept      3.814247216
temperature   -0.055068768
pressure       0.003428843
launch_id     -0.016734090
```

This model predicts the number of O-ring failures versus temperature, pressure, and the launch ID number. The negative coefficients for the temperature and launch ID variables suggests that as temperature or the launch ID increases, the number of expected O-ring failures decreases. Applying the same interpretation to the coefficient for pressure, we learn that as the pressure increases, the number of O-ring failures is expected to increase.

> Even if you are not a rocket scientist, these findings seem reasonable. Cold temperatures make the O-rings more brittle and higher pressure will likely increase the strain on the part. But why would launch ID be associated with fewer O-ring failures? One explanation is that perhaps later launches used O-rings composed from a stronger or more flexible material.

So far, we've only scratched the surface of linear regression modeling. Although our work was useful to help understand exactly how regression models are built, R's functions for fitting linear regression models are not only likely faster than ours, but also more informative. Real-world regression packages provide a wealth of output to aid model interpretation. Let's apply our knowledge of regression to a more challenging learning task.

# Example – predicting medical expenses using linear regression

In order for an insurance company to make money, it needs to collect more in yearly premiums than it spends on medical care to its beneficiaries. As a result, insurers invest a great deal of time and money to develop models that accurately forecast medical expenses.

Medical expenses are difficult to estimate because the most costly conditions are rare and seemingly random. Still, some conditions are more prevalent for certain segments of the population. For instance, lung cancer is more likely among smokers than non-smokers, and heart disease may be more likely among the obese.

The goal of this analysis is to use patient data to estimate the average medical care expenses for such population segments. These estimates could be used to create actuarial tables which set the price of yearly premiums higher or lower depending on the expected treatment costs.

# Step 1 – collecting data

For this analysis, we will use a simulated dataset containing medical expenses for patients in the United States. These data were created for this book using demographic statistics from the U.S. Census Bureau, and thus approximately reflect real-world conditions.

> If you would like to follow along interactively, download the insurance.csv file from the Packt Publishing's website and save it to your R working folder.

The insurance.csv file includes 1,338 examples of beneficiaries currently enrolled in the insurance plan, with features indicating characteristics of the patient as well as the total medical expenses charged to the plan for the calendar year. The features are:

- age: This is an integer indicating the age of the primary beneficiary (excluding those above 64 years, since they are generally covered by the government).

- sex: This is the policy holder's gender, either male or female.

- bmi: This is the **body mass index** (**BMI**), which provides a sense of how over or under-weight a person is relative to their height. BMI is equal to weight (in kilograms) divided by height (in meters) squared. An ideal BMI is within the range of 18.5 to 24.9.

- children: This is an integer indicating the number of children / dependents covered by the insurance plan.

- smoker: This is yes or no depending on whether the insured regularly smokes tobacco.

- region: This is the beneficiary's place of residence in the U.S., divided into four geographic regions: northeast, southeast, southwest, or northwest.

It is important to give some thought to how these variables may be related to billed medical expenses. For instance, we might expect that older people and smokers are at higher risk of large medical expenses. Unlike many other machine learning methods, in regression analysis, the relationships among the features are typically specified by the user rather than detected automatically. We'll explore some of these potential relationships in the next section.

# Step 2 – exploring and preparing the data

As we have done before, we will use the `read.csv()` function to load the data for analysis. We can safely use `stringsAsFactors = TRUE` because it is appropriate to convert the three nominal variables to factors:

```
> insurance <- read.csv("insurance.csv", stringsAsFactors = TRUE)
```

The `str()` function confirms that the data are formatted as we had expected:

```
> str(insurance)
'data.frame': 1338 obs. of  7 variables:
 $ age      : int  19 18 28 33 32 31 46 37 37 60 ...
 $ sex      : Factor w/ 2 levels "female","male": 1 2 2 2 2 1 ...
 $ bmi      : num  27.9 33.8 33 22.7 28.9 ...
 $ children : int  0 1 3 0 0 0 1 3 2 0 ...
 $ smoker   : Factor w/ 2 levels "no","yes": 2 1 1 1 1 1 ...
 $ region   : Factor w/ 4 levels "northeast","northwest", ...
 $ charges  : num  16885 1726 4449 21984 3867 ...
```

Since the dependent variable is `charges`, let's take a look to see how it is distributed:

```
> summary(insurance$charges)
   Min. 1st Qu.  Median    Mean 3rd Qu.    Max.
   1122    4740    9382   13270   16640   63770
```

Because the mean value is greater than the median, this implies that the distribution of insurance charges is right-skewed. We can confirm this visually using a histogram:

```
> hist(insurance$charges)
```

**Histogram of insurance$charges**

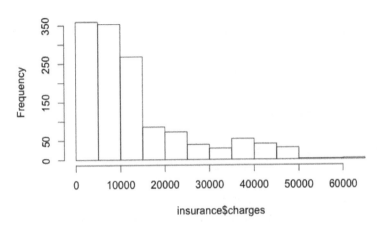

The large majority of individuals in our data have yearly medical expenses between zero and $15,000, although the tail of the distribution extends far past these peaks. Because linear regression assumes a normal distribution for the dependent variable, this distribution is not ideal. In practice, the assumptions of linear regression are often violated. If needed, we may be able to correct this later on.

Another problem at hand is that regression models require that every feature is numeric, yet we have three factor type in our data frame. We will see how R's linear regression function treats our variables shortly.

The sex variable is divided into male and female levels, while smoker is divided into yes and no. From the summary() output, we know that region has four levels, but we need to take a closer look to see how they are distributed.

```
> table(insurance$region)
northeast northwest southeast southwest
      324       325       364       325
```

Here, we see that the data have been divided nearly evenly among four geographic regions.

# Exploring relationships among features – the correlation matrix

Before fitting a regression model to data, it can be useful to determine how the independent variables are related to the dependent variable and each other. A **correlation matrix** provides a quick overview of these relationships. Given a set of variables, it provides a correlation for each pairwise relationship.

To create a correlation matrix for the four numeric variables in the insurance data frame, use the cor() command:

```
> cor(insurance[c("age", "bmi", "children", "charges")])
                age        bmi    children    charges
age       1.0000000 0.1092719 0.04246900 0.29900819
bmi       0.1092719 1.0000000 0.01275890 0.19834097
children  0.0424690 0.0127589 1.00000000 0.06799823
charges   0.2990082 0.1983410 0.06799823 1.00000000
```

At the intersection of each row and column pair, the correlation is listed for the variables indicated by that row and column. The diagonal is always 1 since there is always a perfect correlation between a variable and itself. The values above and below the diagonal are identical since correlations are symmetrical. In other words, cor(x, y) is equal to cor(y, x).

None of the correlations in the matrix are considered strong, but there are some notable associations. For instance, age and bmi appear to have a moderate correlation, meaning that as age increases, so does bmi. There is also a moderate correlation between age and charges, bmi and charges, and children and charges. We'll try to tease out these relationships more clearly when we build our final regression model.

# Visualizing relationships among features – the scatterplot matrix

It can also be helpful to visualize the relationships among features, perhaps by using a scatterplot. Although we could create a scatterplot for each possible relationship, doing so for a large number of features might become tedious.

An alternative is to create a **scatterplot matrix** (sometimes abbreviated as **SPLOM**), which is simply a collection of scatterplots arranged in a grid. It is used to detect patterns among three or more variables. The scatterplot matrix is not a true multi-dimensional visualization because only two features are examined at a time. Still, it provides a general sense of how the data may be interrelated.

We can use R's graphical capabilities to create a scatterplot matrix for the four numeric features: age, bmi, children, and charges. The pairs() function is provided in a default R installation and provides basic functionality for producing scatterplot matrices. To invoke the function, simply provide it the data frame to present. Here, we'll limit the insurance data frame to the four numeric variables of interest:

```
> pairs(insurance[c("age", "bmi", "children", "charges")])
```

This produces the following diagram:

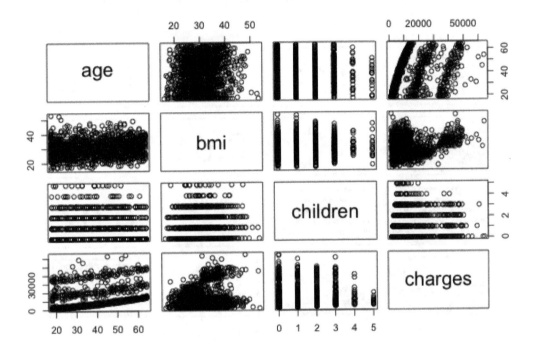

As with the correlation matrix, the intersection of each row and column holds the scatterplot of the variables indicated by the row and column pair. The diagrams above and below the diagonal are transpositions since the x axis and y axis have been swapped.

Do you notice any patterns in these plots? Although some look like random clouds of points, a few seem to display some trends. The relationship between age and charges displays several relatively straight lines, while bmi and charges has two distinct groups of points. It is difficult to detect trends in any of the other plots.

If we add more information to the plot, it can be even more useful. An enhanced scatterplot matrix can be created with the `pairs.panels()` function in the `psych` package. If you do not have this package installed, type `install packages("psych")` to install it on your system then load it using the `library(psych)` command. Then, we can create a scatterplot matrix as we had done previously:

```
> pairs.panels(insurance[c("age", "bmi", "children", "charges")])
```

This produces a slightly more informative scatterplot matrix, as follows:

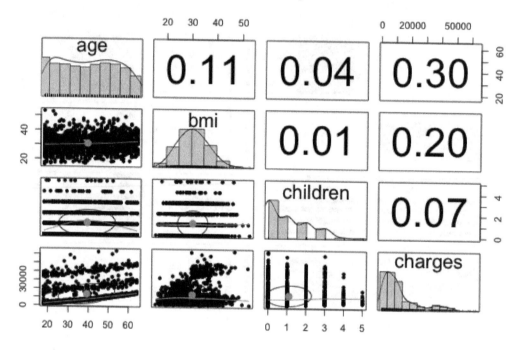

Above the diagonal, the scatterplots have been replaced with a correlation matrix. On the diagonal, a histogram depicting the distribution of values for each feature is shown. Finally, the scatterplots below the diagonal now are presented with additional visual information.

The oval-shaped object on each scatterplot is a **correlation ellipse**. It provides a visualization of how strongly correlated the variables are. The dot at the center of the ellipse indicates the point of the mean value for the x axis variable and y axis variable. The correlation between the two variables is indicated by the shape of the ellipse; the more it is stretched, the stronger the correlation. An almost perfectly round oval, as with `bmi` and `children`, indicates a very weak correlation (in this case 0.01).

The curve drawn on the scatterplot is called a **loess smooth**. It indicates the general relationship between the x axis and y axis variables. It is best understood by example. The curve for `age` and `children` is an upside-down U, peaking around middle age. This means that the oldest and youngest people in the sample have fewer children than those around middle age. Because this trend is non-linear, this finding could not have been inferred from the correlations alone. On the other hand, the loess smooth for `age` and `bmi` is a line sloping gradually up, implying that BMI increases with age, but we had already inferred this from the correlation matrix.

# Step 3 – training a model on the data

To fit a linear regression model to data with R, the `lm()` function can be used. This is included in the `stats` package, which should be included and loaded by default with your R installation. The `lm()` syntax is as follows:

---

**Multiple regression modeling syntax**

using the `lm()` function in the `stats` package

**Building the model:**

```
m <- lm(dv ~ iv, data = mydata)
```

- `dv` is the dependent variable in the `mydata` data frame to be modeled
- `iv` is an R formula specifying the independent variables in the `mydata` data frame to use in the model
- `data` specifies the data frame in which the `dv` and `iv` variables can be found

The function will return a regression model object that can be used to make predictions. Interactions between independent variables can be specified using the `*` operator.

**Making predictions:**

```
p <- predict(m, test)
```

- `m` is a model trained by the `lm()` function
- `test` is a data frame containing test data with the same features as the training data used to build the model.

The function will return a vector of predicted values.

**Example:**

```
ins_model <- lm(charges ~ age + children + sex + smoker,
                          data = insurance)

ins_pred <- predict(ins_model, insurance_test)
```

---

The following command fits a linear regression model called `ins_model`, which relates the six independent variables to the total medical charges. The R formula syntax uses the tilde character ~ to describe the model; the dependent variable `charges` goes to the left of the tilde while the independent variables go to the right, separated by the + sign. There is no need to specify the regression model's intercept term, as it is assumed by default:

```
> ins_model <- lm(charges ~ age + children + bmi + sex +
    smoker + region, data = insurance)
```

Because the . character can be used to specify all features (excluding those already specified in the formula), the following command is equivalent to the preceding command:

```
> ins_model <- lm(charges ~ ., data = insurance)
```

After building the model, simply type the name of the model object to see the estimated beta coefficients:

```
> ins_model3

Call:
lm(formula = charges ~ age + children + bmi + sex +
    smoker + region, data = insurance)

Coefficients:
    (Intercept)            age              children
       -11938.5          256.9                 475.5

            bmi          sexmale               smokeryes
          339.2          -131.3                 23848.5

  regionnorthwest   regionsoutheast    regionsouthwest
         -353.0          -1035.0               -960.1
```

Understanding the regression coefficients is fairly straightforward. The intercept tells us the value of `charges` when the independent variables are equal to zero.

As is the case here, quite often the intercept is difficult to interpret because it is impossible to have values of zero for all features. For example, since no person exists with age zero and BMI zero, the slope has no inherent meaning. For this reason, in practice, the intercept is often ignored.

The estimated beta coefficients indicate the increase in charges for an increase of one in each of the features when the other features are held constant. For instance, for each year that age increases, we would expect $256.90 higher medical expenses on average, assuming everything else is equal. Similarly, each additional child results in an average of $475.50 in additional medical expenses each year, and each unit of BMI increase is associated with an increase of $339.20 in yearly medical costs.

You might notice that although we only specified six features in our model formula, there are eight coefficients reported in addition to the intercept. This happened because the lm() function automatically applied a technique known as **dummy coding** to each of the factor type variables we included in the model.

Dummy coding allows a nominal feature to be treated as numeric by creating a binary variable for each category of the feature, which is set to 1 if the observation falls into that category or 0 otherwise. For instance, the sex variable has two categories, male and female. This will be split into two binary values, which R names sexmale and sexfemale. For observations where sex = male, then sexmale = 1 and sexfemale = 0; if sex = female, then sexmale = 0 and sexfemale = 1. The same coding applies to variables with three or more categories. The four-category feature region can be split into four variables: regionnorthwest, regionsoutheast, regionsouthwest, and regionnortheast.

When adding a dummy-coded variable to a regression model, one category is always left out to serve as the reference category. The estimates are then interpreted relative to the reference. In our model, R automatically held out the sexfemale, smokerno, and regionnortheast variables, making female non-smokers in the northeast region the reference group. Thus, males have $131.30 less medical costs each year relative to females and smokers cost an average of $23,848.50 more than non-smokers. Additionally, the coefficient for each of the other three regions in the model is negative, which implies that the northeast region tends to have the highest average medical expenses.

By default, R uses the first level of the factor variable as the reference. If you would prefer to use another level, the relevel() function can be used to specify the reference group manually. Use the ?relevel command in R for more information.

The results of the linear regression model make logical sense; old age, smoking, and obesity tend to be linked to additional health issues, while additional family member dependents may result in an increase in physician visits and preventive care such as vaccinations and yearly physical exams. However, we currently have no sense of how well the model is fitting the data. We'll answer this question in the next section.

# Step 4 – evaluating model performance

The parameter estimates we obtained by typing `ins_model` tell us about how the independent variables are related to the dependent variable, but they tell us nothing about how well the model fits our data. To evaluate the model performance, we can use the `summary()` command on the stored model:

```
> summary(ins_model)
```

This produces the following output:

```
Call:
lm(formula = charges ~ age + children + bmi + sex + smoker +
    region, data = insurance)

Residuals:
    Min      1Q  Median      3Q     Max
-11304.9 -2848.1  -982.1  1393.9 29992.8    ①

Coefficients:
                 Estimate Std. Error t value Pr(>|t|)
(Intercept)      -11938.5      987.8 -12.086  < 2e-16 ***  ②
age                 256.9       11.9  21.587  < 2e-16 ***
children            475.5      137.8   3.451 0.000577 ***
bmi                 339.2       28.6  11.860  < 2e-16 ***
sexmale            -131.3      332.9  -0.394 0.693348
smokeryes         23848.5      413.1  57.723  < 2e-16 ***
regionnorthwest    -353.0      476.3  -0.741 0.458769
regionsoutheast   -1035.0      478.7  -2.162 0.030782 *
regionsouthwest    -960.0      477.9  -2.009 0.044765 *
---
Signif. codes:  0 '***' 0.001 '**' 0.01 '*' 0.05 '.' 0.1

Residual standard error: 6062 on 1329 degrees of freedom
Multiple R-squared: 0.7509,    Adjusted R-squared: 0.7494    ③
F-statistic: 500.8 on 8 and 1329 DF,  p-value: < 2.2e-16
```

The `summary()` output may seem confusing at first, but the basics are easy to pick up. As indicated by the numbered labels in the preceding output, the output provides three key ways to evaluate the performance (that is, fit) of our model:

1.  The `Residuals` section provides summary statistics for the errors in our predictions, some of which are apparently quite substantial. Since a residual is equal to the true value minus the predicted value, the maximum error of `29992.8` suggests that the model under-predicted expenses by nearly $30,000 for at least one observation. On the other hand, 50 percent of errors fall within the 1Q and 3Q values (the first and third quartile), so the majority of predictions were between $2,850 over the true value and $1,400 under the true value.

2.  The stars (for example, ***) indicate the predictive power of each feature in the model. The significance level (as listed by the `Signif.` codes in the footer) provides a measure of how likely the true coefficient is zero given the value of the estimate. The presence of three stars indicates a significance level of `0`, which means that the feature is extremely unlikely to be unrelated to the dependent variable. A common practice is to use a significance level of 0.05 to denote a statistically significant variable. If the model had few features that were statistically significant, it may be cause for concern, since it would indicate that our features are not very predictive of the outcome. Here, our model has several significant variables, and they seem to be related to the outcome in logical ways.

3.  The `Multiple R-squared` value (also called the coefficient of determination) provides a measure of how well our model as a whole explains the values of the dependent variable. It is similar to the correlation coefficient in that the closer the value is to 1.0, the better the model perfectly explains the data. Since the R-squared value is `0.7494`, we know that nearly 75 percent of the variation in the dependent variable is explained by our model. Because models with more features always explain more variation, the `Adjusted R-squared` value corrects R-squared by penalizing models with a large number of independent variables. It is useful for comparing the performance of models with different numbers of explanatory variables.

Given the preceding three performance indicators, our model is performing fairly well. It is not uncommon for regression models of real-world data to have fairly low R-squared values; a value of 0.75 is actually quite good. The size of some of the errors is a bit concerning, but not surprising given the nature of medical expense data. However, as shown in the next section, we may be able to improve the model's performance by specifying the model in a slightly different way.

# Step 5 – improving model performance

As mentioned previously, a key difference between regression modeling and other machine learning approaches is that regression typically leaves feature selection and model specification to the user. Consequently, if we have subject matter knowledge about how a feature is related to the outcome, we can use this information to inform the model specification and potentially improve the model's performance.

# Model specification – adding non-linear relationships

In linear regression, the relationship between an independent variable and the dependent variable is assumed to be linear, yet this may not necessarily be true. For example, the effect of age on medical expenditures may not be constant throughout all age values; the treatment may become disproportionately expensive for the oldest populations.

If you recall, a typical regression equation follows a form similar to this:

$$y = \alpha + \beta_1 x$$

To account for a non-linear relationship, we can add a higher order term to the regression model, treating the model as a polynomial. In effect, we will be modeling a relationship like this:

$$y = \alpha + \beta_1 x + \beta_2 x^2$$

The difference between these two models is that a separate beta will be estimated, which is intended to capture the effect of the $x$-squared term. This allows the impact of age to be measured as a function of age squared.

To add the non-linear age to the model, we simply need to create a new variable:

```
> insurance$age2 <- insurance$age^2
```

Then, when we produce our improved model, we'll add both age and age2 to the lm() formula, for example, charges ~ age + age2.

# Transformation – converting a numeric variable to a binary indicator

Suppose we have a hunch that the effect of a feature is not cumulative, but rather it has an effect only once a specific threshold has been reached. For instance, BMI may have zero impact on medical expenditures for individuals in the normal weight range, but it may be strongly related to higher costs for the obese (that is, BMI of 30 or above).

We can model this relationship by creating a binary indicator variable that is 1 if the BMI is at least 30 and 0 otherwise. The estimated beta for this binary feature would then indicate the average net impact on medical expenses for individuals with BMI of 30 or above, relative to those with BMI less than 30.

To create the feature, we can use the `ifelse()` function, which for each element in a vector tests a specified condition and returns a value depending on whether the condition is true or false. For BMI greater than or equal to 30, we will return `1`, otherwise `0`:

```
> insurance$bmi30 <- ifelse(insurance$bmi >= 30, 1, 0)
```

We can then include the `bmi30` variable in our improved model, either replacing the original `bmi` variable or in addition, depending on whether or not we think the effect of obesity occurs in addition to a separate BMI effect. Without good reason to do otherwise, we'll include both in our final model.

> If you have trouble deciding whether or not to include a variable, a common practice is to include it and examine the significance level. Then, if the variable is not statistically significant, you have evidence to support excluding it in the future.

# Model specification – adding interaction effects

So far, we have only considered each feature's individual contribution to the outcome. What if certain features have a combined impact on the dependent variable? For instance, smoking and obesity may have harmful effects separately, but it is reasonable to assume that their combined effect may be worse than the sum of each one alone.

When two features have a combined effect, this is known as an **interaction**. If we suspect that two variables interact, we can test this hypothesis by adding their interaction to the model. Interaction effects can be specified using the R formula syntax. To interact the obesity indicator (`bmi30`) with the smoking indicator (`smoker`), we would write a formula in the form `charges ~ bmi30*smoker`

The `*` operator is shorthand that instructs R to model `charges ~ bmi30 + smokeryes + bmi30:smokeryes`

The `:` (colon) operator in the expanded form indicates that `bmi30:smokeryes` is the interaction between the two variables. Note that the expanded form automatically also included the `bmi30` and `smoker` variables as well as the interaction.

> Interactions should never be included in a model without also adding each of the interacting variables. If you always create interactions using the `*` operator, this will not be a problem since R will add the required components for you automatically.

# Putting it all together – an improved regression model

Based on a bit of subject matter knowledge of how medical costs may be related to patient characteristics, we developed what we think is a more accurately-specified regression formula. To summarize the improvements, we:

- Added a non-linear term for age
- Created an indicator for obesity
- Specified an interaction between obesity and smoking

We'll train the model using the `lm()` function as before, but this time we'll add the newly constructed variables and the interaction term:

```
> ins_model2 <- lm(charges ~ age + age2 + children + bmi + sex +
                    bmi30*smoker + region, data = insurance)
```

Next, we summarize the results:

```
> summary(ins_model2)

Call:
lm(formula = charges ~ age + age2 + children + bmi + sex + bmi30 *
    smoker + region, data = insurance)

Residuals:
    Min      1Q   Median       3Q      Max
-17296.4  -1656.0  -1263.3   -722.1  24160.2

Coefficients:
                   Estimate Std. Error t value Pr(>|t|)
(Intercept)        134.2509  1362.7511   0.099 0.921539
age                -32.6851    59.8242  -0.546 0.584915
age2                 3.7316     0.7463   5.000 6.50e-07 ***
children           678.5612   105.8831   6.409 2.04e-10 ***
bmi                120.0196    34.2660   3.503 0.000476 ***
sexmale           -496.8245   244.3659  -2.033 0.042240 *
bmi30            -1000.1403   422.8402  -2.365 0.018159 *
smokeryes        13404.6866   439.9491  30.469  < 2e-16 ***
regionnorthwest   -279.2038   349.2746  -0.799 0.424212
regionsoutheast   -828.5467   351.6352  -2.356 0.018604 *
regionsouthwest  -1222.6437   350.5285  -3.488 0.000503 ***
bmi30:smokeryes  19810.7533   604.6567  32.764  < 2e-16 ***
---
Signif. codes:  0 '***' 0.001 '**' 0.01 '*' 0.05 '.' 0.1 ' ' 1

Residual standard error: 4445 on 1326 degrees of freedom
Multiple R-squared: 0.8664,   Adjusted R-squared: 0.8653
F-statistic: 781.7 on 11 and 1326 DF,  p-value: < 2.2e-16
```

The model fit statistics help to determine whether our changes improved the performance of the regression model. Relative to our first model, the R-squared value has improved from 0.75 to about 0.87. Our model is now explaining 87 percent of the variation in medical treatment costs. Additionally, our theories about the model's functional form seem to be validated. The higher-order `age2` term is statistically significant, as is the obesity indicator, `bmi30`. The interaction between obesity and smoking suggests a massive effect; in addition to the increased costs of over $13,404 for smoking alone, obese smokers spend another $19,810 per year. This may suggest that smoking exacerbates diseases associated with obesity.

# Understanding regression trees and model trees

If you recall from *Chapter 5, Divide and Conquer – Classification Using Decision Trees and Rules*, a decision tree builds a model much like a flowchart in which decision nodes, leaf nodes, and branches define a series of decisions that can be used to classify examples. Such trees can also be used for numeric prediction by making only small adjustments to the tree growing algorithm. In this section, we will consider only the ways in which trees for numeric prediction differ from trees used for classification.

Trees for numeric prediction fall into two categories. The first, known as **regression trees**, were introduced in the 1980s as part of the seminal **Classification and Regression Tree (CART)** algorithm. Despite the name, regression trees do not use linear regression methods as described earlier in this chapter; rather, they make predictions based on the average value of examples that reach a leaf.

 The CART algorithm is described in detail in *Classification and Regression Trees* by *L. Breiman, J.H. Friedman, C.J. Stone,* and *R.A. Olshen* (Chapman & Hall, 1984).

The second type of trees for numeric prediction is known as **model trees**. Introduced several years later than regression trees, they are less widely-known but perhaps more powerful. Model trees are grown in much the same way as regression trees, but at each leaf, a multiple linear regression model is built from the examples reaching that node. Depending on the number of leaf nodes, a model tree may build tens or even hundreds of such models. This may make model trees more difficult to understand than the equivalent regression tree, with the benefit that they may result in a more accurate model.

The earliest model tree algorithm, **M5**, is described in *Learning with Continuous Classes, Proceedings of the 5th Australian Joint Conference on Artificial Intelligence*, pp. 343-348, by *J.R. Quinlan* (1992).

# Adding regression to trees

Trees that can perform numeric prediction offer a compelling yet often overlooked alternative to regression modeling. The strengths and weaknesses of regression trees and model trees relative to the more common regression methods are listed in the following table:

| Strengths | Weaknesses |
|---|---|
| • Combines the strengths of decision trees with the ability to model numeric data | • Not as commonly-used as linear regression |
| • Does automatic feature selection, which allows the approach to be used with a very large number of features | • Requires a large amount of training data |
| • Does not require the user to specify the model in advance | • Difficult to determine the overall net effect of individual features on the outcome |
| • May fit some types of data much better than linear regression | • May be more difficult to interpret than a regression model |
| • Does not require knowledge of statistics to interpret the model | |

Though traditional regression methods are typically the first choice for numeric prediction tasks, in some cases, numeric decision trees offer distinct advantages. For instance, decision trees may be better suited for tasks with many features or many complex, non-linear relationships among features and the outcome; these situations present challenges for regression. Regression modeling also makes assumptions about how numeric data are distributed that are often violated in real-world data; this is not the case for trees.

Trees for numeric prediction are built in much the same way as they are for classification. Beginning at the root node, the data are partitioned using a divide-and-conquer strategy according to the feature that will result in the greatest increase in homogeneity in the outcome after a split is performed. In classification trees, you will recall that homogeneity is measured by entropy, which is undefined for numeric data. For numeric decision trees, homogeneity can be measured by statistics such as variance, standard deviation, or absolute deviation from the mean. Depending on the tree growing algorithm used, the homogeneity measure may vary, but the principles are basically the same.

A common splitting criterion is called the **standard deviation reduction (SDR)**. It is defined by the following formula:

$$\text{SDR} = sd(T) - \sum_i \frac{|T_i|}{|T|} \times sd(T_i)$$

In this formula, the *sd(T)* function refers to the standard deviation of the values in set *T*, while $T_1, T_2 \dots T_n$ are sets of values resulting from a split on a feature. The $|T|$ term refers to the number of observations in set *T*. Essentially, the formula measures the reduction in standard deviation from the original value to the weighted standard deviation post-split.

For example, consider the following case, in which a tree is deciding whether to perform a split on binary feature A or a split on binary feature B:

| original data | 1 1 1 2 2 3 4 5 5 6 6 7 7 7 7 |
|---|---|
| split on feature A | 1 1 1 2 2 3 4 5 5 \| 6 6 7 7 7 7 |
| split on feature B | 1 1 1 2 2 3 4 \| 5 5 6 6 7 7 7 7 |

$$T_1 \qquad\qquad\qquad T_2$$

Using the groups that would result from the proposed splits, we can compute the SDR for A and B as follows. The `length()` function used here returns the number of elements in a vector. Note that the overall group T is named `tee` to avoid overwriting R's built in `T()` and `t()` functions.

```
> tee <- c(1, 1, 1, 2, 2, 3, 4, 5, 5, 6, 6, 7, 7, 7, 7)
> at1 <- c(1, 1, 1, 2, 2, 3, 4, 5, 5)
> at2 <- c(6, 6, 7, 7, 7, 7)
> bt1 <- c(1, 1, 1, 2, 2, 3, 4)
> bt2 <- c(5, 5, 6, 6, 7, 7, 7, 7)
```

```
> sdr_a <- sd(tee) - (length(at1) / length(tee) * sd(at1) +
          length(at2) / length(tee) * sd(at2))
> sdr_b <- sd(tee) - (length(bt1) / length(tee) * sd(bt1) +
          length(bt2) / length(tee) * sd(bt2))
```

Let's compare the SDR of A against the SDR of B:

```
> sdr_a
[1] 1.202815
> sdr_b
[1] 1.392751
```

The SDR for the split on A was about 1.2 versus 1.4 for the split on B. Since the standard deviation was reduced more for B, the decision tree would use B first. It results in slightly more homogeneous sets than does A.

Suppose that the tree stopped growing here using this one and only split. The regression tree's work is done. It can make predictions for new examples depending on whether they fall into group $T_1$ or $T_2$. If the example ends up in $T_1$, the model would predict *mean(bt1)* = 2, otherwise it would predict *mean(bt2)* = 6.25.

In contrast, the model tree would go one step further. Using the seven training examples falling in group bt1 and the eight in bt2, the model tree could build a linear regression model of the outcome versus feature A. (Feature B is of no help in the regression model because all examples at the leaf have the same value of B.) The model tree can then make predictions for new examples using either of the two linear models.

To further illustrate the differences between these two approaches, let's work through a real-world example.

# Example – estimating the quality of wines with regression trees and model trees

Winemaking is a challenging and competitive business that offers the potential for great profit. However, there are numerous factors that contribute to the profitability of a winery. As an agricultural product, variables as diverse as the weather and the growing environment impact the quality of a varietal. The bottling and manufacturing can also affect the flavor, for better or worse. Even the way the product is marketed, from the bottle design to the price point, can affect the customer's perception of taste.

As a consequence, the winemaking industry has invested heavily in data collection and machine learning methods that may assist with the decision science of winemaking. For example, machine learning has been used to discover key differences in the chemical composition of wines from different regions, or to identify the chemical factors that lead a wine to taste sweeter.

More recently, machine learning has been employed to assist with rating the quality of wine—a notoriously difficult task. A review written by a renowned wine critic often determines whether the product ends up on the top or bottom-shelf, in spite of the fact that even expert judges are inconsistent when rating a wine in a blinded test.

In this case study, we will use regression trees and model trees to create a system capable of mimicking expert ratings of wine. Because trees result in a model that is readily understood, this could allow winemakers to identify key factors that contribute to better-rated wines. Perhaps more importantly, the system does not suffer from the human elements of tasting, such as the rater's mood or palate fatigue. Computer-aided wine testing may therefore result in a better product as well as more objective, consistent, and fair ratings.

# Step 1 – collecting data

To develop the wine rating model, we will use data donated to the **UCI Machine Learning Data Repository** by *P. Cortez, A. Cerdeira, F. Almeida, T. Matos*, and *J. Reis*. The data include examples of red and white Vinho Verde wines from Portugal—one of the world's leading wine-producing countries. Because the factors that contribute to a highly-rated wine may differ between the red and white varieties, for this analysis, we will examine only the more popular white wines.

 To follow along with this example, download the whitewines.csv file from the Packt Publishing's website and save it to your R working directory. The redwines.csv file is also available in case you would like to explore these data on your own.

The white wine data includes information on 11 chemical properties of 4,898 wine samples. For each wine, a laboratory analysis measured characteristics such as the acidity, sugar content, chlorides, sulfur, alcohol, pH, and density. The samples were then rated in a blind tasting by panels of no less than three judges on a quality scale ranging from zero (very bad) to 10 (excellent). In the case that the judges disagreed on the rating, the median value was used.

The study by *Cortez* evaluated the ability of three machine learning approaches to model the wine data: multiple regression, artificial neural networks, and support vector machines. We covered multiple regression earlier in this chapter, and we will learn about neural networks and support vector machines in *Chapter 7, Black Box Methods – Neural Networks and Support Vector Machines*. The study found that the support vector machine offered significantly better results than the linear regression model. However, unlike regression, the support vector machine model is difficult to interpret. Using regression trees and model trees, we may be able to improve the regression results while still having a model that is easy to understand.

> To read more about the wine study, please refer to the publication *Modeling wine preferences by data mining from physicochemical properties, Decision Support Systems, Vol. 47,* pp. 547-553, by *P. Cortez, A. Cerdeira, F. Almeida, T. Matos,* and *J. Reis* (2009).

# Step 2 – exploring and preparing the data

As usual, we will use the `read.csv()` function to load the data into R. Since all of the features are numeric, we can safely ignore the `stringsAsFactors` parameter.

```
> wine <- read.csv("whitewines.csv")
```

The `wine` data include 11 features and the `quality` outcome, as follows:

```
> str(wine)
'data.frame': 4898 obs. of  12 variables:
 $ fixed.acidity       : num  6.7 5.7 5.9 5.3 6.4 7 7.9 ...
 $ volatile.acidity    : num  0.62 0.22 0.19 0.47 0.29 0.12 ...
 $ citric.acid         : num  0.24 0.2 0.26 0.1 0.21 0.41 ...
 $ residual.sugar      : num  1.1 16 7.4 1.3 9.65 0.9 ...
 $ chlorides           : num  0.039 0.044 0.034 0.036 0.041 ...
 $ free.sulfur.dioxide : num  6 41 33 11 36 22 33 17 34 40 ...
 $ total.sulfur.dioxide: num  62 113 123 74 119 95 152 ...
 $ density             : num  0.993 0.999 0.995 0.991 0.993 ...
 $ pH                  : num  3.41 3.22 3.49 3.48 2.99 3.25 ...
 $ sulphates           : num  0.32 0.46 0.42 0.54 0.34 0.43 ...
 $ alcohol             : num  10.4 8.9 10.1 11.2 10.9 ...
 $ quality             : int  5 6 6 4 6 6 6 6 6 7 ...
```

Compared to other types of machine learning models, one of the advantages of trees is that they can handle many types of data without preprocessing. This means we do not need to normalize or standardize the features.

However, a bit of effort to examine the distribution of the outcome variable is needed to inform our evaluation of the model's performance. For instance, suppose that there was very little variation in quality from wine-to-wine, or that wines fell into a bimodal distribution: either very good or very bad. These cases may pose trouble for our model. To check for such extremes, we can examine the distribution of quality using a histogram:

```
> hist(wine$quality)
```

This produces the following figure:

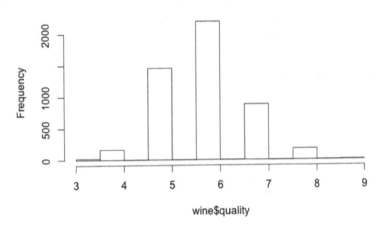

The wine quality values appear to follow a fairly normal, bell-shaped distribution, centered around a value of six. This makes sense intuitively, because most wines are of average quality; few are particularly bad or good. Although the results are not shown here, it is also useful to examine the `summary(wine)` output for outliers or other potential data problems. Even though trees are fairly robust to messy data, it is always prudent to check for severe problems. For now, we'll assume that the data are reliable.

Our last step then is to divide into training and testing datasets. Since the `wine` data were already sorted into random order, we can partition into two sets of contiguous rows as follows:

```
> wine_train <- wine[1:3750, ]
> wine_test <- wine[3751:4898, ]
```

In order to mirror the conditions used by *Cortez*, we used sets of 75 percent and 25 percent for training and testing, respectively. We'll evaluate the performance of our tree-based models on the testing data to see if we can obtain results comparable to the prior research study.

# Step 3 – training a model on the data

We will begin by training a regression tree model. Although almost any implementation of decision trees can be used to perform regression tree modeling, the rpart (recursive partitioning) package offers perhaps the most faithful implementation of regression trees as they were described by the CART team. As the classic R implementation of CART, the rpart package is also well-documented and supported with functions for visualizing and evaluating rpart models.

Install the rpart package using the install.packages(rpart) command. It can then be loaded into your R session using the command library("rpart"). The included rpart() function can fit classification trees or regression trees using the following syntax. This will train a tree using the default settings, which typically work fairly well. If you need more finely-tuned settings, refer to the documentation for the control parameters using the command ?rpart.control.

---

**Regression trees syntax**

using the `rpart()` function in the rpart package

**Building the model:**

```
m <- rpart(dv ~ iv, data = mydata)
```

- dv is the dependent variable in the `mydata` data frame to be modeled
- iv is an R formula specifying the independent variables in the `mydata` data frame to use in the model
- data specifies the data frame in which the dv and iv variables can be found

The function will return a regression tree model object that can be used to make predictions.

**Making predictions:**

```
p <- predict(m, test, type = "vector")
```

- m is a model trained by the `rpart()` function
- test is a data frame containing test data with the same features as the training data used to build the model
- type specifies the type of prediction to return, either **"vector"** (for predicted numeric values), **"class"** for predicted classes, or **"prob"** (for predicted class probabilities)

The function will return a vector of predictions depending on the type parameter.

**Example:**

```
wine_model <- rpart(quality ~ alcohol + sulfates,
                          data = wine_train)
wine_predictions <- predict(wine_model, wine_test)
```

---

Using the R formula interface, we can specify `quality` as the outcome variable and use the dot notation to allow all other columns in the `wine_train` data frame to be used as predictors. The resulting model object is named `m.rpart` to distinguish it from the model tree we will train later:

```
> m.rpart <- rpart(quality ~ ., data = wine_train)
```

For basic information about the tree, simply type the name of the model object:

```
> m.rpart
n= 3750


node), split, n, deviance, yval
      * denotes terminal node


 1) root 3750 2945.53200 5.870933
   2) alcohol< 10.85 2372 1418.86100 5.604975
     4) volatile.acidity>=0.2275 1611  821.30730 5.432030
       8) volatile.acidity>=0.3025 688  278.97670 5.255814 *
       9) volatile.acidity< 0.3025 923  505.04230 5.563380 *
     5) volatile.acidity< 0.2275 761  447.36400 5.971091 *
   3) alcohol>=10.85 1378 1070.08200 6.328737
     6) free.sulfur.dioxide< 10.5 84   95.55952 5.369048 *
     7) free.sulfur.dioxide>=10.5 1294  892.13600 6.391036
      14) alcohol< 11.76667 629  430.11130 6.173291
        28) volatile.acidity>=0.465 11   10.72727 4.545455 *
        29) volatile.acidity< 0.465 618  389.71680 6.202265 *
      15) alcohol>=11.76667 665  403.99400 6.596992 *
```

For each node in the tree, the number of examples reaching the decision point is listed. For instance, all 3750 examples begin at the root node, of which 2372 have `alcohol < 10.85` and 1378 have `alcohol >= 10.85`. Because `alcohol` was used first in the tree, it is the single most important predictor of wine quality.

Nodes indicated by `*` are terminal or leaf nodes, which means that they result in a prediction (listed here as `yval`). For example, node 5 has a `yval` of 5.971091. When the tree is used for predictions, any wine samples with `alcohol < 10.85` and `volatile.acidity < 0.2275` would therefore be predicted to have a quality value of 5.97.

A more detailed summary of the tree's fit, including the mean squared error for each of the nodes and an overall measure of feature importance, can be obtained using the command `summary(m.rpart)`.

## Visualizing decision trees

Although the tree can be understood using only the preceding output, it is often more readily understood using visualization. The `rpart.plot` package by *Stephen Milborrow* provides an easy-to-use function that produces publication-quality decision trees.

> For more information on `rpart.plot`, including additional examples of the types of decision tree diagrams the function can produce, refer to the author's website at http://www.milbo.org/rpart-plot/.

After installing the package using the command `install.packages("rpart plot")`, the `rpart.plot()` function produces a tree diagram from any `rpart` model object. The following commands plot the regression tree we built earlier:

```
> library(rpart.plot)
> rpart.plot(m.rpart, digits = 3)
```

The resulting tree diagram is as follows:

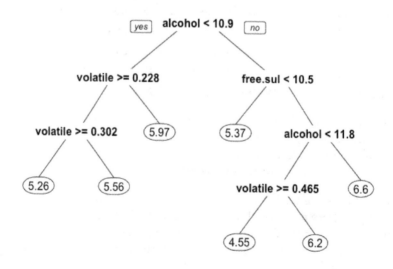

In addition to the `digits` parameter that controls the number of numeric digits to include in the diagram, many other aspects of the visualization can be adjusted. The following command shows just a few of the useful options. The `fallen.leaves` parameter forces the leaf nodes to be aligned at the bottom of the plot, while the `type` and `extra` parameters affect the way the decisions and nodes are labeled :

```
> rpart.plot(m.rpart, digits = 4, fallen.leaves = TRUE,
              type = 3, extra = 101)
```

The result of these changes is a very different looking tree diagram:

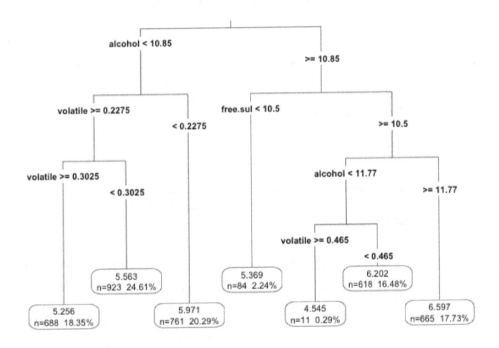

# Step 4 – evaluating model performance

To use the regression tree model to make predictions on the test data, we use the `predict()` function. By default, this returns the estimated numeric value for the outcome variable, which we'll save in a vector named `p.rpart`:

```
> p.rpart <- predict(m.rpart, wine_test)
```

A quick look at the summary statistics of our predictions suggests a potential problem; the predictions fall on a much narrower range than the true values:

```
> summary(p.rpart)
   Min. 1st Qu.  Median    Mean 3rd Qu.    Max.
  4.545   5.563   5.971   5.893   6.202   6.597
> summary(wine_test$quality)
   Min. 1st Qu.  Median    Mean 3rd Qu.    Max.
  3.000   5.000   6.000   5.901   6.000   9.000
```

This finding suggests that the model is not correctly identifying the extreme cases, in particular the best and worst wines. On the other hand, between the first and third quartile, we may be doing well.

The correlation between the predicted and actual `quality` values provides a simple way to gauge the model's performance. Recall that the `cor()` function can be used to measure the relationship between two equal-length vectors. We'll use this to compare how well the predicted values correspond to the true values:

```
> cor(p.rpart, wine_test$quality)
[1] 0.5369525
```

A correlation of 0.54 is certainly acceptable. However, the correlation only measures how strongly the predictions are related to the true value; it is not a measure of how far off the predictions were from the true values.

# Measuring performance with mean absolute error

Another way to think about the model's performance is to consider how far, on average, its prediction was from the true value. This measurement is called the **mean absolute error** (**MAE**). The equation for MAE is as follows, where $n$ indicates the number of predictions and $e$ indicates the error for prediction $i$:

$$\text{MAE} = \frac{1}{n} \sum_{i=1}^{n} |e_i|$$

Essentially, this equation takes the mean of the absolute value of the errors. Since the error is just the difference between the predicted and actual values, we can create a simple `MAE()` function as follows:

```
> MAE <- function(actual, predicted) {
    mean(abs(actual - predicted))
}
```

The MAE for our predictions is then:

```
> MAE(p.rpart, wine_test$quality)
[1] 0.5872652
```

This implies that, on average, the difference between our model's predictions and the true quality score was about 0.59. On a quality scale from zero to 10, this seems to suggest that our model is doing fairly well.

On the other hand, recall that most wines were neither very good nor very bad; the typical quality score was around 5 to 6. Therefore, a classifier that did nothing but predict the mean value may still do fairly well according to this metric.

The mean quality rating in the training data is as follows:

```
> mean(wine_train$quality)
[1] 5.870933
```

If we predicted the value 5.87 for every wine sample, we would have a mean absolute error of only about 0.67:

```
> mean_abserror(5.87, wine_test$quality)
[1] 0.6722474
```

Our regression tree(MAE = 0.59) comes closer on average to the true quality score than the imputed mean (MAE = 0.67), but not by much. In comparison, *Cortez* reported an MAE of 0.58 for the neural network model and an MAE of 0.45 for the support vector machine. This suggests that there is room for improvement.

# Step 5 – improving model performance

To improve the performance of our learner, let's try to build a model tree. Recall that a model tree improves on regression trees by replacing the leaf nodes with regression models. This often results in more accurate results than regression trees, which use only a single value for prediction at the leaf nodes.

The current state-of-the-art in model trees is the **M5' algorithm (M5-prime)** by *Wang and Witten*, which is an enhancement of the original M5 model tree algorithm proposed by *Quinlan* in 1992.

> For more information on the M5' algorithm, see *Induction of model trees for predicting continuous classes, Proceedings of the Poster Papers of the European Conference on Machine Learning* by Y. Wang and I.H. Witten (1997).

The M5' algorithm is available in R via the `RWeka` package and the `M5P()` function. The syntax of this function is shown in the following table. Be sure to install the `RWeka` package if you have not already; because of its dependence on Java, installation instructions are included in *Chapter 1, Introducing Machine Learning*.

---

**Model trees syntax**

using the `M5P()` function in the `RWeka` package

**Building the model:**

```
m <- M5P(dv ~ iv, data = mydata)
```

- `dv` is the dependent variable in the `mydata` data frame to be modeled
- `iv` is an R formula specifying the independent variables in the `mydata` data frame to use in the model
- `data` specifies the data frame in which the `dv` and `iv` variables can be found

The function will return a model tree object that can be used to make predictions.

**Making predictions:**

```
p <- predict(m, test)
```

- `m` is a model trained by the `M5P()` function
- `test` is a data frame containing test data with the same features as the training data used to build the model

The function will return a vector of predicted numeric values.

**Example:**

```
wine_model <- M5P(quality ~ alcohol + sulfates,
                              data = wine_train)
wine_predictions <- predict(wine_model, wine_test)
```

---

We'll fit the model tree using essentially the same syntax as we used for the regression tree:

```
> library(RWeka)
> m.m5p <- M5P(quality ~ ., data = wine_train)
```

The tree itself can be examined by typing its name. In this case, the tree is very large and only the first few lines of output are shown:

```
> m.m5p
M5 pruned model tree:
(using smoothed linear models)
```

```
alcohol <= 10.85 :
|    volatile.acidity <= 0.238 :
|    |    fixed.acidity <= 6.85 : LM1 (406/66.024%)
|    |    fixed.acidity >  6.85 :
|    |    |    free.sulfur.dioxide <= 24.5 : LM2 (113/87.697%)
```

You will note that the splits are very similar to the regression tree we built earlier. Alcohol is the most important variable, followed by volatile acidity and free sulfur dioxide. A key difference, however, is that the nodes terminate not in a numeric prediction, but a linear model (shown here as LM1 and LM2).

The linear models themselves are shown later in the output. For instance, the model for LM1 is as follows. The values can be interpreted exactly the same as the multiple regression models we built earlier in this chapter. Each number is the net effect of the associated feature on the predicted wine quality. The coefficient of 0.266 for fixed acidity implies that for an increase of 1 unit of acidity, the wine quality is expected to increase by 0.266:

```
LM num: 1
quality =
    0.266 * fixed.acidity
    - 2.3082 * volatile.acidity
    - 0.012 * citric.acid
    + 0.0421 * residual.sugar
    + 0.1126 * chlorides
    + 0 * free.sulfur.dioxide
    - 0.0015 * total.sulfur.dioxide
    - 109.8813 * density
    + 0.035 * pH
    + 1.4122 * sulphates
    - 0.0046 * alcohol
    + 113.1021
```

It is important to note that the estimated effects apply only to wine samples reaching this node; a total of 36 linear models were built in this model tree, each with different estimations of the impact of fixed acidity and the 10 other features.

For statistics on how well the model fits the training data, the `summary()` function can be applied to the M5P model. However, keep in mind that since these statistics are based on the training data, they should be used only as a rough diagnostic:

```
> summary(m.m5p)
```

```
=== Summary ===
```

| | |
|---|---|
| Correlation coefficient | 0.6666 |
| Mean absolute error | 0.5151 |
| Root mean squared error | 0.6614 |
| Relative absolute error | 76.4921 % |
| Root relative squared error | 74.6259 % |
| Total Number of Instances | 3750 |

Instead, we'll look at how well the model performs on the unseen test data. The `predict()` function gets us a vector of predicted values:

```
> p.m5p <- predict(m.m5p, wine_test)
```

The model tree appears to be predicting a wider range of values than the regression tree:

```
> summary(p.m5p)
   Min. 1st Qu.  Median    Mean 3rd Qu.    Max.
  4.389   5.430   5.863   5.874   6.305   7.437
```

The correlation also seems to be substantially higher:

```
> cor(p.m5p, wine_test$quality)
[1] 0.6272973
```

Furthermore, the model slightly improved the mean absolute error:

```
> MAE(wine_test$quality, p.m5p)
[1] 0.5463023
```

Although we did not improve a great deal beyond the regression tree, we surpassed the performance of the neural network model published by *Cortez*, and we are getting closer to the published mean absolute error value of 0.45 for the support vector machine model, all while using a much simpler learning method.

Not surprisingly, we have confirmed that predicting the quality of wines is a difficult problem; wine tasting, after all, is inherently subjective. If you would like additional practice, you may try revisiting this problem after reading *Chapter 11, Improving Model Performance*, which covers additional techniques that may lead to better results.

# Summary

In this chapter, two methods for modeling numeric data were presented. The first method, linear regression, involves fitting straight lines to data. The second method uses decision trees for numeric prediction. The latter comes in two forms: regression trees, which use the average value of examples at leaf nodes to make numeric predictions, and model trees, which build a regression model at each leaf node in a hybrid approach that is in some ways the best of both worlds.

We used linear regression modeling to calculate the expected medical costs for various segments of the population. Because the relationship between the features and the target variable are well-described by the estimated regression model, we were able to identify certain demographics, such as smokers and the obese, who may need to be charged higher insurance rates to cover the higher-than-average medical expenses.

Regression trees and model trees were used to model the subjective quality of wines from measureable characteristics. In doing so, we learned how regression trees offer a simple way to explain the relationship between features and a numeric outcome, but the more complex model trees may be more accurate. Along the way, we learned several methods for evaluating the performance of numeric models.

In stark contrast to this chapter, which covered machine learning methods that result in a clear understanding of the relationships between the input and the output, the next chapter covers methods that result in nearly-incomprehensible models. The upside is that they are extremely powerful techniques—among the most powerful stock classifiers—that can be applied to both classification and numeric prediction problems.

# Black Box Methods – Neural Networks and Support Vector Machines

The late science fiction author *Arthur C. Clarke* once wrote that "any sufficiently advanced technology is indistinguishable from magic." This chapter covers a pair of machine learning methods that may, likewise, appear at first glance to be magic. As two of the most powerful machine learning algorithms, they are applied to tasks across many domains. However, their inner workings can be difficult to understand.

In engineering, these are referred to as **black box** processes because the mechanism that transforms the input into the output is obfuscated by a figurative box. The reasons for the opacity can vary; for instance, black box closed source software intentionally conceals proprietary algorithms, the black box of sausage-making involves a bit of purposeful (but tasty) ignorance, and the black box of political lawmaking is rooted in bureaucratic processes. In the case of machine learning, the black box is because the underlying models are based on complex mathematical systems and the results are difficult to interpret.

Although it may not be feasible to interpret black box models, it is dangerous to apply the methods blindly. Therefore, in this chapter, we'll peek behind the curtain and investigate the statistical sausage-making involved in fitting such models. You'll discover that:

- Neural networks use concepts borrowed from an understanding of human brains in order to model arbitrary functions
- Support Vector Machines use multidimensional surfaces to define the relationship between features and outcomes
- In spite of their complexity, these models can be easily applied to real-world problems such as modeling the strength of concrete or reading printed text

With any luck, you'll realize that you don't need a black belt in statistics to tackle black box machine learning methods — there's no need to be intimidated!

# Understanding neural networks

An **Artificial Neural Network (ANN)** models the relationship between a set of input signals and an output signal using a model derived from our understanding of how a biological brain responds to stimuli from sensory inputs. Just as a brain uses a network of interconnected cells called **neurons** to create a massive parallel processor, the ANN uses a network of artificial neurons or **nodes** to solve learning problems.

The human brain is made up of about 85 billion neurons, resulting in a network capable of storing a tremendous amount of knowledge. As you might expect, this dwarfs the brains of other living creatures. For instance, a cat has roughly a billion neurons, a mouse has about 75 million neurons, and a cockroach has only about a million neurons. In contrast, many ANNs contain far fewer neurons, typically only several hundred, so we're in no danger of creating an artificial brain anytime in the near future — even a fruit fly brain with 100,000 neurons far exceeds the current ANN state-of-the-art.

Though it may be infeasible to completely model a cockroach's brain, a neural network might provide an adequate heuristic model of its behavior, such as in an algorithm that can mimic how a roach flees when discovered. If the behavior of a roboroach is convincing, does it matter how its brain works? This question is the basis of the controversial **Turing test**, which grades a machine as intelligent if a human being cannot distinguish its behavior from a living creature's.

Rudimentary ANNs have been used for over 50 years to simulate the brain's approach to problem solving. At first, this involved learning simple functions, like the logical AND function or the logical OR. These early exercises were used primarily to construct models of how biological brains might function. However, as computers have become increasingly powerful in recent years, the complexity of ANNs has likewise increased such that they are now frequently applied to more practical problems such as:

- Speech and handwriting recognition programs like those used by voicemail transcription services and postal mail sorting machines
- The automation of smart devices like an office building's environmental controls or self-driving cars and self-piloting drones
- Sophisticated models of weather and climate patterns, tensile strength, fluid dynamics, and many other scientific, social, or economic phenomena

Broadly speaking, ANNs are versatile learners that can be applied to nearly any learning task: classification, numeric prediction, and even unsupervised pattern recognition.

> Whether deserving or not, ANN learners are often reported in the media with great fanfare. For instance, an "artificial brain" developed by Google was recently touted for its ability to identify cat videos on YouTube. Such hype may have less to do with anything unique to ANNs and more to do with the fact that ANNs are captivating because of their similarities to living minds.

ANNs are best applied to problems where the input data and output data are well-understood or at least fairly simple, yet the process that relates the input to output is extremely complex. As a black box method, they work well for these types of black box problems.

# From biological to artificial neurons

Because ANNs were intentionally designed as conceptual models of human brain activity, it is helpful to first understand how biological neurons function. As illustrated in the following figure, incoming signals are received by the cell's **dendrites** through a biochemical process that allows the impulse to be weighted according to its relative importance or frequency. As the cell body begins to accumulate the incoming signals, a threshold is reached at which the cell fires and the output signal is then transmitted via an electrochemical process down the **axon**. At the axon's terminals, the electric signal is again processed as a chemical signal to be passed to the neighboring neurons across a tiny gap known as a **synapse**.

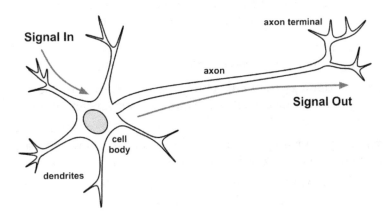

The model of a single artificial neuron can be understood in terms very similar to the biological model. As depicted in the following figure, a directed network diagram defines a relationship between the input signals received by the dendrites (*x* variables) and the output signal (*y* variable). Just as with the biological neuron, each dendrite's signal is weighted (*w* values) according to its importance—ignore for now how these weights are determined. The input signals are summed by the cell body and the signal is passed on according to an **activation function** denoted by *f*.

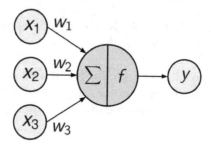

A typical artificial neuron with *n* input dendrites can be represented by the formula that follows. The *w* weights allow each of the *n* inputs, (*x*), to contribute a greater or lesser amount to the sum of input signals. The net total is used by the activation function *f(x)*, and the resulting signal, *y(x)*, is the output axon.

$$y(x) = f\left(\sum_{i=1}^{n} w_i x_i\right)$$

Neural networks use neurons defined in this way as building blocks to construct complex models of data. Although there are numerous variants of neural networks, each can be defined in terms of the following characteristics:

- An **activation function**, which transforms a neuron's net input signal into a single output signal to be broadcasted further in the network

- A **network topology** (or architecture), which describes the number of neurons in the model as well as the number of layers and manner in which they are connected

- The **training algorithm** that specifies how connection weights are set in order to inhibit or excite neurons in proportion to the input signal

Let's take a look at some of the variations within each of these categories to see how they can be used to construct typical neural network models.

# Activation functions

The activation function is the mechanism by which the artificial neuron processes information and passes it throughout the network. Just as the artificial neuron is modeled after the biological version, so too is the activation function modeled after nature's design.

In the biological case, the activation function could be imagined as a process that involves summing the total input signal and determining whether it meets the firing threshold. If so, the neuron passes on the signal; otherwise, it does nothing. In ANN terms, this is known as a **threshold activation function**, as it results in an output signal only once a specified input threshold has been attained.

The following figure depicts a typical threshold function; in this case, the neuron fires when the sum of input signals is at least zero. Because of its shape, it is sometimes called a **unit step activation function**.

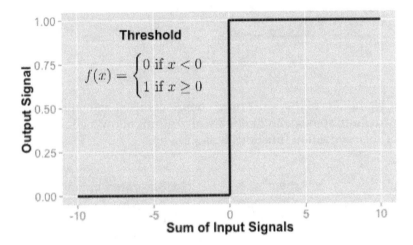

Although the threshold activation function is interesting due to its parallels with biology, it is rarely used in artificial neural networks. Freed from the limitations of biochemistry, ANN activation functions can be chosen based on their ability to demonstrate desirable mathematical characteristics and model relationships among data.

Perhaps the most commonly used alternative is the **sigmoid activation function** (specifically the logistic sigmoid) shown in the following figure, where $e$ is the base of natural logarithms (approximately 2.72). Although it shares a similar step or S shape with the threshold activation function, the output signal is no longer binary; output values can fall anywhere in the range from 0 to 1. Additionally, the sigmoid is **differentiable**, which means that it is possible to calculate the derivative across the entire range of inputs. As you will learn later, this feature is crucial for creating efficient ANN optimization algorithms.

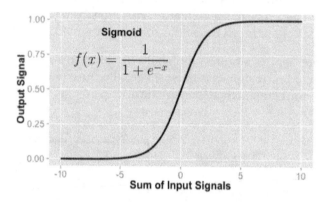

Although the sigmoid is perhaps the most commonly used activation function and is often used by default, some neural network algorithms allow a choice of alternatives. A selection of such activation functions is as shown:

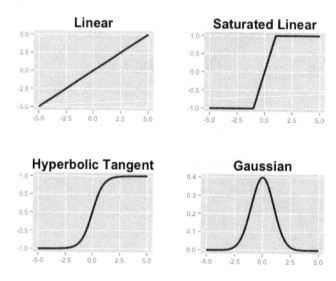

The primary detail that differentiates among these activation functions is the output signal range. Typically, this is one of *(0, 1)*, *(-1, +1)*, or *(-inf, +inf)*. The choice of activation function biases the neural network such that it may fit certain types of data more appropriately, allowing the construction of specialized neural networks. For instance, a linear activation function results in a neural network very similar to a linear regression model, while a Gaussian activation function results in a model called a **Radial Basis Function (RBF) network**.

It's important to recognize that for many of the activation functions, the range of input values that affect the output signal is relatively narrow. For example, in the case of the sigmoid, the output signal is always 0 or always 1 for an input signal below -5 or above +5, respectively. The compression of the signal in this way results in a saturated signal at the high and low ends of very dynamic inputs, just as turning a guitar amplifier up too high results in a distorted sound due to clipping the peaks of sound waves. Because this essentially squeezes the input values into a smaller range of outputs, such activation functions (like the sigmoid) are sometimes called squashing functions.

The solution to the squashing problem is to transform all neural network inputs such that the feature values fall within a small range around 0. Typically, this is done by standardizing or normalizing the features. By limiting the input values, the activation function will have action across the entire range, preventing large-valued features such as household income from dominating small-valued features such as the number of children in the household. A side benefit is that the model may also be faster to train, since the algorithm can iterate more quickly through the actionable range of input values.

Although theoretically a neural network can adapt to a very dynamic feature by adjusting its weight over many iterations, in extreme cases many algorithms will stop iterating long before this occurs. If your model is making predictions that do not make sense, double-check that you've correctly standardized the input data.

# Network topology

The capacity of a neural network to learn is rooted in its **topology**, or the patterns and structures of interconnected neurons. Although there are countless forms of network architecture, they can be differentiated by three key characteristics:

- The number of layers
- Whether information in the network is allowed to travel backward
- The number of nodes within each layer of the network

The topology determines the complexity of tasks that can be learned by the network. Generally, larger and more complex networks are capable of identifying more subtle patterns and complex decision boundaries. However, the power of a network is not only a function of the network size, but also the way units are arranged.

## The number of layers

To define topology, we need a terminology that distinguishes artificial neurons based on their position in the network. The figure that follows illustrates the topology of a very simple network. A set of neurons called **Input Nodes** receive unprocessed signals directly from the input data. Each input node is responsible for processing a single feature in the dataset; the feature's value will be transformed by the node's activation function. The signals resulting from the input nodes are received by the **Output Node**, which uses its own activation function to generate a final prediction (denoted here as $p$).

The input and output nodes are arranged in groups known as **layers**. Because the input nodes process the incoming data exactly as received, the network has only one set of connection weights (labeled here as $w1$, $w2$, and $w3$). It is therefore termed a **single-layer network**. Single-layer networks can be used for basic pattern classification, particularly for patterns that are linearly separable, but more sophisticated networks are required for most learning tasks.

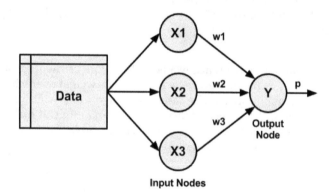

As you might expect, an obvious way to create more complex networks is by adding additional layers. As depicted here, a **multilayer network** adds one or more **hidden layers** that process the signals from the input nodes prior to reaching the output node. Most multilayer networks are **fully connected**, which means that every node in one layer is connected to every node in the next layer, but this is not required.

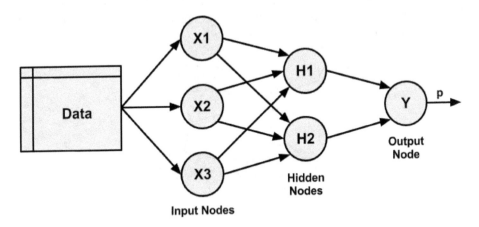

# The direction of information travel

You may have noticed that in the prior examples arrowheads were used to indicate signals traveling in only one direction. Networks in which the input signal is fed continuously in one direction from connection-to-connection until reaching the output layer are called **feedforward networks**.

In spite of the restriction on information flow, feedforward networks offer a surprising amount of flexibility. For instance, the number of levels and nodes at each level can be varied, multiple outcomes can be modeled simultaneously, or multiple hidden layers can be applied (a practice that is sometimes referred to as **deep learning**).

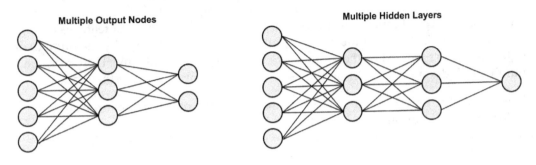

In contrast, a **recurrent network** (or feedback network) allows signals to travel in both directions using loops. This property, which more closely mirrors how a biological neural network works, allows extremely complex patterns to be learned. The addition of a short term memory (labeled **Delay** in the following figure) increases the power of recurrent networks immensely. Notably, this includes the capability to understand sequences of events over a period of time. This could be used for stock market prediction, speech comprehension, or weather forecasting. A simple recurrent network is depicted as shown:

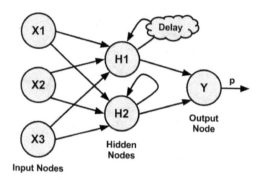

In spite of their potential, recurrent networks are still largely theoretical and are rarely used in practice. On the other hand, feedforward networks have been extensively applied to real-world problems. In fact, the multilayer feedforward network (sometimes called the **Multilayer Perceptron (MLP)** is the de facto standard ANN topology. If someone mentions that they are fitting a neural network without additional clarification, they are most likely referring to a multilayer feedforward network.

# The number of nodes in each layer

In addition to variations in the number of layers and the direction of information travel, neural networks can also vary in complexity by the number of nodes in each layer. The number of input nodes is predetermined by the number of features in the input data. Similarly, the number of output nodes is predetermined by the number of outcomes to be modeled or the number of class levels in the outcome. However, the number of hidden nodes is left to the user to decide prior to training the model.

Unfortunately, there is no reliable rule to determine the number of neurons in the hidden layer. The appropriate number depends on the number of input nodes, the amount of training data, the amount of noisy data, and the complexity of the learning task among many other factors.

In general, more complex network topologies with a greater number of network connections allow the learning of more complex problems. A greater number of neurons will result in a model that more closely mirrors the training data, but this runs a risk of overfitting; it may generalize poorly to future data. Large neural networks can also be computationally expensive and slow to train.

A best practice is to use the fewest nodes that result in adequate performance on a validation dataset. In most cases, even with only a small number of hidden nodes—often as few as a handful—the neural network can offer a tremendous amount of learning ability.

> It has been proven that a neural network with at least one hidden layer of sufficiently many neurons is a **universal function approximator**. Essentially, this means that such a network can be used to approximate any continuous function to an arbitrary precision over a finite interval.

# Training neural networks with backpropagation

The network topology is a blank slate that by itself has not learned anything. Like a newborn child, it must be trained with experience. As the neural network processes the input data, connections between the neurons are strengthened or weakened similar to how a baby's brain develops as he or she experiences the environment. The network's connection weights reflect the patterns observed over time.

Training a neural network by adjusting connection weights is very computationally intensive. Consequently, though they had been studied for decades prior, ANNs were rarely applied to real-world learning tasks until the mid-to-late 1980s, when an efficient method of training an ANN was discovered. The algorithm, which used a strategy of back-propagating errors, is now known simply as **backpropagation**.

> Interestingly, several research teams of the era independently discovered the backpropagation algorithm. The seminal paper on backpropagation is arguably *Learning representations by back-propagating errors, Nature Vol. 323*, pp. 533-566, by *D.E. Rumelhart, G.E. Hinton*, and *R.J. Williams* (1986).

Although still notoriously slow relative to many other machine learning algorithms, the backpropagation method led to a resurgence of interest in ANNs. As a result, multilayer feedforward networks that use the backpropagation algorithm are now common in the field of data mining. Such models offer the following strengths and weaknesses:

| Strengths | Weaknesses |
| --- | --- |
| • Can be adapted to classification or numeric prediction problems<br><br>• Among the most accurate modeling approaches<br><br>• Makes few assumptions about the data's underlying relationships | • Reputation of being computationally intensive and slow to train, particularly if the network topology is complex<br><br>• Easy to overfit or underfit training data<br><br>• Results in a complex black box model that is difficult if not impossible to interpret |

In its most general form, the backpropagation algorithm iterates through many cycles of two processes. Each iteration of the algorithm is known as an **epoch**. Because the network contains no *a priori* (existing) knowledge, typically the weights are set randomly prior to beginning. Then, the algorithm cycles through the processes until a stopping criterion is reached. The cycles include:

- A **forward phase** in which the neurons are activated in sequence from the input layer to the output layer, applying each neuron's weights and activation function along the way. Upon reaching the final layer, an output signal is produced.

- A **backward phase** in which the network's output signal resulting from the forward phase is compared to the true target value in the training data. The difference between the network's output signal and the true value results in an error that is propagated backwards in the network to modify the connection weights between neurons and reduce future errors.

Over time, the network uses the information sent backward to reduce the total error of the network. Yet one question remains: because the relationship between each neuron's inputs and outputs is complex, how does the algorithm determine how much (or whether) a weight should be changed?

The answer to this question involves a technique called **gradient descent**. Conceptually, it works similarly to how an explorer trapped in the jungle might find a path to water. By examining the terrain and continually walking in the direction with the greatest downward slope, he or she is likely to eventually reach the lowest valley, which is likely to be a riverbed.

In a similar process, the backpropagation algorithm uses the derivative of each neuron's activation function to identify the gradient in the direction of each of the incoming weights—hence the importance of having a differentiable activation function. The gradient suggests how steeply the error will be reduced or increased for a change in the weight. The algorithm will attempt to change the weights that result in the greatest reduction in error by an amount known as the **learning rate**. The greater the learning rate, the faster the algorithm will attempt to descend down the gradients, which could reduce training time at the risk of overshooting the valley.

Although this process seems complex, it is easy to apply in practice. Let's apply our understanding of multilayer feedforward networks to a real-world problem.

# Modeling the strength of concrete with ANNs

In the field of engineering, it is crucial to have accurate estimates of the performance of building materials. These estimates are required in order to develop safety guidelines governing the materials used in the construction of buildings, bridges, and roadways.

Estimating the strength of concrete is a challenge of particular interest. Although it is used in nearly every construction project, concrete performance varies greatly due to the use of a wide variety of ingredients that interact in complex ways. As a result, it is difficult to accurately predict the strength of the final product. A model that could reliably predict concrete strength given a listing of the composition of the input materials could result in safer construction practices.

## Step 1 – collecting data

For this analysis, we will utilize data on the compressive strength of concrete donated to the UCI Machine Learning Data Repository (http://archive.ics.uci.edu/ml) by *I-Cheng Yeh*. As he found success using neural networks to model these data, we will attempt to replicate Yeh's work using a simple neural network model in R.

For more information on Yeh's approach to this learning task, refer to: *Modeling of strength of high performance concrete using artificial neural networks, Cement and Concrete Research, Vol. 28,* pp. 1797-1808, by *I-C Yeh* (1998).

According to the website, the concrete dataset contains 1,030 examples of concrete, with eight features describing the components used in the mixture. These features are thought to be related to the final compressive strength, and they include the amount (in kilograms per cubic meter) of cement, slag, ash, water, superplasticizer, coarse aggregate, and fine aggregate used in the product, in addition to the aging time (measured in days).

> To follow along with this example, download the concrete.csv file from the Packt Publishing's website and save it to your R working directory.

# Step 2 – exploring and preparing the data

As usual, we'll begin our analysis by loading the data into an R object using the read.csv() function and confirming that it matches the expected structure:

```
> concrete <- read.csv("concrete.csv")
> str(concrete)
'data.frame': 1030 obs. of  9 variables:
 $ cement       : num  141 169 250 266 155 ...
 $ slag         : num  212 42.2 0 114 183.4 ...
 $ ash          : num  0 124.3 95.7 0 0 ...
 $ water        : num  204 158 187 228 193 ...
 $ superplastic: num  0 10.8 5.5 0 9.1 0 0 6.4 0 9 ...
 $ coarseagg    : num  972 1081 957 932 1047 ...
 $ fineagg      : num  748 796 861 670 697 ...
 $ age          : int  28 14 28 28 28 90 7 56 28 28 ...
 $ strength     : num  29.9 23.5 29.2 45.9 18.3 ...
```

The nine variables in the data frame correspond to the eight features and one outcome we expected, although a problem has become apparent. Neural networks work best when the input data are scaled to a narrow range around zero, and here we see values ranging anywhere from zero up to over a thousand.

Typically, the solution to this problem is to rescale the data with a normalizing or standardization function. If the data follow a bell-shaped curve (a normal distribution as described in *Chapter 2, Managing and Understanding Data*), then it may make sense to use standardization via R's built-in scale() function. On the other hand, if the data follow a uniform distribution or are severely non-normal, then normalization to a 0-1 range may be more appropriate. In this case, we'll use the latter.

In *Chapter 3, Lazy Learning – Classification Using Nearest Neighbors*, we defined our own normalize() function as:

```
> normalize <- function(x) {
    return((x - min(x)) / (max(x) - min(x)))
  }
```

After executing this code, our normalize() function can be applied to every column in the concrete data frame using the lapply() function as follows:

```
> concrete_norm <- as.data.frame(lapply(concrete, normalize))
```

To confirm that the normalization worked, we can see that the minimum and maximum strength are now 0 and 1, respectively:

```
> summary(concrete_norm$strength)
      Min.   1st Qu.    Median      Mean   3rd Qu.      Max.
0.0000000 0.2663511 0.4000872 0.4171915 0.5457207 1.0000000
```

In comparison, the original minimum and maximum values were 2.33 and 82.6:

```
> summary(concrete$strength)
    Min.  1st Qu.    Median      Mean   3rd Qu.      Max.
 2.33000 23.71000 34.44500 35.81796 46.13500 82.60000
```

Any transformation applied to the data prior to training the model will have to be applied in reverse later on in order to convert back to the original units of measurement. To facilitate the rescaling, it is wise to save the original data, or at least the summary statistics of the original data.

Following the precedent of *I-Cheng Yeh* in the original publication, we will partition the data into a training set with 75 percent of the examples and a testing set with 25 percent. The CSV file we used was already sorted in random order, so we simply need to divide it into two portions:

```
> concrete_train <- concrete_norm[1:773, ]
> concrete_test <- concrete_norm[774:1030, ]
```

We'll use the training dataset to build the neural network and the testing dataset to evaluate how well the model generalizes to future results. As it is easy to overfit a neural network, this step is very important.

# Step 3 – training a model on the data

To model the relationship between the ingredients used in concrete and the strength of the finished product, we will use a multilayer feedforward neural network. The `neuralnet` package by *Stefan Fritsch* and *Frauke Guenther* provides a standard and easy-to-use implementation of such networks. It also offers a function to plot the network topology. For these reasons, the `neuralnet` implementation is a strong choice for learning more about neural networks, though that's not to say that it cannot be used to accomplish real work as well—it's quite a powerful tool, as you will soon see.

There are several other commonly used packages to train ANN models in R, each with unique strengths and weaknesses. Because it ships as part of the standard R installation, the `nnet` package is perhaps the most frequently cited ANN implementation. It uses a slightly more sophisticated algorithm than standard backpropagation. Another strong option is the `RSNNS` package, which offers a complete suite of neural network functionality, with the downside being that it is more difficult to learn.

As neuralnet is not included in base R, you will need to install it by typing install.packages("neuralnet") and load it with the library(neuralnet) command. The included neuralnet() function can be used for training neural networks for numeric prediction using the following syntax:

---

**Neural network syntax**

using the neuralnet() function in the neuralnet package

**Building the model:**

```
m <- neuralnet(target ~ predictors, data = mydata, hidden = 1)
```

- **target** is the outcome in the **mydata** data frame to be modeled
- **predictors** is an R formula specifying the features in the **mydata** data frame to use for prediction
- **data** specifies the data frame in which the **target** and **predictors** variables can be found
- **hidden** specifies the number of neurons in the hidden layer (by default, 1)

The function will return a neural network object that can be used to make predictions.

**Making predictions:**

```
p <- compute(m, test)
```

- **m** is a model trained by the **neuralnet()** function
- **test** is a data frame containing test data with the same features as the training data used to build the classifier

The function will return a list with two components: **$neurons**, which stores the neurons for each layer in the network, and **$net.result**, which stores the model's predicted values.

**Example:**

```
concrete_model <- neuralnet(strength ~ cement + slag + ash,
                            data = concrete)

model_results <- compute(concrete_model, concrete_data)
strength_predictions <- model_results$net.result
```

---

We'll begin by training the simplest multilayer feedforward network with only a single hidden node:

```
> concrete_model <- neuralnet(strength ~ cement + slag +
                        ash + water + superplastic +
                        coarseagg + fineagg + age,
                        data = concrete_train)
```

We can then visualize the network topology using the `plot()` function on the
`concrete_model` object:

```
> plot(concrete_model)
```

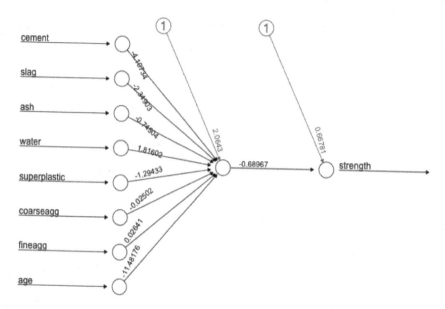

Error: 6.916822   Steps: 3222

In this simple model, there is one input node for each of the eight features, followed
by a single hidden node and a single output node that predicts the concrete strength.
The weights for each of the connections are also depicted, as are the bias terms
(indicated by the nodes with a **1**). The plot also reports the number of training steps
and a measure called, the **Sum of Squared Errors** (**SSE**). These metrics will be useful
when we are evaluating the model performance.

# Step 4 – evaluating model performance

The network topology diagram gives us a peek into the black box of the ANN,
but it doesn't provide much information about how well the model fits our data.
To estimate our model's performance, we can use the `compute()` function to
generate predictions on the testing dataset:

```
> model_results <- compute(concrete_model, concrete_test[1:8])
```

Note that the `compute()` function works a bit differently from the `predict()` functions we've used so far. It returns a list with two components: `$neurons`, which stores the neurons for each layer in the network, and `$net.results`, which stores the predicted values. We'll want the latter:

```
> predicted_strength <- model_results$net.result
```

Because this is a numeric prediction problem rather than a classification problem, we cannot use a confusion matrix to examine model accuracy. Instead, we must measure the correlation between our predicted concrete strength and the true value. This provides an insight into the strength of the linear association between the two variables.

Recall that the `cor()` function is used to obtain a correlation between two numeric vectors:

```
> cor(predicted_strength, concrete_test$strength)
            [,1]
[1,] 0.7170368646
```

 Don't be alarmed if your result differs. Because the neural network begins with random weights, the predictions can vary from model to model.

Correlations close to 1 indicate strong linear relationships between two variables. Therefore, the correlation here of about 0.72 indicates a fairly strong relationship. This implies that our model is doing a fairly good job, even with only a single hidden node.

 A neural network with a single hidden node can be thought of as a distant cousin of the linear regression models we studied in *Chapter 6, Forecasting Numeric Data – Regression Methods*. The weight between each input node and the hidden node is similar to the regression coefficients, and the weight for the bias term is similar to the intercept. In fact, if you construct a linear model in the same vein as the previous ANN, the correlation is 0.74.

Given that we only used one hidden node, it is likely that we can improve the performance of our model. Let's try to do a bit better.

# Step 5 – improving model performance

As networks with more complex topologies are capable of learning more difficult concepts, let's see what happens when we increase the number of hidden nodes to five. We use the `neuralnet()` function as before, but add the parameter `hidden = 5`:

```
> concrete_model2 <- neuralnet(strength ~ cement + slag +
                               ash + water + superplastic +
                               coarseagg + fineagg + age,
                               data = concrete_train, hidden = 5)
```

Plotting the network again, we see a drastic increase in the number of connections. How did this impact performance?

```
> plot(concrete_model2)
```

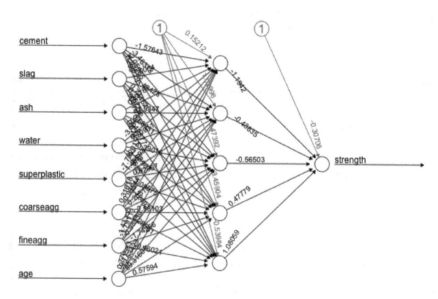

Error: 2.443754   Steps: 7230

Notice that the reported error (measured again by SSE) has been reduced from 6.92 in the previous model to 2.44 here. Additionally, the number of training steps rose from 3222 to 7230, which is no surprise given how much more complex the model has become.

Applying the same steps to compare the predicted values to the true values, we now obtain a correlation around 0.80, which is a considerable improvement over the previous result:

```
> model_results2 <- compute(concrete_model2, concrete_test[1:8])
> predicted_strength2 <- model_results2$net.result
> cor(predicted_strength2, concrete_test$strength)
            [,1]
[1,] 0.801444583
```

Interestingly, in the original publication, *I-Cheng Yeh* reported a mean correlation of 0.885 using a very similar neural network. For some reason, we fell a bit short. In our defense, he is a civil engineering professor; therefore, he may have applied some subject matter expertise to the data preparation. If you'd like more practice with neural networks, you might try applying the principles learned earlier in this chapter to beat his result, perhaps by using different numbers of hidden nodes, applying different activation functions, and so on. The `?neuralnet` help page provides more information on the various parameters that can be adjusted.

# Understanding Support Vector Machines

A **Support Vector Machine (SVM)** can be imagined as a surface that defines a boundary between various points of data which represent examples plotted in multidimensional space according to their feature values. The goal of an SVM is to create a flat boundary, called a **hyperplane**, which leads to fairly homogeneous partitions of data on either side. In this way, SVM learning combines aspects of both the instance-based nearest neighbor learning presented in *Chapter 3, Lazy Learning – Classification Using Nearest Neighbors*, and the linear regression modeling described in *Chapter 6, Forecasting Numeric Data – Regression Methods*. The combination is extremely powerful, allowing SVMs to model highly complex relationships.

Although the basic mathematics that drive SVMs have been around for decades, they have recently exploded in popularity. This is of course rooted in their state-of-the-art performance, but perhaps also due to the fact that award winning SVM algorithms have been implemented in several popular and well-supported libraries across many programming languages, including R. This has led SVMs to be adopted by a much wider audience who previously might have passed it by due to the somewhat complex math involved with SVM implementation. The good news is that although the math may be difficult, the basic concepts are understandable.

SVMs can be adapted for use with nearly any type of learning task, including both classification and numeric prediction. Many of the algorithm's key successes have come in pattern recognition. Notable applications include:

- Classification of microarray gene expression data in the field of bioinformatics to identify cancer or other genetic diseases

- Text categorization, such as identification of the language used in a document or organizing documents by subject matter

- The detection of rare yet important events like combustion engine failure, security breaches, or earthquakes

SVMs are most easily understood when used for binary classification, which is how the method has been traditionally applied. Therefore, in the remaining sections we will focus only on SVM classifiers. Don't worry, however, as the same principles you learn here will apply when adapting SVMs to other learning tasks such as numeric prediction.

## Classification with hyperplanes

As noted previously, SVMs use a linear boundary called a hyperplane to partition data into groups of similar elements, typically as indicated by the class values. For example, the following figure depicts a hyperplane that separates groups of circles and squares in two and three dimensions. Because the circles and squares can be divided by the straight line or flat surface, they are said to be **linearly separable**. At first, we'll consider only the simple case where this is true, but SVMs can also be extended to problems were the data are not linearly separable.

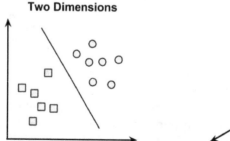
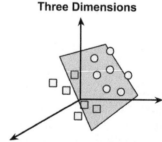

**Two Dimensions**　　　　**Three Dimensions**

For convenience, the hyperplane is traditionally depicted as a line in 2D space, but this is simply because it is difficult to illustrate space in greater than two dimensions. In reality, the hyperplane is a flat surface in a high-dimensional space — a concept that can be difficult to get your mind around.

The task of the SVM algorithm is to identify a line that separates the two classes. As shown in the following figure, there is more than one choice of dividing line between the groups of circles and squares. Three such possibilities are labeled **a**, **b**, and **c**. How does the algorithm choose?

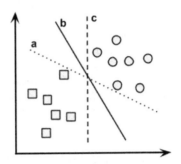

# Finding the maximum margin

The answer to that question involves a search for the **Maximum Margin Hyperplane** (**MMH**) that creates the greatest separation between the two classes. Although any of the three lines separating the circles and squares would correctly classify all the data points, it is likely that the line that leads to the greatest separation will generalize the best to future data. This is because slight variations in the positions of the points near the boundary might cause one of them to fall over the line by chance.

The **support vectors** (indicated by arrows in the figure that follows) are the points from each class that are the closest to the MMH; each class must have at least one support vector, but it is possible to have more than one. Using the support vectors alone, it is possible to define the MMH. This is a key feature of SVMs; the support vectors provide a very compact way to store a classification model, even if the number of features is extremely large.

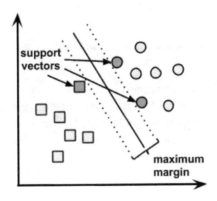

The algorithm to identify the support vectors relies on vector geometry and involves some fairly tricky math which is outside the scope of this book. However, the basic principles of the process are fairly straightforward.

 More information on the mathematics of SVMs can be found in the classic paper: *Support-vector network, Machine Learning, Vol. 20, pp. 273-297*, by C. Cortes and V. Vapnik (1995). A beginner level discussion can be found in *Support vector machines: hype or hallelujah, SIGKDD Explorations, Vol. 2, No. 2, pp. 1-13*, by K.P. Bennett and C. Campbell (2003). A more in-depth look can be found in: *Support Vector Machines* by I. Steinwart and A. Christmann (Springer Publishing Company, 2008).

## The case of linearly separable data

It is easiest to understand how to find the maximum margin under the assumption that the classes are linearly separable. In this case, the MMH is as far away as possible from the outer boundaries of the two groups of data points. These outer boundaries are known as the **convex hull**. The MMH is then the perpendicular bisector of the shortest line between the two convex hulls. Sophisticated computer algorithms that use a technique known as **quadratic optimization** are capable of finding the maximum margin in this way.

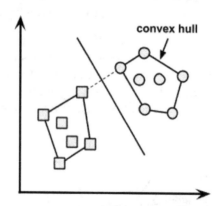

An alternative (but equivalent) approach involves a search through the space of every possible hyperplane in order to find a set of two parallel planes which divide the points into homogeneous groups yet themselves are as far apart as possible. Stated differently, this process is a bit like trying to find the largest mattress that can fit up the stairwell to your bedroom.

To understand this search process, we'll need to define exactly what we mean by a hyperplane. In $n$-dimensional space, the following equation is used:

$$\vec{w} \cdot \vec{x} + b = 0$$

If you aren't familiar with this notation, the arrows above the letters indicate that they are vectors rather than single numbers. In particular, $w$ is a vector of $n$ weights, that is, {w1, w2, ..., wn}, and $b$ is a single number known as the bias.

If you're confused or having trouble imagining the plane, don't worry about the details. Simply think of the equation as a way to specify a line, much like the slope-intercept form ($y = mx + b$) is used to specify lines in 2D space.

Using this formula, the goal of the process is to find a set of weights that specify two hyperplanes, as follows:

$$\vec{w} \cdot \vec{x} + b \geq +1$$
$$\vec{w} \cdot \vec{x} + b \leq -1$$

We will also require that these hyperplanes are specified such that all the points of one class fall above the first hyperplane and all the points of the other class fall beneath the second hyperplane. This is possible so long as the data are linearly separable.

Vector geometry defines the distance between these two planes as:

$$\frac{2}{\|\vec{w}\|}$$

Here, $\|w\|$ indicates the **Euclidean norm** (the distance from the origin to vector $w$). Therefore, in order to maximize distance, we need to minimize $\|w\|$. In order to facilitate finding the solution, the task is typically reexpressed as a set of constraints:

$$\min \frac{1}{2} \|\vec{w}\|^2$$
$$s.t. \; y_i \left( \vec{w} \cdot \vec{x}_i - b \right) \geq 1, \forall \vec{x}_i$$

Although this looks messy, it's really not too complicated if you think about it in pieces. Basically, the idea is to minimize the previous formula subject to (*s.t.*) the condition each of the $y_i$ data points is correctly classified. Note that $y$ indicates the class value (transformed to either +1 or -1) and the upside down "A" is shorthand for "for all."

As with the other method for finding the maximum margin, finding a solution to this problem is a job for quadratic optimization software. Although it can be processor-intensive, specialized algorithms are capable of solving these problems quickly even on fairly large datasets.

## The case of non-linearly separable data

As we've worked through the theory behind SVMs, you may be wondering about the elephant in the room: what happens in the case that the data are not linearly separable? The solution to this problem is the use of a **slack variable**, which creates a soft margin that allows some points to fall on the incorrect side of the margin. The figure that follows illustrates two points falling on the wrong side of the line with the corresponding slack terms (denoted with the Greek letter Xi):

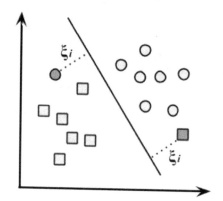

A cost value (denoted as C) is applied to all points that violate the constraints, and rather than finding the maximum margin, the algorithm attempts to minimize the total cost. We can therefore revise the optimization problem to:

$$\min \frac{1}{2} \|\vec{w}\|^2 + C \sum_{i=1}^{n} \xi_i$$
$$s.t.\ y_i \left( \vec{w} \cdot \vec{x}_i - b \right) \geq 1 - \xi_i, \forall \vec{x}_i, \xi_i \geq 0$$

If you're confused by now, don't worry, you're not alone. Luckily, SVM packages will happily optimize this for you without you having to understand the technical details. The important piece to understand is the addition of the cost parameter, C. Modifying this value will adjust the penalty for examples that fall on the wrong side of the hyperplane. The greater the cost parameter, the harder the optimization will try to achieve 100 percent separation. On the other hand, a lower cost parameter will place the emphasis on a wider overall margin. It is important to strike a balance between these two in order to create a model that generalizes well to future data.

# Using kernels for non-linear spaces

In many real-world applications, the relationships between variables are non-linear. As we just discovered, a SVM can still be trained on such data through the addition of a slack variable, which allows some examples to be misclassified. However, this is not the only way to approach the problem of non-linearity. A key feature of SVMs is their ability to map the problem into a higher dimension space using a process known as the **kernel trick**. In doing so, a non-linear relationship may suddenly appear to be quite linear.

Though this seems like nonsense, it is actually quite easy to illustrate by example. In the following figure, the scatterplot on the left depicts a non-linear relationship between a weather class (sunny or snowy) and two features: **Latitude** and **Longitude**. The points at the center of the plot are members of the **Snowy** class, while the points at the margins are all **Sunny**. Such data could have been generated from a set of weather reports, some of which were obtained from stations near the top of a mountain, while others were obtained from stations around the base of the mountain.

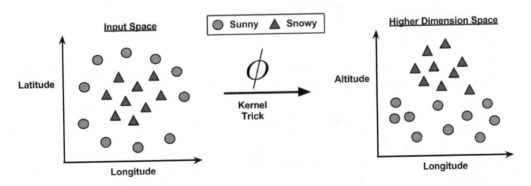

On the right side of the figure, after the kernel trick has been applied, we look at the data through the lens of a new dimension: **Altitude**. With the addition of this feature, the classes are now perfectly linearly separable. This is possible because we have obtained a new perspective on the data; in the left figure, we are viewing the mountain from a bird's-eye view, while on the right we are viewing the mountain from ground level. Here, the trend is obvious: snowy weather is found at higher altitudes.

SVMs with non-linear kernels add additional dimensions to the data in order to create separation in this way. Essentially, the kernel trick involves a process of adding new features that express mathematical relationships between measured characteristics. For instance, the altitude feature can be expressed mathematically as an interaction between latitude and longitude—the closer the point is to the center of each of these scales, the greater the altitude. This allows the SVM to learn concepts that were not explicitly measured in the original data.

SVMs with non-linear kernels are extremely powerful classifiers, although they do have some downsides as shown in the following table:

| Strengths | Weaknesses |
|---|---|
| • Can be used for classification or numeric prediction problems<br><br>• Not overly influenced by noisy data and not very prone to overfitting<br><br>• May be easier to use than neural networks, particularly due to the existence of several well-supported SVM algorithms<br><br>• Gaining popularity due to its high accuracy and high-profile wins in data mining competitions | • Finding the best model requires testing of various combinations of kernels and model parameters<br><br>• Can be slow to train, particularly if the input dataset has a large number of features or examples<br><br>• Results in a complex black box model that is difficult if not impossible to interpret |

Kernel functions, in general, are of the following form. Here, the function denoted by the Greek letter phi, that is, $\phi(x)$, is a mapping of the data into another space:

$$K\left(\vec{x}_i, \vec{x}_j\right) = \phi\left(\vec{x}_j\right) \cdot \phi\left(\vec{x}_j\right)$$

Using this form, kernel functions have been developed for many different domains of data. A few of the most commonly used kernel functions are listed as follows. Nearly all SVM software packages will include these kernels, among many others.

The **linear kernel** does not transform the data at all. Therefore, it can be expressed simply as the dot product of the features:

$$K\left(\vec{x}_i, \vec{x}_j\right) = \vec{x}_i \cdot \vec{x}_j$$

The **polynomial kernel** of degree *d* adds a simple non-linear transformation of the data:

$$K\left(\vec{x}_i, \vec{x}_j\right) = \left(\vec{x}_i \cdot \vec{x}_j + 1\right)^d$$

The **sigmoid kernel** results in a SVM model somewhat analogous to a neural network using a sigmoid activation function. The Greek letters kappa and delta are used as kernel parameters:

$$K\left(\vec{x}_i, \vec{x}_j\right) = \tanh\left(k\, \vec{x}_i \cdot \vec{x}_j - \delta\right)$$

The **Gaussian RBF kernel** is similar to a RBF neural network. The RBF kernel performs well on many types of data and is thought to be a reasonable starting point for many learning tasks:

$$K\left(\vec{x}_i, \vec{x}_j\right) = e^{\dfrac{-\left\|\vec{x}_i - \vec{x}_j\right\|^2}{2\sigma^2}}$$

There is no reliable rule for matching a kernel to a particular learning task. The fit depends heavily on the concept to be learned as well as the amount of training data and the relationships among the features. Often, a bit of trial and error is required by training and evaluating several SVMs on a validation dataset. That said, in many cases, the choice of kernel is arbitrary, as the performance may vary only slightly. To see how this works in practice, let's apply our understanding of SVM classification to a real-world problem.

# Performing OCR with SVMs

Image processing is a difficult task for many types of machine learning algorithms. The relationships linking patterns of pixels to higher concepts are extremely complex and hard to define. For instance, it's easy for a human being to recognize a face, a cat, or the letter A, but defining these patterns in strict rules is difficult. Furthermore, image data is often noisy. There can be many slight variations in how the image was captured depending on the lighting, orientation, and positioning of the subject.

SVMs are well-suited to tackle the challenges of image data. Capable of learning complex patterns without being overly sensitive to noise, they are able to recognize visual patterns with a high degree of accuracy. Moreover, the key weakness of SVMs — the black box model representation — is less critical for image processing. If an SVM can differentiate a cat from a dog, it does not much matter how it is doing so.

In this section, we will develop a model similar to those used at the core of the **Optical Character Recognition (OCR)** software often bundled with desktop document scanners. The purpose of such software is to process paper-based documents by converting printed or handwritten text into an electronic form to be saved in a database. Of course, this is a difficult problem due to the many variants in handwriting style and printed fonts. Even so, software users expect perfection, as errors or typos can result in embarrassing or costly mistakes in a business environment. Let's see whether our SVM is up to the task.

# Step 1 – collecting data

When OCR software first processes a document, it divides the paper into a matrix such that each cell in the grid contains a single **glyph**, which is just a fancy way of referring to a letter, symbol, or number. Next, for each cell, the software will attempt to match the glyph to a set of all characters it recognizes. Finally, the individual characters would be combined back together into words, which optionally could be spell-checked against a dictionary in the document's language.

In this exercise, we'll assume that we have already developed the algorithm to partition the document into rectangular regions each consisting of a single character. We will also assume the document contains only alphabetic characters in English. Therefore, we'll simulate a process that involves matching glyphs to one of the 26 letters, A through Z.

Toward this end, we'll use a dataset donated to the UCI Machine Learning Data Repository (http://archive.ics.uci.edu/ml) by *W. Frey* and *D. J. Slate*. The dataset contains 20,000 examples of 26 English alphabet capital letters as printed using 20 different randomly reshaped and distorted black and white fonts.

>  For more information about these data, refer to: *Letter recognition using Holland-style adaptive classifiers, Machine Learning, Vol. 6,* pp. 161-182, by *W. Frey* and *D.J. Slate* (1991).

The following image, published by *Frey* and *Slate*, provides an example of some of the printed glyphs. Distorted in this way, the letters are challenging for a computer to identify, yet are easily recognized by a human being:

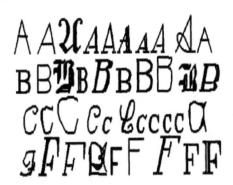

# Step 2 – exploring and preparing the data

According to the documentation provided by *Frey* and *Slate*, when the glyphs are scanned into the computer, they are converted into pixels and 16 statistical attributes are recorded.

The attributes measure such characteristics as the horizontal and vertical dimensions of the glyph, the proportion of black (versus white) pixels, and the average horizontal and vertical position of the pixels. Presumably, differences in the concentration of black pixels across various areas of the box should provide a way to differentiate among the 26 letters of the alphabet.

 To follow along with this example, download the `letterdata.csv` file from the Packt Publishing's website and save it to your R working directory.

Reading the data into R, we confirm that we have received the data with the 16 features that define each example of the letter class. As expected, `letter` has 26 levels:

```
> letters <- read.csv("letterdata.csv")
> str(letters)
'data.frame': 20000 obs. of 17 variables:
 $ letter: Factor w/ 26 levels "A","B","C","D",..
 $ xbox  : int  2 5 4 7 2 4 4 1 2 11 ...
 $ ybox  : int  8 12 11 11 1 11 2 1 2 15 ...
 $ width : int  3 3 6 6 3 5 5 3 4 13 ...
 $ height: int  5 7 8 6 1 8 4 2 4 9 ...
```

```
$ onpix : int   1 2 6 3 1 3 4 1 2 7 ...
$ xbar  : int   8 10 10 5 8 8 8 8 10 13 ...
$ ybar  : int   13 5 6 9 6 8 7 2 6 2 ...
$ x2bar : int   0 5 2 4 6 6 6 2 2 6 ...
$ y2bar : int   6 4 6 6 6 9 6 2 6 2 ...
$ xybar : int   6 13 10 4 6 5 7 8 12 12 ...
$ x2ybar: int   10 3 3 4 5 6 6 2 4 1 ...
$ xy2bar: int   8 9 7 10 9 6 6 8 8 9 ...
$ xedge : int   0 2 3 6 1 0 2 1 1 8 ...
$ xedgey: int   8 8 7 10 7 8 8 6 6 1 ...
$ yedge : int   0 4 3 2 5 9 7 2 1 1 ...
$ yedgex: int   8 10 9 8 10 7 10 7 7 8 ...
```

Recall that SVM learners require all features to be numeric, and moreover, that each feature is scaled to a fairly small interval. In this case, every feature is an integer, so we do not need to convert any factors into numbers. On the other hand, some of the ranges for these integer variables appear fairly wide. This would seem to suggest that we need to normalize or standardize the data. In fact, we can skip this step because the R package that we will use for fitting the SVM model will perform the rescaling for us automatically.

Given that the data preparation has been largely done for us, we can skip directly to the training and testing phases of the machine learning process. In previous analyses, we randomly divided the data between the training and testing sets. Although we could do so here, *Frey* and *Slate* have already randomized the data and therefore suggest using the first 16,000 records (80 percent) for building the model and the next 4,000 records (20 percent) for testing. Following their advice, we can create training and testing data frames as follows:

```
> letters_train <- letters[1:16000, ]
> letters_test  <- letters[16001:20000, ]
```

With our data ready to go, let's start building our classifier.

# Step 3 – training a model on the data

When it comes to fitting an SVM model in R, there are several outstanding packages to choose from. The `e1071` package from the Department of Statistics at the Vienna University of Technology (TU Wien) provides an R interface to the award winning LIBSVM library, a widely-used open source SVM program written in C++. If you are already familiar with LIBSVM, you may want to start here.

 For more information on LIBSVM, refer to the authors' website at:
`http://www.csie.ntu.edu.tw/~cjlin/libsvm/`

Similarly, if you're already invested in the SVMlight algorithm, the `klaR` package from the Department of Statistics at the Dortmund University of Technology (TU Dortmund) provides functions to work with this SVM implementation directly from R.

 For information on SVMlight, have a look at
`http://svmlight.joachims.org/.`

Finally, if you are starting from scratch, it is perhaps best to begin with the SVM functions in the `kernlab` package. An interesting advantage of this package is that it was developed natively in R rather than C or C++, which allows it to be easily customized; none of the internals are hidden behind the scenes. Perhaps even more importantly, unlike the other options, `kernlab` can be used with the `caret` package, which allows SVM models to be trained and evaluated using a variety of automated methods (covered in depth in *Chapter 11, Improving Model Performance*).

 For a more thorough introduction to `kernlab`, please refer to the author's paper at:
`http://www.jstatsoft.org/v11/i09/`

The syntax for training SVM classifiers with `kernlab` is as follows. If you do happen to be using one of the other packages, the commands are largely similar. By default, the `ksvm()` function uses the Gaussian RBF kernel, but a number of other options are provided.

---

**Support vector machine syntax**

using the `ksvm()` function in the `kernlab` package

**Building the model:**

```
m <- ksvm(target ~ predictors, data = mydata,
          kernel = "rbfdot", C = 1)
```

- **target** is the outcome in the **mydata** data frame to be modeled
- **predictors** is an R formula specifying the features in the **mydata** data frame to use for prediction
- **data** specifies the data frame in which the **target** and **predictors** variables can be found
- **kernel** specifies a nonlinear mapping such as **"rbfdot"** (radial basis), **"polydot"** (polynomial), **"tanhdot"** (hyperbolic tangentsigmoid), or **"vanilladot"** (linear)
- C is a number that specifies the cost of violating the constraints, i.e., how big of a penalty there is for the "soft margin." Larger values will result in narrower margins

The function will return a SVM object that can be used to make predictions.

**Making predictions:**

```
p <- predict(m, test, type = "response")
```

- m is a model trained by the `ksvm()` function
- **test** is a data frame containing test data with the same features as the training data used to build the classifier
- **type** specifies whether the predictions should be **"response"** (the predicted class) or **"probabilities"** (the predicted probability, one column per class level).

The function will return a vector (or matrix) of predicted classes (or probabilities) depending on the value of the type parameter.

**Example:**

```
letter_classifier <- ksvm(letter ~ ., data = letters_train,
                          kernel = "vanilladot")
letter_prediction <- predict(letter_classifier, letters_test)
```

---

To provide a baseline measure of SVM performance, let's begin by training a simple linear SVM classifier. If you haven't already, install the `kernlab` package to your library using the command `install.packages("kernlab")`. Then, we can call the `ksvm()` function on the training data and specify the linear (that is, `vanilla`) kernel using the `vanilladot` option as follows:

```
> library(kernlab)
> letter_classifier <- ksvm(letter ~ ., data = letters_train,
                            kernel = "vanilladot")
```

Depending on the performance of your computer, this operation may take some time to complete. When it finishes, type the name of the stored model to see some basic information about the training parameters and the fit of the model.

```
> letter_classifier
Support Vector Machine object of class "ksvm"

SV type: C-svc  (classification)
 parameter : cost C = 1

Linear (vanilla) kernel function.

Number of Support Vectors : 7037

Objective Function Value : -14.1746 -20.0072 -23.5628 -6.2009 -7.5524
-32.7694 -49.9786 -18.1824 -62.1111 -32.7284 -16.2209...

Training error : 0.130062
```

This information tells us very little about how well the model will perform in the real world. We'll need to examine its performance on the testing dataset to know whether it generalizes well to unseen data.

# Step 4 – evaluating model performance

The `predict()` function allows us to use the letter classification model to make predictions on the testing dataset:

```
> letter_predictions <- predict(letter_classifier, letters_test)
```

Because we didn't specify the `type` parameter, the default `type = "response"` was used. This returns a vector containing a predicted letter for each row of values in the testing data. Using the `head()` function, we can see that the first six predicted letters were U, N, V, X, N, and H:

```
> head(letter_predictions)
[1] U N V X N H
Levels: A B C D E F G H I J K L M N O P Q R S T U V W X Y Z
```

In order to examine how well our classifier performed, we need to compare the predicted letter to the true letter in the testing dataset. We'll use the `table()` function for this purpose (only a portion of the full table is shown here):

```
> table(letter_predictions, letters_test$letter)
letter_predictions   A    B    C    D    E
                A  144    0    0    0    0
                B    0  121    0    5    2
                C    0    0  120    0    4
                D    2    2    0  156    0
                E    0    0    5    0  127
```

The diagonal values of `144`, `121`, `120`, `156`, and `127` indicate the total number of records where the predicted letter matches the true value. Similarly, the number of mistakes is also listed. For example, the value of `5` in row `B` and column `D` indicates that there were five cases where the letter D was misidentified as a B.

Looking at each type of mistake individually may reveal some interesting patterns about the specific types of letters the model has trouble with, but this is also time consuming. We can simplify our evaluation by instead calculating the overall accuracy. This considers only whether the prediction was correct or incorrect and ignores the type of error.

The following command returns a vector of TRUE or FALSE values indicating whether the model's predicted letter agrees with (that is, matches) the actual letter in the test dataset:

```
> agreement <- letter_predictions == letters_test$letter
```

Using the `table()` function, we see that the classifier correctly identified the letter in 3,357 out of the 4,000 test records:

```
> table(agreement)
agreement
FALSE   TRUE
  643   3357
```

In percentage terms, the accuracy is about 84 percent:

```
> prop.table(table(agreement))
agreement
    FALSE      TRUE
  0.16075   0.83925
```

Note that when Frey and *Slate* published the dataset in 1991, they reported a recognition accuracy of about 80 percent. Using just a few lines of R code, we were able to surpass their result, although we also have the benefit of over two decades of additional machine learning research. With that in mind, it is likely that we are able to do even better.

# Step 5 – improving model performance

Our previous SVM model used the simple linear kernel function. By using a more complex kernel function, we can map the data into a higher dimensional space and potentially obtain a better model fit.

It can be challenging, however, to choose from the many different kernel functions. A popular convention is to begin with the Gaussian RBF kernel, which has been shown to perform well for many types of data. We can train an RBF-based SVM using the `ksvm()` function as shown here:

```
> letter_classifier_rbf <- ksvm(letter ~ ., data = letters_train,
                                kernel = "rbfdot")
```

From there, we make predictions as before:

```
> letter_predictions_rbf <- predict(letter_classifier_rbf,
                                letters_test)
```

Finally, we'll compare the accuracy to our linear SVM:

```
> agreement_rbf <- letter_predictions_rbf == letters_test$letter
> table(agreement_rbf)
agreement_rbf
FALSE   TRUE
  281   3719
> prop.table(table(agreement_rbf))
agreement_rbf
    FALSE      TRUE
  0.07025   0.92975
```

By simply changing the kernel function, we were able to increase the accuracy of our character recognition model from 84 percent to 93 percent. If this level of performance is still unsatisfactory for the OCR program, other kernels could be tested or the cost of the constraints parameter $c$ could be varied to modify the width of the decision boundary. As an exercise, you should experiment with these parameters to see how they impact the success of the final model.

## Summary

In this chapter, we examined two machine learning methods that offer a great deal of potential but are often overlooked due to their complexity. Hopefully you now realize that this reputation is at least somewhat undeserved. The basic concepts that drive ANNs and SVMs are fairly easy to understand.

On the other hand, because ANNs and SVMs have been around for many decades, each of them has numerous variations. This chapter just scratches the surface of what is possible with these methods. Yet by utilizing the terminology you learned here, you should be capable of picking up the nuances that distinguish the many advancements that are being developed every day.

Now that we have spent some time learning about many different types of predictive models from simple to sophisticated, in the next chapter we will begin to consider methods for other types of learning tasks. These unsupervised learning techniques will bring to light fascinating patterns within the data.

# 8
# Finding Patterns – Market Basket Analysis Using Association Rules

Think back to the last time you made an impulse purchase. Maybe you were waiting in the grocery store checkout lane and bought a pack of chewing gum or a candy bar. Perhaps on a late-night trip to a convenience store for diapers and formula you picked up a caffeinated beverage or a six-pack of beer. You might have even bought this book on a whim after it was recommended to you by your favorite bookseller. In any case, it is no coincidence that gum and candy are located in checkout lanes, convenience stores stock beer in addition to diapers, and the bookstore seems to know exactly which book will catch your interest.

In years past, these type of recommendation systems were based on the subjective experience of marketing professionals and inventory managers or buyers. More recently, machine learning has been used to learn these patterns of purchasing behavior. Barcode scanners, computerized inventory systems, and online shopping have led to a wealth of transactional data ripe for such data mining.

This chapter covers machine learning methods for identifying associations among items in transactional data—a practice commonly known as **market basket analysis** due to its widespread use among retail stores. By the time you finish, you will have learned:

- Methods for finding useful associations in large databases using simple statistical performance measures
- How to manage the peculiarities of working with transactional data
- The start-to-finish steps needed for using association rules to perform a market basket analysis on real-world data

To learn how machine learning locates interesting patterns, keep reading. From there, you'll have the foundations to try a market basket analysis of your own.

# Understanding association rules

The result of a market basket analysis is a set of **association rules** that specify patterns of relationships among items. A typical rule might be expressed in the form:

$$\{peanut\ butter,\ jelly\} \rightarrow \{bread\}$$

In plain language, this association rule states that if peanut butter and jelly are purchased, then bread is also likely to be purchased. In other words, "peanut butter and jelly imply bread." Groups of one or more items are surrounded by brackets to indicate that they form a set, or more specifically, an **itemset** that appears in the data with some regularity. Association rules are learned from subsets of itemsets. For example, the preceding rule was identified from the set of *{peanut butter, jelly, bread}*.

Developed in the context of Big Data and database science, association rules are not used for prediction, but rather for unsupervised knowledge discovery in large databases, unlike the classification and numeric prediction algorithms presented in previous chapters. Even so, you will find that association rule learners are closely related to and share many features of the classification rule learners presented in *Chapter 5, Divide and Conquer – Classification Using Decision Trees and Rules*.

Because association rule learners are unsupervised, there is no need for the algorithm to be trained; data does not need to be labeled ahead of time. The program is simply unleashed on a dataset in the hope that interesting associations are found. The downside, of course, is that there isn't an easy way to objectively measure the performance of a rule learner, aside from evaluating them for qualitative usefulness—typically an eyeball test of some sort.

Although association rules are most often used for market basket analysis, they are helpful for finding patterns in many different types of data. Other potential applications include:

- Searching for interesting and frequently occurring patterns of DNA and protein sequences in an analysis of cancer data
- Finding patterns of purchases or medical claims that occur in combination with fraudulent credit card or insurance use
- Identifying combinations of behavior that proceed customers dropping their cellular phone service or upgrading their cable television package

Association rule analysis is used to search for interesting connections among a very large number of variables. Human beings are capable of such insight quite intuitively, but it often takes expert-level knowledge or a great deal of experience to do what a rule-learning algorithm can do in minutes or even seconds. Additionally, some data is simply too large and complex for a human being to find the needle in the haystack.

# The Apriori algorithm for association rule learning

The complexity of transactional data is largely what makes association rule mining a challenging task for computers and humans alike. Transactional datasets are typically extremely large, both in terms of the number of transactions as well as the number of features (that is, items) that are monitored. Adding difficulty is the fact that the number of potential itemsets grows exponentially with the number of features; given $k$ items that can appear or not appear in a set, there are on the order of $2^k$ possible itemsets that must be searched for rules. A retailer that sells only 100 different items could have about $2^{100} = 1e+30$ itemsets that a learner would have to evaluate—a seemingly impossible task.

Rather than evaluate each of these itemsets one-by-one, a smarter rule-learning algorithm takes advantage of the fact that in reality, many of the potential combinations of items are rarely, if ever, found in practice. For instance, even if a store sells both automotive items and women's cosmetics, a set of *{motor oil, lipstick}* is likely to be extraordinarily uncommon. By ignoring these rare (and therefore perhaps less important) combinations, it is possible to limit the scope of the search for rules to a more manageable size.

Much work has been done to identify heuristic algorithms for reducing the number of itemsets to search. Perhaps the most-widely used approach for efficiently searching large databases for rules is known as **Apriori**. This algorithm was introduced in 1994 by *R. Agrawal* and *R. Srikant*, and has become somewhat synonymous with association rule learning since then. The name is derived from the fact that the algorithm utilizes a simple prior (that is, *a priori*) belief about the properties of frequent itemsets.

Before we get into that, it's worth noting that this algorithm, like all learning algorithms, is not without its strengths and weaknesses. Some of these are listed as follows:

| Strengths | Weaknesses |
|-----------|------------|
| • Is ideally suited for working with very large amounts of transactional data <br><br> • Results in rules that are easy to understand <br><br> • Useful for "data mining" and discovering unexpected knowledge in databases | • Not very helpful for small datasets <br><br> • Takes effort to separate the insight from the common sense <br><br> • Easy to draw spurious conclusions from random patterns |

As noted earlier, the Apriori algorithm employs a simple *a priori* belief as guideline for reducing the association rule search space: *all subsets of a frequent itemset must also be frequent*. This heuristic is known as the **Apriori property**. Using this astute observation, it is possible to dramatically limit the number of rules to search. For example, the set *{motor oil, lipstick}* can only be frequent if both *{motor oil}* and *{lipstick}* occur frequently as well. Consequently, if either motor oil or lipstick is infrequent, then any set containing these items can be excluded from the search.

For additional details on the Apriori algorithm, refer to: *Fast algorithms for mining association rule*, in *Proceedings of the 20th International Conference on Very Large Databases*, pp. 487-499, by *R. Agrawal*, and *R.Srikant*, (1994).

To see how this principle can be applied in a more realistic setting, let's consider a simple transaction database. The following table shows five completed transactions at an imaginary hospital's gift shop:

| Transaction number | Purchased items |
|--------------------|-----------------|
| 1 | *{flowers, get well card, soda}* |
| 2 | *{plush toy bear, flowers, balloons, candy bar}* |
| 3 | *{get well card, candy bar, flowers}* |
| 4 | *{plush toy bear, balloons, soda}* |
| 5 | *{flowers, get well card, soda}* |

By looking at the sets of purchases, one can infer that there are a couple of typical buying patterns. A person visiting a sick friend or family member tends to buy a get well card and balloons, while visitors to new mothers tend to buy plush toy bears and balloons. Such patterns are notable because they appear frequently enough to catch our interest; we simply apply a bit of logic and subject-matter experience to explain the rule.

In a similar fashion, the Apriori algorithm uses statistical measures of an itemset's "interestingness" to locate association rules in much larger transaction databases. In the sections that follow, we will discover how Apriori computes such measures of interest, and how they are combined with the Apriori property to reduce the number of rules to be learned.

# Measuring rule interest – support and confidence

Whether or not an association rule is deemed interesting is determined by two statistical measures: support and confidence. By providing minimum thresholds for each of these metrics and applying the Apriori principle, it is easy to drastically limit the number of rules reported, perhaps even to the point where only the obvious, or common sense, rules are identified. For this reason, it is important to carefully understand the types of rules that are excluded under these criteria.

The **support** of an itemset or rule measures how frequently it occurs in the data. For instance, the itemset *{get well card, flowers}* has support of *3 / 5 = 0.6* in the hospital gift shop data as explained previously. Similarly, the support for *{get well card} ->* *{flowers}* is also *0.6*. Support can be calculated for any itemset, or even a single item; for instance, the support for *{candy bar}* is *2/5 = 0.4*, since candy bars appear in 40 percent of purchases. A function defining support for itemset $X$ could be defined as:

$$support(X) = \frac{count(X)}{N}$$

Where $N$ is the number of transactions in the database and *count(X)* indicates the number of transactions the itemset $X$ appears in.

A rule's **confidence** is a measurement of its predictive power or accuracy. It is defined as the support of the itemset containing both $X$ and $Y$ divided by the support of the itemset containing only $X$:

$$confidence(X \rightarrow Y) = \frac{support(X,Y)}{support(X)}$$

Essentially, the confidence tells us the proportion of transactions where the presence of item or itemset $X$ results in the presence of item or itemset $Y$. Keep in mind that the confidence that $X$ leads to $Y$ is not the same as the confidence that $Y$ leads to $X$. For example, the confidence of *{flowers} -> {get well card}* is $0.6 / 0.8 = 0.75$. In comparison, the confidence of *{get well card} -> {flowers}* is $0.6 / 0.6 = 1.0$. This means that a purchase involving flowers results is accompanied by a purchase of a get well card 75 percent of the time, while a purchase of a get well card is associated with flowers 100 percent of the time. This information could be quite useful to the gift shop management.

You may have noticed similarities between support, confidence, and the Bayesian probability rules covered in *Chapter 4*, *Probabilistic Learning – Classification Using Naive Bayes*. In fact, *support(A, B)* is the same as $P(A \cap B)$ and *confidence(A → B)* is the same as $P(B \mid A)$. It is just the context that differs.

Rules like *{get well card} -> {flowers}* are known as **strong rules** because they have both high support and confidence. One way to find more strong rules would be to examine every possible combination of items in the gift shop, measure the support and confidence, and report back only those rules that meet certain levels of interest. However, as noted before, this strategy is generally not feasible for anything but the smallest of datasets.

In the next section, you will see how the Apriori algorithm uses minimum levels of support and confidence with the Apriori principle to quickly find strong rules by reducing the number of rules to a more manageable level.

# Building a set of rules with the Apriori principle

Recall that the Apriori principle states that all subsets of a frequent itemset must also be frequent. In other words, if *{A, B}* is frequent, then *{A}* and *{B}* both must be frequent. Recall also that by definition, the support metric indicates how frequently an itemset appears in the data. Therefore, if we know that *{A}* does not meet a desired support threshold, there is no reason to consider *{A, B}* or any itemset containing *{A}*; it cannot possibly be frequent.

The Apriori algorithm uses this logic to exclude potential association rules prior to actually evaluating them. The actual process of creating rules occurs in two phases:

- Identifying all itemsets that meet a minimum support threshold
- Creating rules from these itemsets that meet a minimum confidence threshold

The first phase occurs in multiple iterations. Each successive iteration involves evaluating the support of storing a set of increasingly large itemsets. For instance, iteration 1 involves evaluating the set of 1-item itemsets (1-itemsets), iteration 2 evaluates the 2-itemsets, and so on. The result of each iteration *i* is a set of all *i*-itemsets that meet the minimum support threshold.

All the itemsets from iteration *i* are combined in order to generate candidate itemsets for evaluation in iteration *i + 1*. But the Apriori principle can eliminate some of them even before the next round begins. If *{A}*, *{B}*, and *{C}* are frequent in iteration 1 while *{D}* is not frequent, then iteration 2 will consider only *{A, B}*, *{A, C}*, and *{B, C}*. Thus, the algorithm needs to evaluate only three itemsets rather than the six that would have been evaluated if sets containing *D* had not been eliminated *a priori*.

Continuing this thought, suppose during iteration 2 it is discovered that *{A, B}* and *{B, C}* are frequent, but *{A, C}* is not. Although iteration 3 would normally begin by evaluating the support for *{A, B, C}*, this step need not occur at all. Why not? The Apriori principle states that *{A, B, C}* cannot possibly be frequent, since the subset *{A, C}* is not. Therefore, having generated no new itemsets in iteration 3, the algorithm may stop.

At this point, the second phase of the Apriori algorithm may begin. Given the set of frequent itemsets, association rules are generated from all possible subsets. For instance, *{A, B}* would result in candidate rules for *{A} -> {B}* and *{B} -> {A}*. These are evaluated against a minimum confidence threshold, and any rules that do not meet the desired confidence level are eliminated.

# Example – identifying frequently purchased groceries with association rules

As noted in this chapter's introduction, market basket analysis is used behind the scenes for the recommendation systems used in many brick-and-mortar and online retailers. The learned association rules indicate combinations of items that are often purchased together in a set. The acquired knowledge might provide insight into new ways for a grocery chain to optimize the inventory, advertise promotions, or organize the physical layout of the store. For instance, if shoppers frequently purchase coffee or orange juice with a breakfast pastry, then it may be possible to increase profit by relocating pastries closer to the coffee and juice.

In this tutorial, we will perform a market basket analysis of transactional data from a grocery store. However, the techniques could be applied to many different types of problems, from movie recommendations, to dating sites, to finding dangerous interactions among medications. In doing so, we will see how the Apriori algorithm is able to efficiently evaluate a potentially massive set of association rules.

# Step 1 – collecting data

Our market basket analysis will utilize purchase data from one month of operation at a real-world grocery store. The data contain 9,835 transactions, or about 327 transactions per day (roughly 30 transactions per hour in a 12 hour business day), suggesting that the retailer is not particularly large, nor is it particularly small.

The data used here was adapted from the `Groceries` dataset in the Apriori R package. For more information on datasets, see: *Implications of probabilistic data modeling for mining association rules*, in *Studies in Classification, Data Analysis, and Knowledge Organization: from Data and Information Analysis to Knowledge Engineering*, pp. 598–605, by *M. Hahsler, K. Hornik, and T. Reutterer*, (2006).

In a typical grocery store, there is a huge variety of items. There might be five brands of milk, a dozen different types of laundry detergent, and three brands of coffee. Given the moderate size of the retailer, we will assume that they are not terribly concerned with finding rules that apply only to a specific brand of milk or detergent. With this in mind, all brand names can be removed from the purchases. This reduces the number of groceries to a more manageable 169 types, using broad categories such as chicken, frozen meals, margarine, and soda.

If you hope to identify highly-specific association rules—like whether customers prefer grape or strawberry jelly with their peanut butter—you will need a tremendous amount of transactional data. Massive chain retailers use databases of many millions of transactions in order to find associations among particular brands, colors, or flavors of items.

Do you have any guesses about which types of items might be purchased together? Will wine and cheese be a common pairing? Bread and butter? Tea and honey? Let's dig into this data and see if we can confirm our guesses.

# Step 2 – exploring and preparing the data

Unlike the datasets we've used previously, transactional data is stored in a slightly different format. Most of our prior analyses utilized data in the form of a matrix where rows indicated example instances and columns indicated features. Given the structure of the matrix format, all examples are required to have exactly the same set of features.

In comparison, transactional data is more free-form. As usual, each row in the data specifies a single example—in this case, a transaction. However, rather than having a set number of features, each record comprises a comma-separated list of any number of items, from one to many. In essence, the features may differ from example to example.

 To follow along with this analysis, download the groceries.csv file from the Packt Publishing's website and save to your R working directory.

The first five rows of the raw grocery.csv data are as follows:

```
citrus fruit,semi-finished bread,margarine,ready soups
tropical fruit,yogurt,coffee
whole milk
pip fruit,yogurt,cream cheese,meat spreads
other vegetables,whole milk,condensed milk,long life bakery product
```

These lines indicate five separate grocery store transactions. The first transaction included four items: citrus fruit, semi-finished bread, margarine, and ready soups. In comparison, the third transaction included only one item, whole milk.

Suppose we tried to load the data using the read.csv() function as we had done in prior analyses. R would happily comply and read the data into a matrix form as follows:

| | V1 | V2 | V3 | V4 |
|---|---|---|---|---|
| 1 | citrus fruit | semi-finished bread | margarine | ready soups |
| 2 | tropical fruit | yogurt | coffee | |
| 3 | whole milk | | | |
| 4 | pip fruit | yogurt | cream cheese | meat spreads |
| 5 | other vegetables | whole milk | condensed milk | long life bakery product |

You will notice that R created four variables to store the items in the transactional data: V1, V2, V3, and V4. Although it was nice of R to do this, if we use the data like this, we will encounter problems later on. First, R chose to create four variables because the first line had exactly four comma-separated values. However, we know that grocery purchases can contain more than four items; these transactions unfortunately will be broken across multiple rows in the matrix. We could try to remedy this by putting the transaction with the largest number of items at the top of the file, but this ignores another, more problematic issue.

The problem is due to the fact that by structuring the data this way, R has constructed a set of features that record not just the items in the transactions, but also the order they appear. If we imagine our learning algorithm as an attempt to find a relationship among V1, V2, V3, and V4, then whole milk in V1 might be treated differently than whole milk appearing in V2. Instead, we need a dataset that does not treat a transaction as a set of positions to be filled (or not filled) with specific items, but rather as a market basket that either contains or does not contain each particular item.

## Data preparation – creating a sparse matrix for transaction data

The solution to this problem utilizes a data structure called a **sparse matrix**. (You may recall that we used a sparse matrix for processing text data in *Chapter 4, Probabilistic Learning – Classification Using Naive Bayes*.) Similar to the preceding dataset, each row in the sparse matrix indicates a transaction. However, there is a column (that is, feature) for every item that could possibly appear in someone's shopping bag. Since there are 169 different items in our grocery store data, our sparse matrix will contain 169 columns.

Why not just store this as a data frame like we have done in most of our analyses? The reason is that as additional transactions and items are added, a conventional data structure quickly becomes too large to fit into memory. Even with the relatively small transactional dataset used here, the matrix contains nearly 1.7 million cells, most of which contain zeros (hence the name "sparse" matrix). Since there is no benefit to storing all these zero values, sparse matrix does not actually store the full matrix in memory; it only stores the cells that are occupied by an item. This allows the structure to be more memory efficient than an equivalently sized matrix or data frame.

In order to create the sparse matrix data structure from transactional data, we can use functionality provided by the association rules (arules) package. Install and load the package using the commands install.packages("arules") and library(arules).

For more information on the `arules` package, refer to: *arules -- A computational environment for mining association rules and frequent item sets, Journal of Statistical Software Vol. 14* by M. Hahsler, B. Gruen, and K. Hornik, (2005).

The `read.transactions()` function we'll employ is similar to `read.csv()` except that it results in a sparse matrix suitable for transactional data. The parameter `sep=","` specifies that items in the input file are separated by a comma. To read the `groceries.csv` data into a sparse matrix named `groceries`, type:

```
> groceries <- read.transactions("groceries.csv", sep = ",")
```

To see some basic information about the `groceries` dataset we just created, use the `summary()` function on the object:

```
> summary(groceries)
transactions as itemMatrix in sparse format with
 9835 rows (elements/itemsets/transactions) and
 169 columns (items) and a density of 0.02609146
```

The first block of information in the output (as shown previously) provides a summary of the sparse matrix we created. `9835 rows` refer to the store transactions, and `169 columns` are features for each of the 169 different items that might appear in someone's grocery basket. Each cell in the matrix is a `1` if the item was purchased for the corresponding transaction, or `0` otherwise.

The **density** value of `0.02609146` (2.6 percent) refers to the proportion of non-zero matrix cells. Since there are *9835 * 169 = 1662115* positions in the matrix, we can calculate that a total of *1662115 * 0.02609146 = 43367* items were purchased during the store's 30 days of operation (assuming no duplicate items were purchased). With an additional step, we can determine that the average transaction contained *43367 / 9835 = 4.409* different grocery items. (Of course, if we look a little further down the output, we'll see that this has already been computed for us.)

The next block of `summary()` output (shown as follows) lists the items that were most commonly found in the transactional data. Since *2513 / 9835 = 0.2555*, we can determine that whole milk appeared in 25.6 percent of transactions. Other vegetables, rolls/buns, soda, and yogurt round out the list of other common items.

```
most frequent items:
   whole milk  other vegetables      rolls/buns
         2513              1903            1809
         soda            yogurt         (Other)
         1715              1372           34055
```

Finally, we are presented with a set of statistics about the size of transactions. A total of 2,159 transactions contained only a single item, while one transaction had 32 items. The first quartile and median purchase size are 2 and 3 items respectively, implying that 25 percent of transactions contained two or fewer items and about half contained more or less than three items. The mean of 4.409 matches the value we calculated manually.

```
element (itemset/transaction) length distribution:
sizes
   1    2    3    4    5    6    7    8    9   10   11   12
2159 1643 1299 1005  855  645  545  438  350  246  182  117
  13   14   15   16   17   18   19   20   21   22   23   24
  78   77   55   46   29   14   14    9   11    4    6    1
  26   27   28   29   32
   1    1    1    3    1


   Min. 1st Qu.  Median    Mean 3rd Qu.    Max.
  1.000   2.000   3.000   4.409   6.000  32.000
```

The `arules` package includes some useful features for examining transaction data. To look at the contents of the sparse matrix, use the `inspect()` function in combination with vector operators. The first five transactions can be viewed as follows:

```
> inspect(groceries[1:5])
  items
1 {citrus fruit,
   margarine,
   ready soups,
   semi-finished bread}
2 {coffee,
   tropical fruit,
   yogurt}
3 {whole milk}
4 {cream cheese,
   meat spreads,
   pip fruit,
   yogurt}
5 {condensed milk,
   long life bakery product,
   other vegetables,
   whole milk}
```

These transactions match our look at the original CSV file. To examine a particular item (that is, a column of data), it is possible use the `row, column` matrix notion. Using this with the `itemFrequency()` function allows us to see the proportion of transactions that contain the item. This allows us, for instance, to view the support level for the first three items in the grocery data:

```
> itemFrequency(groceries[, 1:3])
abrasive cleaner artif. sweetener    baby cosmetics
    0.0035587189     0.0032536858      0.0006100661
```

Notice that the items in the sparse matrix are sorted in columns by alphabetical order. Abrasive cleaner and artificial sweeteners are found in about 0.3 percent of transactions while baby cosmetics are found in about 0.06 percent.

## Visualizing item support – item frequency plots

To present these statistics visually, use the `itemFrequencyPlot()` function. This allows you to produce at a bar chart depicting the proportion of transactions containing certain items. Since transactional data contains a very large number of items, you will often need to limit those appearing in the plot in order to produce a legible chart.

If you would like to require those items to appear in a minimum proportion of transactions, use `itemFrequencyPlot()` with the `support` parameter:

```
> itemFrequencyPlot(groceries, support = 0.1)
```

As shown in the following plot, this results in a histogram showing the eight items in the `groceries` data with at least 10 percent support:

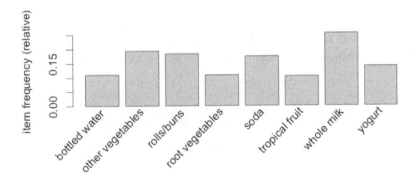

If you would rather limit the plot to a specific number of items, the `topN` parameter can be used with `itemFrequencyPlot()`:

```
> itemFrequencyPlot(groceries, topN = 20)
```

The histogram is then sorted by decreasing support, as shown in the following diagram for the top 20 items in the `groceries` data:

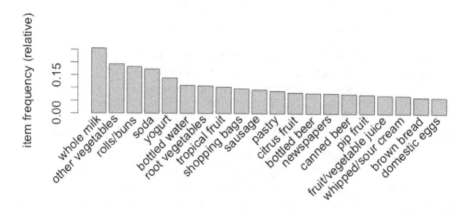

# Visualizing transaction data – plotting the sparse matrix

In addition to looking at items, it's also possible to visualize the entire sparse matrix. To do so, use the `image()` function. The sparse matrix for the first five transactions is as follows:

```
> image(groceries[1:5])
```

The resulting diagram depicts a matrix with five rows and 169 columns, indicating the five transactions and 169 possible items we requested. Cells in the matrix are filled with black for transactions (rows) where the item (column) was purchased.

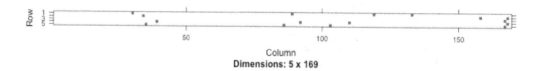

Although the figure is small and may be slightly hard to read, you can see that the first, fourth, and fifth transactions contained four items each, since their rows have four cells filled in. You can also see that rows three, five, two, and four have an item in common (on the right side of the diagram).

This visualization can be a useful tool for exploring the data. For one, it may help with the identification of potential data issues. Columns that are filled all the way down could indicate items that are purchased in every transaction—a problem that could arise, perhaps, if a retailer's name or identification number was inadvertently included in the transaction dataset.

Additionally, patterns in the diagram may help reveal interesting segments of transactions or items, particularly if the data is sorted in interesting ways. For example, if the transactions are sorted by date, patterns in the black dots could reveal seasonal effects in the number or types of items people purchase. Perhaps around Christmas or Hanukkah, toys are more common; around Halloween, perhaps candy becomes popular. This type of visualization could be especially powerful if the items were also sorted into categories. In most cases, however, the plot will look fairly random, like static on a television screen.

Keep in mind that this visualization will not be as useful for extremely large transaction databases because the cells will be too small to discern. Still, by combining it with the `sample()` function, you can view the sparse matrix for a randomly sampled set of transactions. Here is what a random selection of 100 transactions looks like:

```
> image(sample(groceries, 100))
```

This creates a matrix diagram with 100 rows and the same 169 columns, as follows:

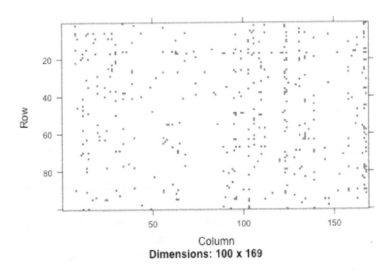

Dimensions: 100 x 169

A few columns seem fairly heavily populated, indicating some very popular items at the store, but overall, the distribution of dots seems fairly random. Given nothing else of note, let's continue with our analysis.

# Step 3 – training a model on the data

With data preparation taken care of, we can now work at finding the associations among shopping cart items. We will use an implementation of the Apriori algorithm in the `arules` package we've been using for exploring and preparing the groceries data. You'll need to install and load this package if you have not done so already. The following table shows the syntax for creating sets of rules with the `apriori()` function:

---

**Association rule syntax**

using the `apriori()` function in the `arules` package

**Finding association rules:**

```
myrules <- apriori(data = mydata,
                   parameter = list(support = 0.1,
                                    confidence = 0.8
                                    minlen = 1))
```

- `data` is a sparse item matrix holding transactional data
- `support` specifies the minimum required rule support
- `confidence` specifies the minimum required rule confidence
- `minlen` specifies the minimum required rule items

The function will return a rules object storing all rules that meet the minimum criteria.

**Examining association rules:**

```
inspect(myrules)
```

- `myrules` is a set of association rules from the `apriori()` function

This will output the association rules to the screen. Vector operators can be used on myrules to choose a specific rule or rules to view.

**Example:**

```
concrete_model <- neuralnet(strength ~ cement + slag + ash,
                            data = concrete)
model_results <- compute(concrete_model, concrete_data)
strength_predictions <- model_results$net.result
```

---

Although running the `apriori()` function is straightforward, there can sometimes be a fair amount of trial and error when finding support and confidence parameters to produce a reasonable number of association rules. If you set these levels too high, then you might find no rules or rules that are too generic to be very useful. On the other hand, a threshold too low might result in an unwieldy number of rules, or worse, the operation might take a very long time or run out of memory during the learning phase.

In this case, if we attempt to use the default settings of `support` = `0.1` and `confidence` = `0.8`, we end up with a set of zero rules:

```
> apriori (groceries)
set of 0 rules
```

Obviously, we need to widen the search a bit.

> If you think about it, this outcome should not have been terribly surprising. With the default support of 0.1, this means that in order to generate a rule, an item must have appeared in at least 0.1 * 9385 = 938.5 transactions. Since only eight items appeared this frequently in our data, it's no wonder we didn't find any rules.

One way to approach the problem of setting support is to think about the minimum number of transactions you would need before you would consider a pattern interesting. For instance, you could argue that if an item is purchased twice a day (about 60 times) then it may be worth taking a look at. From there, it is possible to calculate the support level needed to find only rules matching at least that many transactions. Since 60 out of 9,835 equals 0.006, we'll try setting the support there first.

Setting the minimum confidence involves a tricky balance. On one hand, if confidence is too low, then we might be overwhelmed with a large number of unreliable rules—such as dozens of rules indicating items commonly purchased with batteries. How would we know where to target our advertising budget then? On the other hand, if we set confidence too high, then we will be limited to rules that are obvious or inevitable—like the fact that a smoke detector is always purchased in combination with batteries. In this case, moving the smoke detectors closer to the batteries is unlikely to generate additional revenue, since the two items were already almost always purchased together.

> The appropriate minimum confidence level depends a great deal on the goals of your analysis. If you start with conservative values, you can always reduce them to broaden the search if you aren't finding actionable intelligence.

We'll start with a confidence threshold of 0.25, which means that in order to be included in the results, the rule has to be correct at least 25 percent of the time. This will eliminate the most unreliable rules while allowing some room for us to modify behavior with targeted promotions.

We are now ready to generate some rules. In addition to the minimum support and confidence, it is helpful to set `minlen = 2` to eliminate rules that contain fewer than two items. This prevents uninteresting rules from being created simply because the item is purchased frequently, for instance, `{} => whole milk`. This rule meets the minimum support and confidence because whole milk is purchased in over 25 percent of transactions, but it isn't a very actionable rule.

The full command for finding a set of association rules using the Apriori algorithm is as follows:

```
> groceryrules <- apriori(groceries, parameter = list(support =
                    0.006, confidence = 0.25, minlen = 2))
```

This saves our rules in a `rules` object, which we can peek into by typing its name:

```
> groceryrules
set of 463 rules
```

Our `groceryrules` object contains a set of 463 association rules. To determine whether any of them are useful, we'll have to dig deeper.

# Step 4 – evaluating model performance

To obtain a high-level overview of the association rules, we can use `summary()` as follows. The rule length distribution tells us how many rules have each count of items. In our rule set, 150 rules have only two items, while 297 have three, and 16 have four. The summary statistics associated with this distribution are also given:

```
> summary(groceryrules)
set of 463 rules

rule length distribution (lhs + rhs):sizes
  2   3   4
150 297  16


   Min. 1st Qu.  Median   Mean 3rd Qu.    Max.
  2.000   2.000   3.000  2.711   3.000   4.000
```

> As noted in the previous output, the size of the rule is calculated as the total of both the left-hand side (`lhs`) and right-hand side (`rhs`) of the rule. This means that a rule like `{bread} => {butter}` is two items and `{peanut butter, jelly} => {bread}` is three.

Next, we see summary statistics for the rule quality measures: support, confidence, and lift. Support and confidence should not be very surprising, since we used these as selection criteria for the rules. However, we might be alarmed if most or all of the rules were very near the minimum thresholds—not the case here.

```
summary of quality measures:
      support            confidence          lift
 Min.   :0.006101   Min.    :0.2500   Min.    :0.9932
 1st Qu.:0.007117   1st Qu.:0.2971    1st Qu.:1.6229
 Median :0.008744   Median :0.3554    Median :1.9332
 Mean   :0.011539   Mean    :0.3786   Mean    :2.0351
 3rd Qu.:0.012303   3rd Qu.:0.4495    3rd Qu.:2.3565
 Max.   :0.074835   Max.    :0.6600   Max.    :3.9565
```

The third column, `lift`, is a metric we have not considered yet. It is a measure of how much more likely one item is to be purchased relative to its typical purchase rate, given that you know another item has been purchased. This is defined by the following equation:

$$\text{lift}(X \rightarrow Y) = \frac{\text{confidence}(X \rightarrow Y)}{\text{support}(Y)}$$

 Unlike confidence where the item order matters, `lift(X -> Y)` is the same as `lift(Y -> X)`.

For example, suppose at a grocery store, most people purchase milk and bread. By chance alone, we would expect to find many transactions with both milk and bread. However, if `lift(milk -> bread)` is greater than 1, this implies that the two items are found together more often than one would expect by chance. A large lift value is therefore a strong indicator that a rule is important, and reflects a true connection between the items.

In the final section of the `summary()` output, we receive mining information, telling us about how the rules were chosen. Here, we see that the `groceries` data, which contained 9,835 transactions, was used to construct rules with a minimum support of 0.006 and minimum confidence of 0.25:

```
mining info:
      data ntransactions support confidence
 groceries          9835   0.006       0.25
```

We can take a look at specific rules using the `inspect()` function. For instance, the first three rules in the `groceryrules` object can be viewed as follows:

```
> inspect(groceryrules[1:3])
```

```
  lhs                 rhs                 support     confidence    lift
1 {potted plants} => {whole milk}      0.006914082  0.4000000  1.565460
2 {pasta}         => {whole milk}      0.006100661  0.4054054  1.586614
3 {herbs}         => {root vegetables} 0.007015760  0.4312500  3.956477
```

The columns indicated by `lhs` and `rhs` refer to the **left-hand side (LHS)** and **right-hand side (RHS)** of the rule. The LHS is the condition that needs to be met in order to trigger the rule, and the RHS is the expected result of meeting that condition.

The first rule can be read in plain language as "if a customer buys potted plants, they will also buy whole milk." With a `support` of about 0.007 and `confidence` of 0.400, we can determine that this rule covers about 0.7 percent of transactions, and is correct in 40 percent of purchases involving potted plants. The `lift` value tells us how much more likely a customer is to buy whole milk relative to the average customer, given that he or she bought a potted plant. Since we know that about 25.6 percent of customers bought whole milk (the support) while 40 percent of customers buying a potted plant bought whole milk (the confidence), we can compute the lift as *0.40 / 0.256 = 1.56*, which matches the value shown. (Note that the column labeled `support` indicates the support for the rule, not the support for the `lhs` or `rhs`).

In spite of the fact that the confidence and lift are high, does {`potted plants`} `=>` {`whole milk`} seem like a very useful rule? Probably not—there doesn't seem to be a logical reason why someone would be more likely to buy milk with a potted plant. Yet our data suggests otherwise. How can we make sense of this fact?

A common approach is to take the result of learning association rules and divide them into three categories:

- Actionable
- Trivial
- Inexplicable

Obviously, the goal of a market basket analysis is to find **actionable** associations, or rules that provide a clear and useful insight. Some rules are clear, others are useful; it is less common to find a combination of both of these factors.

**Trivial** rules include any rules that are so obvious that they are not worth mentioning—they are clear, but not useful. Suppose you were a marketing consultant being paid large sums of money to identify new opportunities for cross-promoting items. If you report the finding that {diapers} => {formula}, you probably won't be invited back for another consulting job.

> Trivial rules can also sneak in disguised as more interesting results. For instance, say you found an association between a particular brand of children's cereal and a certain DVD movie. This finding is not very interesting if the movie's main character is on the front of the cereal box.

Rules are **inexplicable** if the connection between the items is so unclear that figuring out how to use the information for action would require additional research. The rule may simply be a random pattern in the data, for instance, a rule stating that {pickles} => {chocolate ice cream} may be due to a single customer whose pregnant wife had regular cravings for strange combinations of foods.

The best rules are the hidden gems—those undiscovered insights into patterns that seem obvious once discovered. Given enough time, one could evaluate each of the 463 rules to find the gems. However, we (the one performing the market basket analysis) may not be the best judge of whether a rule is actionable, trivial, or inexplicable. In the next section, we'll improve the utility of our work by employing methods for sorting and sharing the learned rules so that the most interesting results might float to the top.

# Step 5 – improving model performance

Subject matter experts may be able to identify useful rules very quickly, but it would be a poor use of their time to ask them to evaluate hundreds or thousands of rules. Therefore, it's useful to be able to sort the rules according to different criteria and get them out of R into a form that can be shared with marketing teams and examined in more depth. In this way, we can improve the performance of our rules by making the results more actionable.

## Sorting the set of association rules

Depending upon the objectives of the market basket analysis, the most useful rules might be those with the highest support, confidence, or lift. The arules package includes a sort() function that can be used to reorder the list of rules so that those with the highest or lowest values of the quality measure come first.

To reorder the `groceryrules`, we can apply `sort()` while specifying a `by` parameter of `"support"`, `"confidence"`, or `"lift"`. By combining the sort with vector operators, we can obtain a specific number of interesting rules. For instance, the best five rules according to the lift statistic can be examined using the following command:

```
> inspect(sort(groceryrules, by = "lift")[1:5])
```

This will look like the following screenshot:

```
  lhs                       rhs                         support confidence     lift
1 {herbs}                => {root vegetables}     0.007015760  0.4312500 3.956477
2 {berries}              => {whipped/sour cream}  0.009049314  0.2721713 3.796886
3 {other vegetables,
   tropical fruit,
   whole milk}           => {root vegetables}     0.007015760  0.4107143 3.768074
4 {beef,
   other vegetables}     => {root vegetables}     0.007930859  0.4020619 3.688692
5 {other vegetables,
   tropical fruit}       => {pip fruit}           0.009456024  0.2634561 3.482649
```

These appear to be more interesting rules than the ones we looked at previously. The first rule, with a lift of `3.956477`, implies that people who buy herbs are nearly four times more likely to buy root vegetables than the typical customer — perhaps for a stew of some sort? Rule two is also interesting. Whipped cream is over three times more likely to be found in a shopping cart with berries versus other carts, suggesting perhaps a dessert pairing?

 By default, the sort order is decreasing, meaning the largest values come first. To reverse this order, add an additional parameter `decreasing = FALSE`.

# Taking subsets of association rules

Suppose that given the preceding rule, the marketing team is excited about the possibilities of creating an advertisement to promote berries, which are now in season. Before finalizing the campaign, however, they ask you to investigate whether berries are often purchased with other items. To answer this question, we'll need to find all the rules that include berries in some form.

The `subset()` function provides a method for searching for subsets of transactions, items, or rules. To use it to find any rules with `berries` appearing in the rule, use the following command. This will store the rules in a new object titled `berryrules`:

```
> berryrules <- subset(groceryrules, items %in% "berries")
```

We can then inspect the rules as we had done with the larger set:

```
> inspect(berryrules)
```

The result is the folllowing set of rules:

```
  lhs            rhs                     support confidence      lift
1 {berries} => {whipped/sour cream} 0.009049314  0.2721713 3.796886
2 {berries} => {yogurt}             0.010574479  0.3180428 2.279848
3 {berries} => {other vegetables}   0.010269446  0.3088685 1.596280
4 {berries} => {whole milk}         0.011794611  0.3547401 1.388328
```

There are four rules involving berries, two of which seem to be interesting enough to call actionable. In addition to whipped cream, berries are also purchased frequently with yogurt—a pairing that could serve well for breakfast or lunch as well as dessert.

The subset() function is very powerful. The criteria for choosing the subset can be defined with several keywords and operators:

- The keyword items, explained previously, matches an item appearing anywhere in the rule. To limit the subset to where the match occurs only on the left or right-hand side, use lhs and rhs instead.

- The operator %in% means that at least one of the items must be found in the list you defined. If you wanted any rules matching either berries or yogurt, you could write items %in% c("berries", "yogurt").

- Additional operators are available for partial matching (%pin%) and complete matching (%ain%). Partial matching allows you to find both citrus fruit and tropical fruit using one search: items %pin% "fruit". Complete matching requires that all listed items are present. For instance, items %ain% c("berries", "yogurt") finds only rules with both berries and yogurt.

- Subsets can also be limited by support, confidence, or lift. For instance, confidence > 0.50 would limit you to rules with confidence greater than 50 percent.

- Matching criteria can be combined with standard R logical operators such as and (&), or (|), and not (!).

Using these options, you can limit the selection of rules to be as specific or general as you would like.

# Saving association rules to a file or data frame

To share the results of your market basket analysis, you can save the rules to a CSV file with the write() function. This will produce a CSV file that can be used in most spreadsheet programs including Microsoft Excel:

```
> write(groceryrules, file = "groceryrules.csv",
      sep = ",", quote = TRUE, row.names = FALSE)
```

Sometimes it is also convenient to convert the rules to an R data frame. This can be accomplished easily using the `as()` function, as follows:

```
> groceryrules_df <- as(groceryrules, "data.frame")
```

This creates a data frame with the rules in factor format, and numeric vectors for `support`, `confidence`, and `lift`:

```
> str(groceryrules_df)
'data.frame': 463 obs. of 4 variables:
 $ rules      : Factor w/ 463 levels "{baking powder} => {other
vegetables}",..: 340 302 207 206 208 341 402 21 139 140 ...
 $ support    : num  0.00691 0.0061 0.00702 0.00773 0.00773 ...
 $ confidence: num  0.4 0.405 0.431 0.475 0.475 ...
 $ lift       : num  1.57 1.59 3.96 2.45 1.86 ...
```

You might choose to do this if you want to perform additional processing on the rules or need to export them to another database.

# Summary

Association rules are one solution to the Big Data problem. As an unsupervised learning algorithm, they are capable of extracting knowledge from large databases without any prior knowledge of what patterns to seek. The catch is that it takes some effort to reduce the wealth of information into a smaller and more manageable set of results. The Apriori algorithm, which we studied in this chapter, does so by setting minimum thresholds of interestingness, and reporting only the associations meeting these criteria.

We put the Apriori algorithm to work while performing a market basket analysis for a month's worth of transactions at a moderately-sized supermarket. Even in this small example, a wealth of associations were identified. Among these, we noted several patterns that may be useful for future marketing campaigns. The same methods applied here are used at much larger retailers on databases many times this size.

In the next chapter, we will examine another unsupervised learning algorithm, which just like association rules, is intended to find patterns within data. But unlike association rules that seek patterns within the features, the methods in the next chapter are concerned with finding connections among the examples.

# 9
# Finding Groups of Data – Clustering with k-means

Have you ever spent time watching large crowds? As a sociologist, this was one of my favorite pastimes. I would choose a busy location, such as a coffee shop, library, or cafeteria, and observe the masses of people for interesting patterns of behavior. The goal was to look for details that reveal an insight into how people, as a general rule, relate to each other and their environment.

The more you perform such observational research, the more you may see recurring personalities. Perhaps a certain type of person, identified by a freshly-pressed suit and a briefcase, comes to typify the white-collar business executive. A twenty-something wearing tight jeans, a flannel shirt, and sunglasses might fall into the hipster category, while a woman unloading children from a minivan could be labeled a soccer mom.

Of course, these types of stereotypes are dangerous to apply to individuals—no two people are exactly alike. Used in aggregate, however, the labels may reflect some underlying pattern of similarity among the individuals falling within the group.

This chapter describes methods to address the machine learning task of clustering, which involves finding natural groupings of data. As you will see, clustering works in a process very similar to the observational research described just now. Along the way, you will learn:

- Ways clustering tasks differ from the classification tasks we've examined previously and how clustering defines groups

- The basic methods used by k-means, a classic and easy-to-understand clustering algorithm

- How to apply clustering to a real-world task of identifying marketing segments within teenage social media users

Before jumping into action, let's begin by taking an in-depth look at exactly what clustering entails.

# Understanding clustering

Clustering is an unsupervised machine learning task that automatically divides the data into **clusters**, or groupings of similar items. It does this without having been told what the groups should look like ahead of time. As we may not even know what we're looking for, clustering is used for knowledge discovery rather than prediction. It provides an insight into the natural groupings found within data.

Without advance knowledge of what comprises a cluster, how could a computer possibly know where one group ends and another begins? The answer is simple. Clustering is guided by the principle that records inside a cluster should be very similar to each other, but very different from those outside. As you will see later, the definition of similarity might vary across applications, but the basic idea is always the same: group the data such that related elements are placed together.

The resulting clusters can then be used for action. For instance, you might find clustering methods employed in applications such as:

- Segmenting customers into groups with similar demographics or buying patterns for targeted marketing campaigns and/or detailed analysis of purchasing behavior by subgroup

- Detecting anomalous behavior, such as unauthorized intrusions into computer networks, by identifying patterns of use falling outside known clusters

- Simplifying extremely large datasets by grouping a large number of features with similar values into a much smaller number of homogeneous categories

Overall, clustering is useful whenever diverse and varied data can be exemplified by a much smaller number of groups. It results in meaningful and actionable structures within data that reduce complexity and provide insight into patterns of relationships.

# Clustering as a machine learning task

Clustering is somewhat different from the classification, numeric prediction, and pattern detection tasks we've examined so far. In each of these cases, the result is a model that relates features to an outcome or features to other features; the model identifies patterns within data. In contrast, clustering creates new data. Unlabeled examples are given a cluster label and inferred entirely from the relationships within the data. For this reason, you will sometimes see the clustering task referred to as **unsupervised classification** because, in a sense, this is classifying unlabeled examples.

The catch is that the class labels obtained from an unsupervised classifier are without intrinsic meaning. Clustering will tell you which groups of examples are closely related—for instance, it might return groups A, B, and C—but it's up to you to apply an actionable and meaningful label. To see how this impacts the clustering task, let's consider a hypothetical example.

Suppose you were organizing a conference on the topic of data science. To facilitate professional networking and collaboration, you planned to seat people in groups according to one of three research specialties: computer and/or database science, math and statistics, and machine learning. Unfortunately, after sending out the conference invitations, you realize that you had forgotten to include a survey asking the discipline the attendee would prefer to be seated with.

In a stroke of brilliance, you realize that you might be able to infer each scholar's research specialty by examining his or her publication history. Toward this end, you begin collecting data on the number of articles each attendee published in computer science-related journals and the number of articles published in math or statistics-related journals. Using the data collected for several scholars, you create a scatterplot:

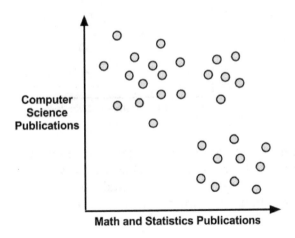

As expected, there seems to be a pattern here. We might guess that the upper-left corner, which represents people with many computer science publications but few articles on math, could be a cluster of computer scientists. Following this logic, the lower-right corner might be a group of mathematicians. Similarly, the upper-right corner, those with both math and computer science experience, may be machine learning experts.

Rather than defining the group boundaries subjectively, it would be nice to use machine learning to define them objectively. Given the axis-parallel splits in the previous figure, this problem seems like an obvious application for decision trees as described in *Chapter 5, Divide and Conquer – Classification Using Decision Trees and Rules*. This would provide us with a clean rule like "if the scholar has few math publications, then he/she is a computer science expert." Unfortunately, there's a problem with this plan. As we do not know the true class value for each point, we cannot deploy supervised learning algorithms.

Our groupings were formed visually; we simply identified clusters as closely grouped data points. In spite of the seemingly obvious groupings, we have no way to know whether they are truly homogeneous without personally asking each scholar about his/her academic specialty. The labels we applied required us to make qualitative, presumptive judgments about the types of people that would fall into the group. For this reason, you might imagine the cluster labels in uncertain terms, as follows:

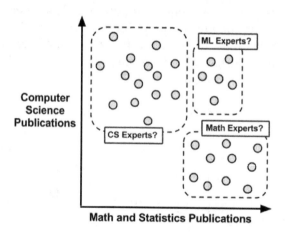

Clustering algorithms use a process very similar to what we did by visually inspecting the scatterplot. Using a measure of how closely the examples are related, they can be assigned to homogeneous groups. In the next section, we'll start looking at how clustering algorithms are implemented.

This example highlights an interesting application of clustering. If you begin with unlabeled data, you can use clustering to create class labels. From there, you could apply a supervised learner such as decision trees to find the most important predictors of these classes. This is called **semi-supervised learning**.

# The k-means algorithm for clustering

The **k-means algorithm** is perhaps the most often used clustering method. Having been studied for several decades, it serves as the foundation for many more sophisticated clustering techniques. If you understand the simple principles it uses, you will have the knowledge needed to understand nearly any clustering algorithm in use today. Many such methods are listed on the following site, the CRAN task view for clustering:

```
http://cran.r-project.org/web/views/Cluster.html
```

As k-means has evolved over time, there are many implementations of the algorithm. One popular approach is described in *A k-means clustering algorithm* in *Applied Statistics, Vol. 28,* pp. 100-108, by *Hartigan, J.A.* and *Wong, M.A.* (1979).

Even though clustering methods have advanced since the inception of k-means, that does not suggest that it is obsolete. In fact, the method may be more popular now than ever. The following table lists some reasons why k-means is still used widely:

| Strengths | Weaknesses |
|---|---|
| • Uses simple principles for identifying clusters which can be explained in non-statistical terms | • It is less sophisticated than more recent clustering algorithms |
| • It is highly flexible and can be adapted to address nearly all of its shortcomings with simple adjustments | • Because it uses an element of random chance, it is not guaranteed to find the optimal set of clusters |
| • It is fairly efficient and performs well at dividing the data into useful clusters | • Requires a reasonable guess as to how many clusters naturally exist in the data |

If the name k-means sounds familiar to you, you may be recalling the kNN algorithm presented in *Chapter 3, Lazy Learning – Classification Using Nearest Neighbors*. As you will soon see, k-means shares more in common with k-nearest neighbors than just the letter k.

The k-means algorithm involves assigning each of the $n$ examples to one of the $k$ clusters, where $k$ is a number that has been defined ahead of time. The goal is to minimize the differences within each cluster and maximize the differences between clusters.

Unless $k$ and $n$ are extremely small, it is not feasible to compute the optimal clusters across all possible combinations of examples. Instead, the algorithm uses a heuristic process that finds locally optimal solutions. Putting it simply, this means that it starts with an initial guess for the cluster assignments then modifies the assignments slightly to see if the changes improve the homogeneity within the clusters.

We will cover the process in depth shortly, but the algorithm essentially involves two phases. First, it assigns examples to an initial set of $k$ clusters. Then, it updates the assignments by adjusting the cluster boundaries according to the examples that currently fall into the cluster. The process of updating and assigning occurs several times until making changes no longer improves the cluster fit. At this point, the process stops and the clusters are finalized.

 Due to the heuristic nature of k-means, you may end up with somewhat different final results by making only slight changes to the starting conditions. If the results vary dramatically, this could indicate a problem. For instance, the data may not have natural groupings or the value of $k$ has been poorly chosen. For this reason, it's a good idea to try a cluster analysis more than once to test the robustness of your findings.

To see how the process of assigning and updating works in practice, let's revisit the example data for the data science conference. Though this is a simple example, it will illustrate the basics of how k-means operates under the hood.

# Using distance to assign and update clusters

As with kNN, k-means treats feature values as coordinates in a multidimensional feature space. For the conference data, there are only two features, so we can represent the feature space as a two-dimensional scatterplot, as depicted previously.

The k-means algorithm begins by choosing *k* points in the feature space to serve as the cluster centers. These centers are the catalyst that spurs the remaining examples to fall into place. Often, the points are chosen by selecting *k* random examples from the training dataset. Because we hope to identify three clusters, *k* = 3 points are selected. These points are indicated by the star, triangle, and diamond in the following figure:

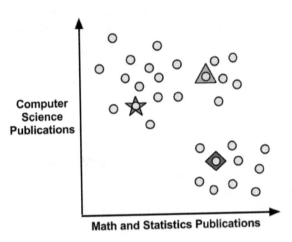

There are several other ways to choose the initial cluster centers. One option is to choose random values occurring anywhere in the feature space (rather than only selecting among values observed in the data). Another option is to skip this step altogether; by randomly assigning each example to a cluster, the algorithm can jump ahead immediately to the update phase. Each of these approaches adds a particular bias to the final set of clusters, which you may be able to use to tailor your results.

After choosing the initial cluster centers, the other examples are assigned to the cluster center that is most similar or nearest according to the distance function. You will remember that we studied distance functions while learning about kNN. Traditionally, k-means uses Euclidean distance, but Manhattan distance or Minkowski distance are also sometimes used.

Recall that if *n* indicates the number of features, the formula for Euclidean distance between example *x* and example *y* is as follows:

$$\text{dist}(x, y) = \sqrt{\sum_{i=1}^{n} (x_i - y_i)^2}$$

For instance, if we are comparing an event guest with five computer science publications and one math publication to a guest with zero computer science papers and two math papers, we could compute this in R as:

```
> sqrt((5 - 0)^2 + (1 - 2)^2)
[1] 5.09902
```

Using this distance function, we find the distance between each example and each cluster center. The example is then assigned to the nearest cluster center.

> Keep in mind that because we are using distance calculations, all data need to be numeric, and the values should be normalized to a standard range ahead of time. The methods presented in *Chapter 3, Lazy Learning – Classification Using Nearest Neighbors*, will prove helpful here.

As shown in the following figure, the three cluster centers partition the examples into three segments labeled Cluster A, B, and C. The dashed lines indicate the boundaries for the **Voronoi diagram** created by the cluster centers. A Voronoi diagram indicates the areas that are closer to one cluster center than any other; the vertex where all three boundaries meet is the maximal distance from all three cluster centers. Using these boundaries, we can easily see the regions claimed by each of the initial k-means seeds:

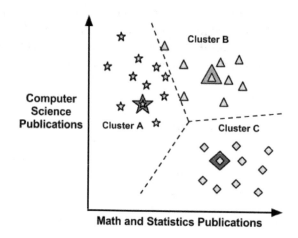

Now that the initial assignment phase has been completed, the k-means algorithm proceeds to the update phase. The first step of updating the clusters involves shifting the initial centers to a new location, known as the **centroid**, which is calculated as the mean value of the points currently assigned to that cluster. The following figure illustrates how the cluster centers shift to the new centroids:

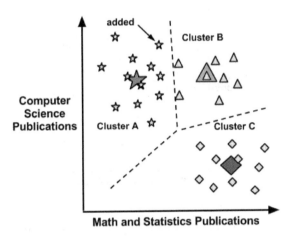

Because the cluster boundaries have been adjusted according to the repositioned centers, Cluster A is able to claim an additional example from Cluster B (indicated by an arrow). Because of this reassignment, the k-means algorithm will continue through another update phase. After recalculating the centroids for the clusters, the figure looks like this:

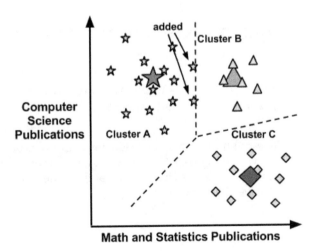

Two more points have been reassigned from Cluster B to Cluster A during this phase, as they are now closer to the centroid for A than B. This leads to another update as shown:

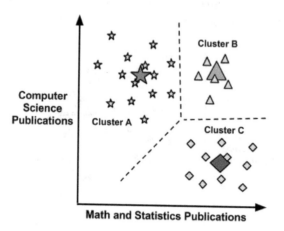

As no points were reassigned during this phase, the k-means algorithm stops. The cluster assignments are now final.

The learned clusters can be reported in one of the two ways. First, you can simply report the cluster assignments for each example. Alternatively, you could report the coordinates of the cluster centroids after the final update. Given either reporting method, you are able to define the cluster boundaries by calculating the centroids and/or assigning each example to its nearest cluster.

## Choosing the appropriate number of clusters

In the introduction to k-means, we learned that the algorithm can be sensitive to randomly chosen cluster centers. Indeed, if we had selected a different combination of three starting points in the previous example, we may have found clusters that split the data differently from what we had expected.

 Choosing the number of clusters requires a delicate balance. Setting the *k* to be very large will improve the homogeneity of the clusters, and at the same time, it risks overfitting the data.

Ideally, you will have some *a priori* knowledge (that is, a prior belief) about the true groupings, and you can begin applying k-means using this information. For instance, if you were clustering movies, you might begin by setting $k$ equal to the number of genres considered for the Academy Awards. In the data science conference seating problem that we worked through previously, $k$ might reflect the number of academic fields of study that were invited.

Sometimes the number of clusters is dictated by business requirements or the motivation for the analysis. For example, the number of tables in the meeting hall could dictate how many groups of people should be created from the data science attendee list. Extending this idea to a business case, if the marketing department only has resources to create three distinct advertising campaigns, it might make sense to set $k = 3$ to assign all the potential customers to one of the three appeals.

Without any *a priori* knowledge at all, one rule of thumb suggests setting $k$ equal to the square root of $(n / 2)$, where $n$ is the number of examples in the dataset. However, this rule of thumb is likely to result in an unwieldy number of clusters for large datasets. Luckily, there are other statistical methods that can assist in finding a suitable k-means cluster set.

A technique known as the **elbow method** attempts to gauge how the homogeneity or heterogeneity within the clusters changes for various values of $k$. As illustrated in the following figures, the homogeneity within clusters is expected to increase as additional clusters are added; similarly, heterogeneity will also continue to decrease with more clusters. Because you could continue to see improvements until each example is in its own cluster, the goal is not to maximize homogeneity or minimize heterogeneity, but rather to find $k$ such that there are diminishing returns beyond that point. This value of $k$ is known as the **elbow point**, because it looks like an elbow.

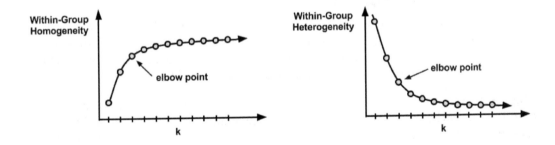

There are numerous statistics to measure homogeneity and heterogeneity within clusters that can be used with the elbow method (have a look at the following information box). Still, in practice, it is not always feasible to iteratively test a large number of $k$ values. This is in part because clustering large datasets can be fairly time consuming; clustering the data repeatedly is even worse. Regardless, applications requiring the exact optimal set of clusters are fairly rare. In most clustering applications, it suffices to choose a $k$ based on convenience rather than strict performance requirements.

 For a very thorough review of the vast assortment of measures of cluster performance, have a look at *On clustering validation techniques, Journal of Intelligent Information Systems Vol. 17*, pp. 107-145, by *M. Halkidi, Y. Batistakis,* and *M. Vazirgiannis* (2001).

The process of setting $k$ itself can sometimes lead to interesting insights. By observing how the characteristics of the clusters change as $k$ is varied, one might infer where the data have naturally defined boundaries. Groups that are more tightly clustered will change little, while less homogeneous groups will form and disband over time.

In general, it may be wise to spend little time worrying about getting $k$ exactly right. The next example will demonstrate how even a tiny bit of subject-matter knowledge borrowed from a Hollywood film can be used to set $k$ such that actionable and interesting clusters are found. Because clustering is unsupervised, the task is really about what you make of it—the insights you take away from the algorithm's findings.

# Finding teen market segments using k-means clustering

Interacting with friends on social networking sites such as Facebook and MySpace has become a rite of passage for teenagers around the world. Having a relatively large amount of disposable income, these adolescents are a coveted demographic for businesses hoping to sell snacks, beverages, electronics, and hygiene products.

The many millions of teenage consumers browsing such sites have attracted the attention of marketers struggling to find an edge in an increasingly competitive market. One way to gain this edge is to identify segments of teenagers who share similar tastes, so that clients can avoid targeting advertisements to teens with no interest in the product being sold. For instance, a sports beverage is likely to be a difficult sell to teens with no interest in sports.

Given the text of teenagers' **Social Networking Service** (**SNS**) pages, we can identify groups that share common interests such as sports, religion, or music. Clustering can automate the process of discovering the natural segments in this population. However, it will be up to us to decide whether or not the clusters are interesting and how we can use them for advertising. Let's try this process from start to finish.

# Step 1 – collecting data

For this analysis, we will be using a dataset representing a random sample of 30,000 U.S. high school students who had profiles on a well-known SNS in 2006. To protect the users' anonymity, the SNS will remain unnamed. However, at the time the data was collected, the SNS was a popular web destination for U.S. teenagers. Therefore, it is reasonable to assume that the profiles represent a fairly wide cross section of American adolescents in 2006.

This dataset was compiled while conducting sociological research on teenage identities at the University of Notre Dame. If you use the data for research purposes, please cite this book chapter. The full dataset is available at the Packt Publishing's website with the filename snsdata.csv. To follow along interactively, this chapter assumes you have saved this file to your R working directory.

The data was sampled evenly across four high school graduation years (2006 through 2009) representing the senior, junior, sophomore, and freshman classes at the time of data collection. Using an automated web crawler, the full text of the SNS profiles were downloaded, and each teen's gender, age, and number of SNS friends was recorded.

A text mining tool was used to divide the remaining SNS page content into words. From the top 500 words appearing across all pages, 36 words were chosen to represent five categories of interests, namely extracurricular activities, fashion, religion, romance, and antisocial behavior. The 36 words include terms such as football, sexy, kissed, bible, shopping, death, and drugs. The final dataset indicates, for each person, how many times each word appeared in the person's SNS profile.

# Step 2 – exploring and preparing the data

We can use the default settings of read.csv() to load the data into a data frame:

```
> teens <- read.csv("snsdata.csv")
```

Let's also take a quick look at the specifics of the data. The first several lines of the `str()` output are as follows:

```
> str(teens)
'data.frame':   30000 obs. of  40 variables:
 $ gradyear    : int  2006 2006 2006 2006 2006 2006 2006 2006 ...
 $ gender      : Factor w/ 2 levels "F","M": 2 1 2 1 NA 1 1 2 ...
 $ age         : num  19 18.8 18.3 18.9 19 ...
 $ friends     : int  7 0 69 0 10 142 72 17 52 39 ...
 $ basketball  : int  0 0 0 0 0 0 0 0 0 0 ...
```

As we had expected, the data include 30,000 teenagers with four variables indicating personal characteristics and 36 words indicating interests.

Do you notice anything strange around the `gender` variable? If you were looking carefully, you may have noticed NA, which is out of place compared to the 1 and 2 values. This is R's way of telling us that the record has a **missing value**—we do not know the person's gender. Until now, we haven't dealt with missing data, but it can be a significant problem for many types of analyses.

Let's see how substantial this problem is. One option is to use the `table()` command, as follows:

```
> table(teens$gender)

    F     M
22054  5222
```

Although this tells us how many F and M values are present, the `table()` function excluded the NA values rather than treating it as a separate value. To include the NA values (if there are any), we simply need to add an additional parameter:

```
> table(teens$gender, useNA = "ifany")

    F     M  <NA>
22054  5222  2724
```

Here, we see that 2,724 records (9 percent) have missing gender data. Interestingly, there are over four times as many females as males in the SNS data, suggesting that males are not as inclined to use SNSs as females.

If you examine the other variables in the `teens` data frame, you will find that besides the `gender` variable, only `age` has missing values. For numeric data, the `summary()` command tells us the number of missing NA values:

```
> summary(teens$age)
   Min. 1st Qu.  Median    Mean 3rd Qu.    Max.    NA's
  3.086  16.310  17.290  17.990  18.260 106.900    5086
```

A total of 5,086 records (17 percent) have missing values for age. Also concerning is the fact that the minimum and maximum values seem to be the suspect; it is unlikely that a 3 year old or a 106 year old is attending high school. To ensure that these extreme values don't cause problems for the analysis, we'll need to clean them up before moving on.

A reasonable range of ages for high school students includes those who are at least 13 years old and not yet 20 years old. Any age value falling outside this range will be treated the same as missing data—we cannot trust the age provided. To recode the age variable, we can use the ifelse() function, assigning teen$age the value of teen$age if the age is at least 13 and less than 20 years; otherwise, it will receive the value NA:

```
> teens$age <- ifelse(teens$age >= 13 & teens$age < 20,
                       teens$age, NA)
```

By rechecking the summary() output, we see that the age range now follows a distribution that looks much more like an actual high school:

```
> summary(teens$age)
   Min. 1st Qu.  Median    Mean 3rd Qu.    Max.    NA's
  13.03   16.30   17.26   17.25   18.22   20.00    5523
```

Unfortunately, now we've created an even larger missing data problem. We'll need to find a way to deal with these values before continuing with our analysis.

# Data preparation – dummy coding missing values

An easy solution for handling missing values is to exclude any record with a missing value. However, if you think through the implications of this practice, you might think twice before doing so. (I said it was easy, I never said it was a good idea!) The problem with this approach is that even if the missingness is not extensive, you can very quickly start to exclude large portions of data.

For example, suppose that in our data the people with NA values for gender are completely different from those with missing age data. This would imply that by excluding those missing either gender or age, you would exclude 26 percent, which is an addition of 9 percent and 17 percent (9% + 17% = 26%), of your data, or over 7,500 records. And this is for missing data on only two variables! The larger the number of missing values present in a dataset, the more likely it is that any given record will be excluded. Fairly soon, you will be left with a tiny subset of data, or worse, the remaining records will be systematically different or non-representative of the full population.

An alternative solution for categorical data like gender is to treat a missing value as a separate category. For instance, rather than limiting to female and male, we can add an additional level for "unknown." At the same time, we should also utilize dummy coding, which is covered in more depth in *Chapter 3, Lazy Learning - Classification Using Nearest Neighbors,* to transform the nominal gender variable into a numeric form that can be used for distance calculations.

Dummy coding involves creating a separate binary 1 or 0 valued dummy variable for each level of a nominal feature except one, which is held out to serve as the reference group. The reason one category can be excluded is because it can be inferred from the other categories. For instance, if someone is not female and not unknown gender, they must be male. Therefore, we need to only create dummy variables for female and unknown gender:

```
> teens$female <- ifelse(teens$gender == "F" &
                         !is.na(teens$gender), 1, 0)
> teens$no_gender <- ifelse(is.na(teens$gender), 1, 0)
```

The first statement assigns `teens$female` the value 1 if gender is equal to F and the gender is not equal to NA, otherwise it assigns the value 0. The `is.na()` function tests whether gender is equal to NA. If `is.na()` returns TRUE, then the `teens$no_gender` variable is assigned 1, otherwise it is assigned the value 0. To confirm that we did the work correctly, let's compare our constructed dummy variables to the original `gender` variable:

```
> table(teens$gender, useNA = "ifany")
    F     M   <NA>
22054  5222  2724
> table(teens$female, useNA = "ifany")
    0     1
 7946 22054
> table(teens$no_gender, useNA = "ifany")
    0     1
27276  2724
```

The number of 1 values for `teens$female` and `teens$no_gender` matches the number of F and NA values in the initial coding, so we should be able to trust our work.

# Data preparation – imputing missing values

Next, let's eliminate the 5,523 missing values on age. As age is numeric, it doesn't make sense to create an additional category for unknown values—where would you rank "unknown" relative to the other age values? Instead, we'll use a different strategy known as **imputation**, which involves filling in the missing data with a guess as to what the true value really is.

Can you think of a way we might be able to use the SNS data to make an educated individual guess about a teenager's age? If you thought about using the graduation year, you've got the right idea. Most people in a graduation cohort were born within a single calendar year. If we can figure out the typical age for each cohort, then we would have a fairly reasonable estimate of the age of a student in that graduation year.

One way to find a typical value is by calculating the average, or mean, value. If we try to apply the `mean()` function as we have done for previous analyses, there's a problem:

```
> mean(teens$age)

[1] NA
```

The issue is that the mean value is undefined for a vector containing missing data. As age contains missing values, `mean(teens$age)` returns a missing value. We can correct this by adding an additional parameter to remove the missing values before calculating the mean:

```
> mean(teens$age, na.rm = TRUE)
[1] 17.25243
```

This reveals that the average student in our data is about 17 years old. This only gets us part of the way there; we actually need the average age for each graduation year. You might be tempted to calculate the mean four times, but one of the benefits of R is that there's usually a more efficient way. In this case, the `aggregate()` function is the tool for the job. It computes statistics for subgroups of data. Here, it calculates the mean age for levels of `gradyear` after removing the `NA` values:

```
> aggregate(data = teens, age ~ gradyear, mean, na.rm = TRUE)
  gradyear      age
1     2006 18.65586
2     2007 17.70617
3     2008 16.76770
4     2009 15.81957
```

The mean age differs by roughly one year per change in graduation year. This is not at all surprising, but a helpful finding for confirming our data is reasonable.

The `aggregate()` output is in a data frame which is human-readable but requires extra work to merge back onto our original data. As an alternative, we can use the `ave()` function, which returns a vector with the group means repeated such that the result is equal in length to the original vector:

```
> ave_age <- ave(teens$age, teens$gradyear, FUN =
                function(x) mean(x, na.rm = TRUE))
```

To impute these means onto the missing values, we need one more `ifelse()` call to use the `ave_age` value only if the original age value was NA:

```
> teens$age <- ifelse(is.na(teens$age), ave_age, teens$age)
```

The `summary()` results show that the missing values have now been eliminated:

```
> summary(teens$age)
   Min. 1st Qu.  Median    Mean 3rd Qu.    Max.
  13.03   16.28   17.24   17.24   18.21   20.00
```

With the data ready for analysis, we are ready to dive into the interesting part of this project. Let's see if our efforts have paid off.

# Step 3 – training a model on the data

To cluster the teenagers into marketing segments, we will use an implementation of k-means in the `stats` package, which should be included in your R installation by default. If by chance you do not have this package, you can install it as you would any other package and load it using the `library(stats)` command. Although there is no shortage of k-means functions available in various R packages, the `kmeans()` function in the `stats` package is widely used and provides a vanilla implementation of the algorithm.

---

**Clustering syntax**

using the kmeans() function in the stats package

**Finding clusters:**

```
myclusters <- kmeans(mydata, k)
```

- mydata is a matrix or data frame with the examples to be clustered
- k specifies the desired number of clusters

The function will return a cluster object that stores information about the clusters.

**Examining clusters:**

- myclusters$cluster is a vector of cluster assignments from the kmeans() function
- myclusters$centers is a matrix indicating the mean values for each feature and cluster combination
- myclusters$size lists the number of examples assigned to each cluster

**Example:**

```
teen_clusters <- kmeans(teens, 5)
teens$cluster_id <- teen_clusters$cluster
```

---

The kmeans() function requires a data frame containing only numeric data and a parameter specifying the desired number of clusters. If you have these two things ready, the actual process of building the model is simple. The trouble is that choosing the right combination of data and clusters can be a bit of an art; sometimes a great deal of trial and error is involved.

We'll start our cluster analysis by considering only the 36 features that represent the number of times various interests appeared on the SNS profiles of teens. For convenience, let's make a data frame containing only these features:

```
> interests <- teens[5:40]
```

A common practice employed prior to any analysis using distance calculations is to normalize or z-score standardize the features such that each utilizes the same scale. By doing so, you can avoid a problem in which some features come to dominate solely because they tend to have larger values than others.

If you recall from *Chapter 3, Lazy Learning – Classification Using Nearest Neighbors*, z-score standardization rescales features such that they have a mean of zero and a standard deviation of one. This transformation changes the interpretation of the feature in a way that may be useful here. Specifically, if someone mentions football a total of 3 times on their profile, without additional information, we have no idea whether this implies they like football more or less than their peers. On the other hand, if the z-score value is 3, we know that that they mentioned football many more times than the average teenager.

To apply z-score standardization to the interests data frame, we can use the `scale()` function with `lapply()`, as follows:

```
> interests_z <- as.data.frame(lapply(interests, scale))
```

 As `lapply()` returns a matrix, it must be coaxed back to data frame form using the `as.data.frame()` function.

Our last decision involves deciding how many clusters to use for segmenting the data. If we use too many clusters, we may find them too specific to be useful; conversely, choosing too few may result in heterogeneous groupings. You should feel comfortable experimenting with the values of *k*. If you don't like the result, you can easily try another value and start over.

 Choosing the number of clusters is easier if you are familiar with the analysis population. Having a hunch about the true number of natural groupings can save you some trial and error.

To help us predict the number of clusters in the data, I'll defer to one of my favorite films, the 1985 *John Hughes* coming-of-age comedy, *The Breakfast Club*. The high-school-age characters in this movie are identified in terms of five stereotypes: a Brain, an Athlete, a Basket Case, a Princess, and a Criminal. Given that these identities prevail throughout popular teen fiction, five seems like a reasonable starting point for *k*.

To divide `teens` into five clusters, we can use the following command:

```
teen_clusters <- kmeans(interests_z, 5)
```

This saves the result of the k-means clustering in an object named `teen_clusters`.

# Step 4 – evaluating model performance

Evaluating the results of clustering can be somewhat subjective. Ultimately, the success or failure of the model hinges on whether the clusters are useful for their intended purpose. As the goal of this analysis was to identify clusters of teenagers with similar interests for marketing purposes, we will largely measure our success in qualitative terms. For other clustering applications, more quantitative measures of success may be needed.

One of the most basic ways to evaluate the utility of a set of clusters is to examine the number of examples falling in each of the groups. If the groups are too large or too small, then they are not likely to be very useful. To obtain the size of the `kmeans()` clusters, use the `teen_clusters$size` component as follows:

```
> teen_clusters$size
[1]   3376   601  1036  3279 21708
```

Here we see the five clusters we requested. The smallest is 601 teenagers (2 percent) while the largest is 21,708 (72 percent). Although the large cluster is slightly concerning, without examining it more carefully, we will not know whether it indicates a problem or not. In good news, we did not find any clusters containing only a single person, which can happen occasionally with k-means.

> Given the random nature of k-means, do not be alarmed if your results differ from those shown here. Instead, consider it as an opportunity to apply your analytic skills to the unique result you obtained!

For a more in-depth look at the clusters, we can examine the coordinates of the cluster centroids using the `teen_clusters$centers` component, which is as follows for the first eight features:

```
> teen_clusters$centers
    basketball     football      soccer     softball
1   0.02447191   0.10550409   0.04357739  -0.02411100
2  -0.09442631   0.06927662  -0.09956009  -0.04697009
3   0.37669577   0.38401287   0.14650286   0.15136541
4   1.12232737   1.03625113   0.53915320   0.87051183
5  -0.18869703  -0.19317864  -0.09245172  -0.13366478
```

| | volleyball | swimming | cheerleading | baseball |
|---|---|---|---|---|
| 1 | 0.04803724 | 0.31298181 | 0.63868578 | -0.03875155 |
| 2 | -0.07806216 | 0.04578401 | -0.10703701 | -0.11182941 |
| 3 | 0.09157715 | 0.24413955 | 0.18678448 | 0.28545186 |
| 4 | 0.78664128 | 0.11992750 | 0.01325191 | 0.86858544 |
| 5 | -0.12850235 | -0.07970857 | -0.10728007 | -0.13570044 |

The rows of the output (numbered 1 to 5) refer to the clusters, while the numbers in the output indicate the average value for the interest listed at the top of the column. As the values are z-score standardized, negative values are below the overall mean for all students and positive values are above the mean.

Given only these eight interests, we can already infer some characteristics of the clusters. Cluster 4 is substantially above the mean on all the listed sports except cheerleading, suggesting that this group may include athletes. Cluster 1 includes the most mentions of cheerleading and is above the average in football interest.

By continuing to examine the clusters in this way, it's possible to construct a table listing the dominant interests of each of the groups. In the following figure, each cluster is shown with the features that most distinguish it from the other clusters. Interestingly, Cluster 5 is distinguished by the fact that it is unremarkable; its members had lower-than-average levels of interest in every measured activity. It is also the single largest group in terms of the number of members. One potential explanation is that these users created a profile on the website but never posted any interests.

| Cluster 1 (N = 3,376) | Cluster 2 (N = 601) | Cluster 3 (N = 1,036) | Cluster 4 (N = 3,279) | Cluster 5 (N = 21,708) |
|---|---|---|---|---|
| swimming<br>cheerleading<br>cute<br>sexy<br>hot<br>dance<br>dress<br>hair<br>mall<br>hollister<br>abercrombie<br>shopping<br>clothes | band<br>marching<br>music<br>rock | sports<br>sex<br>sexy<br>hot<br>kissed<br>dance<br>music<br>band<br>die<br>death<br>drunk<br>drugs | basketball<br>football<br>soccer<br>softball<br>volleyball<br>baseball<br>sports<br>god<br>church<br>Jesus<br>bible | ??? |
| Princesses | Brains | Criminals | Athletes | Basket Cases |

When sharing the results of a segmentation analysis, it is often helpful to apply informative labels that capture the essence of the groups like *The Breakfast Club* typology applied here. The risk in adding such labels is that they can obscure the groups' nuances by stereotyping the group members.

Given the table, a marketing executive would have a clear depiction of five types of teenage visitors to the social networking website. Based on these profiles, the executive could sell targeted advertising impressions to businesses with products relevant to one or more of the clusters. In the next section, we will see how the cluster labels can be applied back to the original population for such uses.

# Step 5 – improving model performance

Because clustering creates new information, the performance of a clustering algorithm depends at least somewhat on both the quality of the clusters themselves as well as what you do with that information. In the prior section, we already demonstrated that the five clusters provided useful and novel insights into the interests of teenagers; by that measure, the algorithm appears to be performing quite well. Therefore, we can now focus our effort on turning these insights into action.

We'll begin by applying the clusters back onto the full dataset. When the k-means clusters were created, the function stored a component called `teens$cluster` that contains the cluster assignments for all 30,000 people in the sample. We can add this as a column on the `teens` data frame using the following command:

```
> teens$cluster <- teen_clusters$cluster
```

Given this information, we can determine which cluster each user has been assigned to. For example, here's the personal information for the first five users in the SNS data:

```
> teens[1:5, c("cluster", "gender", "age", "friends")]
```

| | cluster | gender | age | friends |
|---|---|---|---|---|
| 1 | 5 | M | 18.982 | 7 |
| 2 | 1 | F | 18.801 | 0 |
| 3 | 5 | M | 18.335 | 69 |
| 4 | 5 | F | 18.875 | 0 |
| 5 | 3 | <NA> | 18.995 | 10 |

Using the `aggregate()` function we had used before, we can also look at the demographic characteristics of the clusters overall. The mean age does not vary much by cluster, although we wouldn't necessarily think that interests should systematically differ by age. This is depicted as follows:

```
> aggregate(data = teens, age ~ cluster, mean)
  cluster       age
1       1 16.99678
2       2 17.38765
3       3 17.10022
4       4 17.09634
5       5 17.29841
```

On the other hand, there are some notable differences in the proportion of females by cluster. This is an interesting finding, as we didn't use gender data to create the clusters, yet the clusters are still very predictive of gender:

```
> aggregate(data = teens, female ~ cluster, mean)
  cluster    female
1       1 0.8942536
2       2 0.7221298
3       3 0.8001931
4       4 0.7130223
5       5 0.7109821
```

Recall that overall about 74 percent of the SNS users are female. Cluster 1, the so-called Princesses, is nearly 90 percent female, while Clusters 2, 4, and 5 are only about 70 percent female.

Given our success in predicting gender, you might also suspect that the clusters are predictive of the number of friends the users have. This hypothesis seems to be supported by the data, which is as follows:

```
> aggregate(data = teens, friends ~ cluster, mean)
  cluster  friends
1       1 38.74733
2       2 32.88186
3       3 30.57046
4       4 36.14029
5       5 27.85314
```

On an average, Princesses have the most friends (38.7), followed by Athletes (36.1) and Brains (32.9). Criminals have only 30.6 while Basket Cases have 27.9. As with gender, this finding is remarkable given that we did not use the number of friends as an input to the clustering algorithm.

The association among group membership, gender, and number of friends suggests that the clusters can be useful predictors. Validating their predictive ability in this way may make the clusters an easier sell when they are pitched to the marketing team, ultimately improving the performance of the algorithm.

# Summary

Our findings support the popular adage that "birds of a feather flock together." By using machine learning methods to cluster teenagers with others who have similar interests, we were able to develop a typology of teen identities that was predictive of personal characteristics like gender and the number of friends. These same methods can be applied to other contexts with similar results.

This chapter covered only the fundamentals of clustering. As a very mature machine learning method, there are a myriad of variants to the k-means algorithm as well as many alternatives which bring unique biases and heuristics to the task. Based on what you have learned here, you will be able to understand and apply other clustering methods to new problems.

In the next chapter, we will begin to look at methods for measuring the success of a learning algorithm that are applicable across many machine learning tasks. While our process has always devoted some effort to evaluating the success of learning, in order to obtain the highest degree of performance, it is crucial to be able to define and measure it in the strictest terms.

# 10
# Evaluating Model Performance

Many years ago, when only the wealthy could afford access to education, tests and examinations were not used to evaluate the students. Instead, they were used to judge the teachers—parents wanted to know whether their children were learning enough to justify the instructors' wages. Obviously, this practice has changed over the years. Now, such evaluations are used to distinguish between high and low-achieving students, filtering them into careers and further educational opportunities.

Given the significance of this process, a great deal of effort is invested in developing accurate student assessments. A fair assessment will have a large number of questions to cover a wide breadth of topics and reward true knowledge over lucky guesses. The assessment should also include some questions requiring the student to think about a problem he or she has never faced before. Correct responses would indicate that the student can apply the knowledge more generally.

A similar process of exam writing can be used to imagine the practice of evaluating machine learners. As different algorithms have varying strengths and weaknesses, it is necessary to use tests that reveal distinctions among the learners when measuring how a learner will perform on future data.

This chapter provides the information needed to assess machine learners, such as:

- The reasons why predictive accuracy is not sufficient to measure performance, and the performance measures you might use instead
- Methods to ensure that the performance measures reasonably reflect a model's ability to predict or forecast unseen data
- How to use R to apply these more useful measures and methods to the predictive models we learned in previous chapters

As you will discover, just as the best way to learn a topic is to attempt to teach it to someone else, the process of teaching machine learners will also provide you with a greater insight into how to better the use of machine learning methods you've learned so far.

# Measuring performance for classification

To measure classification performance in previous chapters, we used a measure of accuracy that divided the proportion of correct predictions by the total number of predictions. This number indicates the percentage of cases in which the learner is right or wrong. For instance, suppose a classifier correctly identified whether or not 99,990 out of 100,000 newborn babies are carriers of a treatable but potentially-fatal genetic defect. This would imply an accuracy of 99.99 percent and an error rate of only 0.01 percent.

Although this would appear to indicate an extremely accurate classifier, it would be wise to collect additional information before trusting your child's life to the test. What if the genetic defect is found in only 10 out of every 100,000 babies? A test that predicts "no defect" regardless of circumstances will still be correct for 99.99 percent of all cases. In this case, even though the predictions are correct for the large majority of data, the classifier is not very useful for its intended purpose, which is to identify children with birth defects.

This is one consequence of the **class imbalance problem**, which refers to the trouble associated with data having a large majority of records belonging to a single class.

The best measure of classifier performance is whether the classifier is successful at its intended purpose. For this reason, it is crucial to have measures of model performance that measure utility rather than raw accuracy. Toward this end, we will begin working with a variety of measures derived from predictions presented in a familiar format: the confusion matrix. Before we get started, however, we need to consider how to prepare classification results for evaluation.

# Working with classification prediction data in R

There are three main types of data that are used to evaluate a classifier:

- Actual class values
- Predicted class values
- Estimated probability of the prediction

We used the first two types in previous chapters. The idea is to maintain two vectors of data: one holding the true, or actual class values and the other holding the predicted class values. Both vectors must have the same number of values stored in the same order. The predicted and actual values may be stored as separate R vectors or columns in a single R data frame. Either of these approaches will work with most R functions.

The actual class values come directly from the target feature in the test dataset. For instance, if your test data are in a data frame named `test_data`, and the target is in a column named `outcome`, we can create a vector of actual values using a command similar to `actual_outcome <- test_data$outcome`.

Predicted class values are obtained using the model. For most machine learning packages, this involves applying the `predict()` function to a model object and a data frame of test data, such as: `predicted_outcome <- predict(model, test_data)`.

Until now, we have only examined classification predictions using these two vectors of data. Yet hidden behind-the-scenes is another piece of useful information. Even though the classifier makes a single prediction about each example, it may be more confident about some decisions than others. For instance, a classifier may be 99 percent certain that a SMS with the words "free" and "ringtones" is 99 percent spam, but is only 51 percent certain that a SMS with the word "tonight" is spam. In both cases, the classifier predicts a spam, but it is far more certain about one decision than the other.

Studying these internal prediction probabilities is useful to evaluate the model performance and is the source of the third type of evaluation data. If two models make the same number of mistakes, but one is more able to accurately assess its uncertainty, then it is a smarter model. It's ideal to find a learner that is extremely confident in making a correct prediction, but timid in the face of doubt. The balance between confidence and caution is a key part of model evaluation.

Unfortunately, obtaining the internal prediction probabilities can be tricky because the method for doing so varies across classifiers. In general, the `predict()` function for the classifier will allow you to specify the type of prediction you want. To obtain a single predicted class, such as spam or ham, you typically specify `"class"` type. To obtain the prediction probability, you typically specify a type such as `prob`, `posterior`, `raw`, or `probability`.

Nearly all of the classifiers presented in this book will provide such probabilities; the parameter for doing so is included in the syntax box introducing each model.

For example, to output the predicted probabilities for a naive Bayes classifier as described in *Chapter 4, Probabilistic Learning – Classification Using Naive Bayes*, you would use `type = "raw"` with the prediction function, such as: `predicted_prob <- predict(model, test_data, type = "raw")`.

Similarly, the command for a C5.0 classifier as described in *Chapter 5, Divide and Conquer – Classification Using Decision Trees and Rules* is: `predicted_prob <- predict(model, test_data, type = "prob")`.

Keep in mind that in most cases the `predict()` function will return a probability for each level of the outcome. For example, in the case of a two-outcome yes/no model, the `predicted_prob` might be a matrix or data frame as shown in the following expression:

```
> head(predicted_prob)
          no         yes
1 0.0808272 0.9191728
2 1.0000000 0.0000000
3 0.7064238 0.2935762
4 0.1962657 0.8037343
5 0.8249874 0.1750126
6 1.0000000 0.0000000
```

Be careful while constructing an evaluation dataset to ensure that you are using the correct probability for the class level of interest. To avoid confusion, in the case of a binary outcome, you might even consider dropping the vector for one of the two alternatives.

To illustrate typical evaluation data, we'll use a data frame containing predicted class values, actual class values, and the estimated probability of a spam as determined by the SMS spam classification model developed in *Chapter 4, Probabilistic Learning: Classification Using Naive Bayes*.

To follow along with the examples here, download the `sms_results.csv` file from the Packt Publishing's website and load to a data frame using the command: `sms_results <- read.csv("sms_results.csv")`

The `sms_results` data frame is simple; shown in the following command and its output, it contains three vectors of 1,390 values. One vector contains values indicating the actual type of SMS message (spam or ham), one vector indicates the model's predicted type, and the third vector indicates the probability that the message was spam:

```
> head(sms_results)
  actual_type predict_type    prob_spam
1        ham          ham 2.560231e-07
2        ham          ham 1.309835e-04
3        ham          ham 8.089713e-05
4        ham          ham 1.396505e-04
5       spam         spam 1.000000e+00
6        ham          ham 3.504181e-03
```

Notice that when the predicted type is ham, the prob_spam value is extremely close to zero. Conversely, when the predicted type was spam, the prob_spam value is equal to one, which implies that the model was 100 percent certain that the SMS was spam. The fact that the estimated probability of spam falls on such extremes suggests that the model was very confident about its decisions. But what happens when the predicted and actual values differ? Using the subset() function, we can identify a few of these records:

```
> head(subset(sms_results, actual_type != predict_type))
    actual_type predict_type    prob_spam
53         spam          ham 0.0006796225
59         spam          ham 0.1333961018
73         spam          ham 0.3582665350
76         spam          ham 0.1224625535
81         spam          ham 0.0224863219
184        spam          ham 0.0320059616
```

Notice that the probabilities are somewhat less extreme, particularly row number 73, which the classifier felt had a 35 percent chance of being spam, yet still classified as ham.

The previous six examples represent six of the mistakes made by the SMS classifier. In spite of such mistakes, is the model still useful? We can answer this question by applying various error metrics to this evaluation data. In fact, many such metrics are based on a tool we've already used extensively in previous chapters.

# A closer look at confusion matrices

A **confusion matrix** is a table that categorizes predictions according to whether they match the actual value in the data. One of the table's dimensions indicates the possible categories of predicted values while the other dimension indicates the same for actual values. Although, we have only seen 2 x 2 confusion matrices so far, a matrix can be created for a model predicting any number of classes. The following figure depicts the familiar confusion matrix for two-class binary model as well as the 3 x 3 confusion matrix for a three-class model.

When the predicted value is the same as the actual value, this is a correct classification. Correct predictions fall on the diagonal in the confusion matrix (denoted by **O**). The off-diagonal matrix cells (denoted by **X**) indicate the cases where the predicted value differs from the actual value. These are incorrect predictions. Performance measures for classification models are based on the counts of predictions falling on and off the diagonal in these tables:

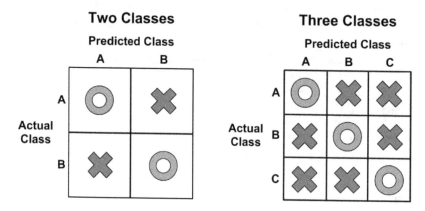

The most common performance measures consider the model's ability to discern one class versus all others. The class of interest is known as the **positive** class, while all others are known as **negative**.

The use of the terminology positive and negative is not intended to imply any value judgment (that is, good versus bad), nor does it necessarily suggest that the outcome is present or absent (that is, birth defect versus none). The choice of the positive outcome can even be arbitrary, as in cases where a model is predicting categories such as sunny versus rainy, or dog versus cat.

The relationship between positive class and negative class predictions can be depicted as a 2 x 2 confusion matrix that tabulates whether predictions fall into one of four categories:

- **True Positive (TP)**: Correctly classified as the class of interest
- **True Negative (TN)**: Correctly classified as not the class of interest
- **False Positive (FP)**: Incorrectly classified as the class of interest
- **False Negative (FN)**: Incorrectly classified as not the class of interest

For the birth defect classifier mentioned previously, the confusion matrix would tabulate whether the model's predicted birth defect status matches the patient's actual birth defect status, as shown in the following diagram:

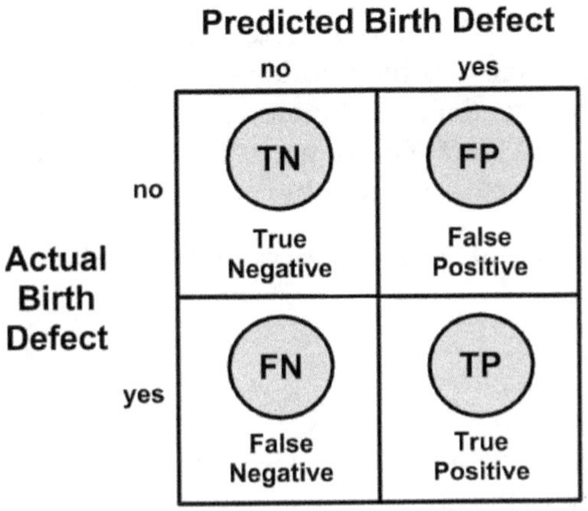

# Using confusion matrices to measure performance

With the 2 x 2 confusion matrix, we can formalize our definition of prediction **accuracy** (sometimes called the success rate) as:

$$accuracy = \frac{TP + TN}{TP + TN + FP + FN}$$

In this formula, the terms *TP, TN, FP,* and *FN* refer to the number of times the model's predictions fell into each of these categories. Therefore, the accuracy is the proportion that represents the number of true positives and true negatives divided by the total number of predictions.

The **error rate**, or the proportion of incorrectly classified examples, is specified as:

$$\text{error rate} = \frac{FP + FN}{TP + TN + FP + FN} = 1 - \text{accuracy}$$

Notice that the error rate can be calculated as one minus the accuracy. Intuitively, this makes sense; a model that is correct 95 percent of the time is incorrect 5 percent of the time.

A quick-and-dirty way to tabulate a confusion matrix is to use the `table()` function. It's easy to remember, and will count the number of occurrences of each combination of values – exactly what we need for a confusion matrix. The command for creating a confusion matrix for the SMS data is shown as follows. The counts in this table could then be used to calculate accuracy and other statistics:

```
> table(sms_results$actual_type, sms_results$predict_type)

        ham  spam
  ham   1202    5
  spam    29  154
```

If you would like to create a confusion matrix with more detailed output, the `CrossTable()` function in the gmodels package offers a highly-customizable solution. If you recall, we first used this function in *Chapter 2, Managing and Understanding Data*. However, if you didn't install the package at that time, you will need to do so using the command `install.packages("gmodels")`.

By default, the `CrossTable()` output includes proportions in each cell that indicate that cell's count as a percentage of the row, column, or total for the table. It also includes row and column totals. As shown in the following code, the syntax is similar to the `table()` function:

```
> library(gmodels)
> CrossTable(sms_results$actual_type, sms_results$predict_type)
```

The result is confusion matrix with much more details:

```
Cell Contents
|-------------------------|
|                       N |
| Chi-square contribution |
|          N / Row Total  |
|          N / Col Total  |
|        N / Table Total  |
|-------------------------|
```

```
Total Observations in Table:  1390


                             | sms_results$predict_type
     sms_results$actual_type |      ham |     spam | Row Total |
     ----------------------- |----------|----------|-----------|
                         ham |     1202 |        5 |      1207 |
                             |   16.565 |  128.248 |           |
                             |    0.996 |    0.004 |     0.868 |
                             |    0.976 |    0.031 |           |
                             |    0.865 |    0.004 |           |
     ----------------------- |----------|----------|-----------|
                        spam |       29 |      154 |       183 |
                             |  109.256 |  845.876 |           |
                             |    0.158 |    0.842 |     0.132 |
                             |    0.024 |    0.969 |           |
                             |    0.021 |    0.111 |           |
     ----------------------- |----------|----------|-----------|
                Column Total |     1231 |      159 |      1390 |
                             |    0.886 |    0.114 |           |
     ----------------------- |----------|----------|-----------|
```

We've used `CrossTable()` in several previous chapters, so by now you should be familiar with the output. If you don't remember, you can refer to the table's key (labeled `Cell Contents`), which provides a description of each number in the table.

We can use the contingency table to obtain the accuracy and error rate. Since accuracy is *(TP + TN) / (TP + TN + FP + FN)*, we can calculate:

```
> (154 + 1202) / (154+ 1202 + 5 + 29)
[1] 0.9755396
```

We can also calculate the error rate, *(FP + FN) / (TP + TN + FP + FN)* as:

```
> (5 + 29) / (154 + 1202 + 5 + 29)
[1] 0.02446043
```

This is the same as one minus accuracy:

```
> 1 - 0.9755396
[1] 0.0244604
```

Although these calculations may seem simple, it can be a helpful exercise to practice thinking about how the components of the confusion matrix relate to one another. In the next section, you will see how these same pieces can be combined in different ways to create a variety of additional performance measures.

# Beyond accuracy – other measures of performance

A comprehensive description of every performance measure is not feasible. Countless measures have been developed and used for specific purposes in disciplines as diverse as medicine, information retrieval, marketing, and signal detection theory, among others. Instead, we'll consider only some of the most commonly-cited measures in machine learning literature.

The Classification and Regression Training (`caret`) package by *Max Kuhn* includes functions for computing many such performance measures. This package provides a large number of tools for preparing, training, evaluating, and visualizing machine learning models and data. In addition to its application here, we will also employ caret extensively in *Chapter 11, Improving Model Performance*. Before proceeding, install the package using the command `install.packages("caret")`.

> For more information on `caret`, please refer to the publication: *Building predictive models in R using the caret package, Journal of Statistical Software, Vol. 28, Iss. 5*, by *Max Kuhn* (2008).

The `caret` package adds yet another function for creating a confusion matrix. As shown in the following commands, the syntax is similar to `table()`, but the positive outcome must be specified. Because the SMS classifier is intended to detect spam, we will set `positive = "spam"`.

```
> library(caret)
> confusionMatrix(sms_results$predict_type, sms_results$actual_type,
    positive = "spam")
```

This results in the following output:

```
Confusion Matrix and Statistics

            Reference
Prediction   ham  spam
      ham   1202    29
      spam     5   154

              Accuracy : 0.9755
                95% CI : (0.966, 0.983)
   No Information Rate : 0.8683
   P-value [ACC > NIR] : < 2.2e-16

                 Kappa : 0.8867
 Mcnemar's Test P-Value : 7.998e-05

           Sensitivity : 0.8415
           Specificity : 0.9959
        Pos Pred Value : 0.9686
        Neg Pred Value : 0.9764
            Prevalence : 0.1317
        Detection Rate : 0.1108
  Detection Prevalence : 0.1144

      'Positive' Class : spam
```

The output includes a confusion matrix and a set of performance measures. Let's take a look at a few of the most commonly used statistics.

# The kappa statistic

The **kappa statistic** (labeled Kappa in the previous output) adjusts accuracy by accounting for the possibility of a correct prediction by chance alone. Kappa values range to a maximum value of 1, which indicates perfect agreement between the model's predictions and the true values—a rare occurrence. Values less than one indicate imperfect agreement.

Depending on how your model is to be used, the interpretation of the kappa statistic might vary. One common interpretation is shown as follows:

- Poor agreement = Less than 0.20

- Fair agreement = 0.20 to 0.40

- Moderate agreement = 0.40 to 0.60

- Good agreement = 0.60 to 0.80

- Very good agreement = 0.80 to 1.00

It's important to note, however, that these categories are subjective. While "good agreement" may be more than adequate for predicting someone's favorite ice cream flavor, "very good agreement" may not suffice if your goal is to land a shuttle safely on the surface of the moon.

> For more information on the previous scale, refer to: *The measurement of observer agreement for categorical data, Biometrics Vol. 33, pp.159-174, by J.R. Landis and G.G. Koch (1977).*

The following is the formula for calculating the kappa statistic. In this formula, *Pr* refers to the proportion of actual (*a*) and expected (*e*) agreement between the classifier and the true values:

$$k = \frac{Pr(a) - Pr(e)}{1 - Pr(e)}$$

> There is more than one way to define the kappa statistic. The most common method, described here, uses Cohen's kappa coefficient, as described in the paper: *A coefficient of agreement for nominal scales, Education and Psychological Measurement Vol. 20, pp. 37-46, by J. Cohen (1960).*

These proportions are easy to obtain from a confusion matrix once you know where to look. Let's consider the confusion matrix for the SMS classification model created with the `CrossTable()` function, duplicated as follows:

| sms_results$actual_type | sms_results$predict_type ham | spam | Row Total |
|---|---|---|---|
| ham | 1202 16.565 0.996 0.976 0.865 | 5 128.248 0.004 0.031 0.004 | 1207 0.868 |
| spam | 29 109.256 0.158 0.024 0.021 | 154 845.876 0.842 0.969 0.111 | 183 0.132 |
| Column Total | 1231 0.886 | 159 0.114 | 1390 |

Remember that the bottom value in each cell indicates the proportion of all instances falling into that cell. Therefore, to calculate the observed agreement *Pr(a)*, we simply add the proportion of all instances where the predicted type and actual SMS type agree. Thus, we can calculate *Pr(a)* as:

```
> pr_a <- 0.865 + 0.111
> pr_a
[1] 0.976
```

For this classifier, the observed and actual values agree 97.6 percent of the time – you will note that this is the same as the accuracy. The kappa statistic adjusts the accuracy relative to the expected agreement, *Pr(e)*, which is the probability that chance alone would lead the predicted and actual values to match, under the assumption that both are selected randomly according to the observed proportions.

To find these observed proportions, we can use the probability rules we learned in *Chapter 4, Probabilistic Learning – Classification Using Naive Bayes*. Assuming two events are independent (meaning one does not affect the other), probability rules note that the probability of both occurring is equal to the product of the probabilities of each one occurring. For instance, we know that the probability of both choosing ham is:

*Pr(actual_type is ham)* * *Pr(predicted_type is ham)*

And the probability of both choosing spam is:

*Pr(actual_type is spam)* * *Pr(predicted_type is spam)*

The probability that the predicted or actual type is spam or ham can be obtained from the row or column totals. For instance, *Pr(actual_type is ham)* = 0.868.

*Pr(e)* can be calculated as the sum of the probabilities that either the predicted and actual values agree that the message is spam, or they agree that the message is ham. Since the probability of either of two mutually exclusive events (that is, they cannot happen simultaneously) occurring is equal to the sum of their probabilities, we simply add both products. In R code, this would be:

```
> pr_e <- 0.868 * 0.886 + 0.132 * 0.114
> pr_e
[1] 0.784096
```

Since pr_e is 0.784096, by chance alone we would expect the observed and actual values to agree about 78.4 percent of the time.

This means that we now have all the information needed to complete the kappa formula. Plugging the pr_a and pr_e values into the kappa formula, we find:

```
> k <- (pr_a - pr_e) / (1 - pr_e)
> k
[1] 0.8888395
```

The kappa is about 0.89, which agrees with the previous confusionMatrix() output (the small difference is due to rounding). Using the suggested interpretation, we note that there is very good agreement between the classifier's predictions and the actual values.

There are a couple of R functions to calculate kappa automatically. The Kappa() function (be sure to note the capital K) in the Visualizing Categorical Data (vcd) package uses a confusion matrix of predicted and actual values. After installing the package using the command install.packages("vcd"), the following commands can be used to obtain kappa:

```
> library(vcd)
> Kappa(table(sms_results$actual_type, sms_results$predict_type))
              value         ASE
Unweighted 0.8867172 0.01918876
Weighted   0.8867172 0.01587936
```

We're interested in the unweighted kappa. The value 0.89 matches what we expected.

> The weighted kappa is used when there are varying degrees of agreement. For example, using a scale of cold, warm, and hot, a value of warm agrees more with hot than it does with the value of cold. In the case of a two-outcome event, such as spam and ham, the weighted and unweighted kappa statistics will be identical.

The kappa2() function in the Inter-Rater Reliability (irr) package can be used to calculate kappa from vectors of predicted and actual values stored in a data frame. After installing the package using the command install.packages("irr"), the following commands can be used to obtain kappa:

```
> library(irr)
> kappa2(sms_results[1:2])
 Cohen's Kappa for 2 Raters (Weights: unweighted)
```

```
Subjects = 1390
   Raters = 2
    Kappa = 0.887


       z = 33.2
 p-value = 0
```

In both cases, the same kappa statistic is reported, so use whichever option you are more comfortable with.

 Be careful not to use the built-in kappa () function. It is unrelated to the Kappa statistic reported previously.

# Sensitivity and specificity

Classification often involves a balance between being overly conservative and overly aggressive in decision making. For example, an e-mail filter could guarantee to eliminate every spam message by aggressively eliminating nearly every ham message at the same time. On the other hand, a guarantee that no ham messages will be inadvertently filtered might allow an unacceptable amount of spam to pass through the filter. This tradeoff is captured by a pair of measures: sensitivity and specificity.

The **sensitivity** of a model (also called the true positive rate), measures the proportion of positive examples that were correctly classified. Therefore, as shown in the following formula, it is calculated as the number of true positives divided by the total number of positives in the data — those correctly classified (the true positives), as well as those incorrectly classified (the false negatives).

$$sensitivity = \frac{TP}{TP + FN}$$

The **specificity** of a model (also called the true negative rate), measures the proportion of negative examples that were correctly classified. As with sensitivity, this is computed as the number of true negatives divided by the total number of negatives — the true negatives plus the false positives.

$$specificity = \frac{TN}{TN + FP}$$

Given the confusion matrix for the SMS classifier, we can easily calculate these measures by hand. Assuming that spam is the positive class, we can confirm that the numbers in the `confusionMatrix()` output are correct. For example, the calculation for sensitivity is:

```
> sens <- 154 / (154 + 29)
> sens
[1] 0.8415301
```

Similarly, for specificity we can calculate:

```
> spec <- 1202 / (1202 + 5)
> spec
[1] 0.9958575
```

The `caret` package provides functions for calculating sensitivity and specificity directly from vectors of predicted and actual values. Be careful to specify the `positive` or `negative` parameter appropriately, as shown in the following lines:

```
> library(caret)
> sensitivity(sms_results$predict_type, sms_results$actual_type,
              positive = "spam")
[1] 0.8415301
> specificity(sms_results$predict_type, sms_results$actual_type,
              negative = "ham")
[1] 0.9958575
```

Sensitivity and specificity range from 0 to 1, with values close to 1 being more desirable. Of course, it is important to find an appropriate balance between the two—a task that is often quite context-specific.

For example, in this case the sensitivity of 0.842 implies that 84 percent of spam messages were correctly classified. Similarly, the specificity of 0.996 implies that 99.6 percent of non-spam messages were correctly classified, or alternatively, 0.4 percent of valid messages were rejected as spam. The idea of rejecting 0.4 percent of valid SMS messages may be unacceptable, or it may be a reasonable tradeoff given the reduction in spam.

Use sensitivity and specificity to provide a tool for thinking about such tradeoffs. Typically, changes are made to the model, and different models are tested until finding one that meets a desired sensitivity and specificity threshold. Visualizations, such as those discussed later in this chapter, can also assist with understanding the tradeoff between sensitivity and specificity.

# Precision and recall

Closely related to sensitivity and specificity are two other performance measures, related to compromises made in classification: precision and recall. Used primarily in the context of information retrieval, these statistics are intended to provide an indication of how interesting and relevant a model's results are, or whether the predictions are diluted by meaningless noise.

The **precision** (also known as the positive predictive value) is defined as the proportion of positive examples that are truly positive; in other words, when a model predicts the positive class, how often is it correct? A precise model will only predict the positive class in cases very likely to be positive. It will be very trustworthy.

Consider what would happen if the model was very imprecise. Over time, the results would be less likely to be trusted. In the context of information retrieval, this would be similar to a search engine such as Google returning unrelated results. Eventually users would switch to a competitor such as Bing. In the case of the SMS spam filter, high precision means that the model is able to carefully target only the spam while ignoring the ham.

$$precision = \frac{TP}{TP + FP}$$

On the other hand, recall is a measure of how complete the results are. As shown in the following formula, this is defined as the number of true positives over the total number of positives. You may recognize that this is the same as sensitivity, only the interpretation differs. A model with high recall captures a large portion of the positive examples, meaning that it has wide breadth. For example, a search engine with high recall returns a large number of documents pertinent to the search query. Similarly, the SMS spam filter has high recall if the majority of spam messages are correctly identified.

$$recall = \frac{TP}{TP + FN}$$

We can calculate precision and recall from the confusion matrix. Again, assuming that spam is the positive class, the precision is:

```
> prec <- 154 / (154 + 5)
> prec
[1] 0.9685535
```

And the recall is:

```
> rec <- 154 / (154 + 29)
> rec
[1] 0.8415301
```

The `caret` package can be used to compute either of these measures from vectors of predicted and actual classes. Precision uses the `posPredValue()` function:

```
> library(caret)
> posPredValue(sms_results$predict_type, sms_results$actual_type,
             positive = "spam")
[1] 0.9685535
```

While recall uses the `sensitivity()` function as we had done before.

Similar to the inherent tradeoff between sensitivity and specificity, for most real-world problems, it is difficult to build a model with both high precision and high recall. It is easy to be precise if you target only the low-hanging fruit—the easy to classify examples. Similarly, it is easy for a model to have high recall by casting a very wide net, meaning that that the model is overly aggressive at predicting the positive cases. In contrast, having both high precision and recall at the same time is very challenging. It is therefore important to test a variety of models in order to find the combination of precision and recall that meets the needs of your project.

## The F-measure

A measure of model performance that combines precision and recall into a single number is known as the **F-measure** (also sometimes called the F1 score or the F-score). The F-measure combines precision and recall using the harmonic mean. The harmonic mean is used rather than the more common arithmetic mean since both precision and recall are expressed as proportions between zero and one. The following is the formula for F-measure:

$$F\text{-}measure = \frac{2 \times precision \times recall}{recall + precision} = \frac{2 \times TP}{2 \times TP + FP + FN}$$

To calculate the F-measure, use the precision and recall values computed previously:

```
> f <- (2 * prec * rec) / (prec + rec)
> f
[1] 0.9005848
```

This is the same as using the counts from the confusion matrix:

```
> f2 <- (2 * 154) / (2 * 154 + 5 + 29)
> f2
[1] 0.9005848
```

Since the F-measure reduces model performance to a single number, it provides a convenient way to compare several models side-by-side. However, this assumes that equal weight should be assigned to precision and recall, an assumption that is not always valid. It is possible to calculate F-scores using different weights for precision and recall, but choosing the weights can be tricky at best and arbitrary at worst. A better practice is to use measures such as the F-score in combination with methods that consider a model's strengths and weaknesses more globally, such as those described in the next section.

# Visualizing performance tradeoffs

Visualizations are often helpful for understanding how the performance of machine learning algorithms varies from situation to situation. Rather than thinking about a single pair of statistics such as sensitivity and specificity, or precision and recall, visualizations allow you to examine how measures vary across a wide range of values. They also provide a method for comparing learners side-by-side in a single chart.

The ROCR package provides an easy-to-use suite of functions for creating visualizations of the performance statistics of classification models. It includes functions for computing a large set of the most common performance measures and visualizations. The ROCR website, http://rocr.bioinf.mpi-sb.mpg.de/, includes a list of the full set of features as well as several examples of the visualization capabilities. Before continuing, install the package using the command install. packages("ROCR").

For more information on the development of ROCR, see: *ROCR: visualizing classifier performance in R, Bioinformatics Vol. 21*, pp. 3940-3941, by *T. Sing, O. Sander, N. Beerenwinkel, and T. Lengauer (2005)*.

To create visualizations with ROCR, two vectors of data are needed. The first must contain the class values predicted, and the second must contain the estimated probability of the positive class. These are used to create a prediction object that can be examined through plotting functions of ROCR.

The prediction object for the SMS classifier uses the classifier's estimated spam probabilities (prob_spam), and the actual class labels (actual_type). These are combined using the prediction() function in the following lines:

```
> library(ROCR)
> pred <- prediction(predictions = sms_results$prob_spam,
                     labels = sms_results$actual_type)
```

ROCR provides a performance() function for computing measures of performance on prediction objects such as pred, which was used in previous code example. The resulting performance object can be visualized using the R plot() function. Given these three functions, a large variety of depictions can be created.

## ROC curves

The **ROC** curve (**Receiver Operating Characteristic**) is commonly used to examine the tradeoff between the detection of true positives, while avoiding the false positives. As you might suspect from the name, ROC curves were developed by engineers in the field of communications around the time of World War II; receivers of radar and radio signals needed a method to discriminate between true signals and false alarms. The same technique is useful today for visualizing the efficacy of machine learning models.

The characteristics of a typical ROC diagram are depicted in the following plot. Curves are defined on a plot with the proportion of true positives on the vertical axis, and the proportion of false positives on the horizontal axis. Because these values are equivalent to **sensitivity** and (**1 – specificity**), respectively, the diagram is also known as a sensitivity/specificity plot:

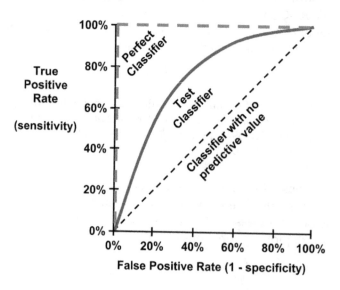

The points comprising ROC curves indicate the true positive rate at varying false positive thresholds. To create the curves, a classifier's predictions are sorted by the model's estimated probability of the positive class, with the largest values first. Beginning at the origin, each prediction's impact on the true positive rate and false positive rate will result in a curve tracing vertically (for a correct prediction), or horizontally (for an incorrect prediction).

To illustrate this concept, three hypothetical classifiers are contrasted in the previous plot. First, the diagonal line from the bottom-left to the top-right corner of the diagram represents a *classifier with no predictive value*. This type of classifier detects true positives and false positives at exactly the same rate, implying that the classifier cannot discriminate between the two. This is the baseline by which other classifiers may be judged; ROC curves falling close to this line indicate models that are not very useful. Similarly, *the perfect classifier* has a curve that passes through the point at 100 percent true positive rate and 0 percent false positive rate. It is able to correctly identify all of the true positives before it incorrectly classifies any negative result. Most real-world classifiers are similar to the *test classifier*; they fall somewhere in the zone between perfect and useless.

The closer the curve is to the perfect classifier, the better it is at identifying positive values. This can be measured using a statistic known as the **area under the ROC curve** (abbreviated AUC). The AUC, as you might expect, treats the ROC diagram as a two-dimensional square and measures the total area under the ROC curve. AUC ranges from 0.5 (for a classifier with no predictive value), to 1.0 (for a perfect classifier). A convention for interpreting AUC scores uses a system similar to academic letter grades:

- *0.9 – 1.0 = A* (outstanding)
- *0.8 – 0.9 = B* (excellent/good)
- *0.7 – 0.8 = C* (acceptable/fair)
- *0.6 – 0.7 = D* (poor)
- *0.5 – 0.6 = F* (no discrimination)

As with most scales similar to this, the levels may work better for some tasks than others; the categorization is somewhat subjective.

It's also worth noting that two ROC curves may be shaped very differently, yet have identical AUC. For this reason, AUC can be extremely misleading. The best practice is to use AUC in combination with qualitative examination of the ROC curve.

Creating ROC curves with the `ROCR` package involves building a performance object for the `pred` prediction object we computed earlier. Since ROC curves plot true positive rates versus false positive rates, we simply call the `performance()` function while specifying the `tpr` and `fpr` measures, as shown in the following code:

```
> perf <- performance(pred, measure = "tpr", x.measure = "fpr")
```

Using the `perf` performance object, we can visualize the ROC curve with R's `plot()` function. As shown in the following code lines, many of the standard parameters for adjusting the visualization can be used, such as `main` (for adding a title), `col` (for changing the line color), and `lwd` (for adjusting the line width):

```
> plot(perf, main = "ROC curve for SMS spam filter",
       col = "blue", lwd = 3)
```

Although the `plot()` command, used in previous lines of code, is sufficient to create a valid ROC curve, it is helpful to add a reference line to indicate the performance of a classifier with no predictive value.

For plotting such a line, we'll use the `abline()` function. This function can be used to specify a line in slope-intercept form, where a is the intercept and b is the slope. Since we need an identity line that passes through the origin, we'll set the intercept to `a=0` and the slope to `b=1` as shown in the following plot. The `lwd` parameter adjusts the line thickness, while the `lty` parameter adjusts the type of line. For example, `lty = 2` indicates a dashed line.

```
> abline(a = 0, b = 1, lwd = 2, lty = 2)
```

The end result is an ROC plot with a dashed reference line:

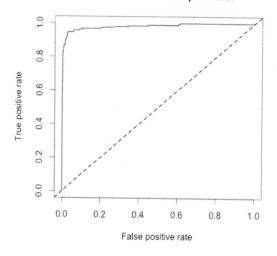

Qualitatively, we can see that this ROC curve appears to occupy the space in the top-left corner of the diagram, which suggests that it is closer to a perfect classifier than the dashed line indicating a useless classifier. To confirm this quantitatively, we can use the ROCR package to calculate the AUC. To do so, we first need to create another performance object, this time specifying `measure = "auc"`, as shown in the following code:

```
> perf.auc <- performance(pred, measure = "auc")
```

Since `perf.auc` is an object (specifically known as an S4 object) we need to use a special type of notation to access the values stored within. S4 objects hold information in positions known as slots. The `str()` function can be used to see all slots for an object:

```
> str(perf.auc)
Formal class 'performance' [package "ROCR"] with 6 slots
  ..@ x.name        : chr "None"
  ..@ y.name        : chr "Area under the ROC curve"
  ..@ alpha.name    : chr "none"
  ..@ x.values      : list()
  ..@ y.values      :List of 1
  .. ..$ : num 0.983
  ..@ alpha.values: list()
```

Notice that slots are prefixed with the @ symbol. To access the AUC value, which is stored as a list in the `y.values` slot, we can use the @ notation along with the `unlist()` function, which simplifies lists to a vector of numeric values:

```
> unlist(perf.auc@y.values)
[1] 0.9829999
```

The AUC for the SMS classifier is 0.98, which is extremely high. But how do we know whether the model is just as likely to perform well on another dataset? In order to answer such questions, we need to better understand how far we can extrapolate a model's predictions beyond the test data.

# Estimating future performance

Some R machine learning packages present confusion matrices and performance measures during the model building process. The purpose of these statistics is to provide insight about the model's **resubstitution error**, which occurs when the training data is incorrectly predicted in spite of the model being built directly from this data. This information is intended to be used as a rough diagnostic, particularly to identify obviously poor performers.

The resubstitution error is not a very useful marker of future performance, however. For example, a model that used rote memorization to perfectly classify every training instance (that is, zero resubstitution error) would be unable to make predictions on data it has never seen before. For this reason, the error rate on the training data can be extremely optimistic about a model's future performance.

Instead of relying on resubstitution error, a better practice is to evaluate a model's performance on data it has not yet seen. We used such a method in previous chapters when we split the available data into a set for training and a set for testing. In some cases, however, it is not always ideal to create training and test datasets. For instance, in a situation where you have only a small pool of data, you might not want to reduce the sample any further by dividing it into training and test sets.

Fortunately, there are other ways to estimate a model's performance on unseen data. The caret package that we used previously for calculating performance measures also, offers a number of functions for this purpose. If you are following along with the R code examples and haven't already installed the caret package, please do so. You will also need to load the package to the R session using the library(caret) command.

# The holdout method

The procedure of partitioning data into training and test datasets that we used in previous chapters is known as the **holdout method**. As shown in the following diagram, the **training dataset** is used to generate the model, which is then applied to the **test dataset** to generate predictions for evaluation. Typically, about one-third of the data is held out for testing and two-thirds used for training, but this proportion can vary depending on the amount of data available. To ensure that the training and test data do not have systematic differences, examples are randomly divided into the two groups.

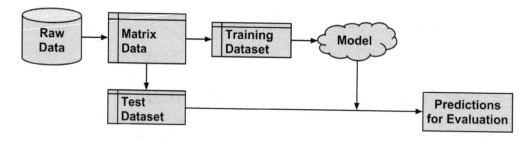

For the holdout method to result in a truly accurate estimate of future performance, at no time should results from the test dataset be allowed to influence the model. It is easy to unknowingly violate this rule by choosing a best model based upon the results of repeated testing. Instead, it is better to divide the original data so that in addition to the training and test datasets, a third validation dataset is available. The validation dataset would be used for iterating and refining the model or models chosen, leaving the test dataset to be used only once as a final step to report an estimated error rate for future predictions. A typical split between training, test, and validation would be 50 percent, 25 percent, and 25 percent respectively.

A keen reader will note that holdout test data was used in previous chapters to compare several models. This would indeed violate the rule as stated previously, and therefore the test data might have been more accurately termed validation data. If we use test data to make a decision, we are cherry-picking results and the evaluation is no longer an unbiased estimate of future performance.

A simple method for creating holdout samples uses random number generators to assign records to partitions. This technique was first used in *Chapter 5, Divide and Conquer – Classification Using Decision Trees and Rules* to create training and test datasets.

If you'd like to follow along with the following examples, download the dataset `credit.csv` from the Packt Publishing's website and load to a data frame using the command `credit <- read.csv("credit.csv")`.

Suppose we have a data frame named credit with 1000 rows of data. We can divide this into three partitions:

```
> random_ids <- order(runif(1000))
> credit_train <- credit[random_ids[1:500],]
> credit_validate <- credit[random_ids[501:750], ]
> credit_test <- credit[random_ids[751:1000], ]
```

The first line creates a vector of randomly ordered row IDs from 1 to 1000. These IDs are then used to divide the credit data frame into 500, 250, and 250 records comprising the training, validation, and test datasets.

One problem with holdout sampling is that each partition may have a larger or smaller proportion of some classes. In certain cases, particularly those in which a class is a very small proportion of the dataset, this can lead a class to be omitted from the training dataset—a significant problem, because the model cannot then learn this class.

In order to reduce the chance that this will occur, a technique called **stratified random sampling** can be used. Although, on average, a random sample will contain roughly the same proportion of class values as the full dataset, stratified random sampling ensures that the generated random partitions have approximately the same proportion of each class as the full dataset.

The `caret` package provides a `createDataPartition()` function that will create partitions based on stratified holdout sampling. Code for creating a stratified sample of training and test data for the `credit` dataset is shown in the following commands. To use the function, a vector of class values must be specified (here, `default` refers to whether a loan went into default), in addition to a parameter `p`, which specifies the proportion of instances to be included in the partition. The `list = FALSE` parameter prevents the result from being stored in list format:

```
> in_train <- createDataPartition(credit$default, p = 0.75,
    list = FALSE)
> credit_train <- credit[in_train, ]
> credit_test <- credit[-in_train, ]
```

The `in_train` vector indicates row numbers included in the training sample. We can use these row numbers to select examples for the `credit_train` data frame. Similarly, by using a negative symbol, we can use the rows not found in the `in_train` vector for the `credit_test` dataset.

> Since models trained on larger datasets generally perform better, a common practice is to retrain the model on the full set of data (that is, training plus test and validation) after a final model has been selected and evaluated, allowing the model maximum use of available data.

Although it distributes the classes evenly, stratified sampling does not guarantee other types of representativeness. Some samples may have too many or too few difficult cases, easy-to-predict cases, or outliers. This is especially true for smaller datasets, which may not have a large enough portion of such cases to divide among training and test sets.

In addition to potentially biased samples, another problem with the holdout method is that substantial portions of data must be reserved for testing and validating the model. Since these data cannot be used to train the model until its performance has been measured, the performance estimates are likely to be overly conservative.

A technique called **repeated holdout** is sometimes used to mitigate the problems of randomly composed training datasets. The repeated holdout method is a special case of the holdout method that uses the average result from several random holdout samples to evaluate a model's performance. As multiple holdout samples are used, it is less likely that the model is trained or tested on non-representative data. We'll expand on this idea in the next section.

# Cross-validation

The repeated holdout is the basis of a technique known as **k-fold cross-validation** (or k-fold CV), which has become the industry standard for estimating model performance. But rather than taking repeated random samples that could potentially use the same record more than once, k-fold CV randomly divides the data into *k* completely separate random partitions called folds.

Although *k* can be set to any number, by far the most common convention is to use **10-fold cross-validation** (10-fold CV). Why 10 folds? Empirical evidence suggests that there is little added benefit to using a greater number. For each of the 10 folds (each comprising 10 percent of the total data), a machine learning model is built on the remaining 90 percent of data. The fold's matching 10 percent sample is then used for model evaluation. After the process of training and evaluating the model has occurred for 10 times (with 10 different training/testing combinations), the average performance across all folds is reported.

An extreme case of k-fold CV is the **leave-one-out method**, which performs k-fold CV using a fold for each one of the data's examples. This ensures that the greatest amount of data is used for training the model. Although this may seem useful, it is so computationally expensive that it is rarely used in practice.

Datasets for cross-validation can be created using the `createFolds()` function in the `caret` package. Similar to the stratified random holdout sampling, this function will attempt to maintain the same class balance in each of the folds as in the original dataset. The following is the command for creating 10 folds:

```
> folds <- createFolds(credit$default, k = 10)
```

The result of the `createFolds()` function is a list of vectors storing the row numbers for each of the k = 10 requested folds. We can peek at the contents using `str()`:

```
> str(folds)
List of 10
 $ Fold01: int [1:100] 1 5 12 13 19 21 25 32 36 38 ...
 $ Fold02: int [1:100] 16 49 78 81 84 93 105 108 128 134 ...
 $ Fold03: int [1:100] 15 48 60 67 76 91 102 109 117 123 ...
 $ Fold04: int [1:100] 24 28 59 64 75 85 95 97 99 104 ...
 $ Fold05: int [1:100] 9 10 23 27 29 34 37 39 53 61 ...
 $ Fold06: int [1:100] 4 8 41 55 58 103 118 121 144 146 ...
 $ Fold07: int [1:100] 2 3 7 11 14 33 40 45 51 57 ...
 $ Fold08: int [1:100] 17 30 35 52 70 107 113 129 133 137 ...
 $ Fold09: int [1:100] 6 20 26 31 42 44 46 63 79 101 ...
 $ Fold10: int [1:100] 18 22 43 50 68 77 80 88 106 111 ...
```

Here, we see that the first fold is named `Fold01`, and stores 100 integers indicating the 100 rows in the `credit` data frame for the first fold. To create training and test datasets to build and evaluate a model, one more step is needed. The following commands show how to create data for the first fold. Just as we had done with stratified holdout sampling, we'll assign the selected examples to the training dataset and use the negative symbol to assign everything else to the test dataset:

```
> credit01_train <- credit[folds$Fold01, ]
> credit01_test <- credit[-folds$Fold01, ]
```

To perform the full 10-fold CV, this step would need to be repeated a total of 10 times, building a model, and then calculating the model's performance each time. At the end, the performance measures would be averaged to obtain the overall performance. Thankfully, we can automate this task by applying several of the techniques we've learned before.

To demonstrate the process, we'll estimate the kappa statistic for a C5.0 decision tree model of the `credit` data using 10-fold CV. First, we need to load `caret` (for creating the folds), `C50` (for the decision tree), and `irr` (for calculating kappa). The latter two packages were chosen for illustrative purposes; if you desire, you can use a different model or a different performance measure with the same series of steps.

```
> library(caret)
> library(C50)
> library(irr)
```

Next, we'll create a list of 10 `folds` as we have done previously. The `set.seed()` function is used here to ensure that the results are consistent if you run the same code again:

```
> set.seed(123)
> folds <- createFolds(credit$default, k = 10)
```

Finally, we will apply a series of identical steps to the list of folds using the `lapply()` function. As shown in the following code, because there is no existing function that does exactly what we need, we must define our own function to pass to `lapply()`. Our custom function divides the `credit` data frame into training and test data, creates a decision tree using the `C5.0()` function on the training data, generates a set of predictions from the test data, and compares the predicted and actual values using the `kappa2()` function:

```
> cv_results <- lapply(folds, function(x) {
    credit_train <- credit[x, ]
    credit_test <- credit[-x, ]
    credit_model <- C5.0(default ~ ., data = credit_train)
    credit_pred <- predict(credit_model, credit_test)
    credit_actual <- credit_test$default
    kappa <- kappa2(data.frame(credit_actual, credit_pred))$value
    return(kappa)
  })
```

The resulting kappa statistics are compiled into a list stored in the `cv_results` object, which we can examine using `str()`:

```
> str(cv_results)
List of 10
 $ Fold01: num 0.283
 $ Fold02: num 0.108
 $ Fold03: num 0.326
 $ Fold04: num 0.162
 $ Fold05: num 0.243
 $ Fold06: num 0.257
 $ Fold07: num 0.0355
 $ Fold08: num 0.0761
 $ Fold09: num 0.241
 $ Fold10: num 0.253
```

In this way, we've transformed our list of IDs for 10 folds into a list of kappa statistics. There's just one more step remaining: we need to calculate the average of these 10 values. Although you will be tempted to type `mean(cv_results)`, because `cv_results` is not a numeric vector the result would be an error. Instead, use the `unlist()` function, which eliminates the list structure and reduces `cv_results` to a numeric vector. From there, we can calculate the mean kappa as expected:

```
> mean(unlist(cv_results))
[1] 0.1984929
```

Unfortunately, this kappa statistic is fairly low — in fact, this corresponds to "poor" on the interpretation scale — which suggests that the credit scoring model does not perform much better than random chance. In the next chapter, we'll examine automated methods based on 10-fold CV that can assist us with improving the performance of this model.

> Perhaps the current gold standard method for reliably estimating model performance is repeated k-fold CV. As you might guess from the name, this involves repeatedly applying k-fold CV and averaging the results. A common strategy is to perform 10-fold CV ten times. Although computationally intensive, this provides a very robust estimate.

# Bootstrap sampling

A slightly less popular, but still fairly widely-used alternative to k-fold CV is known as **bootstrap sampling**, the **bootstrap**, or **bootstrapping** for short. Generally speaking, these refer to statistical methods of using random samples of data to estimate properties of a larger set. When this principle is applied to machine learning model performance, it implies the creation of several randomly-selected training and test datasets, which are then used to estimate performance statistics. The results from the various random datasets are then averaged to obtain a final estimate of future performance.

So, what makes this procedure different from k-fold CV? Where cross-validation divides the data into separate partitions, in which each example can appear only once, the bootstrap allows examples to be selected multiple times through a process of sampling with replacement. This means that from the original dataset of *n* examples, the bootstrap procedure will create one or more new training datasets that also contain *n* examples, some of which are repeated. The corresponding test datasets are then constructed from the set of examples that were not selected for the respective training datasets.

Using sampling with replacement as described previously, the probability that any given instance is included in the training dataset is 63.2 percent. Consequently, the probability of any instance being in the test dataset is 36.8 percent. In other words, the training data represents only 63.2 percent of available examples, some of which are repeated. In contrast with 10-fold CV, which uses 90 percent of examples for training, the bootstrap sample is less representative of the full dataset.

As a model trained on only 63.2 percent of the training data is likely to perform worse than a model trained on a larger training set, the bootstrap's performance estimates may be substantially lower than what will be obtained when the model is later trained on the full dataset. A special case of bootstrapping known as the **0.632 bootstrap** accounts for this by calculating the final performance measure as a function of performance on both the training data (which is overly optimistic) and the test data (which is overly pessimistic). The final error rate is then estimated as:

$$\text{error} = 0.632 \times \text{error}_{test} + 0.368 \times \text{error}_{train}$$

One advantage of the bootstrap over cross-validation is that it tends to work better with very small datasets. Additionally, bootstrap sampling has applications beyond performance measurement. In particular, in the following chapter we'll learn how the principles of bootstrap sampling can be used to improve model performance.

# Summary

This chapter presented a number of the most common measures and techniques for evaluating the performance of machine learning classification models. Although accuracy provides a simple method for examining how often a model is correct, this can be misleading in the case of rare events because the real-life cost of such events may be inversely proportional to how frequently they appear in the data.

A number of measures based on confusion matrices better capture the balance among the costs of various types of errors. Closely examining the tradeoffs between sensitivity and specificity or precision and recall can be a useful tool for thinking about the implications of errors in the real world. Visualizations such as the ROC curve are also helpful toward this end.

It is also worth mentioning that sometimes the best measure of a model's performance is to consider how well it meets or doesn't meet other objectives. For instance, you may need to explain a model's logic in simple language, which would eliminate some models from consideration. Additionally, even if it performs very well, a model that is too slow or difficult to scale to a production environment is completely useless.

An obvious extension of measuring performance is to identify automated ways to find the best models for a particular task. In the next chapter, we will build upon our work so far to investigate ways to make smarter models by systematically iterating, refining, and combining learning algorithms.

# 11
# Improving Model Performance

When a sports team falls short of meeting its goal — whether it is to obtain an Olympic gold medal, a league championship, or a world record time — it must begin a process of searching for improvements to avoid a similar fate in the future. Imagine that you're the coach of such a team. How would you spend your practice sessions? Perhaps you'd direct the athletes to train harder or train differently in order to maximize every bit of their potential. Or, you might place a greater emphasis on teamwork, which could utilize the athletes' strengths and weaknesses more smartly.

Now imagine that you're the coach tasked with finding a world champion machine learning algorithm — perhaps to enter a competition, such as those posted on the Kaggle website (http://www.kaggle.com/competitions), to win the million dollar Netflix Prize (http://www.netflixprize.com/), or simply to improve the bottom line for your business. Where do you begin?

Although the context of the competition may differ, many strategies one might use to improve a sports team's performance can also be used to improve the performance of statistical learners. As the coach, it is your job to find the combination of training techniques and teamwork skills that allow you to meet your performance goals.

This chapter builds upon the material covered in this book so far to introduce a set of techniques for improving the predictive performance of machine learners. You will learn:

- How to fine-tune the performance of machine learning models by searching for the optimal set of training conditions
- Methods for combining models into groups that use teamwork to tackle the most challenging problems
- Cutting edge techniques for getting the maximum level of performance out of machine learners

Not all of these methods will be successful on every problem. Yet if you look at the winning entries to machine learning competitions, you're likely to find at least one of them has been employed. To remain competitive, you too will need to add these skills to your repertoire.

# Tuning stock models for better performance

Some learning problems are well suited to the stock models presented in previous chapters. In such cases, you may not need to spend much time iterating and refining the model; it may perform well enough as it is. On the other hand, some problems are inherently more difficult. The underlying concepts to be learned may be extremely complex, requiring an understanding of many subtle relationships, or it may have elements of random chance, making it difficult to define the signal within the noise.

Developing models that perform extremely well on such difficult problems is every bit an art as it is a science. Sometimes, a bit of intuition is helpful when trying to identify areas where performance can be improved. In other cases, finding improvements will require a brute-force, trial and error approach. Of course, the process of searching numerous possible improvements can be aided by the use of automated programs.

In *Chapter 5, Divide and Conquer – Classification Using Decision Trees and Rules*, we attempted a difficult problem: identifying loans that were likely to enter into default. Although we were able to use performance tuning methods to obtain a respectable classification accuracy of about 72 percent, upon a more careful examination in *Chapter 10, Evaluating Model Performance*, we realized that the high accuracy was a bit misleading. In spite of the reasonable accuracy, the kappa statistic was only about 0.20, which suggested that the model was actually performing somewhat poorly. In this section, we'll revisit the credit scoring model to see if we can improve the results.

 To follow along with the examples, download the `credit.csv` file from the Packt Publishing's website and save it to your R working directory. Load the file into a data frame using the command: `credit <- read.csv("credit.csv")`

You will recall that we first used a stock C5.0 decision tree to build the classifier for the credit data. We then attempted to improve its performance by adjusting the `trials` parameter to increase the number of boosting iterations. By increasing the trials from the default of 1 up to the values of 10 and 100, we were able to increase the model's accuracy. This process of adjusting the model fit options is called **parameter tuning**.

Parameter tuning is not limited to decision trees. For instance, we tuned k-nearest neighbor models when we searched for the best value of $k$, and used a number of options for neural networks and support vector machines, such as adjusting the number of nodes, hidden layers, or choosing different kernel functions. Most machine learning algorithms allow you to adjust at least one parameter, and the most sophisticated models offer a large number of ways to tweak the model fit to your liking. Although this allows the model to be tailored closely to the data, the complexity of all the possible options can be daunting. A more systematic approach is warranted.

# Using caret for automated parameter tuning

Rather than choosing arbitrary values for each of the model's parameters—a task that is not only tedious but somewhat unscientific—it is better to conduct a search through many possible parameter values to find the best combination.

The `caret` package, which we used extensively in *Chapter 10, Evaluating Model Performance*, provides tools to assist with automated parameter tuning. The core functionality is provided by a `train()` function that serves as a standardized interface to train 150 different machine learning models for both classification and regression tasks. By using this function, it is possible to automate the search for optimal models using a choice of evaluation methods and metrics.

Do not feel overwhelmed by the large number of models—we've already covered many of them in earlier chapters. Others are simple variants or extensions of the base concepts. Given what you've learned so far, you should be confident that you have the ability to understand all of the 150 choices.

Automated parameter tuning requires you to consider three questions:

- What type of machine learning model (and/or specific implementation of the algorithm) should be trained on the data?
- Which model parameters can be adjusted, and how extensively should they be tuned to find the optimal settings?
- What criteria should be used to evaluate the models to find the best candidate?

To answer the first question involves finding a well-suited match between the machine learning task and one of the 150 models. Obviously, this requires an understanding of the breadth and depth of machine learning models. This book provides the background needed for the former, while additional practice will help with the latter. Additionally, it can help to work through a process of elimination: nearly half of the models can be eliminated depending on whether the task is classification or regression; others can be excluded based on the format of the data or the need to avoid black box models, and so on. In any case, there's also no reason you can't try several approaches and compare the best result of each.

Addressing the second question is a matter largely dictated by the choice of model, since each algorithm utilizes a unique set of parameters. The available tuning parameters for each of the predictive models covered in this book are listed in the following table. Keep in mind that although some models have additional options not shown, only those listed in the table are supported by `caret` for automatic tuning.

 For a complete list of the 150 models and corresponding tuning parameters covered by `caret`, refer to the table provided by package author *Max Kuhn* at: `http://caret.r-forge.r-project.org/modelList.html`

| Model | Learning task | Method name | Parameters |
|---|---|---|---|
| k-Nearest Neighbors | Classification | knn | k |
| Naïve Bayes | Classification | nb | fL, usekernel |
| Decision Trees | Classification | C5.0 | model, trials, winnow |
| OneR Rule Learner | Classification | OneR | None |
| RIPPER Rule Learner | Classification | JRip | NumOpt |
| Linear Regression | Regression | lm | None |
| Regression Trees | Regression | rpart | cp |
| Model Trees | Regression | M5 | pruned, smoothed, rules |
| Neural Networks | Dual use | nnet | size, decay |
| Support Vector Machines (Linear Kernel) | Dual use | svmLinear | C |
| Support Vector Machines (Radial Basis Kernel) | Dual use | svmRadial | C, sigma |
| Random Forests | Dual use | rf | mtry |

The goal of automatic tuning is to search a set of candidate models comprising a matrix, or **grid**, of possible combinations of parameters. Because it is impractical to search every conceivable parameter value, only a subset of possibilities is used to construct the grid. By default, `caret` searches at most three values for each of $p$ parameters, which means that $3^p$ candidate models will be tested. For example, by default, the automatic tuning of k-nearest neighbors will compare $3^1 = 3$ candidate models, for instance, one each of `k=5`, `k=7`, and `k=9`. Similarly, tuning a decision tree could result in a comparison of up to 27 different candidate models, comprising the grid of $3^3 = 27$ possible combinations of `model`, `trials`, and `winnow` settings. In practice, however, only 12 models are actually tested. This is because the `model` and `winnow` parameters can only take two values (`tree` versus `rules` and `TRUE` versus `FALSE`, respectively), which makes the grid size $3*2*2 = 12$.

Since the `caret` package's default search grid may not be ideal for your learning problem, it also allows you to provide a custom search grid, defined by a simple command which we will cover later.

The third and final step in automatic model tuning involves choosing an approach to identify the best model among the candidates. This uses the methods discussed in *Chapter 10, Evaluating Model Performance* such as the choice of resampling strategy to create training and test datasets, and the use of model performance statistics to measure the predictive accuracy.

All of the resampling strategies and many of the performance statistics we've learned are supported by `caret`. These include statistics such as accuracy and kappa (for classifiers) and R-squared or RMSE (for numeric models). Cost-sensitive measures like sensitivity, specificity, and area under the ROC curve (AUC) can also be used if desired.

By default, when choosing the best model, `caret` will select the model with the largest value of the desired performance measure. Because this practice sometimes results in the selection of models that achieve marginal performance improvements via large increases in model complexity, alternative model selection functions are provided.

Given the wide variety of options, it is helpful that many of the defaults are reasonable. For instance, it will use prediction accuracy on a bootstrap sample to choose the best performer for classification models. Beginning with these default values, we can then tweak the `train()` function to design a wide variety of experiments.

# Creating a simple tuned model

To illustrate the process of tuning a model, let's begin by observing what happens when we attempt to tune the credit scoring model using the caret package's default settings. From there, we will learn how adjust the options to our liking.

The simplest way to tune a learner requires only that you specify a model type via the method parameter. Since we used C5.0 decision trees previously with the credit model, we'll continue our work by optimizing this learner. The basic train() command for tuning a C5.0 decision tree using the default settings is as follows:

```
> library(caret)

> set.seed(300)

> m <- train(default ~ ., data = credit, method = "C5.0")
```

First, the set.seed() function is used to initialize R's random number generator to a set starting position. You may recall that we have used this function in several prior chapters. By setting the seed parameter (in this case to the arbitrary number 300), the random numbers will follow a predefined sequence. This allows simulations like train(), which use random sampling, to be repeated with identical results—a very helpful feature if you are sharing code or attempting to replicate a prior result.

Next, the R formula interface is used to define a tree as default ~ .. This models loan default status (yes or no) using all of the other features in the credit data frame. The parameter method = "C5.0" tells caret to use the C5.0 decision tree algorithm.

After you've entered the preceding command, there may be a significant delay (dependent upon your computer's capabilities) as the tuning process occurs. Even though this is a fairly small dataset, a substantial amount of calculation must occur. R is repeatedly generating random samples of data, building decision trees, computing performance statistics, and evaluating the result.

The result of the experiment is saved in an object, which we named m. If you would like a peek at the object's contents, the command str(m) will list all the associated data—but this can be quite overwhelming. Instead, simply type the name of the object for a condensed summary of the results. For instance, typing m yields the following output:

**1** 1000 samples
    16 predictors
     2 classes: 'no', 'yes'

**2** No pre-processing
    Resampling: Bootstrap (25 reps)

Summary of sample sizes: 1000, 1000, 1000, 1000, 1000, 1000, ...

**3** Resampling results across tuning parameters:

| model | trials | winnow | Accuracy | Kappa | Accuracy SD | Kappa SD |
|-------|--------|--------|----------|-------|-------------|----------|
| rules | 1  | FALSE | 0.685 | 0.258 | 0.0256 | 0.0562 |
| rules | 1  | TRUE  | 0.689 | 0.255 | 0.0268 | 0.057  |
| rules | 10 | FALSE | 0.711 | 0.309 | 0.0209 | 0.0459 |
| rules | 10 | TRUE  | 0.711 | 0.304 | 0.0195 | 0.0448 |
| rules | 20 | FALSE | 0.722 | 0.326 | 0.0198 | 0.0451 |
| rules | 20 | TRUE  | 0.723 | 0.327 | 0.0184 | 0.0371 |
| tree  | 1  | FALSE | 0.677 | 0.229 | 0.0303 | 0.07   |
| tree  | 1  | TRUE  | 0.677 | 0.222 | 0.027  | 0.0596 |
| tree  | 10 | FALSE | 0.722 | 0.288 | 0.0206 | 0.056  |
| tree  | 10 | TRUE  | 0.717 | 0.278 | 0.017  | 0.0436 |
| tree  | 20 | FALSE | 0.73  | 0.307 | 0.0201 | 0.0562 |
| tree  | 20 | TRUE  | 0.729 | 0.306 | 0.015  | 0.0415 |

**4** Accuracy was used to select the optimal model using the largest value.
The final values used for the model were model = tree, trials = 20
and winnow = FALSE.

The summary includes four main components:

1. **A brief description of the input dataset**: If you are familiar with your data and have applied the `train()` function correctly, none of this information should come as a surprise.

2. **A report of preprocessing and resampling methods applied**: Here we see that 25 bootstrap samples, each including 1000 examples, were used to train the models.

3. **A list of candidate models evaluated**: In this section, we can confirm that 12 different models were tested, based on combinations of three C5.0 tuning parameters: `model`, `trials`, and `winnow`. The average and standard deviation (labeled SD) of the accuracy and kappa statistics for each candidate model are also shown.

4. **The choice of best model**: As noted, the model with the largest accuracy value (`0.73`) was chosen as the best. This was the model that used a `model = tree`, `trials = 20`, and `winnow = FALSE`.

The `train()` function uses the tuning parameters from the best model (as indicated by #4 previously) to build a model on the full input dataset, which is stored in the m object as `m$finalModel`. In most cases, you will not need to work directly with the `finalModel` sub-object. Instead, using the `predict()` function with the m object will generate predictions as expected, while also providing added functionality that will be described shortly. For example, to apply the best model to make predictions on the training data, you would use the following commands:

```
> p <- predict(m, credit)
```

The resulting vector of predictions works just as we have done many times before:

```
> table(p, credit$default)


p       no yes
  no   700   2
  yes    0 298
```

Of the 1000 examples used for training the final model, only two were misclassified. Keep in mind that this is the resubstitution error and should not be viewed as indicative of performance on unseen data. The bootstrap estimate of 73 percent (shown in the summary output) is a more realistic estimate of future performance.

As mentioned previously, there are additional benefits of using `predict()`, directly on `train()` objects rather than using the stored `finalModel` directly or training a new model using the optimized parameters.

First, any data preprocessing steps that the `train()` function applied to the data will be similarly applied to the data used for generating predictions. This includes transformations like centering and scaling (that is, when using k-nearest neighbors), missing value imputation, and others. This ensures that the data preparation steps used for developing the model remain in place when the model is deployed.

Second, the `predict()` function for `caret` models provides a standardized interface for obtaining predicted class values and predicted class probabilities — even for models that ordinarily would require additional steps to obtain this information. The predicted classes are provided by default as follows:

```
> head(predict(m, credit))
[1] no  yes no  no  yes no
Levels: no yes
```

To obtain the estimated probabilities for each class, add an additional parameter specifying `type = "prob"`:

```
> head(predict(m, credit, type = "prob"))
          no          yes
1 0.9606970 0.03930299
2 0.1388444 0.86115561
3 1.0000000 0.00000000
4 0.7720279 0.22797208
5 0.2948062 0.70519385
6 0.8583715 0.14162851
```

Even in cases where the underlying model refers to the prediction probabilities using a different string (for example, `"raw"` for a `naiveBayes` model), `caret` automatically translates `type = "prob"` to the appropriate string behind the scenes.

## Customizing the tuning process

The decision tree we created previously demonstrates the `caret` package's ability to produce an optimized model with minimal intervention. The default settings allow strongly performing models to be created easily. However, without digging deeper, you may miss out on the upper echelon of performance. Or perhaps you want to change the default evaluation criteria to something more appropriate for your learning problem. Each step in the process can be customized to your learning task.

To illustrate this flexibility, let's modify our work on the credit decision tree explained previously to mirror the process we had used in *Chapter 10, Evaluating Model Performance*. If you recall from that chapter, we had estimated the kappa statistic using 10-fold cross-validation. We'll do the same here, using kappa to optimize the boosting parameter of the decision tree (boosting the accuracy of decision trees was previously covered in *Chapter 5, Divide and Conquer – Classification Using Decision Trees and Rules*).

The `trainControl()` function is used to create a set of configuration options known as a control object, which can be used with the `train()` function. These options allow for the management of model evaluation criteria such as the resampling strategy and the measure used for choosing the best model. Although this function can be used to modify nearly every aspect of a tuning experiment, we'll focus on two important parameters: `method` and `selectionFunction`.

 If you're eager for more details, you can use the `?trainControl` help command for a list of all parameters.

For the `trainControl()` function, the `method` parameter is used to set the resampling method, such as holdout sampling or k-fold cross-validation. The following table lists the shortened name string `caret` uses to call the method, as well as any additional parameters for adjusting the sample size and number of iterations. Although the default options for these resampling methods follow popular convention, you may choose to adjust these depending upon the size of your dataset and the complexity of your model.

| Resampling method | Method name | Additional options and default values |
|---|---|---|
| Holdout sampling | LGOCV | `p = 0.75` (training data proportion) |
| k-fold cross-validation | cv | `number = 10` (number of folds) |
| Repeated k-fold cross-validation | repeatedcv | `number = 10` (number of folds) |
| | | `repeats = 10` (number of iterations) |
| Bootstrap sampling | boot | `number = 25` (resampling iterations) |
| 0.632 bootstrap | boot632 | `number = 25` (resampling iterations) |
| Leave-one-out cross-validation | LOOCV | None |

The `trainControl()` parameter `selectionFunction` can be used to choose a function that selects the optimal model among the various candidates. Three such functions are included. The `best` function simply chooses the candidate with the best value on the specified performance measure. This is used by default. The other two functions are used to choose the most parsimonious (that is, simplest) model that is within a certain threshold of the best model's performance. The `oneSE` function chooses the simplest candidate within one standard error of the best performance, and `tolerance` uses the simplest candidate within a user-specified percentage.

 Some subjectivity is involved with the `caret` pacakage's ranking of models by simplicity. For information on how models are ranked, see the help page for the selection functions by typing `?best` at the R command prompt.

To create a control object named `ctrl` that uses 10-fold cross-validation and the `oneSE` selection function, use the following command. Note that `number = 10` is included only for clarity; since this is the default value for `method = "cv"`, it could have been omitted.

```
> ctrl <- trainControl(method = "cv", number = 10,
                   selectionFunction = "oneSE")
```

We'll use the result of this function shortly.

In the meantime, the next step in defining our experiment is to create a grid of parameters to optimize. The grid must include a column for each parameter in the desired model, prefixed by a period. Since we are using a C5.0 decision tree, this means we'll need columns with the names .model, .trials, and .winnow. For other models, refer to the table presented earlier in this chapter. Each row in the data frame represents a particular combination of parameter values.

Rather than creating this data frame ourselves—a difficult task if there are many possible combinations of parameter values—we can use the expand.grid() function, which creates data frames from the combinations of all values supplied. For example, suppose we would like to hold constant model = "tree" and winnow = "FALSE" while searching eight different values of trials. This can be created as:

```
> grid <- expand.grid(.model = "tree",
                       .trials = c(1, 5, 10, 15, 20, 25, 30, 35),
                       .winnow = "FALSE")
```

The resulting grid data frame contains *1\*8\*1 = 8* rows:

```
> grid
  .model .trials .winnow
1   tree       1   FALSE
2   tree       5   FALSE
3   tree      10   FALSE
4   tree      15   FALSE
5   tree      20   FALSE
6   tree      25   FALSE
7   tree      30   FALSE
8   tree      35   FALSE
```

Each row will be used to generate a candidate model for evaluation, built using that row's combination of model parameters.

Given this search grid and the control list created previously, we are ready to run a thoroughly customized train() experiment. As before, we'll set the random seed to ensure repeatable results. But this time, we'll pass our control object and tuning grid while adding a parameter metric = "Kappa", indicating the statistic to be used by the model evaluation function—in this case, "oneSE". The full command is as follows:

```
> set.seed(300)
> m <- train(default ~ ., data = credit, method = "C5.0",
             metric = "Kappa",
             trControl = ctrl,
             tuneGrid = grid)
```

This results in an object that we can view as before:

```
> m
```

```
 1000 samples
   16 predictors
    2 classes: 'no', 'yes'

No pre-processing
Resampling: Cross-Validation (10 fold)

Summary of sample sizes: 900, 900, 900, 900, 900, 900, ...

Resampling results across tuning parameters:

   trials  Accuracy  Kappa  Accuracy SD  Kappa SD
   1       0.724     0.312  0.0255       0.059
   5       0.713     0.292  0.0211       0.0602
   10      0.719     0.295  0.0311       0.0672
   15      0.721     0.301  0.0197       0.0511
   20      0.717     0.293  0.0279       0.0791
   25      0.728     0.315  0.0322       0.0937
   30      0.729     0.31   0.0277       0.0807
   35      0.741     0.339  0.0314       0.0935

Tuning parameter 'model' was held constant at a value of 'tree'
Tuning parameter 'winnow' was held constant at a value of 'FALSE'
Kappa was used to select the optimal model using  the one SE rule.
The final values used for the model were model = tree, trials = 1
and winnow = FALSE.
```

Although much of the output is similar to the previously tuned model, there are a few differences of note. Because 10-fold cross-validation was used, the sample size to build each candidate model was reduced to 900 rather than the 1000 used in the bootstrap. As we requested, eight candidate models were tested. Additionally, because model and winnow were held constant, their values are no longer shown in the results; instead, they are listed as a footnote.

The best model here differs quite significantly from the prior trial. Before, the best model used trials = 20 whereas here, the best used trials = 1. This seemingly odd finding is due to the fact that we used the oneSE rule rather the best rule to select the optimal model. Even though the 35-trial model offers the best raw performance according to kappa, the 1-trial model offers nearly the same performance yet is a much simpler model. Not only are simple models more computationally efficient, simple models are preferable because they reduce the chance of overfitting the training data.

# Improving model performance with meta-learning

As an alternative to increasing the performance of a single model, it is possible to combine several models to form a powerful team. Just as the best sports teams have players with complementary rather than overlapping skillsets some of the best machine learning algorithms utilize teams of complementary models. Because a model brings a unique bias to a learning task, it may readily learn one subset of examples but have trouble with another. Therefore, by intelligently using the talents of several diverse team members, it is possible to create a strong team of multiple weak learners.

This technique of combining and managing the predictions of multiple models falls within a wider set of **meta-learning** methods that broadly encompass any technique that involves learning how to learn. This might include anything from simple algorithms that gradually improve performance by automatically iterating over design decisions—for instance, the automated parameter tuning used earlier in this chapter—to highly complex algorithms that use concepts borrowed from evolutionary biology and genetics for self-modifying and adapting to learning tasks.

For the remainder of this chapter, we'll focus on meta-learning only as it pertains to modeling a relationship between the predictions of several models and the desired outcome. The teamwork-based techniques covered here are quite powerful, and are used quite often to build more effective classifiers.

# Understanding ensembles

Suppose you were a contestant on a television trivia show that allowed you to choose a panel of five friends to assist you with answering the final question for the million-dollar prize. Most people would try to stack the panel with a diverse set of subject-matter experts. For instance, a panel containing professors of literature, science, history, and art, along with a current pop-culture expert would be a safely well-rounded group. Given their breadth of knowledge, it would be unlikely to find a question that stumps the panel.

The meta-learning approach that utilizes a similar principle of creating a varied team of experts is known as an **ensemble**. All ensemble methods are based on the idea that by combining multiple weaker learners, a stronger learner is created. Using this simple principle, a large variety of algorithms has been developed distinguished largely by two questions:

- How are the weak learning models chosen and/or constructed?
- How are the weak learners' predictions combined to make a single final prediction?

When answering these questions, it can be helpful to imagine the ensemble in terms of the process diagram as follows; nearly all ensemble approaches follow this pattern.

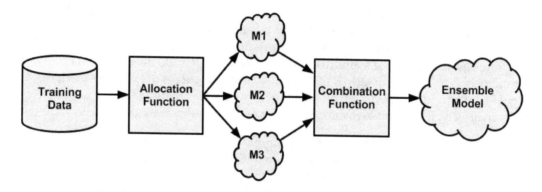

First, input training data is used to build a number of models. The **allocation function** dictates whether each model receives the full training dataset or merely a sample. Since the ideal ensemble includes a diverse set of models, the allocation function could increase diversity by artificially varying the input data to train a variety of learners. For instance, it might use bootstrap sampling to construct unique training datasets or pass on a different subset of features or examples to each model. On the other hand, if the ensemble already includes a diverse set of algorithms — such as a neural network, a decision tree, and a kNN classifier — then the allocation function might pass on the data relatively unchanged.

After the models are constructed, they can be used to generate a set of predictions, which must be managed in some way. The **combination function** governs how disagreements among the predictions are reconciled. For example, the ensemble might use a majority vote to determine the final prediction, or it could use a more complex strategy such as weighting each model's votes based on its prior performance.

Some ensembles even utilize another model to learn a combination function from various combinations of predictions. For example, when *M1* and *M2* both vote yes the actual class value is usually no, then the ensemble might ignore the votes of *M1* and *M2* and instead predict no. This process of using the predictions of several models to train a final arbiter model is known as **stacking**.

One of the benefits of using ensembles is that they may allow you to spend less time in pursuit of a single best model. Instead, you can train a number of reasonably strong candidates and combine them. Yet convenience isn't the only reason why ensemble-based methods continue to rack up wins in machine learning competitions; ensembles also offer a number of performance advantages over single models:

- **Better generalizability to future problems**: Because the opinions of several learners are incorporated into a single final prediction, no single bias is able to dominate. This reduces the chance of overfitting to a learning task.

- **Improved performance on massive or miniscule datasets**: Many models run into memory or complexity limits when an extremely large set of features or examples are used, making it more efficient to train several small models than a single full model. Additionally, it is often trivial to parallelize an ensemble using distributed computing methods. Conversely, ensembles also do well on the smallest datasets because resampling methods like bootstrapping are inherently part of many ensemble designs.

- **The ability to synthesize of data from distinct domains**: Since there is no one-size-fits-all learning algorithm — recall the No Free Lunch theorem — the ensemble's ability to incorporate evidence from multiple types of learners is increasingly important as Big Data continues to draw from disparate domains.

- **A more nuanced understanding of difficult learning tasks**: Real-world phenomena are often extremely complex with many interacting intricacies. Models that divide the task into smaller portions are likely to more accurately capture subtle patterns that a single global model might miss.

None of these benefits would be very helpful if you weren't able to easily apply ensemble methods in R, and there are many packages available to do just that. Let's take a look at several of the most popular ensemble methods and how they can be used to improve the performance of the credit model we've been working on.

# Bagging

One of the first ensemble methods to gain widespread acceptance used a technique called **bootstrap aggregating**, or **bagging** for short. As described by *Leo Breiman* in 1994, bagging generates a number of training datasets by bootstrap sampling the original training data. These datasets are then used to generate a set of models using a single learning algorithm. The models' predictions are combined using voting (for classification) or averaging (for numeric prediction).

 For additional information on bagging, refer to: *Bagging predictors, Machine Learning, Vol. 24*, pp. 123-140, by L. Breiman (1996).

Although bagging is a relatively simple ensemble, it can perform quite well as long as it is used with relatively **unstable** learners, that is, those generating models that tend to change substantially when the input data changes only slightly. Unstable models are essential to ensure the ensemble's diversity in spite of only minor variations between the bootstrap training datasets. For this reason, bagging is often used with decision trees, which have the tendency to vary dramatically given minor changes in input data.

The `ipred` package offers a classic implementation of bagged decision trees. To train the model, the `bagging()` function works similar to many of the models used previously. The `nbagg` parameter is used to control the number of decision trees voting in the ensemble (with a default value of 25). Depending on the difficulty of the learning task and the amount of training data, increasing this number may improve the model's performance, up to a limit. The downside is that this comes at the expense of additional computational expense; a large number of trees may take some time to train.

After installing the `ipred` package, we can create the ensemble as follows: We'll stick to the default value of 25 decision trees:

```
> library(ipred)
> set.seed(300)
> mybag <- bagging(default ~ ., data = credit, nbagg = 25)
```

The resulting model works as expected with the `predict()` function:

```
> credit_pred <- predict(mybag, credit)
> table(credit_pred, credit$default)
```

```
credit_pred   no yes
        no   699   2
       yes     1 298
```

Given the preceding results, the model seems to have fit the training data extremely well. To see how this translates into future performance, we can use the bagged trees with 10-fold CV via the `train()` function in the `caret` package. Note that the method name for the `ipred` bagged trees function is `treebag` as follows:

```
> library(caret)
> set.seed(300)
> ctrl <- trainControl(method = "cv", number = 10)
> train(default ~ ., data = credit, method = "treebag",
        trControl = ctrl)
```

```
1000 samples
  16 predictors
   2 classes: 'no', 'yes'


No pre-processing
Resampling: Cross-Validation (10 fold)


Summary of sample sizes: 900, 900, 900, 900, 900, 900, ...


Resampling results


  Accuracy  Kappa  Accuracy SD  Kappa SD
  0.735     0.33   0.0344       0.0859
```

The kappa statistic of `0.33` for this model suggests that the bagged tree model performs on par with our best-tuned C5.0 decision tree.

To get beyond bags of decision trees, the `caret` package also provides a more general `bag()` function. It includes out-of-the-box support for a handful of models, though it can be adapted to more types with a bit of additional effort. The `bag()` function uses a control object to configure the bagging process. It requires the specification of three functions: one for fitting the model, one for making predictions, and one for aggregating the votes.

For example, suppose we wanted to create a bagged **support vector machine (SVM)** model, using the `ksvm()` function in the `kernlab` package we used in *Chapter 7, Black Box Methods – Neural Networks and Support Vector Machines*. The `bag()` function requires us to provide functionality for training the SVMs, making predictions, and counting votes.

Rather than writing these ourselves, the `caret` package's built-in `svmBag` list object supplies three functions we can use for this purpose:

```
> str(svmBag)
List of 3
 $ fit      :function (x, y, ...)
 $ pred     :function (object, x)
 $ aggregate:function (x, type = "class")
```

By looking at the `svmBag$fit` function, we see that it simply calls the `ksvm()` function from the `kernlab` package and returns the result:

```
> svmBag$fit
function (x, y, ...)
{
    library(kernlab)
    out <- ksvm(as.matrix(x), y, prob.model = is.factor(y), ...)
    out
}
<environment: namespace:caret>
```

The `pred` and `aggregate` functions for `svmBag` are also similarly straightforward. By studying these functions and creating your own in the same format, it is possible to use bagging with any machine learning algorithm you would like.

 The `caret` package also includes example objects for bags of naive Bayes models (nbBag), decision trees (ctreeBag), and neural networks (nnetBag).

Applying the three functions in the `svmBag` list, we can create a bagging control object:

```
> bagctrl <- bagControl(fit = svmBag$fit,
                        predict = svmBag$pred,
                        aggregate = svmBag$aggregate)
```

By using this with the `train()` function and the training control object (`ctrl`) defined earlier, we can evaluate the bagged SVM model as follows. Keep in mind that the `kernlab` package is required for this to work; you may need to install it if you have not done so previously.

```
> set.seed(300)
> svmbag <- train(default ~ ., data = credit, "bag",
                  trControl = ctrl, bagControl = bagctrl)
> svmbag
1000 samples
  16 predictors
   2 classes: 'no', 'yes'

No pre-processing
Resampling: Cross-Validation (10 fold)
```

```
Summary of sample sizes: 900, 900, 900, 900, 900, 900, ...


Resampling results


  Accuracy  Kappa  Accuracy SD  Kappa SD
  0.728     0.293  0.0444       0.132


Tuning parameter 'vars' was held constant at a value of 35
```

Given that the kappa statistic is below 0.30, it seems that the bagged SVM model performs more poorly than the bagged decision tree model. It's worth pointing out that the standard deviation of the kappa statistic (labeled `Kappa SD`) is fairly large compared to the bagged decision tree model. This suggests that the performance varies substantially among the folds in the cross-validation. Such variation may imply that the performance could be improved further by upping the number of models in the ensemble.

# Boosting

Another popular ensemble-based method is called **boosting**, because it boosts the performance of weak learners to attain the performance of stronger learners. This method is based largely on the work of *Rob Schapire* and *Yoav Freund*, who have published extensively on the topic.

 For additional information on boosting, refer to: *Boosting – Foundations and Algorithms Understanding Rule Learners* by R. Schapire, and Y. Freund, (The MIT Press, 2012).

Given a number of classifiers, each with an error rate less than 50 percent; *Schapire* and *Freund* discovered that boosting will result in performance often quite better and certainly no worse than the best of these models. Essentially, this allows one to increase performance to an arbitrary threshold simply by adding more weak learners. Given the obvious utility of this finding, boosting is thought to be one of the most significant discoveries in machine learning.

Similar to bagging, boosting uses ensembles of models trained on resampled data and a vote to determine the final prediction. The key difference is that the resampled datasets in boosting are constructed specifically to generate complementary learners, and the vote is weighted based on each model's performance rather than giving each an equal vote.

A boosting algorithm called **AdaBoost**, or **adaptive boosting**, was proposed in 1997. The algorithm is based on the idea of generating weak leaners that iteratively learn a larger portion of the difficult-to-classify examples in the training data by paying more attention (that is, giving more weight) to often misclassified examples.

Beginning from an unweighted dataset, the first classifier attempts to model the outcome. Examples that the classifier predicted correctly will be less likely to appear in the training dataset for the following classifier, and conversely, the difficult-to-classify examples will appear more frequently. As additional rounds of weak learners are added, they are trained on data with successively more difficult examples. The process continues until the desired overall error rate is reached or performance no longer improves. At that point, each classifier's vote is weighted according to its accuracy on the training data on which it was built.

Though boosting principles can be applied to nearly any type of model, the principles are most commonly used with decision trees. We already used boosting in this way in *Chapter 5, Divide and Conquer – Classification Using Decision Trees and Rules*, as a method to improve the performance of a C5.0 decision tree.

The AdaBoost.M1 algorithm provides an alternative tree-based implementation of AdaBoost for classification. Due to its similarity to the boosted trees we created earlier, AdaBoost.M1 is not covered here.

The AdaBoost.M1 algorithm can be found in the adabag R package. For more information refer to *adabag – an R package for classification with boosting and bagging, Journal of Statistical Software, Vol 54(2)*, pp. 1-35, by *E. Alfaro, M. Gamez, and N. Garcia (2013)*.

# Random forests

Another ensemble-based method called **random forests** (or **decision tree forests**) focus only on ensembles of decision trees. This method was championed by *Leo Breiman* and *Adele Cutler,* and combines the base principles of bagging with random feature selection to add additional diversity to the decision tree models. After the ensemble of trees (the forest) is generated, the model uses a vote to combine the trees' predictions.

For more detail on how random forests are constructed, refer to *Random forests, Machine Learning, Vol. 45*, pp. 5-32, by *L. Breiman (2001)*.

Random forests combine versatility and power into a single machine learning approach. Because the ensemble uses only a small, random portion of the full feature set, random forests can handle extremely large datasets, where the so-called "curse of dimensionality" might cause other models to fail. At the same time, its error rates for most learning tasks are on par with nearly any other method.

 Although the term "Random Forests" is trademarked by *Breiman* and *Cutler* (see http://www.stat.berkeley. edu/~breiman/RandomForests/ for details), the term is used sometimes colloquially to refer to any type of decision tree ensemble. A pedant would use the more general term "decision tree forests" except when referring to the algorithm by *Breiman* and *Cutler*.

The following table lists the general strengths and weaknesses of random forest models. It's worth noting that relative to other ensemble-based methods, random forests are quite competitive and offer key advantages relative to the competition. For instance, random forests tend to be easier to use and less prone to overfitting.

| Strengths | Weaknesses |
|---|---|
| • An all-purpose model that performs well on most problems | • Unlike a decision tree, the model is not easily interpretable |
| • Can handle noisy or missing data; categorical or continuous features | • May require some work to tune the model to the data |
| • Selects only the most important features | |
| • Can be used on data with an extremely large number of features or examples | |

Due to their power, versatility, and ease of use, random forests are quickly becoming one of the most popular machine learning methods. Later on in this chapter, we'll compare a random forest model head-to-head against the boosted C5.0 tree.

# Training random forests

Though there are several packages to create random forests in R, the `randomForest` package is perhaps the implementation most faithful to the specification by *Breiman* and *Cutler*. An added benefit is that it is supported by `caret` for automated tuning. The syntax for training this model is as follows:

---

**Random forest syntax**

using the `randomForest()` function in the `randomForest` package

**Building the classifier:**

```
m <- randomForest(train, class, ntree = 500, mtry = sqrt(p))
```

- `train` is a data frame containing training data
- `class` is a factor vector with the class for each row in the training data
- `ntree` is an integer specifying the number of trees to grow
- `mtry` is an optional integer specifying the number of features to randomly select at each split (uses `sqrt(p)` by default, where `p` is the number of features in the data)

The function will return a random forest object that can be used to make predictions.

**Making predictions:**

```
p <- predict(m, test, type = "response")
```

- `m` is a model trained by the `randomForest()` function
- `test` is a data frame containing test data with the same features as the training data used to build the classifier
- `type` is either `"response"`, `"prob"`, or `"votes"` and is used to indicate whether the predictions vector should contain the predicted class, the predicted probabilities, or a matrix of vote counts, respectively.

The function will return predictions according to the value of the `type` parameter.

**Example:**

```
credit_model <- randomForest(credit_train, loan_default)
credit_prediction <- predict(credit_model, credit_test)
```

---

As noted previously, by default, the `randomForest()` function creates an ensemble of 500 trees that consider `sqrt(p)` random features at each split (where p is the number of features in the training dataset). Whether or not these parameters are appropriate depends on the nature of the learning task and training data. Generally, more complex learning problems and larger datasets (both more features as well as more examples) work better with a larger number of trees.

The goal of using a large number of trees is to train enough that each feature has a chance to appear in several models. This is the basis of the sqrt (p) default value for the mtry parameter; using this value limits the features sufficiently such that substantial random variation occurs from tree-to-tree. For example, since the credit data has 16 features, each tree would be limited to splitting on sqrt (16) = 4 features at any time.

Let's see how the default randomForest () parameters work with the credit data. We'll train the model just as we have done with other learners (the set.seed () function ensures that the result can be repeated).

```
> library(randomForest)
> set.seed(300)
> rf <- randomForest(default ~ ., data = credit)
```

To look at a summary of the model's performance, we can simply type the resulting object's name:

```
> rf


Call:
 randomForest(formula = default ~ ., data = credit)
               Type of random forest: classification
                     Number of trees: 500
No. of variables tried at each split: 4


        OOB estimate of error rate: 23.8%
Confusion matrix:
        no yes class.error
no   640  60  0.08571429
yes 178 122  0.59333333
```

As expected, the output notes that the random forest included 500 trees and tried 4 variables at each split. You might be alarmed at the seemingly poor resubstitution error according to the display confusion matrix—the error rate of 23.8 percent is far worse than any of the other ensemble methods so far. In fact, this confusion matrix is not resubstitution error at all. Instead, it reflects the **out-of-bag error rate** (labeled OOB estimate of error rate), which is an unbiased estimate of the test set error. This means that it should be a fairly reasonable estimate of future performance.

The out-of-bag estimate is computed during the construction of the random forest. Essentially, any example not selected for a single tree's bootstrap sample can be used as a way to test the model's performance on unseen data. At the end of the forest construction, the predictions for each example each time it was held out are tallied, and a vote is taken to determine the final prediction for the example. The total error rate of such predictions becomes the out-of-bag error rate.

# Evaluating random forest performance

As mentioned previously, the `randomForest()` function is also supported by `caret`, which allows us to optimize the model while at the same time calculating performance measures beyond the out-of-bag error rate. To make things interesting, let's compare an auto-tuned random forest to the best auto-tuned boosted C5.0 model we've been working on. We'll treat this experiment as if we were hoping to identify a candidate model for submission to a machine learning competition.

We must first load `caret` and set our training control options. For the most accurate comparison of model performance, we'll use repeated 10-fold cross-validation: 10 times 10-fold CV. While this means that the models will take a much longer time and be more computationally intensive to evaluate; since this is our final comparison, we should be *very* sure that we're making the right choice—the winner of this showdown will be our only entry into the machine learning competition.

```
> library(caret)
> ctrl <- trainControl(method = "repeatedcv",
                       number = 10, repeats = 10)
```

Next, we'll set up the tuning grid for the random forest. The only tuning parameter for this model is `mtry`, which defines how many features are randomly selected at each split. By default, we know that the random forest will use `sqrt(16)` = 4 features. To be thorough, we'll also test values half of that, twice that, as well as the full set of features. Thus, we need to create a grid with values of 2, 4, 8, and 16 as follows:

```
> grid_rf <- expand.grid(.mtry = c(2, 4, 8, 16))
```

 A random forest that considers the full set of features at each split is essentially the same as a bagged decision tree model.

We can supply the resulting grid to the `train()` function with the `ctrl` object as follows. We'll use the kappa metric to select the best model.

```
> set.seed(300)
> m_rf <- train(default ~ ., data = credit, method = "rf",
                metric = "Kappa", trControl = ctrl,
                tuneGrid = grid_rf)
```

The preceding command may take some time to complete as it has quite a bit of work to do! When it finishes, we'll compare that to a boosted tree using 10, 20, 30, and 40 iterations:

```
> grid_c50 <- expand.grid(.model = "tree",
                          .trials = c(10, 20, 30, 40),
                          .winnow = "FALSE")
> set.seed(300)
> m_c50 <- train(default ~ ., data = credit, method = "C5.0",
                 metric = "Kappa", trControl = ctrl,
                 tuneGrid = grid_c50)
```

When the C5.0 decision tree finally completes, we can compare the two approaches side-by-side. For the random forest model the results are:

```
> m_rf
```

```
Resampling results across tuning parameters:
```

| mtry | Accuracy | Kappa | Accuracy SD | Kappa SD |
|------|----------|-------|-------------|----------|
| 2    | 0.725    | 0.128 | 0.0169      | 0.0636   |
| 4    | 0.75     | 0.293 | 0.0299      | 0.0877   |
| 8    | 0.754    | 0.338 | 0.0311      | 0.0835   |
| 16   | 0.756    | 0.361 | 0.0338      | 0.0889   |

For the boosted C5.0 model the results are:

```
> m_c50
```

```
Resampling results across tuning parameters:
```

| trials | Accuracy | Kappa | Accuracy SD | Kappa SD |
|--------|----------|-------|-------------|----------|
| 10     | 0.732    | 0.322 | 0.0402      | 0.0952   |
| 20     | 0.734    | 0.327 | 0.0403      | 0.0971   |
| 30     | 0.738    | 0.334 | 0.0367      | 0.0894   |
| 40     | 0.739    | 0.334 | 0.0393      | 0.0975   |

With a kappa of 0.361, the random forest model with mtry = 16 was the winner among these eight models. It was marginally higher than the best C5.0 decision tree, which had a kappa of 0.334. Based on these results, we would submit the random forest as our final model. Without actually evaluating the model on the competition data, we have no way of knowing for sure whether it will end up winning; but given our performance estimates, it's the safer bet. With a bit of luck, perhaps we'll come away with the prize.

# Summary

After reading this chapter, you now know the base techniques that can be used to win data mining and machine learning competitions. Automated tuning methods can assist with squeezing every bit of performance out of a single model. On the other hand, performance gains are also possible by creating groups of machine learning models that work together.

Although this chapter was designed to help you prepare competition-ready models keep in mind that your fellow competitors have access to the same techniques. You won't be able to get away with stagnancy; you have to keep working to add proprietary methods to your bag of tricks. Perhaps you can bring unique subject-matter expertise to the table, or perhaps your strengths include an eye for detail in data preparation. In any case, practice makes perfect, so take advantage of open competitions to test, evaluate, and improve your own machine learning skillset.

In the next chapter—the last in this book—we'll take a bird's eye look at ways to apply machine learning to some highly specialized and difficult domains using R. You'll gain the knowledge needed to apply machine learning to tasks at the cutting edge of the field.

# 12
# Specialized
# Machine Learning Topics

By now, you are probably eager to start applying machine learning to your own projects—you may have even already done so. If you have attempted a project on your own, you likely found that, the task of turning data into action is more difficult than this book made it appear.

As you attempted to gather data, you might have realized that the information was trapped in a proprietary spreadsheet format or spread across pages on the Web. Making matters worse, after spending hours manually reformatting the data, perhaps your computer slowed to a crawl after running out of memory. Perhaps R even crashed or froze your machine. Hopefully you were undeterred; it does get easier with time.

This chapter covers techniques that may not apply to every machine learning project, but could prove useful for certain types of work. You might find the information particularly useful if you tend to work with data that are:

- Stored in unstructured or proprietary formats such as web pages, web APIs, or spreadsheets
- From a domain such as bioinformatics or social network analysis, which presents additional challenges
- So extremely large that R cannot store the dataset in memory or machine learning takes a very long time to complete

You're not alone if you suffer from any of these problems. Although there is no panacea—these issues are the bane of the data scientist as well as the reason for data skills to be in high demand—through the dedicated efforts of the R community, a number of R packages provide a head start toward solving the problem.

This chapter provides a cookbook of such solutions. Even if you are an experienced R veteran, you may discover a package that simplifies your workflow, or perhaps one day you will author a package that makes work easier for everybody else!

# Working with specialized data

Unlike the analyses in this book, real-world data are rarely packaged in a simple CSV form that can be downloaded from a website. Instead, significant effort is needed to prepare data for analysis. Data must be collected, merged, sorted, filtered, or reformatted to meet the requirements of the learning algorithm. This process is known informally as **data munging**. Munging has become even more important as the size of typical datasets has grown from megabytes to gigabytes and data are gathered from unrelated and messy sources, many of which are domain-specific. Several packages and resources for working with specialized or domain-specific data are listed in the following sections.

# Getting data from the Web with the RCurl package

The RCurl package by *Duncan Temple Lang* provides an R interface to the **curl** (client for URLs) utility, a command-line tool for transferring data over networks. The curl utility is useful for web scraping, which refers to the practice of harvesting data from websites and transforming it into a structured form.

 Documentation for the RCurl package can be found on the Web at http://www.omegahat.org/RCurl/.

After installing the RCurl package, downloading a page is as simple as typing:

```
> library(RCurl)
> webpage <- getURL("http://www.packtpub.com/")
```

This will save the full text of the Packt Publishing's homepage (including all web markup) into the R character object named webpage. As shown in the following lines, this is not very useful as-is:

```
> str(webpage)
 chr "<!DOCTYPE html>\n<html xmlns=\"http://www.w3.org/1999/xhtml\"
lang=\"en\" xml:lang=\"en\" >\n<head>\n    <title>Home | Packt Pu"|  __
truncated__
```

Because most websites use web-specific formats such as XML/HTML and JSON, the web data must be processed before it is useful in R. Two functions for doing so are discussed in the following sections.

# Reading and writing XML with the XML package

XML is a plaintext, human-readable, but structured markup language upon which many document formats have been based. In particular, many web-based documents utilize XML formatting. The XML package by *Duncan Temple Lang* provides a suite of functionality based on the popular C-based libxml2 parser for reading and writing XML documents. Combined with the Rcurl package (noted previously), it is possible to download and process documents directly from the web.

> More information on the XML package, including simple examples to get you started quickly, can be found at the project's website: http://www.omegahat.org/RSXML/.

# Reading and writing JSON with the rjson package

The rjson package by *Alex Couture-Beil* can be used to read and write files in the **JavaScript Object Notation (JSON)** format. JSON is a standard, plaintext format, most often used for data structures and objects on the Web. The format has become popular recently due to its utility in creating web applications, but despite the name, it is not limited to web browsers.

> For details about the JSON format, go to http://www.json.org/.

The JSON format stores objects in plain text strings. After installing the rjson package, to convert from JSON to R:

```
> library(rjson)
> r_object <- fromJSON(json_string)
```

To convert from an R object to a JSON object:

```
> json_string <- toJSON(r_object)
```

Used with the Rcurl package (noted previously), it is possible to write R programs that utilize JSON data directly from many online data stores.

# Reading and writing Microsoft Excel spreadsheets using xlsx

The xlsx package by *Adrian A. Dragulescu* offers functions to read and write to spreadsheets in the Excel 2007 (or earlier) format—a common task in many business environments. The package is based on the Apache POI Java API for working with Microsoft's documents.

>  For more information on xlsx, including a quick start document, go to https://code.google.com/p/rexcel/.

# Working with bioinformatics data

Data analysis in the field of bioinformatics offers a number of challenges relative to other fields due to the unique nature of genetic data. The use of DNA and protein microarrays has resulted in datasets that are often much wider than they are long (that is, they have more features than examples). This creates problems when attempting to apply conventional visualizations, statistical tests, and machine learning-methods to such data.

>  A CRAN task view for statistical genetics/bioinformatics is available at http://cran.r-project.org/web/views/Genetics.html.

The **Bioconductor** project (http://www.bioconductor.org/) of the Fred Hutchinson Cancer Research Center in Seattle, Washington, provides a centralized hub for methods of analyzing genomic data. Using R as its foundation, Bioconductor adds packages and documentation specific to the field of bioinformatics.

Bioconductor provides workflows for analyzing microarray data from common platforms such as for analysis of microarray platforms, including Affymetrix, Illumina, Nimblegen, and Agilent. Additional functionality includes sequence annotation, multiple testing procedures, specialized visualizations, and many other functions.

# Working with social network data and graph data

Social network data and graph data present many challenges. These data record connections, or links, between people or objects. With $N$ people, an $N$ by $N$ matrix of links is possible, which creates tremendous complexity as the number of people grows. The network is then analyzed using statistical measures and visualizations to search for meaningful patterns of relationships.

The `network` package by *Carter T. Butts*, *David Hunter*, and *Mark S. Handcock* offers a specialized data structure for working with such networks. A closely-related package, `sna`, allows analysis and visualization of the `network` objects.

 For more information on `network` and `sna`, refer to the project website hosted by the University of Washington: `http://www.statnet.org/`.

# Improving the performance of R

R has a reputation for being slow and memory inefficient, a reputation that is at least somewhat earned. These faults are largely unnoticed on a modern PC for datasets of many thousands of records, but datasets with a million records or more can push the limits of what is currently possible with consumer-grade hardware. The problem is worsened if the data have many features or if complex learning algorithms are being used.

 CRAN has a high performance computing task view that lists packages pushing the boundaries on what is possible in R: `http://cran.r-project.org/web/views/HighPerformanceComputing.html`.

Packages that extend R past the capabilities of the base package are being developed rapidly. This work comes primarily on two fronts: some packages add the capability to manage extremely large datasets by making data operations faster or by allowing the size of data to exceed the amount of available system memory; others allow R to work faster, perhaps by spreading the work over additional computers or processors, by utilizing specialized computer hardware, or by providing machine learning optimized to Big Data problems. Some of these packages are listed as follows.

# Managing very large datasets

Very large datasets can sometimes cause R to grind to a halt when the system runs out of memory to store the data. Even if the entire dataset can fit in memory, additional RAM is needed to read the data from disk, which necessitates a total memory size much larger than the dataset itself. Furthermore, very large datasets can take a long amount of time to process for no reason other than the sheer volume of records; even a quick operation can add up when performed many millions of times.

Years ago, many would suggest performing data preparation of massive datasets outside R in another programming language, then using R to perform analyses on a smaller subset of data. However, this is no longer necessary, as several packages have been contributed to R to address these Big Data problems.

## Making data frames faster with data.table

The data.table package by *Dowle*, *Short*, and *Lianoglou* provides an enhanced version of a data frame called a **data table**. The data.table objects are typically much faster than data frames for subsetting, joining, and grouping operations. Yet, because it is essentially an improved data frame, the resulting objects can still be used by any R function that accepts a data frame.

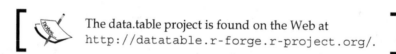

The data.table project is found on the Web at
http://datatable.r-forge.r-project.org/.

One limitation of data.table structures is that like data frames, they are limited by the available system memory. The next two sections discuss packages that overcome this shortcoming at the expense of breaking compatibility with many R functions.

# Creating disk-based data frames with ff

The ff package by *Daniel Adler, Christian Glaser, Oleg Nenadic, Jens Oehlschlagel,* and *Walter Zucchini* provides an alternative to a data frame (ffdf) that allows datasets of over two billion rows to be created, even if this far exceeds the available system memory.

The ffdf structure has a physical component that stores the data on disk in a highly efficient form and a virtual component that acts like a typical R data frame but transparently points to the data stored in the physical component. You can imagine the ffdf object as a map that points to a location of data on a disk.

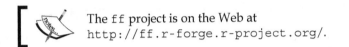

> The ff project is on the Web at
> http://ff.r-forge.r-project.org/.

A downside of ffdf data structures is that they cannot be used natively by most R functions. Instead, the data must be processed in small chunks, and the results should be combined later on. The upside of chunking the data is that the task can be divided across several processors simultaneously using the parallel computing methods presented later in this chapter.

The ffbase package by *Edwin de Jonge, Jan Wijffels,* and *Jan van der Laan* addresses this issue somewhat by adding capabilities for basic statistical analyses using ff objects. This makes it possible to use ff objects directly for data exploration.

> The ffbase project is hosted at
> http://github.com/edwindj/ffbase.

# Using massive matrices with bigmemory

The bigmemory package by *Michael J. Kane* and *John W. Emerson* allows extremely large matrices that exceed the amount of available system memory. The matrices can be stored on disk or in shared memory, allowing them to be used by other processes on the same computer or across a network. This facilitates parallel computing methods, such as those covered later in this chapter.

> Additional documentation on the bigmemory package
> can be found at http://www.bigmemory.org/.

Because `bigmemory` matrices are intentionally unlike data frames, they cannot be used directly with most of the machine learning methods covered in this book. They also can only be used with numeric data. That said, since they are similar to a typical R matrix, it is easy to create smaller samples or chunks that can be converted to standard R data structures.

The authors also provide `bigalgebra`, `biganalytics`, and `bigtabulate` packages, which allow simple analyses to be performed on the matrices. Of particular note is the `bigkmeans()` function in the `biganalytics` package, which performs k-means clustering as described in *Chapter 9, Finding Groups of Data – Clustering with k-means*.

# Learning faster with parallel computing

In the early days of computing, programs were entirely **serial**, which limited them to performing a single task at a time. The next instruction could not be performed until the previous instruction was complete. However, many tasks can be completed more efficiently by allowing work to be performed simultaneously.

**Serial computing:**

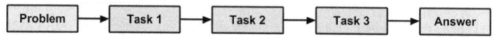

This need was addressed by the development of **parallel computing** methods, which use a set of two or more processors or computers to solve a larger problem. Many modern computers are designed for parallel computing. Even in the case that they have a single processor, they often have two or more **cores** which are capable of working in parallel. This allows tasks to be accomplished independently from one another.

**Parallel computing:**

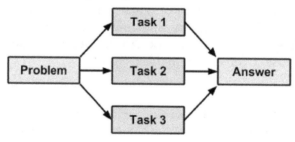

Networks of multiple computers called clusters can also be used for parallel computing. A large cluster may include a variety of hardware and be separated over large distances. In this case, the cluster is known as a **grid**. Taken to an extreme, a cluster or grid of hundreds or thousands of computers running commodity hardware could be a very powerful system.

The catch, however, is that not every problem can be parallelized; certain problems are more conducive to parallel execution than others. You might expect that adding 100 processors would result in 100 times the work being accomplished in the same amount of time (that is, the execution time is 1/100), but this is typically not the case. The reason is that it takes effort to manage the workers; the work first must be divided into non-overlapping tasks and second, each of the workers' results must be combined into one final answer.

So-called **embarrassingly parallel** problems are the ideal. These tasks are easy to reduce into non-overlapping blocks of work, and the results are easy to recombine. An example of an embarrassingly parallel machine learning task would be 10-fold cross-validation; once the samples are decided, each of the 10 evaluations is independent, meaning that its result does not affect the others. As you will soon see, this task can be sped up quite dramatically using parallel computing.

## Measuring execution time

Efforts to speed up R will be wasted if it is not possible to systematically measure how much time was saved. Although you could sit and observe a clock, an easier solution is to wrap the offending code in a `system.time()` function.

For example, on the author's laptop, the `system.time()` function notes that it takes about 0.13 seconds to generate a million random numbers:

```
> system.time(rnorm(1000000))
   user   system elapsed
   0.13    0.00    0.13
```

The same function can be used for evaluating improvement in performance, obtained with the methods that were just described or any R function.

## Working in parallel with foreach

The `foreach` package by *Steve Weston* of Revolution Analytics provides perhaps the easiest way to get started with parallel computing, particularly if you are running R on the Windows operating system, as some of the other packages are platform-specific.

The core of the package is a new `foreach` looping construct. If you have worked with other programming languages, this may be familiar. Essentially, it allows looping over a number of items in a set, without explicitly counting the number of items; in other words, for each item in the set, do something.

 In addition to the `foreach` package, Revolution Analytics has developed high-performance, enterprise-ready R builds. Free versions are available for trial and academic use. For more information, see their website at `http://www.revolutionanalytics.com/`.

If you're thinking that R already provides a set of `apply` functions to loop over sets of items (for example, `apply()`, `lapply()`, `sapply()`, and so on), you are correct. However, the `foreach` loop has an additional benefit: iterations of the loop can be completed in parallel using a very simple syntax.

The sister package `doParallel` provides a parallel backend for `foreach` that utilizes the `parallel` package included with R (Version 2.14.0 and later). The `parallel` package includes components of the `multicore` and `snow` packages described in the following sections.

## Using a multitasking operating system with multicore

The `multicore` package by *Simon Urbanek* allows parallel processing on single machines that have multiple processors or processor cores. Because it utilizes multitasking capabilities of the operating system, it is not supported natively on Windows systems. An easy way to get started with the code package is using the `mcapply()` function, which is a parallelized version of `lapply()`.

 The multicore project is hosted at `http://www.rforge.net/multicore/`.

## Networking multiple workstations with snow and snowfall

The `snow` package (simple networking of workstations) by *Luke Tierney*, *A. J. Rossini*, *Na Li*, and *H. Sevcikova* allows parallel computing on multicore or multiprocessor machines as well as on a network of multiple machines. The `snowfall` package by *Jochen Knaus* provides an easier-to-use interface for `snow`.

For more information on code, including a detailed FAQ and information on how to configure parallel computing over a network, see `http://www.imbi.uni-freiburg.de/parallel/`.

# Parallel cloud computing with MapReduce and Hadoop

The **MapReduce** programming model was developed at Google as a way to process their data on a large cluster of networked computers. MapReduce defined parallel programming as a two-step process:

- A map step, in which a problem is divided into smaller tasks that are distributed across the computers in the cluster
- A reduce step, in which the results of the small chunks of work are collected and synthesized into a final solution to the original problem

A popular open source alternative to the proprietary MapReduce framework is Apache **Hadoop**. The Hadoop software comprises of the MapReduce concept plus a distributed filesystem capable of storing large amounts of data across a cluster of computers.

Packt Publishing has published quite a number of books on Hadoop. To view the list of books on this topic, refer to the following URL: `http://www.packtpub.com/books?keys=Hadoop`.

Several R projects that provide an R interface to Hadoop are in development. One such project is RHIPE by *Saptarshi Guha*, which attempts to bring the divide and recombine philosophy into R by managing the communication between R and Hadoop.

The RHIPE package is not yet available at CRAN, but it can be built from the source available on the Web at `http://www.datadr.org`.

The RHadoop project by Revolution Analytics provides an R interface to Hadoop. The project provides a package, `rmr`, intended to be an easy way for R developers to write MapReduce programs. Additional RHadoop packages provide R functions for accessing Hadoop's distributed data stores.

At the time of publication, development of RHadoop is progressing very rapidly. For more information about the project, see `https://github.com/RevolutionAnalytics/RHadoop/wiki`.

# GPU computing

An alternative to parallel processing uses a computer's graphics processing unit (GPU) to increase the speed of mathematical calculations. A GPU is a specialized processor that is optimized for rapidly displaying images on a computer screen. Because a computer often needs to display complex 3D graphics (particularly for video games), many GPUs use hardware designed for parallel processing and extremely efficient matrix and vector calculations. A side benefit is that they can be used for efficiently solving certain types of mathematical problems. Where a computer processor may have on the order of 16 cores, a GPU may have thousands.

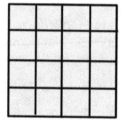

**CPU with 16 cores**

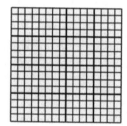

**GPU with 1000+ cores**

The downside of GPU computing is that it requires specific hardware that is not included with many computers. In most cases, a GPU from the manufacturer Nvidia is required, as they provide a proprietary framework called CUDA (Complete Unified Device Architecture) that makes the GPU programmable using common languages such as C++.

For more information on Nvidia's role in GPU computing, go to `http://www.nvidia.com/object/what-is-gpu-computing.html`.

The `gputools` package by *Josh Buckner*, *Mark Seligman*, and *Justin Wilson* implements several R functions, such as matrix operations, clustering, and regression modeling using the Nvidia CUDA toolkit. The package requires a CUDA 1.3 or higher GPU and the installation of the Nvidia CUDA toolkit.

# Deploying optimized learning algorithms

Some of the machine learning algorithms covered in this book are able to work on extremely large datasets with relatively minor modifications. For instance, it would be fairly straightforward to implement naive Bayes or the Apriori algorithm using one of the Big Data packages described previously. Some types of models such as ensembles, lend themselves well to parallelization, since the work of each model can be distributed across processors or computers in a cluster. On the other hand, some algorithms require larger changes to the data or algorithm, or need to be rethought altogether before they can be used with massive datasets.

In this section, we will examine packages that provide optimized versions of the learning algorithms we've worked with so far.

## Building bigger regression models with biglm

The `biglm` package by *Thomas Lumley* provides functions for training regression models on datasets that may be too large to fit into memory. It works by an iterative process in which the model is updated little-by-little using small chunks of data. The results will be nearly identical to what would have been obtained running the conventional `lm()` function on the entire dataset.
The `biglm()` function allows use of a SQL database in place of a data frame. The model can also be trained with chunks obtained from data objects created by the `ff` package described previously.

## Growing bigger and faster random forests with bigrf

The `bigrf` package by *Aloysius Lim* implements the training of random forests for classification and regression on datasets that are too large to fit into memory using `bigmemory` objects as described earlier in this chapter. The package also allows faster parallel processing using the `foreach` package described previously. Trees can be grown in parallel (on a single computer or across multiple computers), as can forests, and additional trees can be added to the forest at any time or merged with other forests.

 For more information, including examples and Windows installation instructions, see the package wiki hosted at GitHub: https://github.com/aloysius-lim/bigrf.

## Training and evaluating models in parallel with caret

The `caret` package by *Max Kuhn* (covered extensively in *Chapter 10, Evaluating Model Performance* and *Chapter 11, Improving Model Performance*) will transparently utilize a parallel backend if one has been registered with R (for instance, using the `foreach` package described previously).

Many of the tasks involved in training and evaluating models, such as creating random samples and repeatedly testing predictions for 10-fold cross-validation are embarrassingly parallel. This makes a particularly good caret.

Configuration instructions and a case study of the performance improvements for enabling parallel processing in caret are available at the project's website: `http://caret.r-forge.r-project.org/parallel.html`.

# Summary

It is certainly an exciting time to be studying machine learning. Ongoing work on the relatively uncharted frontiers of parallel and distributed computing offers great potential for tapping the knowledge found in the deluge of Big Data. And the burgeoning data science community is facilitated by the free and open source R programming language, which provides a very low barrier for entry—you simply need to be willing to learn.

The topics you have learned, both in this chapter as well as previous chapters, provide the foundation for understanding more advanced machine learning methods. It is now your responsibility to keep learning and adding tools to your arsenal. Along the way, be sure to keep in mind the No Free Lunch theorem—no learning algorithm can rule them all. There will always be a human element to machine learning, adding subject-specific knowledge and the ability to match the appropriate algorithm to the task at hand.

In the coming years, it will be interesting to see how the human side changes as the line between machine learning and human learning is blurred. Services such as Amazon's Mechanical Turk provide crowd-sourced intelligence, offering a cluster of human minds ready to perform simple tasks at a moment's notice. Perhaps one day, just as we have used computers to perform tasks that human beings cannot do easily, computers will employ human beings to do the reverse; food for thought.

# Index

# O

OCR, performing with SVMs
  about 233
  data, collecting 234
  data, exploring 235, 236
  data, preparing 235, 236
  model performance, evaluating 239-241
  model performance, improving 241, 242
  model, training on data 237, 239
ODBC 41
odbcConnect() function 41
One Rule algorithm
  about 146
  strengths 146
  weaknesses 146
one-way table 56
Open Database Connectivity. *See* ODBC
optimized learning algorithms
  deploying 363
optimized learning algorithms deployment
  caret package, used for evaluating models
      in parallel 364
  random forests, building with bigrf
      package 363
  regression models, building with biglm
      package 363
Oracle 41
order() function 132
ordinary least squares estimation 164-167
ordinary least squares (OLS) 164
out-of-bag error rate 347
Output Node 212
overfitting 16

# P

pairs() function 177
parallel computing methods 358
parameter estimates 163
parameter tuning 326, 327
pattern discovery 21
Pearson's Chi-squared test 63
Pearson's correlation 167
performance
  improving, of R 355, 356

measuring, confusion matrices
      used 299-301
performance() function 314
performance measures
  about 302
  F-measure 311
  kappa statistic 303-306
  precision 309
  recall 309, 310
  sensitivity 307, 308
  specificity 307, 308
performance tradeoffs
  visualizing 311
plot() function 59, 314
point-and-click interface
  used, for installing R package 25
poisonous mushrooms
  identifying, with rule learners 150
poisonous mushrooms example, with rule
      learners
  data, collecting 150
  data, exploring 151
  data, preparing 151
  model performance, evaluating 154, 155
  model performance, improving 155-157
  model, training on data 152, 153
Poisson regression 161
polynomial kernel 233
posPredValue() function 310
posterior probability 94
PostgreSQL 41
post-pruning 128
precision 309
pred function 342
predict() function 295, 332 340
predictive model 20
pre-pruning 128
prior probability 93
probability 91

# Q

quadratic optimization 228
quantile() function 48
quartiles 48

# R

R
CSV file, loading into 40
data structures 30
JSON, converting to 353
performance, improving 355, 356
used, for managing data 39
using, for machine learning 23
working with classification prediction
data 294-297
Radial Basis Function (RBF) network 211
randomForest() function 346, 348
randomForest package 346
random forests
about 344, 345
performance, evaluating 348-350
strengths 345
training 346-348
weaknesses 345
range 47
range() function 47
RCurl package
about 352
URL, for documentation 352
used, for obtaining data from web 352
real-world data 352
recall 309
Receiver Operating Characteristic. See
ROC curve
recurrent network 214
recursive partitioning 121
reg() function 171
regression
about 160
adding, to trees 188-190
correlation 167, 168
multiple linear regression 168-172
ordinary least squares estimation 164-167
simple linear regression 162-164
regression analysis
use cases 160
regression equations 160
regression models
building, with biglm package 363

regression trees
about 187
strengths 188
weaknesses 188
relationships
examining 61, 63
exploring, between variables 58
visualizing 59, 60
residuals 164
resubstitution error 316
RHIPE package 361
right hand side (RHS) 262
RIPPER algorithm
about 147, 148
strengths 148
weaknesses 148
risky bank loans
identifying, C5.0 decision trees
used 128, 129
rjson package
about 353
used, for reading JSON 353
used, for writing JSON 353
rmr package 361
ROC curve
about 312, 313
creating 314, 315
ROCR package 311
RODBC package 41
rote learning 75
round() function 57
R package
installing 24
installing, point-and-click interface used 25
loading 27
R performance
GPU computing 362
large datasets, managing 356
learning, with parallel computing 358, 359
optimized learning algorithms,
deploying 363
rudimentary ANNs 206
runif() function 132
RWeka package
about 124
loading 27
using 24

## S

save() function 39
scale() function 85
scatterplot 59
Scoville scale 72
sd() function 55, 167
semi-supervised learning 271
sensitivity() function 310
sensor 6
separate-and-conquer 142-145
seq() function 49
Short Message Service (SMS) 101
sigmoid activation function 210
sigmoid kernel 233
simple linear regression 162-164
simple tuned model
  creating 330-333
single-layer network 212
skew 53
slack variable 230
slope 160
sna package
  URL, for info 355
snowfall package
  multiple workstations, networking 360
snow package
  about 360
  multiple workstations, networking 360
social network data
  working with 355
Social Networking Service (SNS) 279
sparse matrix
  about 107, 252
  creating, for transaction data 252-255
specialized data
  working with 352
SQL databases
  data, importing from 41, 42
SQLite 41
sqlQuery() function 42
stacking 338
standard deviation 54
standard deviation reduction (SDR) 189
stock models
  tuning, for better performance 326, 327
stop words 106

str() function 43, 174
stringsAsFactors option 35
subset() function 297
summary() function 44
summary statistics 44
Sum of Squared Errors (SSE) 222
supervised learning 20
Support Vector Machine (SVM)
  about 225, 341
  applications 226
  classifications, with hyperplanes 226, 227
  maximum margin, finding 227
  OCR, performing with 233
support vectors 227
synapse 207

## T

table() function 56, 300
Tab-Separated Value (TSV) 41
target feature 20
teen market segments search, with k-means
      clustering
  about 278
  data, collecting 279
  data, exploring 279, 281
  data, preparing 279-284
  model performance, evaluating 287-289
  model performance, improving 289, 291
  model, training on data 284-286
threshold activation function 209
tm package 104
token 106
tokenization 106
topology 211
trainControl() function 333
train() function 327, 332
training 13
transaction data
  sparse matrix, creating for 252-255
transpose 170
trees
  regression, adding to 188-190
tree structure 120
trial 91
trivial rules 263

tuning process
  customizing 333-336
Turing test 206
two-way cross-tabulation 61-63

# U

UCI Machine Learning Data Repository
  about 191
  URL 129, 217
uniform distribution 53
unimodal 58
unit of observation phrase 18
unit step activation function 209
univariate statistics 58
universal function approximator 215
unsupervised classification 269
unsupervised learning 21
usedcars.csv dataset 42

# V

var() function 55, 166
variables
  relationships, exploring between 58
variance 54
vector 30, 31
vector types
  character 30
  integer 30
  logical 30
  numeric 30
Venn diagram 92
Voronoi diagram 274

# W

web
  data, obtaining from 352
weighted voting process 72

wine quality estimation, with regression
    trees
  about 190
  data, collecting 191
  data, exploring 192, 193
  data, preparing 192, 193
  decision trees, visualizing 196, 197
  model performance, evaluating 197, 198
  model performance, improving 199-202
  model, training on data 194, 195
  performance, measuring with mean
      absolute error 198
word cloud 108

# X

xlsx package
  about 354
  URL 354
  used, for reading Microsoft Excel
      spreadsheets 354
  used, for writing Microsoft Excel
      spreadsheets 354
XML
  about 353
  reading, XML package used 353
  writing, XML package used 353
XML package
  about 353
  URL, for info 353
  used, for reading XML 353
  used, for writing XML 353

# Z

ZeroR 145
z-score standardization 73

## Thank you for buying
# Machine Learning with R

## About Packt Publishing

Packt, pronounced 'packed', published its first book "*Mastering phpMyAdmin for Effective MySQL Management*" in April 2004 and subsequently continued to specialize in publishing highly focused books on specific technologies and solutions.

Our books and publications share the experiences of your fellow IT professionals in adapting and customizing today's systems, applications, and frameworks. Our solution based books give you the knowledge and power to customize the software and technologies you're using to get the job done. Packt books are more specific and less general than the IT books you have seen in the past. Our unique business model allows us to bring you more focused information, giving you more of what you need to know, and less of what you don't.

Packt is a modern, yet unique publishing company, which focuses on producing quality, cutting-edge books for communities of developers, administrators, and newbies alike. For more information, please visit our website: www.packtpub.com.

## About Packt Open Source

In 2010, Packt launched two new brands, Packt Open Source and Packt Enterprise, in order to continue its focus on specialization. This book is part of the Packt Open Source brand, home to books published on software built around Open Source licences, and offering information to anybody from advanced developers to budding web designers. The Open Source brand also runs Packt's Open Source Royalty Scheme, by which Packt gives a royalty to each Open Source project about whose software a book is sold.

## Writing for Packt

We welcome all inquiries from people who are interested in authoring. Book proposals should be sent to author@packtpub.com. If your book idea is still at an early stage and you would like to discuss it first before writing a formal book proposal, contact us; one of our commissioning editors will get in touch with you.

We're not just looking for published authors; if you have strong technical skills but no writing experience, our experienced editors can help you develop a writing career, or simply get some additional reward for your expertise.

## Statistical Analysis with R Beginner's Guide

ISBN: 978-1-84951-208-4          Paperback: 300 pages

Take control of your data and produce superior statistical analyses with R

1.  An easy introduction for people who are new to R, with plenty of strong examples for you to work through

2.  This book will take you on a journey to learn R as the strategist for an ancient Chinese kingdom!

3.  A step-by-step guide to understand R, its benefits, and how to use it to maximize the impact of your data analysis

## R Graphs Cookbook

ISBN: 978-1-84951-306-7          Paperback: 272 pages

Detailed hands-on recipes for creating the most useful types of graphs in R — starting from the simplest versions to more advanced applications

1.  Learn to draw any type of graph or visual data representation in R

2.  Filled with practical tips and techniques for creating any type of graph you need; not just theoretical explanations

3.  All examples are accompanied with the corresponding graph images, so you know what the results look like

Please check **www.PacktPub.com** for information on our titles

**Learning SciPy for Numerical and
Scientific Computing**

ISBN: 978-1-78216-162-2      Paperback: 150 pages

A practical tutorial that guarantees fast, accurate,
and easy-to-code solutions to your numerical and
scientific computing problems with the power of
SciPy and Python

1. Perform complex operations with large
   matrices, including eigenvalue problems,
   matrix decompositions, or solution to large
   systems of equations

2. Step-by-step examples to easily implement
   statistical analysis and data mining that rivals
   in performance any of the costly specialized
   software suites

**Unity 4.x Game AI Programming**

ISBN: 978-1-84969-340-0      Paperback: 232 pages

Learn and implement game AI in Unity3D with a lot
of sample projects and next-generation techniques to
use in your Unity3D projects

1. A practical guide with step-by-step instructions
   and example projects to learn Unity3D scripting

2. Learn pathfinding using A* algorithms as well
   as Unity3D pro features and navigation graphs

3. Implement finite state machines (FSMs), path
   following, and steering algorithms

Please check **www.PacktPub.com** for information on our titles

CPSIA information can be obtained
at www.ICGtesting.com
Printed in the USA
FSHW01n0159170818
51439FS